LANGUAGE AND PSYCHOLOGY IN *Pepita Jiménez*

LANGUAGE AND PSYCHOLOGY IN *Pepita Jiménez*

by Robert E. Lott

University of Illinois Press
URBANA
CHICAGO
LONDON

MANUFACTURED IN THE UNITED STATES OF AMERICA
LIBRARY OF CONGRESS CATALOG CARD NO. 72-114726

252-00113-3

Para Isabelita,
aun más hechicera que Pepita.

Preface

Pepita Jiménez is one of those fortunate works which combines the best of an author's ability and the convergence of the most important artistic trends and ideological concerns of the time. What, in the Spain of the 1870's, could have been more characteristic than the struggle between the demands of the natural world, however ideally conceived, and religious, even mystical zeal? To Valera's credit, he was able to impart to the love story of Luis and Pepita the qualities that make of it a modern classic, as well as doubly "classical," in both its capture of the true spirit of the ancients and of Renaissance-derived classicism and the distillation of outstanding Spanish *Siglo de Oro* literary and stylistic traditions, including especially the Biblical-mystical and the ironic manners of writing.

Pepita Jiménez has many facets worthy of study; only some of them have been treated in this book. It would, of course, be possible to study the entire novel from other points of view and to devise an entirely different configuration of data and commentaries. I believe, however, to have chosen the essential features and to have placed them in their proper perspectives. Valera's masterly utilization of *Siglo de Oro* forms of parody, irony, and elegant mitigation is matched only by his full awareness of the delightful ironies and ambiguities involved in the fusion of the worldly and the spiritual, the pagan and the Biblical, the classical and the romantic, the old and the new in language and in deed. One of Valera's great achievements is to have juxtaposed so well these different aspects of psychic life and different levels of stylistic expression, all in keeping with the added spice of nineteenth-century refinement and sophistication.

To avoid the ambiguities involved in terms like "classicism" and "Golden Age," on the one hand, and yet to provide some flexibility, I have chosen the term "*Siglo de Oro*" to describe the at least dominant characteristics of "classical" Spanish prose style (which, of course, has exercised a constant influence ever since), as seen most especially in the works of Fray Luis de León and Cervantes, and hence covering, roughly, the second half of the sixteenth century and the early years of the seventeenth. I am cognizant of the division of the historical *Siglo de Oro* into diverse and frequently competing period styles, from the Renaissance to near the end of the seventeenth century, but for obvious reasons felt no need to enter into a discussion of these problems and of terms like "mannerism" and "baroque." I must say that my task was made no easier by the prevailing paucity of new, modern treatments of *Siglo de Oro* prose style, although there do exist older landmark studies that were indispensable to me, as my documentation will make clear.

The immediate predecessor of this book, *"Siglo de Oro" Tradition and Modern Adolescent Psychology in "Pepita Jiménez": A Stylistic Study*, was originally my dissertation and was published in a rudimentary form by the Catholic University of America Press in 1958. This book presents that study and additional material, especially in the appendix, which is entirely new, in a revised and greatly improved form.

I am grateful to the University of Illinois Research Board and to the University of Illinois Press for their support of the project. I am also indebted to my former professor, Helmut A. Hatzfeld, for his aid in the conception of some of the ideas found in my interpretation of *Pepita Jiménez* and to many friends and colleagues, among them Cyrus C. DeCoster, J. E. Varey, Germán Bleiberg, and E. Inman Fox, for their encouragement. My special thanks go to Mr.

Miodrag Muntyan (Director) and Miss Martha Bergland and others of the Illinois Press for their patience and aid, and to my capable and dedicated assistants, Miss Suzanne E. Goldsmith, Mrs. Elizabeth Q. Espadas, and Miss Gresilda A. Tilley, for helping to bring this project to fruition.

Contents

INTRODUCTION: *The Critical Reaction to Valera and* Pepita Jiménez

It is paradoxical that, with one notable exception, no study has been made of the style of the man who is universally hailed as the best Spanish prose writer of the nineteenth century. It is equally surprising that no one has thoroughly studied his most outstanding novel and a recognized classic, *Pepita Jiménez*, as a work of art. Much of the abundant criticism on Juan Valera has been focused on the man himself, on his interesting life, on the genesis of his works, and on his purposes, philosophy, views, and theories about his work as represented in his extensive critical writings and correspondence, which have then been compared to his creative writings; or, conversely, the latter have been studied as the expression, or rather, alleged proof of his attitudes and theories. In such criticism what to me is the main object of the literary critic's attention, the aesthetic value of the work itself, has either been neglected or, at best, has received only superficial treatment. My intention in the present work is to fill this gap by studying in detail the language (vocabulary and style) and the total aesthetic structure of *Pepita Jiménez*. But in order to do so and to insert my work within the framework of Valerian scholarship, it is imperative first to survey the general criticism on Valera and *Pepita Jiménez*.

I. VALERA VIEWED BY HIS CONTEMPORARIES

Although focusing his comments around the conflict between liberalism and conservatism, Luis Vidart refuted early charges that Valera was wrong to allow natural instincts to overcome Luis's religious vocation, since matrimony and the family formed the bases of society and Christianity.[1] To Manuel de la Revilla the critical faculty was so dominant in Valera's literary production that the novels, the characters, and their speech suffered as a consequence.[2] He also pointed out Valera's skepticism, complexity, and humorism, all of which led him to play with ideas rather than taking them seriously.

One of the earliest and best interpretations of Valera is that of Menéndez Pelayo, who spoke of Valera's classical qualities and refined paganism. He interpreted *Pepita Jiménez* as a lesson against pseudomysticism, while recognizing that many thought the novel showed the triumph of man's sinful nature over asceticism and religious zeal.[3] Brunetière spoke very highly of Valera's early novels and praised especially his casuistry and skill in the presentation of psychological and moral problems.[4] Leopoldo Alas, who along with Menéndez Pelayo was one of Valera's most ardent and steadfast champions, immediately took exception to Brunetière, rightly claiming that his emphasis on casuistry and morality distorted Valera's artistry. Valera's true attitude, Alas said, was humoristic.[5] Emilia Pardo Bazán claimed that Valera's excellent though rather archaic style was based less on Cervantes than on the Spanish mystics, who

[1] Luis Vidart, "Recuerdos de una polémica acerca da la novela de don Juan Valera—'Pepita Jiménez,'" *Revista de España*, LIII (Nov.-Dec., 1876), 269–284.

[2] Manuel de la Revilla, "Don Juan Valera," *Obras* (Madrid: Víctor Saiz, 1883), pp. 47–55.

[3] Marcelino Menéndez [y] Pelayo, *Historia de los heterodoxos españoles*, ed. Enrique Sánchez Reyes, 8 vols. (Santander: Aldus, 1946–1948), VI, 483.

[4] Ferdinand Brunetière, "La casuistique dans le roman," *Revue des Deux Mondes*, 3rd Period, XLVIII (Nov. 15, 1881), 453–464.

[5] Leopoldo Alas, "Don Juan Valera en Francia," in *La literatura en 1881*, written in part by Armando Palacio Valdés (Madrid: Alfredo de Carlos Hierro, Editor, 1882), pp. 175–180.

also taught him psychological analysis.[6] Her harshest criticism, one that was to be echoed over and over, was that Valera's characters all talked like him and that women did not speak like his heroines. Alas, although sometimes critical of the lack of verisimilitude in the speech of Valera's characters, was invariably high in his praise of Valera as a novelist, psychologist, stylist, and, in the broad sense, poet.[7] Curiously, he found him more revolutionary than Galdós, and added that Valera possessed "toda la graciosa voluptuosidad de un espíritu del Renacimiento y todo el eclecticismo, un tanto escéptico de un hombre de mundo-filósofo del siglo XIX."[8] Alas also claimed that Valera's curiosity and humorism had led him to treat subjects entirely new in Spanish literature.[9]

Armando Palacio Valdés considered Valera a masterful stylist and conversationalist and was intrigued by his complexity.[10] In another essay, while generally praising *Pepita Jiménez* as a true masterpiece, Palacio Valdés said that Valera followed traditional Spanish satirists in attitudes and style, but with a modern content: "El molde de sus obras es antiguo. Es el mismo que usaron Cervantes, Quevedo y Diego Hurtado de Mendoza. . . . Confesando que tal estilo es buscado y que palpita bajo sus laberintos el esfuerzo, para mí es el lenguaje del artista. . . . El contenido es moderno. Está constituído por un fondo contradictorio de filosofía, aspiraciones tradicionales, escep-

[6] Emilia Pardo Bazán, *La cuestión palpitante, Obras completas* (Madrid, 1891), I, 262–265. Her charge that Valera was unpalatable to the French would have to be modified today by Robert Pageard's article, "*Pepita Jiménez* en France," *Bulletin Hispanique*, LXIII (1961), 28–37. Pageard shows that despite Th. Bentzon's poorly translated and badly cut adaptations of *Pepita Jiménez* and *Las ilusiones del doctor Faustino—Récits andalous* (Paris: Calmann-Lévy, 1879), Albert Savine, who did a much more satisfactory translation of *El Comendador Mendoza*, had a better appreciation of Valera. Savine's comments on Valera's art of casuistry led Brunetière, in turn, to treat this topic and motivate Valera's modest success in France.

[7] See, for example, Leopoldo Alas's "Valera," *Obras selectas* (Madrid: Biblioteca Nueva, 1947), pp. 1191–1195.

[8] Leopoldo Alas, "El libre examen de nuestra literatura presente," *Solos de Clarín*, 2nd ed. (Madrid: Alfredo de Carlos Hierro, Editor, 1881), pp. 51–62. In this collection there are several reviews of Valera's works of the 1870's, though not of *Pepita Jiménez*.

[9] *Ibid.*, p. 59.

[10] Armando Palacio Valdés, "Don Juan Valera," *Obras completas* (Madrid: Aguilar, 1945), II, 1179–1182.

ticismo, frivolidad, ironía y profundidad, caracteres los más extraños y difíciles de explicar."[11] Like the Golden Age satirists, Valera insisted upon "una libertad celosa y prevenida contra toda regla, en una mezcla de sagacidad y gracia, de frivolidad y fuerza, de crueldad y delicadeza."[12] Palacio Valdés's strongest criticisms are that Valera, because of a curious sort of positivism, lacked feeling and painted cold, self-seeking characters who were drawn irresistibly to worldly things and expressed themselves, especially during solemn moments, in excessively formal dialogue. But he also saw the great merits of Luis de Vargas's characterization, his elaborate rationalizations, and his ambiguous use of Biblical references.

Juan Fernández Luján's analysis of *Pepita Jiménez* is one of the most judicious and best balanced of the older studies. To him, *Pepita Jiménez*, "una condenación del misticismo," has a satirical note as strong, though less obvious, as the *Quijote* has: "El *Quijote* ridiculiza un género de la literatura; *Pepita Jiménez* una forma de la religiosidad."[13] He pointed out Valera's worth as a psychologist in his epistolary portrayal of Luis's character as a blending of self-conscious and pedantic erudition and naiveté, which were the results of "las sofisticaciones de un ascetismo exagerado y de una religiosidad impía" and "una falsa idea de la divinidad" vis-à-vis an incipient carnal love.[14] Valera is classified as an idealist, although psychologically a realist. Valera's style is described as varying considerably from the first to the second part of *Pepita Jiménez*, becoming simpler, without losing its elegance and symmetry. Later, as he compared Pardo Bazán's, Pereda's, and Valera's styles, Fernández Luján added about Valera: ". . . su estilo tiene un sabor clásico, que en la novela

[11] *Ibid.*, pp. 1210–1217.

[12] *Ibid.*, p. 1212.

[13] Juan Fernández Luján, *Pardo Bazán, Valera y Pereda (Estudios críticos)* (Barcelona: Luis Tasso, 1889), pp. 31–43 *passim*. The quotation is from p. 31.

Fernández Luján intended to show in this analysis of, primarily, Pardo Bazán's *Un viaje de novios*, *Pepita Jiménez*, and Pereda's *Sotileza* something about the transition from idealism to realism, the persistence of the former in the latter, the curiously common idyllic note in the three works, and similarities in the protagonists. "Sotileza" is considered as overrefined in her argumentative ability as Pepita, and Artegui is considered less real than Pepita.

[14] Fernández Luján, *Pardo Bazán, Valera y Pereda*, pp. 32–36.

perjudica alguna vez a sus caracteres. Quien ha dicho [Pardo Bazán] que está culpado de arcaísmo se engaña: no conozco prosista más castizo y elegante en nuestro tiempo. Su dicción es pura, escultural la frase, y el período lleno, pero no ampuloso: tiene párrafos soberbios, como columnas salomónicas."[15]

Francisco Blanco García pointed out Valera's skepticism and his mixing of Christian mysticism with the theories of Plato and the Neoplatonists and said: "El misticismo insidioso de esta obra es un misticismo al revés, una rehabilitación muy velada del deleite sensual frente a las aspiraciones del espíritu, un ensayo de conciliación entre la moral cristiana y la epicúrea."[16] He added that Valera's psychological analyses were penetrating and praised his classical language and lack of affectation.

As the author of *Pepita Jiménez*, Valera achieved a certain literary fame abroad, though more in English-speaking countries than in France. Two of his most fervent supporters, William Dean Howells and Havelock Ellis, may be mentioned as samples of this foreign reaction. Howells, who had no trouble in fitting Valera among the realists, and while agreeing in principle with Valera's advocacy of art for art's sake, said that nevertheless "no reader . . . could read his Pepita Ximenez without finding himself in possession of a great deal of serious thinking on a very serious subject, which is none the less serious because it is couched in terms of a delicate irony," and that, "in spite of himself . . . Valera has proved a thesis in his story": the primacy of the right to love and marry over religious vocation (whether true or false, according to Howells).[17] But Howells objected to Pepita's trickery in winning Luis and believed that a bad marriage would result from such a basis. In what is still a most useful and fair synthesis of Valera, Ellis found Valera to be truly classical

[15] *Ibid.*, p. 71.

[16] Padre Francisco Blanco García, *La literatura española en el siglo XIX*, 3 vols., 2nd ed. (Madrid: Sáenz de Jubera Hermanos, Editores, 1899–1903), II, 147 and 480, respectively.

[17] William Dean Howells, *Criticism and Fiction and Other Essays*, ed. C. M. Kirk and R. Kirk (New York: New York Univ. Press, 1959), pp. 41–43. The original edition of *Criticism and Fiction* was made in 1891 and the comments on Valera are still earlier (1886).

in a double sense: in the fact that his harmonious blending of the real and the ideal reflected the ideals of the ancients and in his following of the best Spanish traditions.[18]

II. VALERA AND *PEPITA JIMÉNEZ* IN THE TWENTIETH CENTURY

The observations of earlier critics, although with some lacunae, provided a solid foundation for the understanding of Valera and *Pepita Jiménez*; but, regrettably, their ideas were not satisfactorily developed by twentieth-century critics, some of whom continued to belabor rather irrelevant and often moralistic considerations. Nevertheless, there are several studies which provide indispensable leads.

In 1910 José Ortega y Gasset wrote an important essay in which he claimed that in Valera there was a kind of positivism as well as an overpowering urge to level all things, great and small, a tendency especially noticeable in Valera's literary criticism, but one which also informed his attitude toward life, philosophy, and literature:

> Valera propendía a nivelar todas las cosas: en su opinión, los grandes errores son de menor talla que se juzga comúnmente, y las verdades no son tan verdaderas que no se puedan considerar como cristalizaciones graciosas de muchos errores pequeños. De esta manera todo viene a ser equivalente, y donde todo vale lo mismo, nada tiene valor. Es un allanamiento feroz del relieve que da plasticidad al mundo de la cultura.
>
> . . . Podría hallarse en Valera, bajo toda la elegancia de su espíritu, algo o mucho de esa manera celtíbera de sentir la democracia como nivelación universal. . . .
>
> La crítica de Valera es una crítica de rebajamiento: movíale a ella un inconsciente positivismo, un positivismo cazurro y extraintelectual, que solemos hallar en los hombres de nuestra raza cuando rascamos un poco su epidermis. Así en Valera había primero un ropaje exquisito de hombre moderno, una amplísima lección, una apostura elegantísima,

[18] Havelock Ellis, "Juan Valera," *The Soul of Spain,* 2nd impression (London: A. Constable, 1908), pp. 244–272.

una ironía gramatical deliciosa; mas tras ello solía aparecer un cortijero andaluz, buen recibidor, anchamente simpático, lleno de facundia y malicia bondadosa.[19]

Several years later Ramón Pérez de Ayala, probably influenced by Ortega's theory, wrote a most brilliant and suggestive essay on Valera.[20] He followed Ortega's line of thought in showing that, unlike Galdós, in whose humblest characters there was always a grain of virtue or courage which could lead to saintliness or heroism, Valera created characters for whom the proverb, "Entre santa y santo, pared de cal y canto," was always applicable, since in Valera the would-be saint (Luis de Vargas), wise man (Faustino), and hero (Morsamor) inevitably fail. But the most important and original part of this essay is the interpretation of Valera's art as a "diversionary art" ("arte de la distracción"), in accordance with which Valera leads up to and plays with, before slyly evading, the treatment of serious problems. Undoubtedly some parallel could be established between this "teasing" art and Valera's ambiguous and complex style, his comic feigning and pirouetting, and his joyful mental gymnastics.

Other Spanish critics of the time treated Valera with varying degrees of success and fairness.[21] Valuable though brief remarks were made by Eduardo Gómez de Baquero on the ". . . finas y amenas disertaciones de mística y de teología moral, escritas en terso y elegante estilo . . ." in *Pepita Jiménez* and on Valera's stylization of popular language, with archaisms and pure Andalusian expressions.[22]

[19] José Ortega y Gasset, "Una polémica," *Obras completas*, 2nd ed. (Madrid: Revista de Occidente, 1950), I, 156–163. The quoted passage is from pp. 161–162.

[20] Ramón Pérez de Ayala, "Don Juan Valera o el arte de la distracción," *Divagaciones literarias* (Madrid: Biblioteca Nueva, 1958), pp. 67–85.

[21] Andrés González-Blanco harshly denied that Valera was even a novelist. See his *Historia de la novela en España* (Madrid: Sáenz de Jubera Hermanos, Editores, 1909), pp. 323–345.

[22] Eduardo Gómez de Baquero, *El renacimiento de la novela española en el siglo XIX* (Madrid: Mundo Latino, 1924), pp. 68–74.

In another essay, on comparing Pardo Bazán's style with that of her contemporaries, Gómez de Baquero is less favorable to Valera: "Valera, lleno de pulcritud y preciosismo, muy siglo XVII en estilo y XVIII en espíritu, muy dado al detallismo y a cierto arcaísmo elegante, es algo artificial y frío" ("Los dos aspectos de Emilia Pardo Bazán," *De Gallardo a Unamuno* [Madrid: Espasa-Calpe, 1926], p. 157).

Manuel Azaña, who treated in detail Valera's youthful experiences in Italy,[23] contributed greatly to Valera's biography and to the overall understanding of his work in relation to his life and family.[24] In what is the widely accepted opinion, Azaña claimed that *Pepita Jiménez* was Spain's first psychological novel and Valera's best.[25] Luis Araujo Costa, in his introduction to Valera's *Obras completas*, briefly mentioned Valera's debt to mystical-ascetical writers and compared his style in *Dafnis y Cloe* to classical sixteenth-century Spanish models.[26]

During the past three or four decades, American interest in Valera has been limited primarily to academic circles. Edith Fishtine made good use of unpublished letters and other material in her good early study of Valera's critical writings, particularly concerning their value in relation to modern criticism and in relation to Valera's theories and work.[27] Typical of the unpublished dissertations on Valera is Frank R. Thompson's.[28] While quite observant about Valera's fiction, especially his characterizations, Thompson overdid his attempt to relate Valera to the classicism of antiquity. Sometimes failing to detect Valera's irony, he thought that Antoñona "harbored noble sentiments" and said: "True to his constant desire for clarity, Valera holds nothing in abeyance in his novels."[29] About the characters' speech he said that it "assumes the tone of a Socratic dialogue . . . ,"[30] though a comparison with the tradition of stylized dialogues in the *Siglo de Oro* would surely be more appropriate. He spoke judiciously of the "polished perfection" of Luis's speech,

[23] Manuel Azaña, *Valera en Italia: amores, política y literatura* (Madrid: Paez, 1929).

[24] See the prologue to Azaña's edition of *Pepita Jiménez*, "Clásicos Castellanos" (Madrid: Espasa-Calpe, 1953), ix–lxviii, and "La novela de Pepita Jiménez," originally published in 1927 (like the prologue) in *Cuadernos Literarios* and now included, along with his other essays on Valera, in his *Obras completas*, ed. Juan Marichal, 4 vols. (México: Oasis, 1966), I, 1035–1058.

[25] Prologue to his edition of *Pepita Jiménez*, p. lx.

[26] Luis Araujo Costa, *Obras completas*, 3 vols.: I, 3rd ed.; II and III, 2nd ed. (Madrid: Aguilar, 1947–1949), I, 25 and 28.

[27] Edith Fishtine, *Don Juan Valera, the Critic* (Bryn Mawr, 1933).

[28] Frank R. Thompson, "The Classicism of Don Juan Valera," Ph.D. Diss., Univ. of Wisconsin, 1941.

[29] *Ibid.*, pp. 110 and 133, respectively.

[30] *Ibid.*, p. 144.

"reminiscent of Spain's classic authors . . . ," of the "lack of figures of speech and the scanty adjectivization" in Valera's nature descriptions, due to his classic restraint and to the painting of scenes from memory.[31] Although his treatment of Valera's style was too general and vague, he saw clearly the psychological nature of Valera's novels: "Valera was far more intrigued by a controlled *spiritual conflict* arising from a dualistic personality, than by a display of unbridled emotions and passions. He studied these spiritual states with the interest of a psychoanalyst and then recorded them, not as case histories, but as works of art."[32]

Sherman H. Eoff classified Valera's critical and literary position as one governed by a "classical idealism" which led him to oppose realism on aesthetic grounds, to seek an "improved copy of nature," and to create characters of universal yet individual qualities.[33] To Eoff:

> *Pepita Jiménez* is a practical demonstration of Valera's theory of classical idealism in that (1) it deliberately paints actualities better than they are, and (2) its whole mechanism is controlled by a single dominating idea—the beauty of love between man and woman, earthly love, in a word, which reflects the divine ideal. In structural technique he adheres to the classical directness of excluding all that is unnecessary to the narrative problem, though he gives the story a philosophical color by concentrating upon an idea rather than a specific mark of human nature. The Platonic concept of individual, earthly experience as a reflection of the Absolute Ideal, a notion of which Valera was fond, becomes a prominent theme in the discussion of aesthetics in the 1880's, and is used to refute realism, which allegedly loses sight of the universal through too much attention to the particular.[34]

Two French Hispanists made particularly suggestive interpretations of Valera. First, a Valerian "philosophy" of aestheticism, ow-

[31] *Ibid.*, p. 145.

[32] *Ibid.*, pp. 148, 158, and 176, respectively.

[33] Sherman H. Eoff, "Pereda's Conception of Realism as Related to His Epoch," *Hispanic Review*, XIV (1946), 281–303. Eoff's classification is perhaps derived from Aubrey F. G. Bell's "Valera and the Classical Idealist Novel," *Contemporary Spanish Literature* (New York: A. Knopf, 1925), pp. 44–48.

[34] Eoff, "Pereda's Conception of Realism," pp. 286–287.

ing much to Santa Teresa and San Juan de la Cruz, was postulated by Jean Krynen.[35] Then, in a related study, Valera's philosophy is said to have centered around his knowledge of poetry; his poetic skepticism; and his optimism, wisdom, and humor. His philosophy supposedly fluctuated between the two poles of his aestheticism—woman and occultism.[36] Too many of the elements pointed out by Krynen, however, such as the interest in the Orient and in occultism, the striving for absolutes, and other vestiges of romanticism, were all part of the atmosphere of the times and would naturally be reflected in Valera's work. Moreover, Valera's concern about the problems of his time and his critical empathy for his characters remove him from pure aestheticism.

More important was R. Romeu's study of Valera's humor. He called *Pepita Jiménez* Valera's best and most characteristic novel, one marked throughout by "ironie sucrée" and the author's "sourire sceptique indéfinissable."[37] Romeu demonstrated that Valera's humor is always present, especially in his ironical treatment of Luis (with his great naïveté), of Pepita (who is falsely religious), and of the Vicar (as an ignorant priest), and concluded: ". . . *Pepita Jiménez* est un chef-d'oeuvre d'humour, et c'est pour cela qu'il est le chef-d'oeuvre de Valera. Humour qui réside dans l'analyse psychologique des divers états d'âme d'un personnage, de ses réactions devant deux grandes questions qui s'opposent: l'amour et la vocation religieuse; humour dans les caractères et dans certains tableaux. Humour malicieux dont la suave et savoureuse ironie ne se départit pas

[35] Jean Krynen, "Juan Valera et la mystique espagnole," *Bulletin Hispanique*, XLVI (1944), 35–72.

[36] Jean Krynen, *L'Esthétisme de Juan Valera, Acta Salmanticensia*, "Filosofía y Letras," vol. II, no. 2 (Salamanca: Universidad de Salamanca, 1946). Cf. also Fermín de Urmeneta, "Sobre la estética valeriana," *Revista de Ideas Estéticas*, XIV, no. 54 (1956), 161–164. Urmeneta characterizes Valera's aesthetics as follows: "Dios, amor, bondad . . . Simetría, conformidad, calidad . . . He aquí el doble tríptico conceptual que ha sido subrayado, . . . y cuyos vigorosos ecos presiden en el integral concepto valeriano de belleza. . . ."

[37] R. Romeu. "Les divers aspects de l'humour dans le roman espagnol moderne," *Bulletin Hispanique*, XLVIII (1946), 97–146, 340–364, and XLIX (1947), 48–83. Valera is discussed in XLVIII, 97–126; the comments quoted are from p. 105.

It has been said that Valera's lack of anguish and a certain serenity in the face of doubt remove him from the ranks of the true humorists. See D. L. Shaw, "*Humorismo* and *Angustia* in Modern Spanish Literature," *Bulletin of Hispanic Studies*, XXXV (1958), 165–176.

un instant du sens de la mesure. . . . Aucune trace de pessimisme, d'amertume ou de sentiment."[38]

Romeu's theory that humor is the informing principle in Valera's work is fundamentally sound; but to me irony is a better term, since there is no humor in which irony is not present and since irony is more appropriate for the description of even minute stylistic elements.

Only a few of the books and essays written by Spanish scholars in the post-Civil War period need be singled out here. Luisa Revuelta y Revuelta's study is the only significant one of Valera's style.[39] It describes, in the French-Swiss *stylistique* tradition, syntactical features and general stylistic means, including formulas, imagery, nature descriptions, and techniques of character portrayal. In general, Valera's style is characterized as *primoroso*, by which is meant a mastery of technique and a charming, graceful sense of proportion.[40] But Revuelta y Revuelta's work has several grave faults: she considered the examples isolated from context, she did not detect Valera's irony, and, while paying lip service to his perfect assimilation of classical style elements, she completely ignored his sources, both Spanish and foreign.

Azorín, although varying from an attitude of hostility to one of praise, made some observations which facilitate the understanding of Valera. In a piece called "Valeriana" he claimed that Valera's poetic vocation was his great "idea fija y pivotal" and stressed the contradiction, which he supposed that Valera enjoyed, between Valera's elegant and erudite poetry (the antithesis of popular poetry) and the great emphasis on "lo cotidiano" and "lo pueblerino" which one finds so prevalent in his novels.[41] Perhaps the key could be found in a comparison with Cervantes: "Cervantes es un hombre de eufemismos, de reticencias, de omisiones. Y Valera usa tales recursos dialécticos: todo Valera, podríamos decir, está en las omi-

[38] Romeu, "Les divers aspects," XLVIII, 119–120.

[39] Luisa Revuelta y Revuelta, "Valera, estilista," *Boletín de la Real Academia de Ciencias, Bellas Letras y Nobles Artes de Córdoba*, XVII (1946), 25–71.

[40] *Ibid.*, p. 63.

[41] José Martínez Ruiz [Azorín], in *De Valera a Miró* (Madrid: A. Aguado, 1959), pp. 25–28. This and the other essays cited from this collection were first published in *ABC* a few years earlier.

siones, en las reticencias y en los eufemismos. Supone todo esto, en Cervantes, una personalidad que se recata. Y sabemos de Valera que era una personalidad que se recataba. Ni Cervantes se da todo en sus libros, ni Valera se da tampoco. Se ha dicho que cuando Valera afirma o niega, hay que mirar mucho cómo lo afirma y cómo lo niega. ¿Y es que en Cervantes no encontramos, a veces, una actitud análoga?"[42] Among other interesting points are Azorín's comments on Valera's style—his elegance, prolixity, frequent use of the pronoun *yo*, and, most notably, his ennobling of colloquial language and his "prosa parlamentaria, prosa de salón."[43]

While Alberto Jiménez made valuable contributions about the background of Valera's novels, his role among his contemporaries, and his philosophical beliefs, the analyses of Valera's novels, mainly concerned with the genesis and interrelations of Valera's works, are unoriginal.[44] Furthermore, he sometimes overemphasized the biographical element in Valera's novels, as well as Valera's own theories and statements of purposes. His interpretation of Valera's artistic merit was rather subjective: "La misma riqueza y finura que Valera eleva a la más alta perfección, imponen limitaciones a su arte y hasta a su propio lenguaje. Está éste colocado también en un punto tal de perfección en que con elementos parciales tomados del lenguaje corriente y de los más sencillos y claros ejemplos clásicos, compone una lengua tan irreal como exquisita y diáfana, que la misma falta de vida y de exuberancia de que ese lenguaje adolece, se nos antojan méritos más que defectos. . . . Es arte maravilloso, buscado, deseado y maravillosamente logrado, pero de escuela."[45] Although Jiménez deplored Valera's lack of the vitality and spontaneity of such writers as Galdós, he conceded that Valera's style was ". . . el que enteramente armoniza con sus novelas, y el que forma con ellas un conjunto tan equilibrado, armónico y bello. . . ."[46]

The best study of Valera's total work and the most complete syn-

42 "Valera y Cervantes," *ibid.*, pp. 29–30.

43 "Nota a Valera," *ibid.*, p. 51.

44 Alberto Jiménez, *Juan Valera y la generación de 1868* (Oxford: Dolphin, 1956).

45 *Ibid.*, pp. 171–172.

46 *Ibid.*, p. 172.

thesis of Valerian scholarship is José F. Montesinos's useful monograph.[47] His intention was to treat Valera as a literary anomaly, a proponent of a highly personal literary art, free from the movements of his time, and to explain his fiction according to Valera's own expressed statements.[48] Such an approach is suggestive but not conclusive, in part because Valera's own comments about his work inadequately explained it. Like Azaña and Jiménez, Montesinos devoted much attention to the genesis and interrelations of Valera's novels, showing clearly the importance of Valera's first novelistic attempt, *Mariquita y Antonio*, and providing a clear account of the circumstances leading to the writing of *Pepita Jiménez* and a good analysis of it. Although he did not treat Valera's style in detail, his comments are always valuable and thought-provoking. He too called Valera the best Spanish prose writer of his time and said that his style, unique among his fellow novelists, was "la integración de un lenguaje literario general, hecho de elementos cultos y populares; algo como lo que fué en el siglo XVI la fórmula nunca expresada de nuestra lengua literaria. . . ."[49] He added that Valera made no attempt at the graphic reproduction of popular language, but adhered to its inner form and that: "Esta lengua hablada—bien hablada—de Andalucía es la principal fuente a que acude Valera. . . ."[50]

As Montesinos, following Azaña's lead, hinted, there might have been a family experience which gave Valera the idea for *Pepita Jiménez*. This hint has been exploited by Mario Maurín to interpret from internal evidence—he found no new biographical facts—an obsessive recurrence in Valera's novels of illegitimacy, with indications that a priest was involved, the *viejo-niña* theme, and love truncated or frustrated until the completion of a mythic labyrinthian ordeal and the disappearance of the dominant maternal figure.[51]

47 José F. Montesinos, *Valera o la ficción libre* (Madrid: Gredos, 1957).
48 *Ibid.*, p. 8.
49 *Ibid.*, pp. 216–217.
50 *Ibid.*, p. 218.
51 Mario Maurín, "Valera y la ficción encadenada," *Mundo Nuevo*, no. 14 (Aug., 1967), 35–44; no. 15 (Sept., 1967), 37–44. See also the article of Paul Smith (who evidently had not seen Maurín's articles), "Juan Valera and the Illegitimacy Motif," *Hispania*, LI, no. 4 (Dec., 1968), 804–811. Smith prefers to treat Luis's illegitimacy (as well as the illegitimacy of other Valerian characters) as the cause of an in-

Books like Montesinos's and collections of Valeriana published recently by Cyrus C. DeCoster have reawakened interest in Valera among Hispanists everywhere. Of the latter's several biographically oriented studies on Valera, one in particular should be mentioned for its general relevance to Valera's novelistic method and relations to literary trends of his time.[52] In it DeCoster documented Valera's ambivalent attitude toward Andalusia, since he was nostalgically drawn to it from afar but incapable of living there permanently, and showed how Valera nevertheless depended more on direct observation of his native region and its inhabitants than on imagination in the writing of his novels. According to DeCoster's appraisal, Valera was only partially a regionalist and *costumbrista*, and there existed only a tenuous relationship between the settings and characters of his novels or between the *costumbrista* material and the main action.

Among the major conclusions to be drawn from the somewhat repetitious criticism on Valera are: that he was influenced by the mystical-ascetical writers of the sixteenth century, that his vocabulary and prose style are classical and elegant, that his novels reveal great psychological penetration, and that irony (or humor) is an important element in his work. All of these points need additional study. It is impossible to treat the first two points without a careful consideration of sources and influences from Spain's Golden Age. Existent criticism and Valera's own frequent statements point consistently toward the greatest of the Spanish mystics, Santa Teresa and San Juan de la Cruz, and to the two most famous of the ascetical writers, Fray Luis de Granada and Fray Luis de León. In defending himself against Pardo Bazán's charges of affectation, Valera disclosed his thorough familiarity with the mystical-ascetical literature of Spain and even said that: "La lectura de los místicos, aún careciendo de la fe que ellos tenían, es, además, muy útil ejercicio para los escri-

---

feriority complex which becomes a stimulus to the seeking of inordinate purity and fame, a seeking which inevitably results in failure.

[52] Cyrus C. DeCoster, "Valera and Andalusia," *Hispanic Review*, XXIX (1961), 200–216. Similar ideas had been expressed by Azaña, "La novela de Pepita Jiménez," *Obras*, I, 1045 ff.

tores de novelas, porque en dicha lectura aprenden a conocer y a describir el alma humana, en cuyos senos nadie penetró nunca más hondo."[53] In the same essay, Valera spoke of theological works, including Fr. Antonio Arbiol's *Desengaños mysticos*,[54] which he had already mentioned in *Pepita Jiménez* and which was no doubt one of the sources of his knowledge of mysticism, both the true and spurious varieties. But since this book, like similar manuals for seminarians, depends so much on Santa Teresa and San Juan de la Cruz and includes such a liberal sprinkling of quotations and paraphrases from their works, it seems advisable to go directly to the mystics, to whom Valera was strongly attracted because of their greater literary merits.

My study will consist of two parts. In Part One I shall point out, first, that Valera subtly parodied mystical-ascetical language of the sixteenth century in his characterization of Luis de Vargas as a false mystic and seminarian without a vocation, that he borrowed from Santa Teresa's *Moradas* and San Juan de la Cruz's *Noche oscura* for special literary effects, and that the style of *Pepita Jiménez* may be characterized in general as mock-spiritual. Then I shall show how Valera expanded the parody to an unobtrusive pastiche of more general *Siglo de Oro* stylistic expressions, mostly taken from *Don Quijote*. All of these elements will be studied in relation to the characters, situations, functions, and values. In Part Two we shall see Valera's excellent psychological penetration in his characterization of Luis as an adolescent. The fourth chapter will consist of a brief study of a kind of critical empathy in Valera and his position in regard to his epoch, and will include a synthesis of refined irony as the informing principle of Valera's style and art in *Pepita Jiménez*. In an appendix, I study more modern aspects of *Pepita Jiménez*'s vocabulary.

To achieve a full aesthetic appreciation of the novel, I shall apply the methods of modern style investigation, particularly according

[53] Juan Valera, *Apuntes sobre el nuevo arte de escribir novelas*, *Obras completas*, ed. Luis Araujo Costa (Madrid: M. Aguilar, 1947–1949), II, 645–646.

[54] Fr. Antonio Arbiol, *Desengaños mysticos* (Barcelona: Thomas Piferrer, 1772).

to Amado Alonso's theory and practice, and shall consider all elements as the subject matter for the work's "expressive system" or "aesthetic structure." As Alonso said, "La estilística estudia la obra literaria como una construcción poética, y esto en sus dos aspectos esenciales: *cómo está construída*, formada, hecha, tanto en su conjunto como en sus elementos, y qué *delicia* estética provoca; o desdoblando de otro modo: como producto creado y como actividad creadora."[55]

Amado Alonso left many practical demonstrations of his theories in several stimulating essays and books. The one most relevant to my study, his analysis of Enrique Larreta's *La gloria de don Ramiro*, will serve me as a practical guide.[56] As a matter of fact, Larreta's novel is in some respects curiously similar to *Pepita Jiménez.* It is a historical novel with overtones of modern psychology and sensibility. Its protagonist, Don Ramiro, is an adolescent and a sensual dreamer with mystical aspirations but without asceticism, like Luis de Vargas, and each young man is more interested in *fama* than in *gloria.*[57] Like *Pepita Jiménez*, Larreta's novel reflects modern Spanish-speaking novelists' great interest in choosing seminarians, priests, or other persons dedicated to ascetic or ecclesiastical life as protagonists for their novels.[58] In this connection, although it will be impractical for me to deviate from my central analysis by drawing general analogies, it is fitting to recall the attention paid to religious problems in Spanish novels of the 1870's, as well as Palacio Valdés's treatment of themes similar to those of *Pepita Jiménez* in *Marta y María* and *La hermana San Sulpicio.* In one important sense, in Spanish writers' propensity to create in beautiful prose a tension between the spiritual and the sensuous, Valera's *Pepita Jiménez* may be considered as a link between the baroque novel and Valle-Inclán's *Sonatas.* It is also informative to place Valera in

[55] Amado Alonso, "La interpretación estilística de los textos literarios," *Materia y forma en poesía* (Madrid: Gredos, 1955), p. 110.

[56] Amado Alonso, *Ensayo sobre la novela histórica: El modernismo en* "*La gloria de don Ramiro*" (Buenos Aires: Instituto de Filología, 1942).

[57] See *ibid.*, pp. 178–179.

[58] See Juan Terlingen, "La novela del sacerdote en las literaturas hispanas," *Clavileño*, vol. VII, no. 39 (1956), 14–18.

Pepita Jiménez somewhere along the trajectory of the development from romanticism and *costumbrismo* to realism, but with strong elements of "classical idealism," which is perhaps the most satisfactory term for his general view of art.

PART ONE

Pseudo-spirituality and Interior Stiltedness Reflected in Siglo de Oro *Stylistic Expressions*

PREMISES

Since its original publication in 1874, *Pepita Jiménez* has been widely acclaimed and is generally considered Valera's best novel. In his prologue to Appleton's English edition, Valera insisted that his aim was to please and denied having any didactic purpose. Nevertheless, he stated, it may happen "que el alma de un autor venga a ser como limpio y hadado espejo, donde se reflejen las ideas y los sentimientos todos que agitan el espíritu colectivo de un pueblo, y pierdan allí la discordancia y se agrupen y combinen en suave conciliación y armonía."[1] His own attitudes toward Krausism, general philosophical trends, and mysticism are a case in point. He had at times made fun of the Krausists and of their involved terminology, in spite of being sympathetic toward their movement, and wished to demonstrate that if the Krausists were pantheistic, so were the Spanish mystics. Montesinos, among other commentators, has pointed out that Valera in his youth shared the ideal of pantheism and Neoplatonism then prevalent in Spain and that he had become disillusioned in them by the time he wrote *Pepita Jiménez*.[2] Within the novel itself, Valera declared the moral lesson to be one against the proud, "con ejemplar escarmiento en la persona de D. Luis" (179), and had the Dean make the following humorous remark about the Krausists: ". . . los krausistas, que ven a Dios, según aseguran, con

[1] *Pepita Jiménez*, ed. Manuel Azaña, "Clásicos Castellanos" (Madrid: Espasa-Calpe, 1953). Subsequent references to *Pepita Jiménez* will be from this edition and page numbers will be indicated within parentheses.

[2] Cf. José F. Montesinos, *Valera o la ficción libre* (Madrid: Gredos, 1957).

vista real, tienen que leerse y aprenderse antes muy bien toda la *Analítica* de Sanz del Río, lo cual es más dificultoso y prueba más paciencia y sufrimiento que abrirse las carnes a azotes y ponérselas como una breva madura" (183).

One must be cautious, however, about placing too much credence in the professed purposes of such a subtle and ironical writer as Valera. Not believing in the sublimation of human love by divine love, he really intended to show that the pseudo-mysticism of his young seminarian could not withstand the onslaughts of his own sensuous nature and of the world around him. Valera went to the mystics for means not only to show up Krausist pantheism as the false mysticism of his day, but to characterize mysticism itself as a similar illusion for all but the very few. Yet, being proud of the mystical-literary heritage of his country, he did not fail to remark that he read all the mystical and devout books possible immediately before writing *Pepita Jiménez.* Valera also made many references to the Spanish mystics in his critical writings, mistakenly including Fray Luis de León among them; but even if he had not openly praised the mystics, internal evidence would indicate how thoroughly familiar he was with their writings. He seems to have been especially influenced by the most classical among them, Santa Teresa and San Juan de la Cruz, to whom he was attracted by their acknowledged merits as mystics, poets, and prose writers. Blanca de los Ríos de Lampérez, combatting the ideas of Blanco García and Julio Cejador y Frauca, took Valera's mysticism more seriously and claimed that Valera was especially impressed by the mystics' psychological penetration: ". . . fue la psicología mística, singularmente, la asombrosa introspección de los místicos . . . que penetró más hondo en el espíritu de Valera, . . . que directamente influyó en la génesis de *Pepita Jiménez*, que hizo a Valera novelista, que le transmitió aquel saber y dominio psicológico. . . ."[3]

There is no doubt that Valera parodied the mystics in a style which constantly evokes the Spanish language of the Golden Age. But it is equally certain that the word "parody" as applied to *Pepita*

[3] Blanca de los Ríos de Lampérez, "De la mística y de la novela de D. Juan Valera," *Raza Española* (Madrid), Año VII, nos. 75–76 (March–April, 1925), 4–18.

Jiménez can only be used in a broad sense; it cannot be applied in the narrower sense of a satirical "takeoff." Nor would the term "pastiche," as it is normally used, be sufficiently broad for *Pepita Jiménez.* Harry Levin, in his essay, "The Example of Cervantes," points out the distinction between pastiche and parody: "His [André Malraux's] dictum—that every artist begins with pastiche—is highly illuminating, so far as it goes; it has to be qualified only by recognizing that *pastiche* implies both activities . . . imitation and parody. The novelist must begin by playing the sedulous ape, assimilating the craft of his predecessors; but he does not master his own form until he has somehow exposed and surpassed them, passing from the imitation of art through parody to the imitation of nature."[4] An essay by Vivian H. S. Mercier likewise sheds light on the nature of parody in literature.[5] Mercier, who calls Joyce's *Ulysses* a thematic and structural parody of the *Odyssey*, says that in it the past as well as the present is being held up to ridicule.[6] He further states that the parody may be of an individual style, of an epoch style, or of a literary or subliterary genre. In this inclusive sense, *Pepita Jiménez* may be viewed as a parody of the Spanish mystics which is couched in language reminiscent of their individual styles and the general style of the *Siglo de Oro*. Its parodistic qualities are discernible in the main action involving Luis and his characterization as well as in the form, particularly in the letters.

4 Harry Levin, "The Example of Cervantes" in "Society and Self in the Novel," *English Institute Essays 1955* (New York: Columbia Univ. Press, 1956), pp. 24–25. Similar ideas are expressed by Levin in his *The Gates of Horn* (New York: Oxford Univ. Press, 1966), pp. 47–48. In general, Levin takes the "parody-novel" as a typical form for the exploration of the relationships between romance and realism, illusion and disillusion.

Additional useful information on parody, whether open and direct or concealed in a narrative, may be found in Gilbert Highet's *The Anatomy of Satire* (Princeton: Princeton Univ. Press, 1962). Highet says that if an imitation or copy "wounds the original (however slightly), pointing out faults, revealing hidden affectations, emphasizing weaknesses and diminishing strengths, then it is satiric parody" (p. 68).

5 Vivian H. S. Mercier in "Society and Self in the Novel," pp. 78–116.

6 *Ibid.*, pp. 83–84.

CHAPTER I: *Pseudo-spiritual Style and the Style of the Mystics*

I. PARALLELS WITH THE MYSTICS

A. *Luis de Vargas: A False Mystic*

Don Luis is more than an ordinary misguided youth; he is also a false mystic who deludes himself into believing that he has been singled out for special favors by God. He would identify his spiritual situation with the mystical stage called "infused contemplation," which is defined by Pascal P. Parente as "a free gift of God, something no effort or preparation of ours can attain for us."[1] The recipient is not active; he merely receives special blessings in a completely passive state, although generally after a life of mortification, which is entirely lacking in Luis's case. Parente quotes the three signs marking the mystical experience as outlined in San Juan de la Cruz's *Subida del Monte Carmelo*.[2] A comparison of this passage by San Juan de la Cruz and Luis's depiction of something like a state of

[1] Pascal P. Parente, *The Mystical Life* (St. Louis: B. Herder, 1946), p. 71. This book is especially useful because in it the contributions of Santa Teresa and San Juan de la Cruz to mystical theology are systematically compared.

[2] *Ibid.*, p. 76.

infused contemplation, to which he aspires, will show the parallelism of ideas as well as general similarities in vocabulary.

Subida del Monte Carmelo (II, 13)

La primera es ver en sí que ya no puede meditar ni discurrir con la imaginación, ni gustar de ello como antes solía; antes halla ya sequedad en lo que antes solía fijar el sentido y sacar jugo. Pero en tanto que sacare jugo y pudiere *discurrir en la meditación*, no la ha de dejar, si no fuere cuando su alma se pusiere en la paz y quietud que se dice en la tercera señal.

La segunda es cuando ve no le da ninguna gana de poner la imaginación ni el sentido en otras cosas particulares, exteriores ni interiores. . . .

La tercera y más cierta es si el alma gusta de estarse a solas con atención amorosa a Dios, sin particular consideración, en paz interior y *quietud, y descanso*, y *sin* actos y *ejercicios de las potencias*, memoria, entendimiento y voluntad, a lo menos discursivos, que es ir de uno en otro, sino sólo con la atención y noticia general amorosa que decimos, sin particular inteligencia y sin entender sobre qué.[3]

Pepita Jiménez (30)

Aunque con poco aprovechamiento en la virtud, aunque nunca libre mi espíritu de los fantasmas de la imaginación, aunque no exento en mí el hombre interior de las impresiones exteriores y del fatigoso método discursivo, aunque incapaz de reconcentrarme por un esfuerzo de amor en el centro mismo de la simple inteligencia, en el ápice de la mente, para ver allí la verdad y la bondad, desnudas de imágenes y de formas, aseguro a usted que *tengo miedo del modo de orar imaginario*, propio de un hombre corporal y tan poco aprovechado como yo soy. *La misma meditación racional me infunde recelo. No quisiera yo hacer discursos para conocer a Dios, ni traer razones de amor para amarle.* Quisiere alzarme de un vuelo a la *contemplación esencial e íntima.* ¿Quién me diese alas como de paloma para volver al seno del que ama mi alma? Pero ¿cuáles son, dónde están mis méritos? ¿Dónde las mortificaciones, la larga oración y el ayuno? ¿Qué he hecho yo, Dios mío, para que Tú me favorezcas?

In the twelfth letter, after he and Pepita have begun to shake hands and to exchange ardent looks, Luis has his first supposed mystical experience; he thinks he has seen Heaven in a mystical vision:

[3] San Juan de la Cruz, *Vida y obras de San Juan de la Cruz*, ed. Crisógono de Jesús, O.C.D. (Madrid: Biblioteca de Autores Cristianos, 1950), p. 639. Future references to San Juan de la Cruz's works will be from this edition. The italics of the text will be supplemented by personal italics; those in quotations from *Pepita Jiménez* will be mine.

"El reino de los cielos cede a la violencia, y yo quiero conquistarlo. Con violencia llamo a sus puertas para que se me abran. Con ajenjo me alimenta Dios para probarme, y en balde le pido que aparte de mí ese cáliz de amargura; pero he pasado y paso en vela muchas noches entregado a la oración, y ha venido a endulzar lo amargo del cáliz una inspiración amorosa del espíritu consolador y soberano. He visto con los ojos del alma la nueva patria y en lo más íntimo de mi corazón ha resonado el cántico nuevo de la Jerusalén celeste" (91). This passage recalls several passages from the Bible which are also mystical in nature,[4] but since all subsequent mystics have drawn inspiration from the prototypical mysticism of the Bible, it is often impossible to separate Spanish and Biblical mysticism and usually unimportant to try to do so.

A few days after he and Pepita kiss for the first time, Luis describes his second experience, which he believes to be an approximation to union with God (here called the Supreme Good), accomplished by means of prayers of quiet, and in which there is a sleep of the powers:

> En todas estas noches he rezado, he velado, me he mortificado mucho.
> La persistencia de mis plegarias, la honda contrición de mi pecho han hallado gracia delante del Señor, quien ha mostrado su gran misericordia.
> El Señor, como dice el Profeta, ha enviado fuego a lo más robusto de mi espíritu, ha alumbrado mi inteligencia, ha encendido lo más alto de mi voluntad y me ha enseñado.
> La actividad del amor divino, que está en la voluntad suprema, ha podido en ocasiones, sin yo merecerlo, llevarme hasta la oración de quietud afectiva. He desnudado las potencias inferiores de mi alma de toda imagen, hasta de la imagen de esa mujer; y he creído, si el orgullo no me alucina, que he conocido y gozado en paz, con la inteligencia y con el afecto, del bien supremo que está en el centro y abismo del alma. (98–99)

This description matches San Juan's imageless, immediate contact, or, to take a modern interpreter, the description given by Parente of one of the infraecstatic states, called the prayer of union: "The

[4] Cf., for example, Apocalypse 21:1–2. On the interrelationships between Spanish and Biblical mysticism, see Helmut Hatzfeld, *Estudios literarios sobre mística española* (Madrid: Gredos, 1955), pp. 29–30.

prayer of union corresponds to the fifth mansion of St. Theresa's *Interior Castle.* This mystical prayer is one step higher than the prayer of quiet. The difference lies merely in the fact that not only the will, as in the former state, but also the intellect is mystically, i.e., passively united; as to the memory there seems to be none left."[5] Luis's two experiences are counterfeit, of course; the stimulus which gives rise to each illusion is physical contact with Pepita. The last example given is from the fourteenth letter and it is worth mentioning that Luis speaks of Pepita before, after, and in the middle of the relation of his supposed experience. Trying in his self-deceiving way to combat the fundamental sensuality of his nature, he only succeeds in creating a curious verbal mixture of eroticism and mystical-spiritual phraseology.

After Luis has fallen victim to Pepita, he finally admits having been a "santo postizo" (172). The author indicates the falsity of Luis's mysticism:

> En cuanto a lo que él llamaba su caída antes de caer, fuerza es confesar que le parecía poco honda y poco espantosa después de haber caído. Su misticismo, bien estudiado con la nueva luz que acababa de adquirir, se le antojó que no había tenido ser ni consistencia; que había sido un producto artificial y vano de sus lecturas, de su petulancia de muchacho y de sus ternuras sin objeto de colegial inocente. Cuando recordaba que a veces había creído recibir favores y regalos sobrenaturales, y había oído susurros místicos, y había estado en conversación interior, y casi había empezado a caminar por la vía unitiva, llegando a la oración de quietud, penetrando en el abismo del alma y subiendo al ápice de la mente, D. Luis se sonreía y sospechaba que no había estado por completo en su juicio. Todo había sido presunción suya. Ni él había hecho penitencia, ni él había vivido largos años en contemplación, ni él tenía ni había tenido merecimientos bastantes para que Dios le favoreciese con distinciones tan altas. La mayor prueba que se daba a sí propio de todo esto, la mayor seguridad de que los regalos sobrenaturales de que había gozado eran sofísticos, eran simples recuerdos de los autores que leía, nacía de que nada de eso había deleitado tanto su alma como un *te amo* de Pepita, como el toque delicadísimo de una mano de Pepita jugando en los negros rizos de su cabeza. (178)

[5] Parente, *The Mystical Life*, p. 129.

Valera reinforces the effect by enumerating mystical terms such as "susurros místicos," "conversación interior," "la vía unitiva," "la oración de quietud," and by the ironically climactic allusion to the well-known *toques* of San Juan de la Cruz, heightened by the absolute superlative, "delicadísimo."[6] These terms occur frequently in the mystics; for instance, the "conversación interior" corresponds to the *hablas interiores* of Santa Teresa. In her *Moradas sextas* she speaks of "unas hablas . . . ; parece que vienen de fuera, otras de lo muy interior del alma, otras tan en lo exterior, que se oyen con los oídos porque parece es voz formada."[7] She says, however, that they may also proceed from the Devil and from the *flaca imaginación.*

The Dean, who realized after the first few letters that his nephew was going astray, remarks in his letter to Don Pedro:

> Luisito me escribe hace días extrañas cartas, donde descubro, al través de su exaltación mística, una inclinación harto terrenal y pecaminosa hacia cierta viudita, guapa, traviesa y coquetísima que hay en ese lugar. Yo me había engañado hasta aquí, creyendo firme la vocación de Luisito, y me lisonjeaba de dar en él a la Iglesia de Dios un sacerdote sabio, virtuoso y ejemplar; pero las cartas referidas han venido a destruir mis ilusiones. Luisito se muestra en ellas más poeta que verdadero varón piadoso, y la viuda, que ha de ser de la piel de Barrabás, le rendirá con poco que haga. Aunque yo escribo a Luisito amonestándole para que huya de la tentación, doy ya por seguro que caerá en ella. (198)

In the supposed note about what Valera calls "la rápida transformación de don Luis de místico en no místico" (181), the Dean expresses no surprise and states: "Pensé que tenía una verdadera vocación, pero luego caí en la cuenta de que era un vano espíritu poético; el misticismo fué la máquina de sus poemas, hasta que se presentó otra máquina más adecuada" (182).

It should be evident from these examples that the ironical treatment of mysticism becomes progressively more marked in the

[6] San Juan de la Cruz usually qualifies the *toques* as being *delicados,* which he often enhances as in the following: "El Verbo es inmensamente sutil y *delicado,* que es el toque que toca al alma . . ."; *Obras,* p. 1209 ("Llama de amor viva," canción 2).

[7] Santa Teresa de Jesús, *Las moradas,* ed. Tomás Navarro Tomás, 6th ed., "Clásicos Castellanos" (Madrid: Espasa-Calpe, 1951), ch. 3, p. 134.

course of the novel, that Valera was well acquainted with mystical literature, that he speculated on the relationship between mysticism and poetry, and that he skillfully depicted the behavior of a false mystic and poetical romantic in the person of Luis.

B. *Imperfections in Luis's Character*

Among the many flaws in Luis that would prevent him from being a mystic, the main one is pride, as Valera himself indicated.[8] Alberto Jiménez commented on this defect: "*Pepita Jiménez* o la Victoria del Amor podría titularse el cuento. ¿Victoria sobre qué? Sobre las falsas vocaciones y el misticismo contrahecho, interpreta Menéndez y Pelayo. Pero de un modo más general podría decirse: sobre el orgullo infundado, sobre la falsa ambición."[9] Quite naturally, these two go together, as is evidenced at the beginning of San Juan de la Cruz's *Noche oscura*, where he points out common imperfections of beginners in mystical life.[10] A listing of these deficiencies in parallel columns with remarks about and excerpts from *Pepita Jiménez* shows Luis to have at least similar faults. (Letters placed in parentheses in the text cited from San Juan de la Cruz correspond to the observations in the right-hand column. It should be borne in mind, however, that the citations from San Juan de la Cruz pertain to the flaws of beginners in quest of mystical favors, while those of Valera's novel concern the behavior of Luis, the *preprincipiante*, in general. Thus the headings are essentially indicative of the divisions of the *Noche oscura* and the particular comparisons drawn are not limited to those of the headings.)

1. *Immaturity* (ch. 1).
Lo cual para que más claramente se vea, y cuán faltos van estos principiantes en las virtudes acerca de lo que con el dicho gusto con facilidad

a. One of the many proofs of Luis's immaturity is his frequent effort to impress people with his "maturity," as in the following passages: "Desde que vivo, desde que soy hombre, y ya

[8] See above, Premises.

[9] Alberto Jiménez, *Juan Valera y la generación de 1868* (Oxford: Dolphin, 1956), p. 134.

[10] San Juan de la Cruz, *Obras*, pp. 815–829. This material is from chapters 1–7; the chapter number will be given in parentheses after each heading.

obran, irémoslo notando por los *siete vicios capitales*, diciendo algunas de las *muchas imperfecciones* que en cada uno de ellos tienen, en que se verá claro cuán de niños (a) es el obrar que éstos obran.

hace años, pues no es tan grande mi mocedad . . ." (164); and "Como salí de aquí tan niño y he vuelto hecho un hombre . . ." (5).

2. *Pride* (ch. 2).

. . . por su imperfección les nace muchas veces cierto ramo de *soberbia oculta* (a), donde viene a tener alguna satisfacción de sus obras y de sí mismos (b). Y de aquí también les nace cierta gana algo vana, y a veces muy rara, de hablar cosas espirituales delante de otros (c), y aun a veces de enseñarlas más que de aprenderlas, y condenan en su corazón a otros cuando no los ven con la manera de devoción que ellos querrían (d). . . . A éstos muchas veces les acrecienta el demonio el fervor y gana de hacer más estas y otras obras, porque les vaya creciendo la soberbia y presunción (e). . . . y a tanto mal suelen llegar algunos de éstos, que no querrían que pareciese bueno otro sino ellos; . . . (d).

. . . Cuando sus maestros espirituales, . . . no les aprueban su espíritu y modo de proceder (porque tienen gana que estimen y alaben sus cosas), juzgan que no les entienden el espíritu (f) . . . ordinariamente desean tratar su espíritu con aquellos que han de alabar y estimar sus cosas (g), y huyen como de la muerte, de aquellos que se las deshacen para ponerlos en camino seguro, y aun a veces toman ojeriza con ellos. Muchos quieren proceder y privar con los confesores y de aquí nacen mil envidias e inquietudes. Tienen empacho de decir sus pecados

a. The most notable illustration of this is Luis's resentful and proud reaction to riding a mule on an excursion (59–61).

b. Luis is self-satisfied: "No me mueve vanidad alguna; no quiero creerme superior a otro hombre" (16).

c. He is fond of discussing religious matters: "todos me refieren sus cuitas y me piden que les muestre el camino que deben seguir" (26). Immediately after this he discusses with the Vicar an "anonymous" case of conscience.

d. Luis criticizes practically everyone, including the Spanish clergy. (See, for instance, the first letter and pages 20–21.)

e. Luis is presumptuous and seems to think his mission is to reform the Spanish clergy: "la escasez de sacerdotes instruidos y virtuosos excita más en mí el deseo de ser sacerdote" (21).

d. (See above.) This may be one of the reasons that Luis is so critical. Another is that, realizing his own deficiencies, he tries to aggrandize himself by comparison.

f. Luis feels that the Dean, who tries to advise him, does not understand him and often defends himself against his charges. (See for example, the entire sixth letter, pages 49–54.)

g. This helps to explain why Luis is so fond of talking with the Vicar, who continually flatters his ego. The

desnudos, porque no los tengan sus confesores en menos, y vanlos coloreando por que no parezcan tan malos, lo cual más es irse a excusar que a acusar (h).

Tambíen algunos de éstos tienen en poco sus faltas, y otras veces se entristecen demasiado de verse caer en ellas, pensando que ya habían de ser santos, y se enojan contra sí mismos con impaciencia (i), lo cual es otra imperfección.

other reason is that the Vicar always talks to him about Pepita. (See page 44.)

h. Luis often uses the verb *confesar* in writing to the Dean and implies that he withholds nothing from him: "le escribo siempre como si estuviese de rodillas delante de V. a los pies del confesionario . . ." (80).

Thus Luis thinks of the Dean as his confessor while writing the letters; his rationalizations will be taken up later.

i. Luis's impatience is evidenced by his wish to be a mystic or saint without going through the arduous preparation. (See page 30.) It is interesting to note that just before this Luis speaks of his "patience" (29).

3. *Lust which comes from spiritual things* (ch. 4). In a description of the causes and qualities of this vice, the following statements are made:

El tercer origen de donde suelen proceder y hacer guerra estos movimientos torpes, suelen ser *el temor que ya tienen cobrado estos tales a estos movimientos* y representaciones torpes . . . (a).

Hay tambíen algunas almas de naturales tan tiernos y deleznables, que, en viniéndoles cualquier gusto de espíritu o de oración, luego es con ellos el espíritu de la lujuria, que de tal manera los embriaga y regala la sensualidad, que se hallan como engolfados en aquel jugo y gusto de este vicio . . . (b).

Cobran algunos de éstos aficiones con algunas personas por via espiritual, que muchas veces nacen de lujuria y no de espíritu; lo cual se

a. Luis frequently speaks of his fear or terror: ". . . no sé qué extraño temor, qué singular escrúpulo, qué apenas perceptible e indeterminado remordimiento me atormenta ahora, cuando tengo, . . . alguna efusión de ternura, algún rapto de entusiasmo . . ." (31).

b. Luis says: "Se me figura a veces que hay en todo esto algo de delectación sensual, algo que me hace olvidar, por un momento al menos, más altas aspiraciones" (31). And later: "Siento una dejadez, un quebranto, un abandono de la voluntad, una facilidad tan grande para las lágrimas; lloro tan fácilmente de ternura al ver una florecilla bonita o al contemplar el rayo misterioso, tenue y ligerísimo de una remota estrella, que casi tengo miedo" (33).

c. (See item 3a, for *remordimiento*.) Although Valera is depicting physi-

conoce ser así cuando con la memoria de aquella afición no crece más la memoria y amor de Dios, sino remordimiento en la conciencia (c).

4. *Wrath* (ch. 5).

. . . se aíran muy fácilmente por cualquier cosilla . . . (a).

También hay otros de estos espirituales que caen en otra manera de ira espiritual, y es que se aíran contra los vicios ajenos con cierto celo desasosegado . . . (b). Todo lo cual es contra la mansedumbre espiritual. . . . De éstos hay muchos que proponen mucho y hacen grandes propósitos (c), y como no son humildes ni desconfían de sí, cuantos más propósitos hacen, tanto más caen y tanto más se enojan. . . .

5. *Spiritual gluttony* (ch. 6).

Todo se les va a éstos en buscar gusto y consuelo de espíritu, y para esto nunca se hartan de leer libros (a), y ahora toman una meditación, ahora otra, andando a caza de este gusto. . . .

6. *Spiritual envy and sloth* (ch. 7).

. . . suelen tener movimientos de pesarles del bien espiritual de los otros, . . . y no querrían verlos alabar; porque se entristecen de las virtudes ajenas, y a veces no lo pueden sufrir sin decir ellos lo contrario (a), . . . y así por esta *acidia* posponen el camino de perfeccíon (que es el de la negación de su voluntad y gusto por Dios) al gusto y sabor de su voluntad . . . (b).

cal lust, the parallel with San Juan de la Cruz shows how Luis confuses religious and erotic feelings.

a. Luis becomes very angry when the Count speaks disparagingly of Pepita: "La sangre de su padre, que hervía en sus venas, le despertaba la cólera y le excitaba a ahorcar los hábitos, como al principio le aconsejaban en el lugar, y dar luego su merecido al señor Conde . . ." (130).

b. This aspect of Luis's makeup has already been indicated. (See above, item 2d.)

c. Luis makes constant references to his calling; all his fanciful plans collapse, however, and, after his fall, he provokes the Count into a duel (187-191).

a. In general, Luis seems to derive sensuous pleasure from religion and evidently read books in search of such enjoyment. He invariably recalls his reading when confronted by a new situation.

a. This could perhaps be one of the motives behind Luis's criticism of others. He contradicts the eulogies of Pepita before he really knows her, for instance, by making fanciful suppositions about her and by referring to her as "esta mujer," "la Pepita," etc. (especially pages 10-14).

b. It should be clear that Luis does not practice self-denial at all and that, in spite of frequent statements to the contrary, he is often idle.

It is apparent that Luis's major defect is his stubborn pride, which is specifically stated by the author to be the only thing that kept Luis from "hanging up the habit" and admitting his love for Pepita

(122–123). The similarities on all the points listed are so striking that San Juan de la Cruz's statements could even have served Valera as an outline for the portrayal of Luis. Although such matters are impossible to ascertain, it is nevertheless quite probable that Valera read and used these or like remarks in his penetrating representation of a pseudo-mystic. Similar remarks can easily be found in the other writings of San Juan de la Cruz, and in those of Santa Teresa as well, by consulting the concordances to their works under the respective words.[11]

c. *Parallels between the Progression of Luis's Love for Pepita and the Ascent of the Mystics toward Union*

Generally speaking, on what may be called a secondary level of parody, the inception, progression, and climax of Luis's love for Pepita have certain affinities with the mystical progression of the *principiantes* to the *perfectos* in their ascent to the transforming union. After his first physical contact with Pepita, the touch of her hand, Luis endeavors to purge himself of his sensual love: "Las mortificaciones, el ayuno, la oración, la penitencia serán las armas de que me revista para combatir y vencer con el auxilio divino" (85). He fails, however, and has to start from the beginning after his first kiss; it is then that he describes his second pseudo-mystical experience (98–99). In the second part of the novel, *Paralipómenos*, something parallel to the preparatory phases of the mystics occurs: on the eve of St. John's Day, Luis goes out into the fields, where everything is conducive to love. Here, as Montesinos has written, "por una vez, Valera se muestra hombre de sensualidad extraordinaria, y no creo que haya en su obra pasaje alguno que pueda compararse al que refiere las sensaciones de D. Luis antes de acudir a la cita. . . ."[12]

Many words and details of this scene and of Luis's ensuing visit

[11] Fr. Luis de San José, *Concordancias de las obras y escritos de Santa Teresa de Jesús* (1945) and *Concordancias de las obras y escritos del Doctor de la Iglesia San Juan de la Cruz* (1948) (Burgos: Tipografía de "El Monte Carmelo").

[12] José F. Montesinos, *Valera o la ficción libre: Ensayo de interpretación de una anomalía literaria* (Madrid: Gredos, 1957), p. 109.

to Pepita's house indicate that Valera may have parodied, although with great subtlety, the mystics in general and Santa Teresa's *Moradas* in particular. The similarity is at first intimated by certain key words, which are like clues to the underlying parody. Luis hears the bells ringing and prays before setting out for Pepita's house: "El lento son de las campanas, amortiguado y semiperdido por la distancia, apenas turbaba el reposo de la tierra, y convidaba a la oración sin distraer los *sentidos* con *rumores*. Don Luis se quitó su sombrero, se hincó de rodillas al pie de la cruz, cuyo pedestal le había servido de asiento, y rezó con profunda devoción el *Angelus Domini*" (145). Noteworthy are the words "sentidos" and "rumores," so often used by the mystics. In a following description, Valera says: "No hay por allí luciérnagas aladas ni cocuyos, pero estos gusanillos de luz abundan y dan un resplandor bellísimo" (146). This remark could be taken as a reference to Santa Teresa's famous metaphor of the silkworm which becomes a butterfly. Words from the following quotation, ". . . a la fuente del río, donde al pie de la sierra brota de una peña viva todo el caudal cristalino que riega las huertas . . ." (146), are reminiscent of San Juan de la Cruz's "cristalina fuente,"[13] of the "ríos caudalosos,"[14] and of the renowned irrigation images of Santa Teresa. While Luis was still outside the town, ". . . sonaron las diez, hora de la cita, en el reloj de la parroquia. Las diez campanadas fueron como diez golpes que le hirieron el corazón. Allí le dolieron materialmente, si bien con un dolor y con un sobresalto mixtos de traidora inquietud y de regalada dulzura" (147). The "golpes" could be compared to the *golpes* used in a mystical sense by Santa Teresa and even to the *toques* of San Juan de la Cruz: "cuantas cosas de él sientes y entiendes, tantos toques y heridas que de amor matan recibes."[15]

Antoñona led the "colegial atortolado y silencioso" (149) into

[13] San Juan de la Cruz, *Obras*, p. 1331 ("Cántico espiritual," canción 12).

[14] Santa Teresa, *Moradas cuartas*, ch. 1, p. 61. For the irrigation images, see especially her *Vida*, ch. 11, in *Obras de Santa Teresa de Jesús*, ed. P. Silverio de Sta. Teresa, 2 vols., 2nd ed. (Buenos Aires: Poblet, 1943), I, 71–72. Hereafter all citations from her works other than *Las moradas* will be from this edition, cited as *Obras*.

[15] San Juan de la Cruz, *Obras*, p. 1008 ("Cántico espiritual," canción 8).

the house. Then they ". . . atravesaron el patio, subieron por la escalera, pasaron luego por unos corredores y por dos salas, y llegaron a la puerta del despacho, que estaba cerrado" (149). Two things are especially significant here. First, the word "atortolado" brings to mind Santa Teresa's "tortolito";[16] and second, they pass through five places to reach the *despacho*, which corresponds to the sixth *morada*. The seventh, of course, will be Pepita's bedroom, which Luis will finally enter. It is meaningful that of all the settings in *Pepita Jiménez*, this inner study and parlor is by far the most fully described and is the place in which the important long dialogues between Pepita and the Vicar and between Pepita and Luis are presented. Santa Teresa's sixth *morada* is likewise the most prominent one; one hundred of the two hundred and fifty-four pages of the *Moradas* (in the "Clásicos Castellanos" edition) are taken up by the sixth *morada*. It is in the center of the spiritual castle, as the *despacho* is in the center of Pepita's house; to it few noises (*rumores*) arrive, as is true of the *despacho*: "En toda la casa reinaba maravilloso silencio. El despacho estaba en lo interior y no llegaban a él los rumores de la calle. Sólo llegaban, aunque confusos y vagos, el resonar de las castañuelas y el son de la guitarra y un leve murmullo, causado todo por los criados de Pepita, que tenían su *jaleo probe* en la casa de campo" (149). It may also be noted that the "criados" mentioned here recall the *criados* and *vasallos* of the spiritual castle. Santa Teresa says of her sixth *morada*: "por poco que sea, es todo mucho lo que hay en este gran Dios, y no quiere estorbo de naide, ni de potencias, ni sentidos; sino de presto manda cerrar las puertas de estas Moradas todas, y sólo en la que El está queda abierto para entrarnos."[17] Is it not perhaps more than coincidental that Valera specifically states that Antoñona closes the door (150) and that the door between the *despacho* and the bedroom is kept open, as is the door between the sixth and seventh *moradas*?[18] Two of the descriptions of the *despacho* stress the following points, several of which also occur in the representation of the sixth *morada*: diffused light,

[16] Santa Teresa, *Moradas cuartas,* ch. 1, p. 59.
[17] Santa Teresa, *Moradas sextas,* ch. 4, p. 152.
[18] Cf. *ibid.*, p. 148.

an inner garden, muted noise (and later, absolute silence), murmur of the fountain, and fragrant aromas (154, 170). The concept of a *morada*, of a secret castle, figures prominently in Luis's daydreams: "No hay duquesa ni marquesa en Madrid, ni emperatriz en el mundo, ni reina ni princesa en todo el orbe, que valgan lo que valen las ideales y fantásticas criaturas con quienes yo he vivido, porque se aparecían en los *alcázares y camarines*, estupendos de lujo, buen gusto y exquisito ornato, que yo edificaba en mis espacios imaginarios, desde que llegué a la adolescencia, y que daba luego por *morada* a mis Lauras, Beatrices, Julietas, Margaritas y Eleonoras, o a mis Cintias, Glíceras y Lesbias" (162). It seems especially significant that he uses the word "morada" here and that he speaks of his personal "*castillo interior*," in which he housed the fancies of his sensuous imagination. He also refers to his and Pepita's future home as their *morada* in a later and similarly fanciful passage (185).

In view of the overall nature of the novel, such a constellation of similarities indicates that Valera may have had Santa Teresa's *Moradas* in mind as a parallel progression when he treated Luis's growing love. Whether or not one accepts this theory, it is clear that Valera borrowed from San Juan de la Cruz and Santa Teresa in the characterization of Luis as a pseudo-mystic, and that, in a general and subtle way, the novel is a mystical parody. The many imperfections in Luis's character and his almost complete lack of the asceticism recognized by the Spanish mystics as the precondition to any mystical experience, make him a false mystic.[19] Without the necessary foundation in asceticism, Luis gives free play to his immature and often feverish imagination whenever aroused by some new situation, which is ordinarily related to the progress of his love for Pepita. Hence the constant recollection of past readings, which included much religious literature, leads him to interpret everything that

[19] Helmut Hatzfeld has commented on the importance of asceticism in true mysticism: ". . . ningún misticismo de ningún pueblo ni de ninguna época ha destacado el elemento ascético con tal energía como los mismos místicos españoles. Tres de las siete *Moradas* de Santa Teresa están consagradas al ejercicio ascético exclusivamente. El golpe maestro de San Juan de la Cruz es su doctrina de que el progreso espiritual, incluso del místico, se halla esencialmente ligado al ascetismo . . ." *Estudios literarios sobre mística española* (Madrid: Gredos, 1955), p. 21.

happens to him in the light of this remembered knowledge and to fill his letters with mystical and spiritual phrases which, in combination with Biblical allusions, make of his speech a stylized theological cant.

II. SPIRITUAL LANGUAGE

Inasmuch as the parody works on a double level, simultaneously exposing a false mystic and the allegedly poor theological training and the misunderstandings of a seminarian, the language is inevitably full of words, phrases, and images from mystical, theological, and general religious writings, thus becoming what may be termed mock-spiritual language. To make true spiritual language mock-spiritual by a fundamentally ironical treatment, Valera has his characters ordinarily mix this language with sensuality or use it for such wrong purposes as rationalization and suasion, or for selfish interests. Even when there is apparent sincerity in the use of spiritual language, the underlying parody is generally discernible. The subtlety of the author is so great, however, that his language, as used by the speakers, is only ironical by allusion to the context; that is to say, separated from the context, it would not appear ironical in itself or discernible from genuinely mystical speech patterns. From the author's perspective, the irony is willed; from the speaker's, it is unwilled. The spiritual language may be studied from the viewpoint of verbal style as well as from that of the ironical structure of the novel. At the same time, both the individual stylistic nuances and the parodistic or ironical functions of the diverse elements within the novel as a whole must constantly be kept in mind.

A. *Spiritual Language from the Viewpoint of Verbal Style*

1. MYSTICAL WORDS AND PHRASES. In addition to the mystical terms previously indicated, many others are used in the novel, sometimes readily perceptible, sometimes half-concealed. In the sixth letter, Luis, attempting to refute his uncle's accusations, sums up what he had said in the third letter about his mystical aspirations:

"Me quejo de *sequedad* de espíritu en la oración, de distraído, de disipar mi ternura en objetos pueriles; ansío volar al *trato íntimo de Dios*, a la *contemplación esencial*, y desdeño la *oración imaginaria* y la *meditación racional y discursiva*. ¿Cómo sin obtener la pureza, cómo sin ver la luz he de lograr el goce del amor?" (49). Although this comment merely repeats earlier remarks (30), it still serves to strengthen the impression of pseudo-mysticism, since all this mystical language is used by Luis for an antispiritual purpose, self-justification. About *sequedad*, constantly referred to by the mystics, for whom it is a necessary trial, Santa Teresa says: "que saquéis de las sequedades humildad, y no inquietud. . . ."[20] This is precisely what Luis fails to do. The different kinds of prayer, meditation, and contemplation are, of course, often treated in mystical and spiritual literature. The motif of raising oneself to God occurs frequently in the novel: "Usted reconoce y aplaude en mí la energía verdaderamente varonil que debe haber en el afecto y en la mente que anhelan *elevarse a Dios* . . . El mismo afecto acendrado y ardiente, que aun en criaturas simples y cuitadas, puede *encumbrarse hasta Dios por un rapto de amor*, logrando conocerle por iluminación sobrenatural, es hijo, a más de la gracia divina, de un carácter firme y entero" (58). This motif reaches its culmination when Luis invites Pepita to join him in the ascent of "esta mística y difícil escala" (168), an evident reminder of San Juan de la Cruz's "escala mística de amor,"[21] which on its part is based on the *scala*-concept of St. John Climacus and St. Bonaventure and is also found at the end of *Il cortegiano*.

Like the mystics, Luis attempts to rid himself of "afectos" and "imágenes": "He procurado *morir* en mí *para vivir* en el *objeto* amado; *desnudar*, no ya sólo los *sentidos*, sino hasta las *potencias* de mi alma, de *afectos* del mundo y de *figuras* y de *imágenes*, para poder decir con razón que no soy yo el que vivo, sino que Cristo vive en mí" (164).[22] The "morir para vivir" idea, though also in other spiritual literature, recalls the famous "muero porque no muero" of Santa Teresa and San Juan de la Cruz, based on the passage indirect-

20 Santa Teresa, *Moradas terceras*, ch. 1, p. 43.
21 San Juan de la Cruz, *Obras*, pp. 900–905 (*Noche oscura*, II, ch. 19).
22 For similar passages, see *Pepita Jiménez*, pp. 75, 98, 99, and 122.

ly quoted (II Cor. 5:15 and Gal. 2:20). Luis often speaks of *objetos*; sometimes, as here, in reference to God; at others, in reference to mundane objects to be driven from the spirit. The great *objeto* in his life, although he refuses to admit it, has become Pepita, his *douça res* in the sense of the Provençal troubadours. The faculties of the soul mentioned here, naturally, cannot be confined to the language of the mystics. Nevertheless, they are so often spoken of in mystical writings that it is difficult not to think of the mystics when encountering in *Pepita Jiménez* repeated comments about the faculties, as well as the frequent occurrence of the words *entendimiento*, *voluntad*, and *memoria* themselves. These words, in combination with *imaginación* and *sentidos*, frequently appearing in close proximity, are especially remindful of Santa Teresa's *Moradas*.[23] Luis has constant recourse to these words in attempting to explain or justify his thoughts: "Desde luego noto, y no me acuse V. de soberbia porque le digo lo que noto, que el imperio de mi *voluntad*, que V. me ha enseñado a ejercer, es omnímodo sobre todos mis *sentidos*" (74). It is interesting to remark the importance of the parenthetical asides in this sentence; they reveal Luis's awareness of his basic self-delusion, thus completely invalidating the main statement.

Aside from such motifs, individual words and phrases also remind one of the mystics. The word "flaqueza," for instance: "Lleno de un provechoso temor de Dios, y con la debida desconfianza de mi *flaqueza*, no olvidaré los consejos y prudentes amonestaciones de V. . . ." (50). And referring to Pepita's kiss, Luis says: "Aún es tiempo de remediarlo todo. Pepita sanará de su amor y olvidará la *flaqueza* que ambos tuvimos" (98). Such phrases as "la música callada" (145) and the "puro amor de Dios" (27), the first of which recalls the identical words of San Juan de las Cruz,[24] serve the same purpose. Luis's comments about light are like the *extremada luz*, *divina luz*, and *luz interior* of Santa Teresa and San Juan de la Cruz. Speaking of Pepita, he remarks: "Es vago, es obscuro, es indescriptible, es como *tiniebla* profunda el más alto concepto, blanco de mi

[23] Santa Teresa, *Moradas segundas*, pp. 27–28, and *Moradas cuartas*, ch. 1, pp. 59–60.

[24] San Juan de la Cruz, *Obras*, p. 1332 ("Cántico espiritual," canción 14).

amor; mientras que ella se me representa con determinados contornos, clara, evidente, luminosa, con la *luz velada* que resisten *los ojos del espíritu*, no luminosa con la otra *luz intensísima* que para *los ojos del espíritu* es *como tinieblas*" (75). Also notable are: the traditional contrast between "luz" and "tinieblas"; the confusion of spirituality and eroticism; and the repetition within one sentence of the comparison, "como tinieblas," and of the phrase, "los ojos del espíritu." Luis, trying to clear himself of his uncle's suspicions, after specifically mentioning San Juan de la Cruz and Santa Teresa, speaks of God as the "esposo" or "dueño" of the soul in a passage particularly reminiscent of the mystics, not only in this central idea, but also in the use of the verb *morar* and of the Biblical words, "siervo" and "hechura": "Porque Dios no más debe ocupar nuestra alma, como su *dueño* y *esposo*, y cualquiera otro ser que en ella *more* ha de ser sólo a título de amigo o *siervo* o *hechura* del *esposo*, y en quien el *esposo* se complace" (50).

In the depiction of Pepita's eyes and of his love, Luis uses the phrases "llama fugaz y devoradora" (81) and "fuego devorante" (86), which recall San Juan de la Cruz's "Llama de amor viva."[25] A similar mingling of courtly love and mystical connotations occurs in the adjective *herido*, not without a trace of irony. Luis tells the Dean in his last letter: "¡Qué mudado va V. a encontrarme! ¡Qué lleno de amargura mi corazón! ¡Cuán perdida la inocencia! ¡Qué herida y qué lastimada mi alma!" (101).[26] This essential ambiguity is found in many other words, which are conventional and, for that very reason, extremely effective in the evocation of different associations. Thus such words as "ejido" (148), "silbo" (31), and "tórtola" (31), typical of San Juan de la Cruz's "Cántico espiritual," may assume an intensified significance. It seems that this secondary level of meaning is often prevalent in whole passages too. Hence when, at the very beginning of the first letter (5), Luis says such things as "con toda felicidad" (used by the mystics for full union

[25] San Juan de la Cruz, *Obras*, p. 1335. More similar remarks, such as "fuego consumidor," may be found in the prose commentary, pp. 1202–1204. On the origin of this metaphor, see Dámaso Alonso, *La poesía de San Juan de la Cruz* (Madrid: Aguilar, 1946), pp. 80–83.

[26] For other uses, see *Pepita Jiménez*, pp. 13, 76, 128, and 129.

with God), “contento,” “me ha embargado el ánimo,” and “todos estos objetos que guardaba en la memoria,” the entire passage takes on a heightened meaning and points to the underlying irony and parody. Similar to this is the use of the verb “impulsar” (141, 142) and of the noun “impulso” (21), which were frequently employed by the mystics. The ironical and even farcical climax in the use of this word comes when Luis follows Pepita into her room: “Pe*p*ita *p*asó la *p*uerta. Su *f*igura se *p*erdió en la o*b*scuridad. Arrastrado D. Luis como *p*or un *p*oder so*b*rehumano, *impulsado* como *p*or una mano invisible, *p*enetró en *p*os de Pe*p*ita en la estancia som*b*ría” (170). The comical elements are further enhanced by the labial, mostly *p*-sounds and by the thereby-provoked use of “en pos de,” instead of the more normal *detrás de*.

Thus it is seen that Valera borrowed all kinds of words and phrases from the mystics, which he used on all levels of the parody. Although some of the parallels may seem faint, the many obvious similarities strengthen and validate the statements made about secondary resemblances.

2. ASCETICAL-SPIRITUAL LANGUAGE. That it is in the main impractical completely to separate mystical language from spiritual language in general has become increasingly evident. Indeed, most writers of literary histories do not separate the mystical from the ascetical writers at all. The reason is that the mystics, of course, had to use general ascetical language in addition to and often simultaneously with strictly mystical language. In Valera’s case the separation would make no sense, in view of the parody’s direction toward nineteenth-century Spain and what Valera undoubtedly considered to be the poor selection and training of candidates for the priesthood. A great deal of the ascetical-spiritual language is used in examinations of conscience, made by Luis of himself and of other characters in the novel. As early as the first letter, Luis mentions this scrutiny of the conscience: “Casi no me atrevo a *confesarme* a mí mismo una cosa; pero *contra mi voluntad*, esta cosa, este pensamiento, esta cavilación *acude a mi mente con frecuencia*, y ya que acude a mi mente, quiero, debo *confesársela* a usted; no me *es lícito ocultarle* ni *mis más*

recónditos e involuntarios pensamientos; usted me ha enseñado a *analizar* lo que el alma siente, a *buscar su origen* bueno o malo, a *escudriñar* los más *hondos senos del corazón*, a hacer, en suma, un *escrupuloso examen de conciencia*" (16). This quotation indicates how remarkably close Valera (in his ironical insistence on what to him was excusable and sin-excluding) came to the modern concept of the unconscious, especially in the phrases "contra mi voluntad" and "mis más recónditos e involuntarios pensamientos." Also noteworthy are the key words used by Luis in his routine examination of conscience. Later the seminarian writes: ". . . pero aseguro a V. que hasta ahora, por más que *ahondo* en mi *conciencia* y *registro* con suspicacia sus más *escondidos senos*, nada descubro que me haga temer lo que V. teme" (51). This passage, like the previous one, occurs in a context of emotional disturbance. When Luis is upset or semiconscious of deviating from the ascetical way of life which he has—in view of his character—wrongly chosen, he resorts to this or like themes, in order to simulate a spirituality which he does not truly possess. What he calls "examen de conciencia" is often nothing more than romantic reverie about his new situation with Pepita: "Aunque me paso todo el día en el campo a caballo, en el casino y en la tertulia, robo algunas horas al sueño, ya voluntariamente, ya porque me desvelo y medito en mi posición y *hago examen de conciencia*. La imagen de Pepita está siempre presente en mi alma. ¿Será esto amor?, me pregunto" (74). In a similarly self-deluding way, Luis frequently makes of his poetical reflections and guilt-revealing rationalizations sham examinations of conscience.[27]

In his suppositions concerning the motivation of the behavior of others, Luis exhibits a tendency to show off his knowledge of casuistry and to meditate and discourse as if he were treating cases of conscience in the role of a father confessor. On a minor scale, many of his remarks about his neighbors are in the same vein; thus he analyzes Pepita's motives, before meeting her (12–13), and states about this analysis: "Como quiera que sea, dejando a un lado estas *investigaciones psicológicas que no tengo derecho a hacer* . . ." (13). But, characteristically, he continues doing so.

[27] See, for example, *Pepita Jiménez*, pp. 80–83 and 92–94.

The outstanding example of examination of conscience is the supposedly anonymous case of conscience (which really concerns Pepita) related to Luis by the Vicar:

> Cuenta el señor Vicario que una *hija* suya *de confesión* tiene grandes *escrúpulos* porque se siente llevada, con irresistible impulso, hacia *la vida solitaria y contemplativa*; pero teme, a veces, que este *fervor de devoción* no venga acompañado de una *verdadera humildad*, sino que en parte le promueva y excite el mismo *demonio del orgullo.*
>
> *Amar a Dios* sobre todas las cosas, buscarle en *el centro del alma donde está*, *purificarse* de todas las pasiones y *afecciones terrenales* para unirse a El, son ciertamente *anhelos piadosos* y *determinaciones buenas*; pero el *escrúpulo* está en saber, en calcular si nacerán o no de un *amor propio* exagerado. ¿Nacerán acaso, parece que piensa la *penitente*, de que *yo*, aunque *indigna y pecadora*, presumo que *vale más mi alma* que las almas de mis *semejantes*; que la *hermosura interior* de mi *mente* y de mi *voluntad* se turbaría y se empañaría con el *afecto* de los seres humanos que conozco y que creo que no me merecen? ¿Amo a Dios, no sobre todas las cosas *de un modo infinito*, sino sobre lo poco conocido que desdeño, que desestimo, que no puede llenar mi corazón? Si *mi devoción* tiene este fundamento, hay en ella dos grandes faltas: la primera, que no está *cimentada en un puro amor de Dios*, lleno de *humildad* y de *caridad*, sino en el *orgullo*; y la segunda, que esa devoción no es firme y valedera, sino que está en el aire, porque ¿quién asegura que no pueda el alma olvidarse del amor a su *Creador*, cuando no le ama *de un modo infinito*, sino porque no hay *criatura* a quien juzgue digna de que el amor en ella se emplee? (26–27)

The italicized words are indicative of the ascetical-spiritual language of this and similar passages. It is particularly meaningful that Luis switches from third person narrative to represented thought (26, line 33), continuing the passage in the first person. Thus he simultaneously presents his own case of conscience and Pepita's; that is, he indirectly identifies himself with her. Everything he says about her, in and after the text cited, applies equally well to himself. The desire for purification and union with God, the idea that this is founded on pride and self-love, and the counsel he offers, all fit his own case perfectly. This fusion is all to the credit of a highly aesthetic sensibility in Valera the novelist.

After an unconvincing profession of humility, Luis advises:

> . . . lo que importa a esta hija de confesión atribulada es mirar con mayor *benevolencia* a los hombres que la rodean, y en vez de *analizar y desentrañar sus faltas con el escalpelo de la crítica*, tratar de *cubrirlas con el manto de la caridad*, haciendo resaltar todas las buenas cualidades de ellos y *ponderándolas* mucho, a fin de *amarlos y estimarlos*; que *debe esforzarse* por ver en cada *ser humano* un *objeto digno de amor*, un verdadero *prójimo*, un *igual* suyo, un *alma* en cuyo fondo hay *un tesoro de* excelentes prendas y *virtudes*, un *ser hecho*, en suma, a *imagen y semejanza de Dios*. Realzado así cuanto *nos* rodea, *amando y estimando* a las *criaturas* por lo que son y por más de lo que son, procurando no tenerse por superior a ellas en nada, antes bien, *profundizando* con valor *en el fondo de nuestra conciencia* para descubrir todas nuestras *faltas y pecados*, y adquiriendo *la santa humildad* y el *menosprecio de uno mismo*, el corazón se sentirá lleno de *afectos humanos*, y no despreciará, sino valuará en mucho *el mérito* de las cosas y de las personas. . . . (27–28)

Here we may point out, in addition to the vocabulary, the ironical juxtaposition of the medical image, "analizar y desentrañar sus faltas con el escalpelo de la crítica," and the Biblical "cubrirlas con el manto de la caridad," and that Luis's change to the first person plural, "nos," reinforces the idea of self-identification with Pepita. In a subsequent letter he states this more explicitly: "A veces me pregunto a mí mismo si al censurar en mi interior esta condición de Pepita no soy yo quien me censuro. . . . ¿Acaso, al creer que veo su alma, no es la mía la que veo?" (39).

Luis is likewise prone to divining the motives of others in the novel. Speaking of his father's affection for him, he writes: "Acaso influya en esto la vanidad. En el amor paterno hay algo de egoísta; es como una *prolongación del egoísmo*. Todo mi valer, si yo le tuviese, mi padre le consideraría como creación suya, como si yo fuera *emanación de su personalidad*, así en el cuerpo como en el espíritu" (18). It is noteworthy that this somewhat cynical claim that love for others is essentially a projection of self-love is in accord with the theories of some modern psychologists.[28] Valera, through the voice of Luis, repeats this idea later, speaking of Pepita: "Es muy cómodo . . . hacer del amor y del afecto a los demás un aditamento y como un complemento del amor propio" (39). By allowing Luis to probe the motives behind the attitudes and actions of those around him, finding in them the faults half-hidden in his own unconsciousness, Valera successfully and artistically anticipates the process called "disowning projection," as defined by Norman Cameron and Ann Margaret: "The assimilative variety of projection is genetically earlier in development than the disowning, and it is more closely related to identification. In its clearest forms, it is no more than *the assumption by a person, without adequate supporting evidence, that others are behaviorally the same or closely similar.* The disowning variety stems from the same implicit assumption; but *it is complicated by a stated or implied denial by the projecting person that he shares the attributes which he ascribes to others.*[29]

Thus Valera, starting from the traditionally Catholic examination of conscience, attains a high degree of psychologically valid penetration into the motives of his characters. This is unobtrusively done by allusion, in an indirect and reflected way; Luis is best portrayed in his own interpretations of others. Such perspicacity is sometimes transmitted through not one, but two or more personalities. All of Luis's remarks in the first letter about Don Gumersindo, Pepita, and her mother are based on second- or even third-hand information, gleaned from conversations with his father, the servants, and perhaps others. Similarly, his interpretation of Pepita's conscience is still primarily dependent on second-hand reports: first, from what the Vicar tells him; and second, from earlier remembered information, already colored by his own personality. An excellent example of this telescoping of character presentation, achieved through a similar telescoping of the examining of others' conscience and motives, occurs in the fifth letter:

[28] Cf. Karl A. Menninger, *The Human Mind*, 3rd ed. (New York: Alfred A. Knopf, 1948), p. 307.

[29] Norman Cameron and Ann Margaret, *Behavior Pathology* (New York: Houghton Mifflin, 1951), pp. 381–382. The italics are of the text.

Por lo que relata el padre Vicario, *entreveo* que en el alma de Pepita Jiménez, en medio de la serenidad y calma que aparenta, . . . hay un amor de pureza contrariado por su vida pasada.

En su devoción a la Virgen se descubre un sentimiento de humillación dolorosa, un torcedor, una melancolía que influye en su mente el recuerdo de *su matrimonio indigno y estéril.*

Hasta en su adoración al niño Dios, . . . interviene el amor maternal sin objeto, *el amor maternal que busca ese objeto en un ser no nacido de pecado y de impureza.*

El padre Vicario dice que Pepita adora al niño Jesús como a su Dios, pero que le ama con las entrañas maternales con que amaría a un hijo. . . . (46)

Two new disturbing factors even further complicate things in this passage: Luis's eroticism and the remembered stain of illegitimacy, which are intimately related in his mind. Thus one character (Luis) is seen making suppositions about another (Pepita), which in turn are based on the suppositions of an intervening character (the Vicar), who is also emotionally involved. All of this is represented in a letter to yet another person (the Dean), likewise affected by what is going on. Therefore, not one, but several personalities and attitudes are simultaneously presented, with a striking condensation and telescoping of means in the service of psychological character portrayal by an aesthetic mirror-technique.

The general introspective and analytical nature of the vocabulary italicized in the preceding examples has doubtlessly already become apparent. Valera is primarily indebted to spiritual literature for this *probing vocabulary*. These words are used to penetrate to "the center of the soul," which, in Valera's novel, often becomes synonymous with the unconscious. For the mystics, it is where the mystical experience takes place: "El centro del alma es Dios. . . ."[30] This is one of the oldest of mystical terms and has been traced back to Plotinus.[31] Valera makes frequent use of the concept, in all of its variant forms: "el centro del alma" (26), "el fondo de mi corazón" (17), "el fondo de su alma" (23), "el fondo de nuestra conciencia"

[30] San Juan de la Cruz, *Obras*, p. 1187 ("Llama de amor viva," canción 1).
[31] Parente, *The Mystical Life*, p. 43.

(28), "los más hondos senos del corazón" (16), "el centro mismo de la simple inteligencia" (30), "el ápice de la mente" (30, 178), and "el abismo del alma" (178, 75). He also employs constructions with *interior*, such as "en mi interior" (39), or with *íntimo*, as in the following: ". . . ¿cómo penetrar en *lo íntimo del corazón*, en el secreto escondido de la mente juvenil de una doncella. . .?" (12).

Of the verbs used in this soul-searching, with the exception of *meditar*, *pensar*, and *reflexionar*, the most common are *asaltar la mente*, *atormentar(se)*, *confesar*, *penetrar*, and *preguntarse*. Valera employs many other introspective and probing verbs: *abatirse*, *abismarse*, *acudir a la mente*, *ahondar*, *analizar*, *desahogarse*, *descubrir*, *desentrañar*, *desnudar*, *entrever*, *escudriñar*, *examinar*, *hundirse*, *infundir*, *profundizar*, *ponderar*, *reconcentrarse*, and *registrar*. By adding the very frequently used verbs of mental exertion, like *esforzarse*, *esmerarse*, *procurar* and *tratar de*, or those of evaluation, with which Luis appraises the actions of others, such as *apreciar*, *aprobar*, *calificar*, *censurar*, *criticar*, *desestimar*, *estimar*, *juzgar*, *tildar*, and *tiznar*, plus the corresponding nouns and adjectives, the list reaches impressive proportions, indicating the general introspective nature of the novel. Although it is by no means implied that Valera did not take advantage of other resources in the Spanish language, the extent and efficacy of his psychologically probing vocabulary are largely a result of his ironical utilization of existing ascetical-spiritual language, particularly that of casuistry.

Much attention is drawn to spiritual language by Luis's references to his imagined mission or calling, which forms one of the novel's leitmotifs. The leitmotif also has the psychological function of serving Luis as a bolster when he is guilty or on the defensive. For instance, he writes in the first letter:

> *Aunque indigno y humilde, me siento llamado al sacerdocio*, y los bienes de la tierra hacen poca mella en mi ánimo. Si hay algo en mí del ardor de la juventud y de la vehemencia de las pasiones propias de dicha edad, todo habrá de emplearse en dar pábulo a una caridad activa y fecunda. Hasta los muchos libros que usted me ha dado a leer, y mi conocimiento de la historia de las antiguas civilizaciones de los pueblos

de Asia, unen en mí la curiosidad científica al deseo de propagar la fe, y me convidan y excitan a irme de *misionero al remoto Oriente.* Yo creo que no bien salga de este lugar, donde usted mismo me envía a pasar algún tiempo con mi padre, y *no bien me vea* elevado a la dignidad del sacerdocio, y *aunque ignorante y pecador como soy, me sienta* revestido por don sobrenatural y gratuito, merced a la soberana bondad del Altísimo, de la facultad de perdonar los pecados y de la misión de enseñar a las gentes, y *reciba* el perpetuo y milagroso favor de traer a *mis manos impuras* al mismo Dios humanado, dejaré a España y me iré a tierras distantes a *predicar el Evangelio.* (15–16)

Also significant are: the three expressions of false humility, "Aunque indigno y humilde," "aunque ignorante y pecador como soy," with their concessive restriction, and "mis manos impuras"; the incongruous juncture of "la curiosidad científica" and the "deseo de propagar la fe"; the rather romantic idea of the Orient; and the involved structure of the last sentence, with the "timid" clauses dependent on "no bien" ("me vea," "me sienta," and "reciba") progressively further separated by intervening phrases. The most disturbing factor is the thought of his relationship with his father, that is, his illegitimate birth, which becomes a feature of his pride, thus causing him to speak so much of humility. He broaches the subject before the text cited, and briefly recurs to it immediately afterwards, only to lapse promptly into an immature and self-conscious discourse on education, not without veiled allusions to his own situation. After finally treating the matter, he again speaks of his vocation, with certain qualms which he manages to settle in his favor (18–19).

He returns to the theme twice in the third letter (29, 32), in which he also speaks of his supposed mystical favors (30). Religious zeal is utilized here to compensate his guilt for having become so emotional, a guilt which is in reality motivated by the beginning of his love for Pepita. He says: "Hace pocos días cumplí veintidós años. Tal ha sido hasta ahora mi fervor religioso, que no he sentido más amor que el inmaculado amor de Dios mismo y de su santa religión, que quisiera difundir y ver triunfante en todas las regiones de la tierra. Confieso que algún sentimiento profano se ha mezclado con esta pureza de afecto" (32). He goes on to formulate some rather curious ideas about the role of knowledge and the love of self-glory in Christianity.

In the midst of his relation to the Dean of the trip to Pepita's *huerta*, after making several revealing remarks about the physical attractiveness of Pepita and of her servants, Luis returns to the idea of his mission, this time to justify Pepita's neatness and his own sense of guilt (39–40). He writes: ". . . se satisfarían no sólo mis nobles y desinteresados deseos, sino también mis deseos egoístas, mi amor a la gloria, mi afán de saber, mi curiosidad de ver tierras distantes, mi anhelo de ganar nombre y fama" (39). Then, before openly defending Pepita, he adds:

> *Yo he recibido ya las órdenes menores*; he desechado de mi alma las vanidades del mundo; *estoy tonsurado*; *me he consagrado al altar*, y, sin embargo, un porvenir de ambición se presenta a mis ojos, y veo con gusto que puedo alcanzarlo y me complazco en dar por ciertas y valederas las condiciones que tengo para ello, por más que a veces llame a la modestia en mi auxilio, a fin de no confiar demasiado. En cambio, esta mujer, ¿a qué aspira ni qué quiere? *Yo la censuro de que se cuida las manos*; de que mira tal vez con complacencia su belleza; *casi la censuro de su pulcritud*, del esmero que pone en vestirse, de yo no sé qué coquetería que hay en la misma modestia y sencillez con que se viste. ¡Pues qué! ¿La virtud ha de ser desaliñada? ¿Ha de ser sucia la santidad? (39–40)

In a subsequent passage, Valera ironically represents Luis's thoughts about his calling, here used in a vain effort to overcome his love (124–125). Valera heightens the effect with enumerations, including such words as "codicia," "ángel," "arcángel," "potestad criada," "dignidad," "rebaño," and "pastor." In general, we may conclude, Luis evinces a rather fanciful concept of the duties of priesthood, since he is more interested in mysteries and adventures than in the assumption of serious charges and obligations.

Many words and phrases from spiritual language used throughout the novel are traditional or even stereotyped, as in the following: "Me alegro de no ser cándido y de ir derecho a la virtud, y en cuanto cabe en lo humano, a la perfección, sabedor de todas las tribulaciones, de todas las asperezas que hay en *la peregrinación* que debemos hacer con [*sic*, por] este *valle de lágrimas*, y no ignorando tampoco lo llano, lo fácil, lo dulce, lo sembrado de flores que está, en apariencia, *el camino que conduce a la perdición* y a la muerte eterna" (17). Other clichéd expressions in the novel, like "con paciencia poco evangélica" (10), "pecar de prolijo" (19, 122), and "predicar en desierto" (130), are used ironically and will be treated later. Even such time-honored sayings as *es un ángel* are often revived by some new usage. Speaking of Pepita's matrimony with Don Gumersindo, Luis calls her the "angel tutelar" (12) of her family and often uses this word in describing her. Since he refers to his mother as "un ángel de bondad y mansedumbre" (18), and since he similarly idealizes each of them, the word *ángel* becomes one of the means by which he gradually identifies Pepita with his (as he believes) martyred mother. When Luis thinks of his "Angel de la Guarda" (147), it is as the voice of his conscience; but Don Pedro's use of the phrase is purely ironical: ". . . tomaría a Pepita por mujer para que me sonriese al morir como si fuera el *ángel de mi guarda que había revestido cuerpo humano* . . ." (200). Curiously, Luis had already expressed a similar thought, saying that Pepita was "como ángel que toma forma humana" (12). The trick of having one character repeat previous remarks of another character is one of the main features of the novel and seems to indicate a general mingling of voices, that is, conscious or unconscious imitation by the speakers of one another, justified by Luis's intermediary reporting.

In regard to formal principles, Valera has a special predilection for spiritual proparoxytones, which he uses for both rhythmical and ironical purposes. A partial list follows: *Angelus*, *apocalíptico*, *apócrifo*, *apostólico*, *catecúmeno*, *cántico*, *evangélico*, *gentílico*, *Líbano*, *mísero*, *neófito*, *Paráclito*, *Paralipómenos*, *sacrílego*, *simoníaco*, *túnica*, and *virgíneo*. The ironical climax in the use of these proparoxytones occurs toward the end of the novel: ". . . Luis se consuela y se conforma con no haber sido un varón *místico, extático y apostólico* . . ." (213).

Rather than citing passages replete with general religious words and phrases, I shall present two selected lists. First, words of high frequency: *caridad*, *contemplación*, *criatura*, *devoción*, *escrúpulo*, *mortificación*, *profano*, *prójimo*, *recogimiento*, *santo*, *sermón*, and *teólogo*. Second, those rare but more varied ones of low frequency: *Artífice*, *soberano*, *bienaventuranza*, *consurrección*, *Cordero*, *Custodia*, *escapulario*, *esclavina*, *evangelizar*, *Extremaunción*, *hermandad*, *homilía*, *hueste*, *incensario*, *iniquidad*, *inmaculado*, *levadura del vicio*, *mancilla*, *mandamiento*, *mansedumbre*, *ministro del Altísimo*, *mitra*, *moralizar*, *oratorio*, *ordenarse*, *pastor*, *pecaminoso*, *penitencia*, *plegaria*, *pontificio*, *potestad*, *purgatorio*, *querubín*, *renacer*, *reverencia*, *sacerdocio*, *sacramento*, *salvación*, *serafín*, *tonsurar*, *vestimentas*, and *virtudes teologales*. These listings, while indicative of the great number of such words employed by Valera, leave out the all-important context, which is rarely, if ever, one of true spirituality. These words are used primarily for purposes of parody, ironical criticism, characterization, and general atmosphere. Yet Valera is skillful enough to make them unobtrusive and only one step removed from the expression of real religious feeling, thus providing multiple opportunities for ambiguity, an important characteristic of his style.

3. THEOLOGICAL LANGUAGE. The characters of *Pepita Jiménez*, especially Luis and the Vicar, employ many terms from general theological language. Luis's fondness for displaying his knowledge of theology often causes his speech to sound affected: "*Para complacerle me violento y procuro aparentar que me gustan las diversiones de aquí*, las jiras campestres y hasta la caza, a todo lo cual le acompaño. Procuro mostrarme más alegre y bullicioso de lo que naturalmente soy. Como en el pueblo, medio de burla, medio en son de elogio, me llaman el *santo*, yo por modestia *trato de disimular estas apariencias de santidad o de suavizarlas y humanarlas con la virtud de la eutropelia* [*sic*, *eutrapelia*], ostentando una alegría serena y decente, la cual nunca estuvo reñida ni con *la santidad* ni con *los santos*" (19–20). His essential hypocrisy is evident here; he attempts to deceive himself, his uncle, and the others. He really enjoys the local diversions and worsens his self-delusion by pretending to have to make a violent effort even to appear happy, so

"devout" is his true nature. Ironically, he uses the verb *humanar*, often meaning "God becoming man," in which sense it had previously occurred (16). It seems that he would have more logically chosen *humanizar*, which is used later by Don Pedro in a similar context (199).

Luis frequently appeals to the Church Fathers for aid in his rationalizations or self-justifications: "Dice V. que la gran victoria en cierto género de batallas consiste en la fuga: que huir es vencer. ¿Cómo he de negar yo lo que el Apóstol y tantos santos Padres y Doctores han dicho?" (56). He then refutes his uncle's and St. John Chrysostom's assertion that it was a "mayor prodigio el que Josef no ardiera, que el que los tres mancebos que hizo poner Nabucodonosor en el horno candente no se redujesen a cenizas" (57). The reason is that his uncle had compared his and Pepita's situation to that of Joseph and Potiphar's wife (Gen. 39:7–20). Luis belittles the fact that Joseph had disdained the lady's love by claiming that the other wonder was greater, thus endeavoring to attenuate the danger of his growing love for Pepita:

> Confieso con ingenuidad que, lo que es en punto a hermosura, no atino a representarme que supere a Pepita Jiménez la mujer de aquel príncipe egipcio, mayordomo mayor o cosa por el estilo del palacio de los Faraones; *pero ni yo soy como Josef*, agraciado con tantos dones y excelencias, *ni Pepita es una mujer sin religión y sin decoro*. Y aunque fuera así, aun suponiendo todos estos horrores, *no me explico la ponderación de San Juan Crisóstomo* sino porque vivía en la capital corrompida, y semi-gentílica aún, del Bajo Imperio; en aquella corte, cuyos vicios tan crudamente censuró y donde la propia emperatriz Eudoxia daba ejemplo de corrupción y de escándalo. Pero hoy, que la *moral evangélica* ha penetrado más profundamente en el seno de la sociedad cristiana, me parece exagerado creer más milagroso el casto desdén del hijo de Jacob que la incombustibilidad material de los tres mancebos de Babilonia. (57)

Although Valera's main intention is to show Luis's specious reasoning, he is also making fun of theological hairsplitting. The humorous artificiality of Luis's speech is indicated by the overly conscious erudition of "incombustibilidad material."

After having "preached" unsuccessfully to the Count in the Casino, Luis consoles himself in a rationalizing soliloquy so full of Biblical reminiscences that it becomes something of a pastiche (132–133). Most of the references, of course, are from the Sermon on the Mount, but since Luis has vengeance in mind, he also paraphrases Isaiah (63:1–3):

¿Por qué me he de dejar vencer de la ira? Muchos santos Padres lo han dicho: "La ira es peor aún que la lascivia en los sacerdotes." La ira de los sacerdotes ha hecho verter muchas lágrimas y ha causado males horribles. Esta ira, consejera tremenda, tal vez los ha persuadido de que era menester que los pueblos sudaran sangre bajo la presión divina, y ha traído a sus encarnizados ojos *la visión de Isaías*, y han visto y han hecho ver a sus secuaces fanáticos al *manso Cordero convertido en vengador inexorable*, descendiendo de la cumbre de Edón, soberbio con la muchedumbre de su fuerza, pisoteando a las naciones como el pisador pisa las uvas en el lagar, y con la vestimenta levantada y cubierto de sangre hasta los muslos. ¡Ah, no, Dios mío! Voy a ser tu ministro; Tú eres un Dios de paz, y mi primera virtud debe ser la *mansedumbre*. Lo que enseñó tu Hijo en el sermón de la Montaña *tiene que ser* mi norma. *No ojo por ojo, ni diente por diente*, sino amar a nuestros enemigos. Tú amaneces sobre justos y pecadores, derramas sobre todos la lluvia fecunda de tus inexhaustas bondades. Tú eres nuestro Padre, que estás en el cielo, y *debemos ser perfectos como Tú*, perdonando a quienes nos ofendan, y pidiéndote que los perdones porque no saben lo que hacen. Yo *debo recordar las bienaventuranzas. Bienaventurados cuando os ultrajaren y persiguieren y dijeren todo mal de vosotros.* El sacerdote, el que va a ser sacerdote, *debe ser* humilde, pacífico, *manso de corazón.* (132–133)

It is easy to see that Luis rearranges things to suit his own purposes and that, although he deludes himself into believing that he has overcome his anger, his behavior immediately afterwards, as well as the fact that he provoked the Count into a duel as soon as he was free to do so, proves that this is not true. The way he uses the verbs *deber* and *tener que* indicates that he is trying, in vain, to convince himself that he must be meek. It is evident that he uses the Sermon on the Mount for his own purposes, because, when he says "Bienaventurados cuando os ultrajaren y persiguieren y dijeren todo mal de vosotros," he significantly leaves out the concluding words of the verse, "mintiendo, por mi causa."[32] Then Luis ends the passage with the traditional comparison of the oak and the reed, symbols of pride and humility. If there were any doubt about Valera's ironical intention, the ensuing remarks about Don Pedro would dispel it: "Su padre, que no iba a cantar misa y que tenía una índole poco sufrida . . ." (133). It is curious to note that when Luis arrives at Pepita's house, Antoñona refers to Pepita as "la sal de la tierra" (149), also from the Sermon on the Mount, but perhaps with an allusion also to such expressions as *tiene salero* (or *sal*).

Theological and philosophical terms and reasoning may merge, as when Luis associates the "idea of God" with the "idea" or "ideal" he has formed of Pepita: "*Esto que yo amo* es V., y V. tal cual es; pero es tan bello, tan limpio, tan delicado esto que yo amo, que no me explico que pase todo por los sentidos de un modo grosero y llegue así hasta mi mente. Supongo, pues, y creo, y tengo por cierto, que estaba antes en mí. Es como la *idea* de Dios, que estaba en mí, *que ha venido a magnificarse* y desenvolverse en mí, y que, sin embargo, *tiene su objeto real, superior, infinitamente superior a la idea.* Como creo que Dios existe, creo que existe usted y que *vale V. mil veces más que la idea* que de usted tengo formada" (161–162). Here again the parody works on a double level: first, of the seminarian's twisted reasoning; second, of the Krausists. While Valera lends Luis the Platonic-Kantian-Krausist concepts of innate ideas, he also ironizes the Germanic idealism in Luis's romantic nature. For the Krausists, the problem of the idea and its corresponding reality was one of great concern. They tried to modify the Platonic concept of the idea as the only genuine reality and to make of it the generating principle of reality and later the ideal. Juan López Morillas comments on this point: "El segundo significado del *Urbild* lo constituye la realización en el tiempo del mentado principio generador. En esta etapa la *idea* se convierte en *ideal*, u objetivo hacia el que se orienta la voluntad racional."[33] Luis says, in effect, "all that I am

[32] Matt. 5:11. *Biblia Sacra iuxta Vulgatam Clementinam* (Madrid: Biblioteca de Autores Cristianos, 1946).

[33] Juan López Morillas, *El krausismo español* (México: Fondo de Cultura Económica, 1956), p. 71.

saying, this idea, is magnificent; but the reality behind it is infinitely superior to the idea." He had previously tried to convert Pepita into an "idea," in an effort not to love her: "Aunque yo me represente a Pepita como una *idea*, como una *poesía*, no deja de ser la *idea*, la *poesía* de algo finito, limitado, concreto, mientras que el amor de Dios y el concepto de Dios todo lo abarcan" (75).

The Vicar's speech also abounds in theological language, which is not always used for pure motives. He is quite fond of Pepita, perhaps excessively so, and is upset when he learns that she and Luis are in love. He advises her to renounce her love for him and to marry Don Pedro, not without an implied emotional involvement:

Esta vida es muy breve y pronto se pasa. En el cielo os reuniréis y os amaréis como se aman los ángeles. Dios aceptará vuestro sacrificio y os premiará y recompensará con usura. Hasta tu amor propio debe estar satisfecho. ¡Cuán honda herida no habrás logrado hacer en su corazón! Bástete con esto. ¡Sé generosa, sé valiente! Compite con él en firmeza. Déjale partir; lanza de tu pecho el fuego del amor impuro; *ámale como a tu prójimo*, por el amor de Dios. *Guarda su imagen* en tu mente, pero *como la de criatura predilecta*, reservando al Creador la más noble parte del alma. No sé lo que te digo, hija mía, porque estoy muy turbado; pero tú tienes mucho talento y mucha discreción, y me comprendes por medias palabras. (114)

In view of Luis's and Pepita's true natures, his advice seems poor. Also, it is not theologically sound because there is no union or betrothal in Heaven and because the promised Christian reward is not to be used for bargaining. A little earlier the Vicar had made a similar statement: "Arrepiéntete tú también, y se acabó. Dios os perdonará y *os hará unos santos*" (112). Later he adds ". . . conservarás de él un grato y melancólico recuerdo que no te hará daño. Será como una hermosa poesía que dorará con su luz tu existencia" (115). The passage following this remark is similarly theological in tone; the Biblical phrases again seem to be put to a wrong use. Valera, clearly wanting to show the Vicar's involvement, says after describing Pepita's hands: ". . . todo era para volver loco a *cualquier hombre*. El *virtuoso* Vicario comprendió, a pesar de sus ochenta años, la caída o tropiezo de D. Luis" (112). Valera seems to be adding to himself, after "a cualquier hombre," "*including* the Vicar." The irony of "virtuoso" is apparent. The Vicar left Pepita's house, ". . . sin poder resistir *ciertos estímulos de vanidad* al considerar la influencia que ejercía sobre el noble espíritu de aquella preciosa muchacha" (117).

Pepita, influenced by the two persons whom she admires the most, Luis and the Vicar, imitates their speech, thus using much of the same theological and spiritual language in a similarly involved and specious way. Speaking to the Vicar, she says: "Usted veía y trazaba en D. Luis el modelo ejemplar del sacerdote, del misionero, del varón apostólico; ya predicando el Evangelio en apartadas regiones y convirtiendo infieles, ya trabajando en España para realzar la cristiandad, tan perdida hoy por la impiedad de los unos y la carencia de virtud, de caridad y de ciencia de los otros. . . . Yo anhelaba cometer un robo sacrílego. Soñaba con robársele a Dios y a su templo, como el ladrón, enemigo del cielo, que roba la joya más rica de la venerada Custodia" (111). The first sentence is a paraphrase of what Luis had written in the second letter (20); it seems likely, therefore, that he or the Vicar must have voiced these ideas in Pepita's presence and that the phraseology and such terms as "varón apostólico" and "robo sacrílego" came to her from them. After the Vicar's departure, she repeats some of his ideas to Antoñona, showing clearly that they, as well as the phrasing of them, are superficial and unconvincing:

Yo había soñado una vida venturosa al lado de este hombre que me enamora; yo me veía ya elevada hasta él por obra milagrosa del amor; mi pobre inteligencia en comunión perfectísima con su inteligencia sublime; mi voluntad siendo una con la suya; con el mismo pensamiento ambos; latiendo nuestros corazones acordes. ¡Dios me le quita y se le lleva, y yo me quedo sola, sin esperanzas ni consuelo! ¿No es verdad que es espantoso? Las razones del padre Vicario son justas, discretas. . . . Al pronto me convencieron. Pero se fué, y *todo el valor de aquellas razones me parece nulo; vano juego de palabras; mentiras, enredos y argucias.* (119)

Luis, as we have seen, had expressed similar thoughts in his letters and, no doubt, in his conversations with Pepita. It is difficult not to think, when reading the last sentence, that this is exactly how Valera feels about the language and reasoning of theologians in general; applied to the Vicar and Luis, of course, the words are literally true. A little later, Pepita more obviously repeats the Vicar's words: "Si muero por él, él me amará, él guardará mi imagen en su memoria, mi amor en su corazón; y *Dios*, que es tan bueno, *hará que yo vuelva a verle en el cielo, con los ojos del alma*, y que allí nuestros espíritus se amen y se confundan" (121). She reveals how alien all of this really is to her when, forgetting her Catholic education, she blasphemously tells Antoñona: ". . . es horrible lo que voy a decir, pero lo siento aquí, en el centro del pecho; me arde aquí, en la frente calenturienta: yo por él daría hasta la salvación de mi alma" (120). In a subsequent dialogue she tells Luis how much she loves him and adds: "No; yo no soy cristiana, sino idólatra materialista" (169). The dominant note in Pepita's makeup is actually sensuality, which is usually hidden under a thin veneer of pseudo-spiritual language that she is influenced to use, contrary to her true nature, by the admiration she feels for Luis and the Vicar. Of course, she may have other reasons for speaking in this way: to make amends for having married Don Gumersindo, to try to mitigate the passion she feels for Luis, or to express an ironical repartee, as in her conversation with Luis: "Cierto es que en *mi humilde inteligencia* no puede usted hallar rivales tan poderosos como yo tengo en la de V. Ni con la *mente*, ni con la *voluntad*, ni con el afecto atino a *elevarme* a Dios inmediatamente. Ni por naturaleza, ni por gracia subo ni me atrevo a querer *subir tan encumbradas esferas*" (165).

In conclusion, the characters of *Pepita Jiménez* often use pseudo-spiritual and theological language for improper purposes and in a manner that seldom indicates true spirituality. Their speech, which could frequently be characterized as cant, reveals the author's ironical-critical attitude. Luis, when confronted by a new situation, invariably relates everything to his knowledge of spiritual literature; and, indeed, to such an extent does he confuse things in his mind that he can no longer separate them, as the author explicitly states: "Estas y otras razones de un orden egoísta militaban también contra la viuda, a par de las razones legítimas y de sustancia; pero *todas las razones se revestían del mismo hábito religioso,* de manera que el propio D. Luis no acertaba a reconocerlas y distinguirlas, creyendo amor de Dios, no sólo lo que era amor de Dios, sino asimismo el amor propio" (123–124). Thus we can say that Luis and the Vicar speak in a stylized cant, and that Pepita is inspired to imitate them and their involved speech habits. Therefore, it would seem more pertinent to observe why and how Pepita uses spiritual language than to censure, as many have done, the "artificiality" of her speech. The apparent artificiality is cleverly arranged by the author for characterization, to expose the partially concealed irony, and to point out the intricate cross-relations among the characters.

B. *Spiritual Language from the Viewpoint of the Ironical Structure*

Within the novel's basically ironical structure, that is, the twofold parody, all the mystical and spiritual language employed is essentially ironical. Luis, the Vicar, the Dean, and Pepita use this language in such a way that, while believing themselves to be truly devout, they unavoidably disclose what for them is unintentional irony; but when the author, Don Pedro, and Antoñona use it, the irony is deliberate. Since the irony has been pointed out incidentally in the examples of the preceding section, only the more obvious cases of the ironical usage of spiritual language need be presented here.

1. KEY WORDS. The words *místico* or *misticismo, santo* or *santidad, sermón, teólogo* or *teología,* and *varón* are almost invariably employed ironically and serve as key words in the parody. Even when Luis refers to the Spanish mystics by name, the irony is easily detectable, as in his attempt to justify Pepita's extreme care of her hands: ". . . pero si tiene esta vanidad, es disculpable en la flaqueza humana, y al fin, si yo no estoy trascordado, creo que Santa Teresa tuvo la misma vanidad cuando era joven, lo cual no le impidió ser una santa tan grande" (36). Reporting what his father told him concerning Pepita, Luis writes: "El aseo y el esmero de su persona poco tenían de *cenobíticos. . . . Ella imagina que su alma está llena de un místico amor de Dios,* y que sólo con Dios se satisface, porque no ha

salido a su paso todavía un mortal bastante discreto y agradable que le haga olvidar hasta a su Niño Jesús" (25). As will be seen, practically everything said in such a vein by Don Pedro is ironical, as are all references to Pepita's *Niño Jesús.*

Luis's concluding remarks to the Vicar on Pepita's case of conscience are ironical in more ways than one: "Si, como sospecho, es Pepita Jiménez la que ha consultado al señor Vicario sobre estas dudas y tribulaciones, me parece que *mi padre no puede lisonjearse todavía de ser muy querido;* pero, si el Vicario acierta a darla mi consejo, y ella le acepta y pone en práctica, o vendrá a hacerse *una María de Agreda o cosa por el estilo,* o, lo que es más probable, dejará a un lado *misticismos y desvíos* y se conformará y contentará con aceptar la mano y el corazón de mi padre, que *en nada es inferior a ella*" (28). The first thing to be noted is that Luis himself jestingly uses the word "misticismos," in this case associated with "desvíos," and that there is a touch of irony in the addition of the informal "o cosa por el estilo" to the name of the mystic visionary, María de Agreda. It is also obvious that, even while attempting to give spiritual advice, he thinks of the situation between Pepita and Don Pedro, making two indirect thrusts: that Pepita does not love his father and that the latter "en nada es inferior a ella," a phrase which, in view of the many critical remarks he has been making about her, is something less than a compliment. A later use of the word *misticismo* in Valera's representation of the Vicar's consternation at the thought of Luis's being in love is also ironical: "Si el santo de su mayor devoción hubiera sido arrojado del altar y hubiera caído a sus pies, y se hubiera hecho cien mil pedazos, no se hubiera el Vicario consternado tanto. Todavía miró a Pepita con incredulidad, como dudando de que aquello fuese cierto y no una alucinación de la vanidad mujeril. Tan de firme creía en la *santidad* de D. Luis y en su *misticismo*" (109). The author's ironical criticism of the Vicar is attributable to the fact that the Vicar does not have sufficient judgment to recognize Luis for what he really is. The sentence beginning with "Si el santo . . ." makes the irony more apparent, as does the Vicar's subsequent humorous remark: "—¡Las mujeres son peores que pateta! . . . Echáis la zancadilla al mismísimo mengue" (109).

Toward the end of the novel the word *misticismo* again marks a scoffing note, here enhanced by the colloquialism, *salir huero*: "Temeroso el señor Deán de que su hermano le embromase demasiado con que el *misticismo* de Luisito había *salido huero* . . ." (203).

The irony is similarly denoted by *santo* and *santidad*, employed in such phrases as "supuesta santidad" (82), "un aspirante a santo" (123), "santa ambición" (123), and "santo postizo" (172). After Luis's duel, his *santidad* is facetiously qualified by the adjective "*burguesa*," italicized by Valera himself: "No había quedado pecado mortal de que no se contaminase. Sus propósitos de *santidad heroica* y perfecta se habían desvanecido primero. Sus propósitos de *santidad* más fácil, cómoda y *burguesa* se desvanecían después. *El diablo desbarataba sus planes.* Se le antojaba que ni siquiera podía ya ser un Filemón cristiano, pues no era buen principio para el idilio perpetuo el de *rasgar la cabeza al prójimo de un sablazo*" (194). The author has Luis characteristically blame the Devil, and culminates the comic effect with the jocular use of "prójimo." Shortly afterwards, Don Pedro relates to Luis the local reaction to his "transformation," humorously using colloquialisms such as the augmentative "santurrón," which characterizes Luis from the popular point of view: "¡Miren el cógelas a tientas y mátalas callando; miren el *santurrón* y el gatito muerto, exclaman las gentes, con lo que ha venido a descolgarse! El padre Vicario, sobre todo, se ha quedado turulato. Todavía *está haciéndose cruces al considerar cuánto trabajaste en la vida* [*sic*, *viña*] *del Señor* en la noche del 23 al 24, y cuán variados y diversos fueron tus trabajos. Pero a mí no me cogieron las noticias de susto, salvo tu herida. Los viejos sentimos crecer la hierba. No es fácil que los pollos engañen a los recoveros" (197).

Another important term in the service of irony is *sermón*, used in the first letter by Luis, who says that Pepita "preached" "un sermón dulcísimo" to Don Pedro (14). Antoñona expresses her indignation at the state in which the Vicar has left Pepita: "Apuesto cualquier cosa a que ese *zanguango de Vicario* te ha echado *un sermón de acíbar* y te ha destrozado el alma a pesadumbres" (118). The author refers to the Count's vituperations of Pepita as "el extraño sermón de honras" (128), that is, a "eulogy." Luis was never content with the letter he tried to write to Pepita: "Ya era seca, fría, pedantesca, como un mal sermón o como la plática de un dómine..." (141–142). When Antoñona interrupts Luis's prolonged visit, with a quick play on words she alludes to the sermon on the seven short utterances of Christ from the Cross and to the sermon of The Forty Hours' Devotion, thus hinting at the unusual length of time Luis has stayed with Pepita: "—¡Vaya una plática larga! Este *sermón* que ha predicado el colegial no ha sido *el de las siete palabras*, sino que ha estado a punto de ser *el de las cuarenta horas*" (174). Finally, in the second encounter of Luis and the Count, these remarks are made: "¿—Viene V. a echarme otro sermón?—exclamó el Conde.—Nada de *sermones* —exclamó D. Luis..." (187). (Also worth noting here is the repetition of "exclamó," which follows up that of "dijo" in the two short sentences preceding those quoted. Valera's satisfaction with the traditional means of reporting conversation indicates, on a small scale, his acceptance of conventional forms and his avoidance of contrived originality.)

The ironical-critical structure of the novel comes particularly to the fore in the words *teólogo* (which, of course, is applied to seminarians in the final stage of their training) and *teología.* Luis is taunted by Currito on the expedition to the Pozo de la Solana: "Mi primo Currito volvió a embromarme sobre mi manera de cabalgar y sobre la mansedumbre de mi mula: me llamó *teólogo* y me dijo que sobre aquella mula parecía que iba yo repartiendo bendiciones" (65). Don Pedro expresses his astonishment at his son's ignorance: "—Tu tío te ha criado . . . debajo de un fanal, haciéndote *tragar teología y más teología*, y dejándote a obscuras de lo demás que hay que saber" (73). Antoñona calls Luis "ese teólogo pisaverde" (120). Currito is impressed by Luis's equestrian feats: "Currito, que no estimaba gran cosa a su primo mientras no fué más que *teólogo*, le veneraba, le admiraba y formaba de él un concepto sobrehumano desde que le había visto montar tan bien en *Lucero*. Saber *teología* y no saber montar desacreditaba a D. Luis a los ojos de Currito..." (125–126). Valera comically refers to Luis as the "joven teólogo" (193) in the narration of the duel. Don Pedro wishes to avenge his son's injury until learning that "D. Luis había sabido tomar venganza por sí, a pesar de su *teología*" (195). And with good-natured humor, Don Pedro writes the Dean: "Ahora comprendo que, al haberse humanizado, al hacerme tantas fiestas y al bailarme el agua delante, no miraba en mí la pícara de Pepita, sino al papá del *teólogo barbilampiño*" (199).

The noun *varón*, in the sense of "holy man," is sometimes employed seriously, as when the Dean says he had hoped Luis would be a "varón perfecto" (183) and a "varón piadoso" (198); but it ordinarily has ironical connotations. Pepita refers to Luis as a "varón apostólico" (111), a phrase later amplified by Don Pedro to "varón místico, extático y apostólico" (213). Don Pedro also makes the following sly remarks in a decidedly ironical passage: "Mucho lamentan todos en el lugar la muerte del padre Vicario, y no faltan personas que le dan por *santo verdadero* y merecedor de estar en los altares, atribuyéndole milagros. Yo no sé de esto; pero sé que era un *varón excelente*, y debe haber ido derechito a los cielos, donde tendremos en él un *intercesor*" (209). The implication of "intercesor" may suggest here that the Vicar had unwittingly been a go-between in the development of Pepita's and Luis's love, as had previously been stated quite explicitly by Don Pedro (202).

2. IRONICAL-SPIRITUAL SINGLE PASSAGES. To supplement the comments that I have already made on the ironical use of spiritual language, including the treatment of key words, it is important to consider other ironical-critical passages. These passages, which increase in intensity as the novel progresses, are particularly revelatory of the novel's parodistic structure. Usually Valera makes the early, half-concealed irony clear in the second part of the novel.

At one point, Luis intimates that Pepita does not differentiate her *Niño Jesús* from her cats and canaries: ". . . me inclino a creer que la viuda se ama a sí misma sobre todo, y que para recreo y para efusión de este amor tiene los gatos, los canarios, las flores y al propio Niño Jesús, que en el fondo de su alma tal vez no esté muy por cima de los canarios y de los gatos" (23). This ironical criticism is made more evident by the author in his depiction of Pepita's preparations for Luis's visit, in which he discloses that she uses religion for selfish interests:

A un Jesús Nazareno, con la cruz a cuestas y la corona de espinas; a un Ecce-Homo, ultrajado y azotado, con la caña por irrisorio cetro y la áspera soga por ligadura de las manos; o a un Cristo crucificado, sangriento y moribundo, Pepita no se hubiera atrevido a pedir lo que pedía a Jesús, pequeñuelo todavía, risueño, lindo, sano y con buenos colores. Pepita le pidió que le dejase a D. Luis; que no se le llevase. . . .

Terminados estos preparativos, que nos será lícito clasificar y dividir en *cosméticos*, indumentarios y religiosos, Pepita se instaló en el despacho. . . . (153)

Any spiritual language spoken by Antoñona or Don Pedro is ironical by definition. Antoñona vividly registers her complaint about the condition in which the Vicar left Pepita: "¡ . . . ese zángano, pelgar, vejete, tonto, qué maña se da para consolar a sus amigas! Habrá largado alguna barbaridad, algún buen par de coces a esta criaturita de mi alma, y me la ha dejado aquí medio muerta, y él se ha vuelto a la iglesia, a preparar lo conveniente para *cantarle el gorigori*, y *rociarla con el hisopo* y enterrármela sin más ni más" (118). She shows her innate cunning when she combats Luis with his own terminology in definite cantlike reasoning: "¿No eres tan santo? Pues los santos son compasivos y además valerosos. No huyas como un cobardón grosero, sin despedirte. Ven a ver a mi niña, que está enferma. Haz esta obra de misericordia" (136). She shrewdly invalidates Luis's weak protest: "—¿ Y por qué ha de ser tentar a Dios? Pues si Dios ve la rectitud y la pureza de tus intenciones, ¿no te dará su favor y su gracia para que no te pierdas en esta ocasión en que te pongo con sobrado motivo? ¿No debes volar a librar a mi niña de la desesperación y a traerla al buen camino?" (137). Valera indicates Antoñona's specious reasoning about why she picked such a late hour for Luis's visit: to avoid scandal, as the Gospel says (139).

Don Pedro's wry comments are often recorded in his son's letters, as in the following passage: "Yo también tenía mis horas canónicas en el cuartel de Guardias de Corps; el cigarro era el incensario, la baraja el libro de coro, y nunca me faltaban otras devociones y ejercicios más o menos espirituales" (73). But it is in the last pages of the book that Don Pedro's ironical-critical role is really accentuated. He prefers for Luis to stay home rather than to go abroad as a missionary: "En vez de ir de misionero y de traerme de Australia, o de Madagascar, o de la India, varios neófitos con jetas de a palmo, negros como la tizne, o amarillos como el estezado y con ojos de mochuelo, ¿no será mejor que Luisito predique en casa y me saque en abundancia una serie de catecumenillos rubios, sonrosados, con ojos como los de Pepita, y que parezcan querubines sin alas? Los catecúmenos que me trajese de por allá sería menester que estuvieran a respetable distancia para que no me inficionasen, y éstos de por acá me olerían a rosas del paraíso . . ." (201). Of himself he says: ". . . como no me he de hacer cenobita, me complazco en esperar que haré el papel de patriarca" (202). Don Pedro, who is fond of making such ironical remarks, does so good-humoredly. The letter in which he expresses these and similar thoughts is a masterpiece of subtle, ironical wit; the criticism is softened by the general levity of his speech.

Reversing the procedure of the first part, in which Luis reported Don Pedro's ironical observations in his letters, Valera now has Don Pedro relate his son's still pseudo-spiritual thoughts:

> *El mundo mayor*, toda esa fábrica grandiosa del Universo, dice él que sin su Dios providente le parecería sublime, pero sin orden, ni belleza, ni propósito. Y en cuanto al *mundo menor*, como suele llamar al hombre, tampoco le amaría si por Dios no fuera. Y esto, no porque Dios le mande amarle, sino porque la dignidad del hombre y el merecer ser amado estriban en Dios mismo, quien no sólo hizo el alma humana a su imagen, sino que ennobleció el cuerpo humano, haciéndole *templo vivo del Espíritu*, comunicando con él *por medio del Sacramento*, y sublimándolo hasta el extremo de *unir con él su Verbo increado.* (212–213)

What makes of this the same kind of cant that Luis has been using in the whole novel is that Luis's actions are quite different from his words. The novel's concluding remarks clearly indicate that Valera wishes to stress that Pepita and Luis are as much pagan as Catholic:

"En la casa de mis hijos hay, pues, algunas salas que parecen preciosas capillitas católicas o devotos oratorios; pero he de confesar que *tienen ambos también su poquito de paganismo*, como poesía rústica amoroso-pastoril, la cual ha ido a refugiarse extramuros" (213). The erotic nature of their outdoor temple, with its paintings of Psyche and Cupid and of Daphnis and Chloe, and with its statue of Venus, is obvious. Valera's belief that Christianity retains many vestiges of pagan antiquity partially accounts for his ironical mixture of Christianity and paganism in *Pepita Jiménez*. Another major example concerns St. John's Eve, of which he says: "La noche y la mañanita de San Juan, aunque fiesta católica, conservan no sé qué resabios del paganismo y naturalismo antiguos" (148). The frequent juxtaposition of Christian and pagan imagery and allusions likewise stems from the author's ironical purposes and not from any close imitation of Greco-Roman classicism.

Don Pedro, telling Luis that the real missionary must know how to ride and be able to use a sword, jocularly cites examples to corroborate his opinion:

> Cita en primer lugar a Santiago, quien sin dejar de ser apóstol, más acuchilla a los moros que les predica y persuade en su caballo blanco; cita a un señor de la Vera que fué con una embajada de los Reyes Católicos para Boabdil, y que en el patio de los Leones se enredó con los moros en disputas teológicas, y, apurado ya de razones, sacó la espada y arremetió contra ellos para acabar de convertirlos; y cita, por último al hidalgo vizcaíno D. Iñigo de Loyola, el cual, en una controversia que tuvo con un moro sobre la pureza de María Santísima, harto ya de las impías y horrorosas blasfemias con que el moro le contradecía, se fué sobre él espada en mano, y si el moro no se salva por pies, le infunde el convencimiento en el alma por estilo tremendo. (69)

After the mortification caused by the Count, Luis finds this ironical theory less absurd and in a similarly humorous passage recalls a Persian philosopher who also believed in physical persuasion (131).

Luis's inability to think in terms other than those related to his education and reading creates much of the ironical humor of the novel. For instance, when Luis says that he understands how the game of cards is played, the Count answers: "—Así es, amiguito, tiene V. *un entendimiento macho*" (188). Luis thinks immediately of the powers of the soul and answers: "—Pues lo mejor es que no tengo sólo *macho el entendimiento*, sino también la voluntad . . ." (188). The passage which relates that Luis wishes to bet everything on one card shows how ignorant he is of these matters, but at the same time how quick he is to learn: "—¿Cómo explicaré—preguntó D. Luis—que juego en un golpe cuanto hay en la banca contra otro tanto? —Eso se explica —respondió Currito—diciendo: *¡copo!*—Pues copo—dijo D. Luis dirigiéndose al Conde—. *Va el copo y la red en este rey de espadas*, cuyo compañero hará de seguro su epifanía antes que su enemigo el tres" (189). His Andalusian wit is seen in the rapidity with which he makes the pun, misinterpreting "copo" (the gambling term from the verb *copar*) as meaning a small fish-net, which he immediately associates with a larger net, a "red." Luis then makes the mental jump from one king to the "Epiphany" (reminiscent of the Magi) of the second, instead of using the normal *salir*.

The above and similar passages, reinforced by isolated phrases such as "clérigo de misa y olla" (45), or "negocios del alma" (176), and by the key words *místico*, *santo*, *sermón*, *teólogo*, and *varón*, are of great importance in the ironical structure of the novel and serve to point out the less obvious examples of irony.

3. CONFUSION OF EROTICISM AND SPIRITUALITY. Luis's evident and constant confusion of eroticism and spirituality is obviously ironical from the author's and the reader's points of view. The pseudo-mystical experiences themselves are erotically motivated and much of the seminarian's rationalizing also reveals a mixture of the two. In a typical case, Luis begins to justify his nascent love by subordinating it, as manifested in a growing sensitivity to the beauties of nature, to the love of God:

Harto sé . . . que el amor divino es la *caridad*, y que amar a Dios es amarlo todo, porque *todo está en Dios*, y *Dios está en todo* por inefable y alta manera. Harto sé que *no peco amando las cosas por el amor de Dios*, lo cual es amarlas por ellas con rectitud; porque, ¿qué son ellas más que la manifestación, la obra del amor de Dios? Y, sin embargo, no sé qué extraño temor, qué singular escrúpulo, qué apenas perceptible e indeterminado remordimiento me atormenta ahora, cuando tengo, como antes, como en otros días de mi juventud, como en la misma niñez, alguna efusión de ternura, algún rapto de entusiasmo, al penetrar en una enramada frondosa, al oír el canto del ruiseñor en el silencio de la noche, al escuchar el pío de las golondrinas, al sentir el arrullo enamorado de la tórtola, al ver las flores o al mirar las estrellas. Se me figura a veces que hay en todo esto algo de *delectación sensual*. . . . (31)

But realizing the trend of his thought, he then says that he does not want worldly things to distract him from "la contemplación de la superior hermosura," or to weaken his love for "quien ha creado esta armoniosa fábrica del mundo" (32).

Writing of his meeting with Pepita in the wood, Luis mentions the "graciosa ligereza de sus movimientos" (62) and adds hesitatingly that she had appeared as if by magic. But he appeases his conscience and pretends there is no danger in this:

La cautela, que recomiendan los ascetas, de pensar en ella, afeada por los años y por las enfermedades, *de figurármela muerta, llena de hedor y podredumbre y cubierta de gusanos*, vino, a pesar mío, a mi imaginación. . . .

Lo que sí me ocurrió fué un argumento para invalidar, al menos en mí, *la virtud de esa cautela*. La hermosura, obra de un arte soberano y divino, puede ser caduca, efímera, desaparecer en el instante; pero *su idea es eterna*, y en la mente del hombre vive vida inmortal, una vez percibida. *La belleza de esta mujer*, tal como hoy se me manifiesta, *desaparecerá* dentro de breves años: *ese cuerpo elegante, esas formas esbeltas*, esa noble cabeza, tan gentilmente erguida sobre los hombros, *todo será pasto de gusanos inmundos*. . . . (62–63)

His attempted rationalization finally breaks down and merely becomes an excuse to say something else about her beauty.

As the novel progresses, Pepita becomes an obsession which Luis tries desperately to counteract: "Bien pudiera conversar con Dios con plena seguridad, *si* el enemigo no viniese a pelear contra mí en el mismo santuario. La imagen de Pepita se me presenta en el alma" (74–75). The *si* clause is so strong that the rest of the sentence becomes laughable. He asks for a symbol of divine love to absorb the image and the memory of this woman. Nothing else can drive out this image, he claims: "Entre el Crucifijo y yo se interpone, sobre la página del libro espiritual que leo viene también a interponerse" (76).

Luis's reaction to Pepita's offered hand again indicates how he relates everything to his knowledge of spiritual literature. Feeling guilty, he tries to invalidate what he recalls:

> No crea V. que no recordé lo que recomiendan tantos y tantos moralistas y ascetas; pero, allá en mi mente, *pensé que exageraban el peligro.* Aquello del Espíritu Santo de que *el que echa mano a una mujer se expone como si cogiera un escorpión,* me pareció dicho en otro sentido. Sin duda que en los libros devotos, con la más sana intención, *se interpretan harto duramente ciertas frases y sentencias de la Escritura.* ¿Cómo entender, si no, que la hermosura de la mujer, obra tan perfecta de Dios, es causa de perdición siempre? ¿Cómo entender tampoco, en sentido general y constante, que la mujer es más amarga que la muerte? ¿Cómo entender que el que toca a una mujer, en toda ocasión y con cualquier pensamiento que sea, no saldrá sin mancha? (78–79)

Luis makes subsequent references to this hand-shaking ceremony, as does Pepita in speaking to the Vicar: ". . . he cuidado con infernal esmero de todo este cuerpo miserable, que ha de hundirse en la sepultura y ha de convertirse en polvo vil . . . y, al estrechar su mano, *he querido transmitir* de mis venas a las suyas *este fuego inextinguible* en que me abraso" (111).

Luis almost deliriously confuses spirituality and eroticism in his dialogue with Pepita. Awkwardly bringing in his knowledge of antiquity, he betrays his innocence and sensuality by referring to his Lesbias and other ideal women, whom he adorned ". . . con la *coa* transparente de las bellas cortesanas de Atenas y Corinto, para que reluciese, bajo la nebulosa velatura, lo blanco y sonrosado del bien torneado cuerpo" (163). He is trying to explain to Pepita that such erotic daydreams should be subordinated to divine love:

> Pero ¿qué valen los deleites del sentido, ni qué valen las glorias todas y las magnificencias del mundo, cuando un alma arde y se consume en el amor divino, como yo entendía, tal vez con sobrada soberbia, que la mía estaba ardiendo y consumiéndose? . . . Lanzaba de sí mi espíritu todo

el peso del universo y de la hermosura creada, que se le ponía encima y le aprisionaba, impidiéndole volar a Dios, como a su centro. . . . El amor profano de la mujer, no sólo ha venido a mi fantasía con cuantos halagos tiene en sí, sino con aquellos hechizos soberanos y casi irresistibles de la más peligrosa de las tentaciones: de la que llaman los moralistas tentación virgínea, cuando la mente, aún no desengañada por la experiencia y el pecado, se finge en el abrazo amoroso un subidísimo deleite, inmensamente superior, sin duda, a toda realidad y a toda verdad. (163–164)

He demonstrates his naiveté by speaking of such things to Pepita and, at the same time, he shows that his sensuality has developed to such a point that he is practically delirious. Rather than convincing Pepita that they should renounce human love, he is actually inciting himself, and her, to this love. He makes a final effort to persuade her that they should have an ideal and mystical love: "¿Por qué no nos amamos entonces *sin vergüenza y sin pecado y sin mancha*? Dios, con el fuego purísimo y refulgente de su amor, penetra las almas santas y las llena por tal arte, que así como un metal que sale de la fragua, sin dejar de ser metal, reluce y deslumbra, y es todo fuego, así *las almas* se hinchen de Dios, y *en todo son Dios*, penetradas por dondequiera de Dios, en gracia del amor divino. *Estas almas se aman y se gozan* entonces, como si *amaran y gozaran* de Dios, *amándole y gozándole*, porque *Dios son ellas*" (167–168). In moments of emotional crisis Luis seems to remember the stain of his birth, as is indicated by the question he asks Pepita. Also of interest is the parallelistic repetition of *amar* and *gozar*, which, although not exclusively, of course, is a typical figure of spiritual literature in general and of the Canticle and the Spanish mystics in particular.

The most concentrated confusion of eroticism and spirituality occurs in letters ten through fifteen, which will be taken up later. One example is of interest here. Luis tells his uncle that he wishes something like a mystical union with Pepita:

Me recomienda V. que piense en lo inestable, en lo inseguro de nuestra existencia y en lo que hay más allá. Pero esta consideración y esta meditación ni me atemorizan ni me arredran. *¿Cómo he de temer la muerte cuando deseo morir?* El amor y la muerte son hermanos. Un sentimiento de abnegación se alza de las profundidades de mi ser, y me llama a sí, y me dice que *todo mi ser debe darse y perderse por el objeto amado. Ansío confundirme en una de sus miradas; diluir y evaporar toda mi esencia en el rayo de luz que sale de sus ojos, quedarme muerto mirándola, aunque me condene.* (87)

Thus we see that Luis's excited sensibility leads him to associate his erotically motivated sensations with his knowledge of mystical and spiritual literature, misinterpreting the desire for the death of the ego and the absorption by God, and mingling the two elements in the expression of his feelings and self-justifications. By doing so, he reveals the author's ironical intent and simultaneously creates emotion-charged, poetical-romantic passages which are among the best in the novel. The reader senses the irony while nevertheless being impressed by the psychological truth and the evocative beauty of these pages.

c. *Style Comparison: Valera and the Mystics*

In addition to phrases, motifs, concepts, and images, there exist certain affinities between Valera's prose style and that of the Spanish mystics. This is not to say that the style of Santa Teresa is identical to San Juan de la Cruz's, of course, since they are actually quite different. Yet the two mystics have some things in common: each has a fundamentally didactic purpose, to explain mystical experiences and to teach beginners; each paradoxically attempts to describe the indescribable, resorting inevitably to symbols and analogies; and each exemplifies a total self-subordination to the love of God. The differences in their prose styles are essentially the same as those in their poetry, as shown by Helmut Hatzfeld.[34] Of the contrasting adjectives he suggests, the most appropriate for their prose styles seem to be: Santa Teresa—paradoxical-contradictory; San Juan de la Cruz—theological-logical; or, in other terms, " . . . Santa Teresa como tipo emotivo-contradictorio; San Juan de la Cruz, como tipo sereno-armonioso."[35] Valera's style has elements

[34] Helmut Hatzfeld, *Estudios literarios sobre mística española* (Madrid: Gredos, 1955), pp. 250–252.

[35] *Ibid.*, p. 252.

similar to those of each of the two mystics. Like San Juan de la Cruz, Valera is usually clear, concise, logical, and, at times, abstract. On the other hand, Valera's style is occasionally paradoxical-contradictory and even somewhat rambling, not unlike what Menéndez Pidal called Santa Teresa's "estilo ermitaño."[36]

The resemblance to Santa Teresa's style is particularly apparent in Luis's paradoxical statements of mixed and contradictory feelings. Such statements are outward manifestations of his interior conflict between human love and divine love. The paradoxes serve primarily to depict his inhibited love, as in: "Yo deseaba y no deseaba a la vez que llegasen los otros. Me complacía y me afligía al mismo tiempo de estar solo con aquella mujer" (63); or "Me prometo a mí mismo fingirme enfermo, buscar cualquier otro pretexto para no ir a la noche siguiente a casa de Pepita, y sin embargo voy" (85). Later Luis says: "Nada le he dicho ni me ha dicho, y, sin embargo, nos lo hemos dicho todo" (87). He has the paradoxical feelings of love: "Si estoy cerca de ella, la amo; si estoy lejos, la odio" (90); and "La aborrezco y casi la adoro" (90). The paradox is sometimes reduced to oxymoronic terms, as in ". . . me inspiró el infierno una maldita *elocuencia muda* . . ." (12), or "piedad funesta" (170). Such phrases are particularly frequent in the works of Santa Teresa; for example, she writes: "Todo no es nada. . . ."[37] Menéndez Pidal has listed similar expressions of hers: ". . . la santa acumula los adjetivos antitéticos para dar a entender aquella *gozosa pena* en que el alma se anega; un *glorioso desatino*, una *celestial locura*, donde se aprende la verdadera sabiduría; una y otra vez repite *desatinos santos*, *borrachez celestial*. . . ."[38] What permits us to associate Luis's paradoxical-contradictory statements, which express his never satisfied psychological inhibitions, with those of Santa Teresa is the pseudo-spiritual context in which they occur.

The Spanish mystics' great humility, frequently found in conjunction with the expression of their difficulty in explaining mystical experiences, forms a central motif in their works. This is especially

[36] Ramón Menéndez Pidal, *La lengua de Cristóbal Colón*, "Colección Austral" (Buenos Aires: Espasa-Calpe Argentina, 1942), p. 133.

[37] Santa Teresa, *Moradas sextas*, ch. 1, p. 124.

[38] Menéndez Pidal, *La lengua de Cristóbal Colón*, p. 152. The italics are his.

true of Santa Teresa, who was theologically less sure and less precise in her didactic writings than San Juan de la Cruz.[39] In the expression of this motif, she often uses the verbs *acertar*, *atinar*, *lograr*, *procurar*, and *saber* with *decir* or *explicar*, as in the following examples:

Plega El, que haya *acertado a dar a entender* lo que en esto he aprendido. . . .[40]

. . . si el Señor fuere servido que *acierte*, en suma, alguna cosa de éstas. . . .[41]

Eso *no sabrá* el alma *decir*, ni puede entender cómo lo entiende, sino que lo sabe con una grandísima certidumbre.[42]

. . . *no alcanza* mi saber *a darme a entender*; hágalo el Señor.[43]

Luis constantly writes as if he were truly humble, although he is not. Valera's frequent use of the same verbs is remindful of Santa Teresa. Some Valerian examples are:

. . . *no acierto a decir* si es buena o mala moralmente. . . . (8)

. . . me parece una mujer singular, cuyas condiciones morales *no atino a determinar con certidumbre.* (21)

Allí se descubren mil inefables misterios de amor, allí se comunican sentimientos que por otro medio o llegarían a saberse, y se citan poesías que no caben en lengua humana, y se cantan canciones que no hay voz que exprese ni acordada cítara que module. (87)

Additional though secondary stylistic resemblances to be found in Valera and Santa Teresa are the appearance of exclamations, especially with *cuán*,[44] and the unusually frequent use of *harto*. But

[39] This occurs in San Juan de la Cruz, but to a lesser degree. See Dámaso Alonso, *La poesía de San Juan de la Cruz*, pp. 141–144.
[40] Santa Teresa, *Moradas sextas*, ch. 3, p. 145.
[41] *Ibid.*, ch. 8, p. 184.
[42] *Ibid.*, p. 188.
[43] Santa Teresa, *Moradas cuartas*, ch. 1, p. 57.
[44] This is one of the characteristics of Luis's speech and of Santa Teresa's style. On the latter, see Guido Mancini Giancarlo, *Espressioni letterarie dell'insegnamento di Santa Teresa de Avila* (Modena: Società Tipografica Modence, 1955), pp. 130–140.

more and greater resemblances exist between Valera and San Juan de la Cruz. A partial listing would include the following features, which appear with high frequency in both writers: binary and ternary sentence structure, doublets, accumulations, and synonymy; logic, precision, and erudition; special rhythmical and sound patterns; parallelism, antithesis, and repetitive figures; and the use of logical connectives and such summation phrases as *en resumen* and *con todo*. The complications and contradictions implied in the listing of these possible topics of comparison suggest, however, why a close comparison would be of little worth. Valera is writing a parody and even if many of the elements listed were the same or similar in appearance, the resemblance would never be more than peripheral. Valera's irony gives to words, phrases, formulas, and concepts that are similar to those of the mystics completely different functions and values. Without regard to the central purposes and informing principles of the three writers, such comparisons are meaningless, for, although Valera borrowed a great deal from mystics, his purpose is diametrically opposed to theirs, and what he borrowed, he used ironically. The mystics tried to explain their mystical experiences and to describe their total self-dedication to the love of God, all of which Valera rejected for the characters of this novel.

In view of the suggested parallels between Valera and the mystics in content, language, vocabulary, etc., one question remains to be asked: Are there sufficient stylistic resemblances to establish with any certainty a fundamental similarity of prose style? The answer would have to be negative for several reasons. First, the differences between Santa Teresa's style and San Juan de la Cruz's are so great that the mere fact that such widely divergent elements are to be found in *Pepita Jiménez* indicates that they only occur in new ironical combinations, for different purposes, and with other total effects. Second, the similarities themselves, if we ignore the subject matter, as we ought to do at this point, are also similarities to the *Siglo de Oro* style in general, and would be more appropriately considered from that vantage point. Third, their works are primarily didactic; aesthetic value is a by-product, though a great one, to be sure. *Pepita*

Jiménez is a work of fiction in which the aesthetic aim is the essential one; didacticism is secondary. Thus we could rightly expect to find more fundamental similarities to Cervantes's prose style than to the mystics'. What Valera primarily took from the mystics were matters of content and words and phrases used for his parody, a certain introspectiveness, and an analogical and symbolical way of thinking, which, as will be seen, is revealed in the imagery and allusions that he used.

III. IMAGERY AND ALLUSIONS

A surprisingly large number of the metaphors and similes in *Pepita Jiménez* is apparently taken from those of Santa Teresa and San Juan de la Cruz. The fact that many of them also belong to traditional love poetry does not detract from the possibility of a direct borrowing from the mystics; rather, it lends to each such image a new ambiguity, which is also based on the inhibitions of love. The image may have exactly its spiritual or mystical meaning (which was often originally expressed in terms of human love); but it usually has a new erotic meaning in relation to Luis's love too. Hence, although Valera's imagery is not invented, it has a new significance. The same could be said about all of his figurative language; he is satisfied to draw from the vast storehouse of imagery already existent in the Spanish language and to use it in new juxtapositions, in new combinations or contexts, for purposes of irony and characterization.

A. *Mystical Imagery*

The main literary value of Santa Teresa and of San Juan de la Cruz consists in their eidetic imagery and convincing symbols. Only by resorting to metaphors, analogies, and symbols could they adequately suggest, if not fully explain, the nature of their mystical experience. About this Hatzfeld has said: "El simbolismo, pues, como fenómeno estilístico, es el principio unificador de todos los escritos místicos."[45] Valera recognized this fact and, while borrowing freely, used what he borrowed so unobtrusively that the secondary meanings in no way impair the poetic beauty of the surface meaning.

Luis de Urbano, in an excellent study of Santa Teresa's imagery, has pointed out that among her favorite metaphors figure those of battles, or what he calls *alegorías marciales*.[46] She often speaks in terms of castles, fortresses, battlefields, flags, vassals, etc. In addition to short references to these military metaphors (some of which Valera could also have seen in St. Ignatius's and Scupoli's writings), Valera has several extended passages similar to Santa Teresa's:

La inteligencia que *pugna* por comprenderla ha de ser briosa; la voluntad que se le somete por completo es porque *triunfa* antes de sí misma, riñendo bravas *batallas*, con todos los apetitos y *derrotando y poniendo en fuga* todas las tentaciones; . . . no he de perderme porque una piedad relajada y muelle abra las puertas de mi corazón a los vicios, transigiendo con ellos. Dios me salvará y yo *combatiré* por salvarme con su auxilio; pero, si me pierdo, los *enemigos* del alma y los pecados mortales no han de entrar disfrazados ni por *capitulación* en la *fortaleza de mi conciencia*, sino con *banderas desplegadas*, llevándolo todo *a sangre y fuego* y después de *acérrimo combate*. (58)

Luis uses similar metaphors to tell how he will fight to overcome his love for Pepita in a text which recalls Jacob's wrestling with the angel as well as closely resembling a passage by Santa Teresa:

Pepita Jiménez (76)

Mientras aquí permanezca, *combatiré* con valor. Combatiré con Dios, para *vencerle por el amor y el rendimiento*. Mis clamores llegarán a El como *inflamadas saetas*, y derribarán el escudo con que se defiende y oculta

Santa Teresa[47]

¡ . . . curáis estas *llagas, que con las saetas del mismo amor habéis hecho*! . . . Vos mi verdadero Amador, comenzáis esta *guerra de amor*. . . . Pues, Señor, comenzada esta *batalla*, ¿a quién han de ir a *combatir*, sino a

[45] Hatzfeld, *Estudios literarios sobre mística española*, p. 30.

[46] Luis de Urbano, "Las alegorías predilectas de Santa Teresa de Jesús," *Ciencia Tomista*, XXVII (1923), 52–71. Continued, with a change in title from *alegorías* to *analogías*, in XXVIII (1923), 364–383, and XXIX (1924), 350–370.

[47] Santa Teresa, *Obras*, II, 81–82 ("Exclamaciones del alma a Dios," ch. 16).

a los ojos de mi alma. Yo *pelearé* como Israel, en el silencio de la noche, y Dios me llagará en el muslo y me quebrantará en ese combate, para que yo sea *vencedor siendo vencido.*

quien se ha hecho señor de esta *fortaleza* adonde moraban, que es lo más superior del alma, y echádolas fuera de ellas, para que tornen a *conquistar a su conquistador?* Y ya, cansadas de haberse visto sin El, presto se dan por vencidas, y se emplean perdiendo todas sus fuerzas y *pelean* mejor; y, en dándose por *vencidas, vencen a su vencedor.*

The resemblances between the Santa Teresa text and the last two citations from *Pepita Jiménez* are truly striking. Luis even uses paradoxes that are like Santa Teresa's.

Luis employs the conventional mirror-metaphor: ". . . si alguna leve mancha ha venido a *empañar el sereno y pulido espejo de mi alma* en que Pepita se reflejaba, ha sido la ruda sospecha de V. . . ." (51); and ". . . la hermosura interior de mi mente y de mi voluntad *se turbaría y se empañaría* con el afecto de los seres humanos que conozco . . ." (27). In the *Moradas séptimas* Santa Teresa says: ". . . no nos vemos en este *espejo* que contemplamos, adonde nuestra imagen está esculpida."[48] Similar mirror-metaphors are found in San Juan de la Cruz.

When Luis, in depicting the struggle between his two loves, resorts to the following metaphorical language, it is immediately reminiscent of San Juan de la Cruz's:

Toda su beldad, todo su resplandor, todo su atractivo no es más que el reflejo de ese sol increado, no es más que la *chispa* brillante, transitoria, inconsciente de aquella *infinita y perenne hoguera.*

Mi alma, abrasada de amor, pugna por criar alas, y *tender el vuelo*, y subir a esa *hoguera*, y consumir allí cuanto hay en ella de impuro. (88)

Among the many similar, though not precisely parallel, passages of San Juan de la Cruz is the following: "Acaecerá que estando el *alma inflamada de amor de Dios*. . . que sienta embestir en ella un serafín con una flecha o dardo encendidísimo en *fuego de amor*, traspasando

[48] Santa Teresa, *Moradas séptimas*, ch. 2, p. 230.

a esta alma que ya está encendida como ascua, o, por mejor decir, como llama, y cauterízala subidamente. Y entonces, en este cauterizar traspasándola con aquella saeta, apresúrase la llama del alma y sube de punto con vehemencia, al modo que *un encendido horno o fragua* cuando le hornaguean o trabucan el fuego y afervoran la llama. . . ."[49] The "chispa" referred to by Luis also belongs to mystical imagery. Valera adds an ironical aside to the *hoguera*-metaphor by having Antoñona use the same word: "Tú sacrificas voluntariamente en el altar a esa mujer que te ama, que es ya tuya, a tu víctima; pero ella, ¿dónde te tiene a ti para sacrificarte? ¿qué joya tira por la ventana, que lindo primor echa en la *hoguera* sino un amor mal pagado?" (136). In the use of these and similar metaphors, Valera can lay no claim to originality, nor do I mean to imply that the mystics were his only source. As a matter of fact, the passage cited above from *Pepita Jiménez* (88) is closer in phraseology to parts of José Zorrilla's *Don Juan Tenorio* (III, iii): "De amor con ella en mi pecho, / brotó una *chispa* ligera, / que han convertido en *hoguera* / . . . no *hoguera* ya, volcán es. / . . . *tender* osastes el *vuelo*. . . ."[50] Nevertheless, it is evident that in Zorrilla nothing like a spiritual meaning is intended, whereas in Valera it is, through the prevailing irony.

One of the most significant images in the novel is that of the net (*red*, *lazo*, *ligar*), closely related to the *caza de amor*. Here, too, the images are very much a part of traditional love poetry.[51] The first major reference (though not an image) to nets and bird-hunting is made by Luis in a moment of emotional intensity during which, as often occurs, he remembers his childhood: "El agua del Pozo de la Solana forma un arroyo claro y abundante, donde vienen a beber todos los pajarillos de las cercanías, y donde *se cazan* a centenares

[49] San Juan de la Cruz, *Obras*, p. 1205 ("Llama de amor viva," canción 2).

[50] José Zorrilla, *Don Juan Tenorio*, "Colección Austral" (México: Espasa-Calpe Mexicana, 1956), p. 67.

[51] See, for example, Dámaso Alonso, *La poesía de San Juan de la Cruz*, pp. 111–117, and his essay, "El misterio técnico en la poesía de San Juan de la Cruz," in *Poesía española*, 3rd ed. (Madrid: Gredos, 1957), pp. 217–305, especially pp. 242–244. These two books, needless to say, are extremely useful, particularly for the relations between traditional and mystical poetry.

por medio de espartos con *liga*, o con *red*, en cuyo centro se colocan el *cimbel* y el *reclamo*. Allí recordé mis diversiones de la niñez y cuántas veces había ido yo a cazar pajarillos de la manera expresada" (61). In a subsequent passage, he speaks of Pepita in the following Biblical terms (Eccl. 7:27): "Eres *lazo de cazadores*, la digo; tu corazón es *red* engañosa, y tus manos *redes que atan*; quien ama a Dios huirá de ti, y el pecador será por ti aprisionado" (92). Then he adds: "Me parece que *soy uno con todo*, y que todo está *enlazado con lazada de amor* por Dios y en Dios" (93). Antoñona comically uses the net-image in speaking to Luis: "Ella, . . . ha venido a caer en tus traidoras *redes*. Esta santidad mentida fué, sin duda, el *señuelo* de que te valiste. Con tus *teologías* y *tiquismiquis celestiales*, has sido como el pícaro y desalmado *cazador*, que atrae con el *silbato* a los zorzales bobalicones para que se ahorquen en la percha" (135). The real "zorzal bobalicón" is Luis; he is the prey and Pepita is the huntress. In mystical imagery the soul is sometimes compared to a bird: "Dos veces trabaja el *pájaro* que se asentó en la *liga*, es a saber: en desasirse y limpiarse de ella."[52] Santa Teresa is also fond of images of *aves* or *pajarillos* and *silbos*, as in the following example, although in a different context: "No parece sino que están en ella muchos ríos caudalosos, . . . muchos *pajarillos y silbos*, y no en los oídos, sino en lo superior de la cabeza. . . ."[53] In *Pepita Jiménez* the net-image shows that Luis is being pursued and trapped; scattered allusions to it may be found on pages 50, 141, 171, and 173. Remembering these references, it is not difficult to detect a note of irony when, after Luis's "capture," Valera says: "Pepita le hizo mejor el *lazo* de la corbata" (175).

Other mystical images or remembrances of mystical images occur in the novel. Luis writes the Dean that ". . . cada una de las impresiones que Pepita produce puede ser como el golpe del *eslabón que hiere el pedernal* y que hace *brotar la chispa* que todo lo incendia y devora . . ." (52). The same metaphor of flint and steel is recorded

[52] San Juan de la Cruz, *Obras*, p. 1285 ("Avisos y sentencias," no. 22). Also cited by Hatzfeld, *Estudios literarios sobre mística española*, p. 157.

[53] Santa Teresa, *Moradas cuartas*, ch. 1, p. 61.

by Hatzfeld: "La meditación hiere con el eslabón el pedernal, la contemplación hace brotar la chispa. . . ."[54] The traditional image of the "knot" in the throat is used: "De repente, como si lograse *desatar un nudo* que le apretaba la garganta, como si quebrase un cordel que la ahogaba, rompió Pepita en lastimeros gemidos . . ." (117). Pepita remarks about Luis's kiss: "Su beso fué marca, fué *hierro candente* con *que me señaló* y selló *como a su esclava*" (113). Santa Teresa has a similar image: "¿Sabéis qué es ser espirituales de veras? Hacerse esclavos de Dios, a quien, *señalados con su hierro*, que es el de la Cruz. . . ."[55] The images of the *vuelo* and of *alas como de paloma* (30) and of San Juan de la Cruz's *mística escala* (168) have already been dealt with. From this sampling, it is clear that Valera, always aware of traditional love poetry and of the erotic implications, drew freely from the imagery of the Spanish mystics.

Although other trends in European literature must not be ignored, Valera may have been led by his knowledge of the mystics to be more aware of symbols and images and to have used them rather frequently. His realization of the importance of analogies to the divine is manifested, first of all, by Luis's constant references to signs and symbols. Luis thought that he should love earthly beauty "como *signo*, como *representación* de una hermosura oculta y divina . . ." (32). And of Pepita's hands he says: ". . . parecen el símbolo del imperio mágico, del dominio misterioso que tiene y ejerce el espíritu humano . . . sobre todas las cosas visibles . . ." (37). Luis sometimes longs for a divine symbol: "Fervorosamente pido al cielo que se despierte en mí la fuerza imaginativa y cree una *semejanza*, un *símbolo* de ese concepto que todo lo comprende, a fin de que absorba y ahogue la imagen, el recuerdo de esta mujer" (75). A similar wish for a sign is expressed the night of his decisive visit to Pepita's house: "Penetraba por lo más sombrío de las enramadas, anhelando ver algún *prodigio* espantable, algún *signo*, algún *aviso* que le retrajese" (147). He would like to turn Pepita into a symbol: "Yo haré de ella, me digo, un *símbolo*, una *alegoría*, una *imagen* de

[54] Hatzfeld, *Estudios literarios sobre mística española,* p. 148. This is drawn from Pedro de Alcántara.

[55] Santa Teresa, *Moradas séptimas,* ch. 4, p. 245.

todo lo bueno y hermoso. Será para mí, como Beatriz para Dante, figura y representación de mi patria, del saber y de la belleza" (93).

Thus we can say that Luis thinks symbolically; but are there any significant symbols in the novel? The answer, in my opinion, is affirmative. For example, the horse Luis rides is a symbol of his manhood, and the significant name of the horse itself, *Lucero*, brings to mind the morning star, or Venus, and other poetic associations. The following passage is in fact charged with symbolic meaning: "Sigue mi padre contentísimo de mí como discípulo de equitación. Dentro de cuatro o cinco días asegura que podré ya montar y montaré en *Lucero*, caballo negro, hijo de un caballo árabe y de una yegua de la casta de Guadalcázar, saltador, corredor, lleno de fuego y adiestrado en todo linaje de corvetas.—Quien eche a *Lucero* los calzones encima—dice mi padre—, ya puede apostarse a montar con los propios centauros; y tú le echarás los calzones encima dentro de poco" (74). The horse may be taken as a symbol of Luis himself. The possibility of such an identification is strengthened by Pepita's use of *lucero* as a traditional term of endearment: "No hay lazo alguno que conmigo te ligue; y si lo hay, yo le desato o le rompo. Eres libre. Básteme el haber hecho caer por sorpresa al *lucero* de la mañana . . ." (171). One might also associate eroticism with the mention of centaurs and the phrase, "echarle los calzones encima." The *Lucero* symbol was already prepared for in the earlier comparison drawn between Luis and Pepita's local suitors: "¿Qué valgo yo al lado de los gallardos mozos, *aunque algo rústicos*, que han pretendido a Pepita: *ágiles jinetes*, . . . cazadores como Nembrot, diestros en todos los ejercicios del cuerpo . . .?" (53). With typical self-delusion, Luis professes humility while his scorn is revealed in the qualifying aside, "aunque algo rústicos." What he really wants is to be, like them, a virile male, exposed to a *caída*. The importance of *Lucero* as a manhood symbol for Luis can hardly be overemphasized.[56] Luis's

[56] Cf. Mario Maurín, "Valera y la ficción encadenada," *Mundo Nuevo*, no. 14, p. 40. "El símbolo sexual de la equitación es patente. . . . El caballo representa tradicionalmente la pasión, pero el buen jinete es el que sabe controlar su montura." Maurín's conclusion that Luis supplanted his father as the aggressive male must be qualified by two considerations: the substitution was desired by the father and Luis is to be the conquered, not the conqueror.

humiliation and loss of prestige in the eyes of Pepita, plus her encouragement, motivate him to learn to ride horseback. After he has successfully ridden the horse, putting on a show in front of Pepita's house (77), his stock with Pepita stands higher than ever. This in turn initiates the handshaking ceremony, his first physical contact with her; and from this moment on, he is lost. Currito also esteems Luis more when he finds out that he was "capaz de sostenerse tan bizarramente en las espaldas de una fiera" (126).

The following traditional similes are used by Luis: "El sacerdote, el que va a ser sacerdote, debe ser humilde, pacífico, manso de corazón. No como la *encina*, que se levanta orgullosa hasta que *el rayo la hiere*, sino como las *hierbecillas* fragantes de las selvas . . ." (133). Luis uses the oak as a symbol of pride; but if the reader remembers a passage shortly prior to this one, he also associates the oak with Luis himself: "Don Luis, . . . se quedó como *herido por un rayo* . . ." (129). In the present framework, it is not necessary to treat other symbols or symbolic actions found in the novel. It is clear, though, that Valera does think symbolically and that the mystical imagery and symbols lend to the novel a poetic and evocative ambiguity not always admitted.

B. *The Novel's Poetical Climax*

Luis's last six letters (83–101), written in a more lyrical tone than the rest of the book and filled with metaphorical language and Biblical allusions, constitute the novel's poetical climax. Here, more than in any other place, Valera allows Luis to attain a level of seriousness and to make a real effort to struggle against his human love. It is in these pages that Luis expresses his full awareness of his sensual love and his now serious though self-deluding attempt to continue his chosen way of life. His heightened sense of awareness is motivated by physical contact with Pepita. Thus in his love crisis he must try more than usual to justify his behavior, a process which he primarily accomplishes by means of his two pseudo-mystical experiences and by the use of Biblical references and allusions.

Luis constantly paraphrases Biblical passages, most of which are from the Psalms:

> Templos del Espíritu Santo son nuestros cuerpos (I Cor. 3:16), mas si se arrima fuego a sus paredes, aunque no ardan, se tiznan.
>
> La primera sugestión es la cabeza de la serpiente. Si no la hollamos con planta valerosa y segura (Gen. 3:15), el ponzoñoso reptil sube a esconderse en nuestro seno.
>
> El licor de los deleites mundanos, por inocentes que sean, suele ser dulce al paladar, y luego se trueca en hiel de dragones y veneno de áspides. . . . (Ps. 139:4; Deut. 32:33)
>
> . . . Como el corzo sediento desea y busca el manantial de las aguas (Ps. 41:2), así mi alma busca a Dios todavía. A Dios se vuelve para que le dé reposo, y anhela beber en el torrente de sus delicias (Ps. 35:9), cuyo ímpetu alegra el Paraíso, y cuyas ondas claras ponen más blanco que la nieve (Ps. 50:9); pero un abismo llama a otro abismo (Ps. 41:8), y mis pies se han clavado en el cieno que está en el fondo. (Ps. 68:3)
>
> Sin embargo, aún me quedan voz y aliento para clamar con el Salmista: ¡Levántate, gloria mía! (Ps. 56:9) Si te pones de mi lado, ¿quién prevalecerá contra mí?
>
> Yo digo a mi alma pecadora, llena de quiméricas imaginaciones y de vagos deseos, que son sus hijos bastardos: ¡Oh hija miserable de Babilonia, bienaventurado el que te dará tu galardón; bienaventurado el que deshará contra las piedras a tus pequeñuelos! (Ps. 136: 8–9) (84–85)

One can see that Luis skips around in using these phrases, as he does later with those from the Sermon on the Mount (132–133), thus forming new combinations. Luis attributes to Pepita's eyes "una atracción magnética inexplicable" (85), and says: "Mis ojos deben arder entonces, como los suyos, con una llama funesta; como los de Amón cuando se fijaban en Tamar (II Sam. 13); como los del príncipe de Siquén cuando se fijaban en Dina" (Gen. 34) (85).

The sensuality of Luis's love is indicated by the following statement, in which he makes one of his frequent references to Pepita as a "maga":

> Al entrar, Pepita y yo nos damos la mano, y al dárnosla *me hechiza.* Todo mi ser se muda. *Penetra hasta mi corazón un fuego devorante,*

y ya no pienso más que en ella. . . . La miro con insano ahinco, por un estímulo irresistible, y a cada instante creo descubrir en ella nuevas perfecciones. Ya los hoyuelos de sus mejillas cuando sonríe, ya la blancura sonrosada de la tez, ya la forma recta de la nariz, ya la pequeñez de la oreja, ya la suavidad de contornos y admirable modelado de la garganta.

Entro en su casa, a pesar mío, *como evocado por un conjuro*; y, no bien entro en su casa, *caigo bajo el poder de su encanto*; veo claramente que estoy dominado por una *maga* cuya fascinación es ineluctable. (86)

Luis concludes the letter with the *hoguera*-metaphor, with an allusion to the Apocalypse, and by saying that he must escape "como un ladrón" (88).

The eleventh letter begins with phrases from the Psalms: "Soy un vil gusano, y no un hombre; soy el oprobio y la abyección de la Humanidad; soy un hipócrita (Ps. 21:7). Me han circundado dolores de muerte, y torrentes de iniquidad me han conturbado" (Ps. 17:5) (89). Luis adds the simile of the falling stone: "El proceso de mi mal es rápido. Como piedra que se desprende de lo alto del templo y va aumentando su velocidad en la caída, así mi espíritu ahora" (89). He thinks of Pepita, comparing her to Judith, Jael, and the bride of the Canticle, and employing epithets from the Canticle: "Su recuerdo me mata. Soñando con ella, sueño que me divide la garganta, como Judit al capitán de los asirios, o que me atraviesa las sienes con un clavo, como Jael a Sisara (Judg. 4:21); pero a su lado, me parece la esposa del *Cantar de los Cantares*, y la llamo con voz interior, y la bendigo, y la juzgo fuente sellada, huerto cerrado, flor del valle, lirio de los campos, paloma mía y hermana" (90). Luis ends the letter with an erotic memory: "A veces, jugando al tresillo, se han tocado por acaso nuestras rodillas, y he sentido un indescriptible sacudimiento" (90).

In the next letter Luis claims to have seen Heaven in a mystical vision and then remarks: "Si al cabo logro vencer, será gloriosa la victoria; pero se la deberé a la Reina de los Angeles, a quien me encomiendo. Ella es mi refugio y mi defensa; torre y alcázar de David, de que penden mil escudos y armaduras de valerosos campeones; cedro del Líbano, que pone en fuga a las serpientes" (91). He is, of course, referring to the Virgin Mary, with attributes from the litany of Loreto and analogies from the Canticle. He pretends that Pepita is dead so that he can make a symbol of her, as Dante did of Beatrice. However, the sensual side of his nature wins out, and he "revives" her in the classic form of Galatea:

Luego la lloro, luego me horrorizo de mi crimen, y me acerco a ella en espíritu, y con el calor de mi corazón *le vuelvo la vida*, y la veo, no vagarosa, diáfana, casi esfumada entre nubes de color de rosa y flores celestiales, como vió el feroz Gibelino a su amada en la cima del Purgatorio, sino consistente, sólida, *bien delineada* en el ambiente sereno y claro, como las obras más perfectas *del cincel helénico*, como Galatea, animada ya por el afecto de Pigmalión, y bajando llena de vida, respirando amor, lozana de juventud y de hermosura, de su pedestal de mármol. (94)

The sensuality, though mitigated by the classical reference, is still detectable. It is curious to note that Luis, in a vain effort to combat his love for Pepita, several times pretends that she is dead (see, for example, pp. 62–63). All of this is typically romantic.[57]

Later, when Luis is alone with Pepita, he sees that she is sad, with tears in her eyes, and says: "Parecía la madre de los dolores" (96). The simile is weakened by familiarity but is nevertheless effective. After kissing her, Luis says:

—¡El primero y el último!

Yo aludía al beso profano; mas, *como si hubieran sido mis palabras una evocación*, se ofreció en mi mente la visión apocalíptica en toda su terrible majestad. Vi al que es por cierto el primero y el último, y con la espada de dos filos que salía de su boca me hería en el alma, llena de maldades, de vicios y de pecados (Apoc. 2:16).

Toda aquella noche la pasé en un *frenesí*, en un *delirio interior*, que no sé como se disimulaba. . . .

. . . Al recordarme de aquel beso y de aquellas palabras de despedida, me comparaba yo con el traidor Judas, que vendía besando, y con el

[57] José Zorrilla expresses a similar thought in *Don Juan Tenorio*: "¡Quién pudiera, doña Inés, / volver a darte la vida!" (2nd part, I, ii, p. 106).

sanguinario y alevoso asesino Joab, cuando, al besar a Amasá, le hundió el hierro agudo en las entrañas. (II Sam. 20:10) (97)

Again we see that Luis habitually relates important events to spiritual literature and that he evokes things remembered in a moment of emotional crisis. His youthful tendency to exaggerate the importance of what happens to him adds a note of humor here, as in other parts of the novel. He seems to enjoy the opportunity to be melodramatic in his letters to his uncle. Yet, *he* is serious and the phrase "delirio interior" is an apt one for his mental state in practically all of these passages.

In the fourteenth letter Luis supposedly experiences mystical knowledge and enjoyment of God and promises himself victory: "Yo haré un azote durísimo de mis oraciones y penitencias, y con él la arrojaré de allí, como Cristo arrojó del templo a los condenados mercaderes" (99).

Thus it is seen that in the midst of his love crisis Luis reaches an emotional intensity, which he expresses in imagery and Biblical phrases, and that, for once, he apparently makes a sincere effort to overcome his human love. But Valera dispels any seriousness of tone when he has Antoñona say to Luis in her "jerga medio gitana": "—¡Anda, fullero de amor, *indinote*, maldecido seas; *malos chuqueles te tagelen el drupo*, que has puesto enferma a la niña y con tus retrecherías la estás matando!" (100).[58] Luis's reaction to Antoñona's pinching is also comical, showing the author's ironical purpose: "No me qu*ej*o, mer*ez*co esta broma brutal, dado que sea broma. Mer*ez*co que me aten*ac*en los demonios con ten*az*as h*ech*as *asc*ua" (100). The italicized sounds likewise contribute to the humorous effect. It seems that Valera has allowed Luis the maximum freedom he intends to and that he is now bringing him down to earth with an ironical thud, thus setting the stage for Luis's eventual acceptance of his sensual nature.

[58] Cf. Carlos Clavería, "En torno a una frase en *caló* de don Juan Valera," *Estudios sobre los gitanismos del español* (Madrid: CSIC, 1951), pp. 97–128. Clavería studies this gypsy curse (which may be translated as "may bad dogs devour your body") and its relations with Valera's customary avoidance of slang and of the graphic representation of dialectal speech habits.

c. *Function and Ironical Treatment of Imagery, References, and Allusions*

The allusions and imagery sometimes have a clear-cut function other than the customary purposes of characterization and evocation of atmosphere. Generally speaking, this function is one of rationalization, because Luis seeks support among historical persons in order to justify each new turn of events.

He hopes to persuade Pepita to renounce human love and to imitate saintly women who, he says: ". . . no ya han desistido de unirse con un amante, sino hasta de unirse con el esposo, viviendo con él como un hermano, según se refiere, por ejemplo, en la vida de San Eduardo, rey de Inglaterra. Y después de pensar en esto, se sentía D. Luis más consolado y animado, y ya se figuraba que *él iba a ser como San Eduardo*, y que *Pepita era como la reina Edita*, su mujer; y bajo la forma y condición de tal reina, *virgen a par de esposa*, le parecía Pepita, si cabe, mucho más gentil, elegante y poética" (142). Part of Luis's stubborn resistance to yielding to Pepita is a result of the hagiographical ideal of unconsummated love which he has formed; at the same time, Pepita's attractiveness to him is largely derived from the fact that she is a widow and still chaste. He makes several allusions to this unusual condition. About Pepita's marriage to Don Gumersindo, he says that if she did not penetrate "en *otros misterios*, salva queda la bondad de lo que hizo" (13). In another place, he speaks of her "casta viudez" (52). One wonders if his ideal is not ultimately attributable to the sinful circumstances of his birth and to his desire for atonement.[59] He again thinks of Saint Edward and his queen later; this time they corroborated his will (147). After giving in to Pepita, he rationalizes his failure to imitate Saint Vincent Ferrer and Saint Edward, saying also that to

[59] Here and elsewhere, I am not in accord with Paul Smith's analysis of Luis's psychological motivation because he shifts the emphasis from awareness of sin, feelings of guilt, and rationalizations of those feelings to an Adlerian type of inferiority complex, which, though relevant to some of Valera's other protagonists, seems to me to have little relevance to Luis's psychology. See Paul Smith, "Juan Valera and the Illegitimacy Motif," *Hispania*, LI, no. 4 (Dec., 1968), 805–806.

have rejected Pepita's love would have been an act of cowardice, as if Booz had given Ruth "un puntapié y la hubiera mandado a paseo": "Así *se disculpaba* D. Luis de no haber imitado a San Vicente y a otros santos no menos ariscos. En cuanto al mal éxito que tuvo la proyectada imitación de San Eduardo, también *trataba de cohonestarle y disculparle*. San Eduardo se casó por razón de Estado, . . . pero en él y en Pepita Jiménez no había razón de Estado, ni grandes ni pequeños, sino amor finísimo de ambas partes" (184).

But, undaunted and not heeding the example of Don Quijote after his defeat at the hands of the Caballero de la Blanca Luna, Luis immediately fashions another illusion: that of perfect married life, in imitation of the ideal couple of antiquity, Philemon and Baucis (184–185). After Luis's duel, the author ironically says: "Se le antojaba que ni siquiera podía ya ser un Filemón cristiano, pues no era buen principio para el idilio perpetuo el de rasgar la cabeza al prójimo de un sablazo" (194). Other recurring references and allusions of the novel are those to Daphnis and Chloe (156–157, 213–214) and to Booz and Ruth (157, 183–184).

The ironical nature and treatment of imagery and allusions are seen in other examples. For instance, Don Pedro says of Pepita's marriage to Luis: "Si no quiere esta fresca y lozana *hiedra enlazarse al viejo tronco*, carcomido ya, trepe por él, me digo, para subir al renuevo tierno y al verde y florido pimpollo" (201). This image, although traditional, is also similar to Luis de Granada's ivy-image: "The *ivy-plant clinging to the tree* grows not more nor throws more widely its lovely branches than the soul grown in virtues and graces when it clings to Thee."[60] Don Pedro, who is given to using conventional spiritual imagery ironically, also says about Pepita: ". . . no es de la piel de Barrabás, . . . sino una criatura remonísima, *más bendita que los cielos* y más apasionada que coqueta" (200). An ironical simile is used in reference to Pepita's rejection of the Count: "El amor se había vuelto odio, y el Conde se desahogaba a menudo, *poniendo a Pepita como chupa de dómine*" (128). Luis's frequent blaming of *demonios* for his behavior is also ironical, as in the follow-

[60] Quoted by E. Allison Peers, *Studies of the Spanish Mystics*, 2 vols. (London: Sheldon Press, 1927), I, 62.

ing: "Se diría que los demonios me agarran de los pies y me llevan allá sin que yo quiera" (89).

Often the irony is achieved by mixing classical and spiritual imagery and references: "Pepita, pues, se me mostraba . . . no como iba . . . sino de un modo ideal y etéreo, en el retiro nemoroso, como a Clímaco Palas, como al pastor bohemio Kroco la sílfide que luego concibió a Libusa, como Diana al hijo de Aristeo, como al Patriarca los ángeles en el valle de Mambré, como a San Antonio el hipocentauro en la soledad del yermo" (66–67). Or it may be achieved by the traditional irony of the reference itself: "Aunque el precio era sin comparación mucho más subido, a D. Luis se le figuraba que si cedía iba a remediar a Esaú, y a vender su primogenitura y a deslustrar su gloria" (123). Or it may be due to the incongruity between the tenor and the vehicle of the comparison: ". . . Pepita lleva áun el luto de viuda. Su compostura, su vivir retirado y su melancolía son tales, que cualquiera pensaría que llora la muerte del marido *como si hubiera sido un hermoso mancebo*" (13). The disparity between the decrepit and miserly Don Gumersindo and the "hermoso mancebo" is so great that a comic effect is produced. Similar incongruity occurs when Luis sees in his room ". . . a la entremetida Antoñona, que había penetrado *como una sombra, aunque tan maciza . . .*" (134). The humor is created here, of course, by a typically ironical aside. In other cases, the effect is attained by ironical understatement, with an implied incongruity, as when the Dean writes of Pepita: ". . . esa muchacha, que al fin no tiene otra culpa que la de haberse enamorado de él *como una loca* con un candor y un ímpetu selváticos" (183). The incongruity can also be on a purely linguistic level, as in the deliberately anachronistic application of modern colloquial expressions to ancient philosophers: "Jámblico no tuvo poder para evocar a los genios del amor . . . sin haberse antes *quemado las cejas* a fuerza de estudio. . . . Apolonio de Tiana se supone que se maceró *de lo lindo* antes de hacer sus falsos milagros" (182–183).

From this study of the language, imagery, and allusions in *Pepita Jiménez*, several conclusions may be drawn. First, Valera took from the mystics and the Bible what he needed for his parody, for his characterizations, and for the creation of the atmosphere. He blended these elements into a new, subtle, and ambiguous novel of refined aesthetic value. Second, Valera made little effort to invent new imagery. Since he was writing a parody, he was better served by the evocative and associative values of the traditional images already in the language; in other words, not having strongly vital emotional feelings or experiences which he felt impelled to express subjectively, he had little need to create personal imagery. Third, the parody of a false mystic and misguided seminarian is written in a pseudo-spiritual style, which, since the primary sources are the mystical-ascetical writers of sixteenth-century Spain, is evocative of *Siglo de Oro* style in general.

CHAPTER II: Siglo de Oro *and Cervantine Stylistic Expressions and Their Use in* Pepita Jiménez

Amado Alonso has said that although style is an expression of the author's individuality, there is no better way to apprehend it than by fixing the extremes within which the individuality is expressed.[1] He was thus able to characterize Enrique Larreta's *La gloria de don Ramiro* as a work which moved between the conditions of the historical novel and those of *modernismo*. In a similar way, *Pepita Jiménez* may be placed within the confines of two distinct kinds of work, the parody and the modern psychological novel. Alonso calls Larreta's novel "una novela histórica hecha con prosa modernista."[2] *Pepita Jiménez* is a psychological novel written in a prose style which is primarily evocative of the prose of the *Siglo de Oro*. En *La gloria de don Ramiro* there are readily discernible archaic words and syntactical constructions, such as *por doquier* and "Cuando hubo cumplido los trece años. . . ."[3] But Valera, who has often been praised for his elegant and *castizo* Spanish, does not employ

[1] Amado Alonso, *Ensayo sobre la novela histórica: El modernismo en "La gloria de don Ramiro,"* "Estudios Estilísticos," vol. III (Buenos Aires: Instituto de Filología, 1942), p. 151.

[2] *Ibid.*

[3] *Ibid.*, pp. 308–309.

language so evidently aberrant from normal usage, nor does he, as a rule, deliberately use archaic words or locutions. This would have led him to what he most abhorred, a mannered style. Yet, being dissatisfied with the Spanish prose of his day and having so thoroughly read and digested the great works of Spanish literature, he was attracted to write as the great "classical" writers of the *Siglo de Oro* (especially those of the late sixteenth and early seventeenth centuries) had written, insofar as this was possible without falling into affectation. His deviation from normal usage is small, much smaller, say, than that of Pereda or Galdós; but what there is points almost inevitably to the *Siglo de Oro.*

Starting from a parody of mystical and general spiritual-Biblical language, Valera was induced by his thorough knowledge of and steadfast admiration for the Spanish classics to expand the parody to the *Siglo de Oro* in general. Thus Luis is made to talk in a stilted way, reflecting in a desultory fashion the ill-assimilated fruits of his studies at the seminary, just as Cervantes had had Don Quijote mimic the speech of the heroes of novels of chivalry. In both cases the aesthetic result became so pleasing that the parodied style or styles, in a mitigated form, overflowed into the normal style of the writer.[4] This is not to say that Valera did not emulate the best Spanish prose writers before writing *Pepita Jiménez*; on the contrary, his early efforts often reveal a conscious imitation of traditional modes of expression, although never in the condensed manner nor with the felicitous outcome of his first complete novel.

Since Valera wanted above all to write pure and elegant prose, the borrowings are not bold ones. They are, on the one hand, archaic or relatively rare in modern general usage and are often evocative of the *Siglo de Oro*; on the other hand, they are manifested in classical stylistic expressions which may be and sometimes are used by Valera's contemporaries, though with less frequency. Before the Generation of 1898 and the *modernistas,* all late nineteenth-century Spanish novelists were largely dependent on time-honored phrases

[4] On this point, especially on the overflow of the colloquial expressions of Sancho's speech into that of other characters and of the author, see Helmut Hatzfeld, *El "Quijote" como obra de arte del lenguaje* (Madrid: Patronato del IV Centenario del Nacimiento de Cervantes, 1949), pp. 80–81.

and devices; but in none of them is there such a constellation of details, themes, and even structural elements belonging to the classical tradition as there is in Valera's *Pepita Jiménez.*

Needless to say, I can only aim for a more total aesthetic appreciation of *Pepita Jiménez* and can make no pretense at a systematic and complete description of *Siglo de Oro* style. Many of the expressions and formulas to be pointed out were not new in the *Siglo de Oro*; but since it was then that they were most successfully used and were fixed into the language, Valera undoubtedly drew his major inspiration from this period. As for the means of determining exactly what constitutes *Siglo de Oro* style, still inadequately described, the standard dictionaries and grammars were consulted, as well as several excellent monographs on individual writers.[5] I shall use Rafael Lapesa's accurate, though lamentably sketchy, historical treatment of Spanish prose style as a guide,[6] to be supplemented by Ramón Menéndez Pidal's valuable but fragmentary observations in his *Antología de prosistas españoles.*[7]

I. CHOICE AMONG SYNONYMIC POSSIBILITIES

A. *Words and Phrases Which Are Archaic or Evocative of the* Siglo de Oro

Valera, wanting to represent Luis's stilted, artificial attitude, has him make a stylistic choice among synonyms which one would not

[5] Particularly: Joan Corominas, *Diccionario crítico etimológico de la lengua castellana,* 4 vols. (Bern: A. Francke, 1954); Julio Cejador y Frauca, *Fraseología o estilística castellana,* 4 vols. (Madrid: Tipografía de la "Revista de arch. bibl. y museos," 1921–1923); Julio Cejador y Frauca, *La lengua de Cervantes,* 2 vols. (Madrid: J. Rates, 1905–1906); Andrés Bello and Rufino J. Cuervo, *Gramática de la lengua castellana,* ed. Niceto Alcalá-Zamora y Torres, 4th ed. (Buenos Aires: Sopena Argentina, 1954).

[6] Rafael Lapesa, *Historia de la lengua española,* 3rd ed. (Madrid: Escelicer, 1955). Martín Alonso's *Evolución sintáctica del español* (Madrid: Aguilar, 1962), while suggestive for the modern period, is disappointing for the *Siglo de Oro.* His treatment of the so-called "sintaxis del buen gusto" among prose writers from Fray Luis de León to Cervantes (pp. 214–227) is of very little help.

[7] Ramón Menéndez Pidal, *Antología de prosistas españoles,* 6th ed., "Colección Austral" (Buenos Aires: Espasa-Calpe Argentina, 1951). See Menéndez Pidal's introductory remarks and his notes to the individual selections.

ordinarily make without a refined erudition based on a thorough knowledge of the Spanish classics. This choice is also that of the author, who is equally fond of the traditional expressions which he lends to his protagonist. The words and phrases, not at all startling or difficult to comprehend, are only one step removed from general usage. Nevertheless, as an examination of several passages and expressions will disclose, they reveal the subtle use of stiltedness and erudition for irony and characterization.

In a description of Pepita, Luis writes, ". . . no se advierten en ella ni *cosméticos* ni *afeites* . . ." (22), thus juxtaposing the normal modern term, "cosméticos," and the old-fashioned one (in this sense), "afeites." Valera's use of "color" as a feminine noun, "La color trigueña" (144), has been pointed out by Amado Alonso as an archaism.[8] Other semiarchaic forms follow: the poetic adjective, "esplendente" (12, 160), where one would expect *esplendoroso* or *resplandeciente*; the absolute superlative of *mezquino*, which already means *muy pequeño* or *pequeñísimo* (in the phrase "un mezquinísimo mayorazgo" [8]); the adjective "mujeril" (in "la vanidad mujeril" [109]), which was widely used in the *Siglo de Oro* and which, although still employed today, is gradually giving way in this usage to *femenino*; the adjective "mundanal" in "el amor mundanal" (142) and "un clérigo . . . mundanal" (158) (evocative of Fray Luis de León's famous *mundanal ruido*), rather than the more natural *mundano*; the adjective "cortesano" in "no era más cortesano el traje de Pepita" (36); and "sobrado" as an adverb in ". . . todavía me aturden y desazonan los dichos de mi padre, *sobrado* libres a veces" (73).

The omission of prefixes, as in older language, gives the adverbs "por bajo" (100, 127), "por cima de" (23, 75, 125), and "a más de" (22, 126) an archaic flavor. Although sometimes used today, primarily for variety, they are ordinarily replaced by *por debajo*, *por encima de*, and *además de*. It is easy to find examples of them in the *Siglo de Oro*; Cervantes wrote, for instance: ". . . *por cima de* la peña . . . pareció la pastora Marcela . . . ."[9] *Cuán*, though occasionally used

[8] Amado Alonso, *Ensayo sobre la novela histórica*, p. 309.

[9] Miguel de Cervantes Saavedra, *Don Quijote de la Mancha*, ed. Francisco Ro-

with adjectives and adverbs, is no longer used with verbs as it is in one case by Luis: "A todo me sometí *de buen talante*, y pronto hasta las bromas de Currito acabaron *al notar cuán* invulnerable *yo era*. Pero ¡*cuán sufrí* por dentro!" (60). Luis seems to have been drawn into the use of "cuán" with "sufrí" by the preceding occurrence of the poetic "cuán" with "invulnerable." His expression of mortification clearly indicates both stiltedness and emotional perturbation. These effects are also reflected in other things: the adverbial phrase, "de buen talante," which, although not archaic, is particularly common in the *Siglo de Oro*; the termination of the first sentence in an active verb form, "era"; and the zeugmatic construction of "al notar," which logically refers to Currito, although it is syntactically dependent on "las bromas." This passage is a good example of how archaic and conventional phrases are used to represent an emotional effect, or, to be more accurate, the stilted reporting of an emotional effect. That the feeling revealed in these words is also ironical may be appreciated by comparison with the self-deceiving statement of resignation which immediately precedes them: "Aplauda V. mi resignación y mi valerosa paciencia." Another clearly antiquated form is "*me doy a* pensar" (20), instead of *me pongo a pensar*. To use *darse a* in such a phrase is not surprising in view of the many other locutions in which it occurs; Cervantes had already employed it as Valera does: ". . . se daba a leer . . ." (*DQ* I, 53). Two additional examples are: "ha menester *de*" in the phrase, "la Iglesia *ha menester de* otros hombres más serios . . . " (158); and the transitive use of *reír* in "se los río" (73). The last example occurs in an ironical and emotional context (immediately after the use of "sobrado libres," cited above), in which Luis says of his father's irreverent remarks: "Aunque no puedo censurár*selos*, tampoco *se los* aplaudo ni *se los río*." It seems that Valera ironically causes Luis to be influenced by the pronouns *se los*, accompanying the first two verbs, and thus to misuse them with *reír*. In the *Lazarillo* the verb *reír* is also

---

dríguez Marín, 8 vols., 6th ed., "Clásicos Castellanos" (Madrid: Espasa-Calpe, 1952–1957), I, 316. Subsequent quotations from the *Quijote* will be indicated in parentheses by the abbreviation *DQ*, followed by the volume and page numbers.

used transitively: ". . . me parescia que hazia sinjusticia en no *se las reyr.*"[10]

To the preceding list may be added words which are still used but which are so *castizos* that they are evocative of older language. In a particularly affected passage, Luis employs the word "cuitas": "No parece sino que la excesiva indulgencia de usted para conmigo ha hecho *cundir* aquí *mi fama* de hombre de consejo; *paso por un pozo de ciencia;* todos me refieren sus *cuitas* y me piden que les muestre el *camino* que deben seguir" (26). The ironical artificiality is augmented by the elevated "cundir mi fama" and by the stereotyped figurative expressions, "paso por un pozo de ciencia" and "camino." The reader may recall such phrases by Cervantes as: ". . . que la vuestra magnificencia sea servida de darle facultad y licencia para entrar *á decirle su cuita*, que es una las más nuevas y más admirables que el más *cuitado* pensamiento del orbe pueda haber pensado" (*DQ* VII, 17). Valera uses the verb *mudar* in speaking of the papers he is to publish: "... he decidido publicarlos . . . , *mudando* sólo *los nombres propios* . . ." (4), where *cambiar* would perhaps be the normal choice. This is reminiscent of the frequent use of the same phrase by Cervantes, as in: "... mudado su nombre en el de Beltenebros . . ." (*DQ* II, 289).

Valera has recourse to other words that are at once *castizos* and evocative of classical prose: the ironically informal "cosa de" in "cosa de sermón o de teología" (3), widely used in the *Siglo de Oro*; "criarse" instead of *cultivarse* (34, 35); "desestimar" (124); "descomponerse," as in "Don Luis, que desde niño había estado acostumbrado a que nadie *se descompusiese* en su presencia . . ." (129); "muy enorme" (141); ". . . *hizo* Antoñona mil *extremos* de furor" (118); and "hermoso *mancebo*" (13). Whole phrases may produce the same effect, as when Luis says: "páseme V. la palabra" (40), rather than *perdóneme* or *dispénseme*; or that his father "... puede *poner envidia* a los más gallardos mozos del lugar" (7), instead of *hacer sentir envidia* or *causar envidia*; or as in "di *sin rebozo*" (196), where *fran-*

[10] *La vida de Lazarillo de Tormes,* ed. Julio Cejador y Frauca, "Clásicos Castellanos" (Madrid: Espasa-Calpe, 1952), p. 100. Future references will be given in parentheses.

camente or *abiertamente* might be expected. The word "suerte" in "De esta suerte" (103, 140), which is apparently being superseded by *manera* and *modo* in this usage, also makes one think of the *Siglo de Oro*.

There are two progressive and repetitive constructions in *Pepita Jiménez* which recall similar ones of classical prose. About the card game, ombre, Luis writes: "*Mediando, como media*, tan poco interés en el juego, lo interrumpimos continuamente . . ." (79); and the author later says: "*Corría, que no andaba*, D. Luis por aquellas sendas, saltando arroyos y fijándose apenas en los objetos, *casi* como toro picado del tábano" (144). In the latter example, the comic note of the introductory phrase is heightened by the traditional device of using *casi* plus a humorous comparison. Something like this is Cervantes's "Y diciendo esto, volvió las espaldas y *comenzó, no digo á correr sino á volar* . . ." (*DQ* VII, 246). Repetitive or semipleonastic constructions like the first example were common in the *Siglo de Oro*; Bello cites the following one: ". . . en trayendo que le trujese . . ." (*DQ* II, 336).[11] But since such constructions are no longer currently used, it is obvious that in *Pepita Jiménez* they are both jocular and reminiscent of old-fashioned language.

B. *Literary and Elegant Locutions*

Certain phrases belonging to refined and classical literary style are employed by Valera in his desire to write pure, elegant prose. At the same time, they indicate that Luis consciously meant to write stylized letters. All of this results in delightful ambiguity: surface elegance that simultaneously and ironically reveals the seminarian's stiltedness. Two notable examples are a particular use of the preposition *a* and the appearance of temporal constructions with *ha*. Instead of the more usual *según* or *por*, Luis uses *a* in the following phrases: "*a* lo que parece" (14) and "*a* lo que yo presumo" (22). That this was common in older language is witnessed by Sancho's statement: "Allí vió él visiones hermosas y apacibles, y yo veré aquí, *á lo que creo*, sapos y culebras" (*DQ* VIII, 9). For variety and elegance, Valera

[11] On these locutions, see Bello y Cuervo, *Gramática*, pp. 796–801.

and other writers sometimes use *ha*, not *hace*, as in: "El señor Deán de la catedral de . . . , muerto pocos años *ha* . . ." (3). This is likewise consecrated by usage among the classical writers: "–Ocho días o diez ha . . ." (*DQ* VIII, 17).

Other phrases obviously belong to literary style: "fuerza es" (12, 44); "de cortas luces" (10, 209); "prendas" (9); "en punto a" (8), which avoids the repetition of "con respecto a"; "en son de" (20); and "a modo de" (3, 20). Often seen in the novel are *cuanto* or *cuantos*, in an apparent avoidance of relative clauses introduced by *que*: "Para que engorde se proponen . . . hacerme comer *cuantos primores* de cocina y de repostería *se confeccionan* en el lugar. Está visto: quieren cebarme" (7). (Here it seems that Luis wishes to be both elegant and witty, because he employs *cebar*, which is ordinarily applied to animals.) A later example of *cuanto* appears in an emotional context: ". . . creo que no soy orgulloso con mi padre; creo que yo aceptaría *todo cuanto* tiene si lo necesitara . . ." (19). Another means of achieving elegance and variety is the use of *tanto* and a noun in the singular where one would expect the plural: ". . . por estas frescas y amenas huertas . . . con *tantos* mansos arroyos y acequias, con *tanto lugar* apartado y esquivo, con *tanto pájaro* que le da música; y con *tantas flores* . . ." (29–30).

The above examples show that Luis makes a synonymic choice of words and phrases which are archaic, pure, elegant, or generally reminiscent of *Siglo de Oro* usage and that, in many cases, these elements appear in an emotional context, thus suggesting a definitive correlation between Luis's interior contradictions and the stylized stiltedness of his mode of self-expression.

c. *Stock Phrases and Comparisons*

Stereotyped phrases and comparisons are indicative of how satisfied Valera is to recur to time-proven phrases which are often evocative of the *Siglo de Oro*. Nevertheless, he uses stock phrases inventively, mainly for irony, as in the following: "Mi padre estuvo *finísimo*; parecía remozado, y sus *extremos* cuidadosos hacia *la dama de sus pensamientos* eran recibidos, *si no* con amor, con gratitud"

(23–24). Luis has already become his father's rival, at least unconsciously; his resentment is reflected by the ironical-critical "finisimo," "extremos" (both of which forms are less frequent today than in older language), and "la dama de sus pensamientos," apparently already a cliché in Cervantes's time. With smug satisfaction, Luis notes that Pepita's reaction is gratitude rather than love, a fact which he states in a typical *Siglo de Oro* restrictive formula: "si no *A*, *B*." He makes one of his frequent thrusts at his father's age in "parecía remozado."

A few of the many such locutions in *Pepita Jiménez* (some with parallels from the *Quijote*) will suffice to suggest Valera's subtle originality, which will become clear if the phrases are viewed in their full context. Don Gumersindo asks Pepita "a boca de jarro" (11) to marry him. Pepita's mother managed to place her son in Havana "en un *empleíllo de mala muerte*, viéndose así libre de él y *con el charco de por medio*" (10). (Here, as often, the popular nature of the colloquialisms contributes a pleasing counterpoint to the novel's refined and elegant phrases.) Pepita's servants were unaware that she was in love with Luis: "Sólo Antoñona, que *era un lince* para todo, y más aún para las cosas de su niña, había penetrado en el misterio" (103). We are told that: "Currito era un holgazán, un perdido, un verdadero *mueble*, pero tenía un corazón afectuoso y leal" (126). A similar metaphor is Cervantes's euphemism for pages, "leños movibles" (*DQ* VII, 24), cited by Hatzfeld.[12] Currito urges Luis to accompany him to the Casino: "¿Qué haces aquí solo, tonteando y *hecho un papamoscas*?" (126). Sancho Panza, in the midst of a string of proverbs, says: ". . . siendo gobernador y juntamente liberal, como lo pienso ser, no habrá falta que se me parezca. No, sino hacer os miel, y *paparos han moscas* . . ." (*DQ* VII, 118). In Luis's quarrel with the Count, there occurs the Biblical "predicar en desierto" (130), already used by Cervantes (*DQ* VIII, 231). Upon leaving Pepita's house, Luis "*dió rienda suelta* a sus pensamientos" (177). Don Gumersindo's clothes were "*saltando de limpias*, aunque *de tiempo inmemorial* se le conocía la misma capa . . ." (9). The latter phrase was already fossilized in the *Siglo de Oro* (cf. *DQ* VIII, 16), of course,

12 Hatzfeld, *El "Quijote" como obra de arte*, p. 244.

and another traditional expression, "trabajos, desvelos y fatigas" (9), is also humorously applied to Don Gumersindo.

The preference for stock phrases is often manifested by clichéd epithet-substantive combinations like "grato murmullo" (6), "amenas huertas" (6), "tierno afecto" (13), "santa paz" (13), and "pompas vanas" (14). Many similar combinations occur in the novel, but usually with other effects. The fact that the examples cited are from the first letter indicates that, in addition to their evocative value, they also have the function of disclosing Luis's stilted but artistic attempt to write in a literary style.

At other times the liking for stock phrases is seen in the use of stereotyped comparisons and similes, some of which have been discussed. Additional examples illustrate this point: "Las paredes estaban *blancas como la nieve* del frecuente enjalbiego . . ." (127; also, 84); ". . . cantan como canarios . . ." (158); ". . . se puso *colorada como una guinda* . . ." (11); "Debí ponerme *encendido como la grana* . . ." (78); "El porvenir de felicidad con que había soñado *se desvanecía como una sombra*" (156; also, 134); "Te estás portando *como un tuno*" (135); ". . . es más noble que el oro y más serena que un coche" (59); ". . . limpios como el oro" (125); ". . . es mejor que el pan" (177); and ". . . tuvo que llevarle a su casa a *dormir la mona*, terciado en una borrica *como un pellejo de vino*" (204). Other traditional figurative expressions follow: ". . . pelando la pava . . ." (177); "sin haber*se* antes *quemado las cejas* a fuerza de estudio . . ." (182); and "El niño *es un sol de bonito* . . ." (210). Precisely because this type of figurative language has little stylistic value in itself, unless used in some new or functional way, it does evince a kind of classical attenuation. But the context alone is often sufficient to vivify these dead figures: "Don Luis había pasado solo toda la mañana, entregado a sus melancólicos pensamientos, y *más firme que roca* en su resolución de borrar de su alma la imagen de Pepita y de consagrarse a Dios por completo" (122). Luis employs a conventional comparison which, although of surface beauty, is nevertheless semi-ironized (perhaps because of the inner tension between his conscience and his inceptive love) by the use of "esta" and "casi": ". . . las manos de *esta* Pepita, que parecen *casi diáfanas como el alabastro*, si bien con leves tintas rosadas . . ." (37). The concluding clause and the rest of the passage show how truly observant he is in spite of his professed disinterest in Pepita. Luis twice says that Pepita's eyes are "verdes como los de Circe" (38, 80), although the second usage is only a recollection of the earlier one. Since he considers Pepita something of a *maga*, and since he often refers to the irresistible, magnetic attraction she exercises upon him, the comparison retains something of its original force.

To sum up, Valera deliberately employed what may be termed borderline archaisms, in view of their narrow divergence from normal usage. Contrariwise, archaisms in the romantic and *costumbrista* novel are ordinarily much more obvious, as has been noted by Lapesa: "La novela histórica, a que tan aficionados fueron los románticos, requería el empleo de arcaísmos para evocar ambientes del pasado: . . . La artificiosa imitación del español aúreo, acompañada por el uso de voces antiguas o regionales, dió lugar a la tendencia casticista, que si en ocasiones procuró notable caudal de palabras jugosas y plásticas, resultó disfraz incómodo llevada al extremo, como en las *Escenas andaluzas* de Estébanez Calderón."[13] Valera's preference for conventional expressions is primarily illustrated by an artistically unerring choice among synonymic possibilities which evokes the *Siglo de Oro* prose style as well as literary reminiscences in the mind of the reader. Lapesa recognized the refined nature of Valera's prose and the role of stock phrases among the nineteenth-century Spanish novelists, of whom he said:

> . . . lograron exactitud y fuerza pictórica en las descripciones, sondearon con profundidad el corazón humano y a veces dieron sencilla viveza al coloquio entre sus personajes. Es cierto que, *a excepción de Valera, prosista esmerado y fino*, atendieron al fondo más que al arte de la palabra; pero si, como reacción contra el atildamiento hinchado, se abandonaron con frecuencia al desaliño y a la frase hecha, *dieron a la novela el tono medio que necesitaba*. Después de ellos, limadas ya las más duras asperezas, ha podido surgir el cuidado estilístico de los prosistas actuales.[14]

Some, like Lapesa, are able to see the aesthetic merit of artistic

[13] Lapesa, *Historia de la lengua española*, p. 269.
[14] *Ibid.*, p. 273. The italics are mine.

renovation among the writers of the Generation of 1898 without thereby denying the achievements of the novelists of the preceding generation and without condemning them for the utilization of conventional stylistic expressions. Others would say with Guillermo Díaz-Plaja that nineteenth-century Spanish prose ". . . ofrece, en general, un lamentable, un increíble descuido. Prosa-cauce, atenta a lo sumo al hilo narrativo, está plagada de *clichés*, de frases hechas. Asombra en efecto, su vulgaridad y su pobreza."[15] It is no doubt more appropriate to try to apprehend the functional value of fossilized images and stock phrases used by nineteenth-century novelists, especially those who, like Valera, accept the limitations of normal and conventional usage. Moreover, traditional forms of expression are evidently much better adapted to an ironical and evocative style, as R. A. Sayce has remarked: ". . . conventional language is a suitable instrument for irony when it is employed consciously."[16] In general, Sayce's approach to the treatment of the cliché is the most logical and valid one: "On the face of it such unoriginal expressions should make a writer's style lifeless and mediocre, but like the conventional metaphor they may be employed for special purposes. In fact the *cliché may be regarded, like the single word, as one of the conventional elements, the combination of which with other such elements constitutes the only way of attaining originality. . . .*"[17]

I have treated this problem at length because the exposing of classical, traditional language and techniques and the establishing of literary parallels with writers of the *Siglo de Oro* in no way minimize Valera's aesthetic accomplishment. An understanding of the use to which Valera put traditional elements leads to a more correct evaluation of his contribution to Spanish literature. Literary sources, in-

[15] Guillermo Díaz-Plaja, *Modernismo frente a noventa y ocho* (Madrid: Espasa-Calpe, 1951), p. 301. In all fairness to Díaz-Plaja, it should be noted that he slightly qualifies this by saying: "Que el uso—sobre todo el uso continuado—de modismos da una impresión de pereza y de pobreza, nos parece irrefutable hoy; sin embargo, muchos escritores del siglo XIX sentían que de este modo se acercaban a las locuciones de la Edad de Oro" (p. 302); he nevertheless shows a marked prejudice for poetic prose. It should also be clarified that he did not make these remarks about Valera directly but about the writers of Valera's time, other than Bécquer.

[16] R. A. Sayce, *Style in French Prose: A Method of Analysis* (Oxford: Oxford Univ. Press, 1953), p. 61.

[17] *Ibid.*, p. 81.

fluences, and even vague reminiscences in the mind of the creative writer all become part of the subject matter for the new creation, or, as Amado Alonso put it: "... lo que una vez ha sido forma—objeto de conciencia—puede luego retornar a ser materia—mera sensación o incitación—que una nueva potencia poética puede sacar a nueva forma."[18] Valera himself expressed similar thoughts on the utilization of sources in his essay, "La originalidad y el plagio":

> Puesto que todos los poetas se copian, ¿en qué consiste la originalidad? ... Llámase a veces original al extravagante, raro y disparatado. De esta originalidad pedimos a Dios que nos libre. La verdadera y buena originalidad ni se pierde ni se gana por copiar pensamientos, ideas o imágenes, o por tomar asunto de otros autores. La verdadera originalidad está en la persona. . . . Para ser, pues, original en el buen sentido no hay que afanarse mucho ni poco en decir y pensar cosas raras. Basta con pensar, sentir y expresar lo que se piensa y se siente, del modo más sencillo. *Entonces sale retratado el alma del que escribe en lo que escribe;* y como el alma es original, original es lo escrito.[19]

It is curious to note that this essay was written in 1876, only two years after *Pepita Jiménez*, and that the italicized words apply perfectly to Luis's self-portrayal in his letters, although Luis, by contrast, does not usually express himself in a "simple" way.

II. GENERAL SIMILARITIES TO THE *SIGLO DE ORO* PROSE STYLE

Most critics have mentioned the classical qualities of Valera and his work, although none has established specific parallels between his style and that of the *Siglo de Oro*, the age of the greatest Spanish prose writers. Frank R. Thompson legitimately said in general terms, for instance: "Restraint, sobriety, naturalness, were qualities of utmost importance in Valera's artistic creed."[20] Thompson also spoke

18 Amado Alonso, "Estilística de las fuentes literarias: Rubén Darío y Miguel Angel," in *Materia y forma en poesía* (Madrid: Gredos, 1955), p. 382.

19 Juan Valera, *Obras completas*, ed. Luis Araujo Costa (Madrid: Aguilar, 1947–1949), II, 467. The italics are mine.

20 Frank R. Thompson, "The Classicism of Don Juan Valera," Ph.D. Diss., Univ. of Wisconsin, 1941, p. 48. See pp. 39–53 for Thompson's ideas on Valera's classicism.

of Valera's universality, idealization of reality, measure, order, common sense, good taste, decorum, cult of the beautiful, and Olympic serenity, which are fitting characteristics, although again somewhat general. These qualities in Valera the man may be related to Greco-Roman classicism, if one so desires; but it seems erroneous to do the same with the stylistic means by which these qualities are manifested in his work, for Valera could and did take ideas and attitudes from various periods of history without thereby going outside his own language and literary heritage for the means with which to express them. Yet is is certain that a sense of moderation, restraint, and an avoidance of the two extremes of romanticism and naturalism characterize Valera's novels; the problem is to discover how this restraint is related to the style of *Pepita Jiménez*.

Classical attenuation in Valera is attained by many of the same devices with which it was attained in the *Siglo de Oro* and most of all by the use of what Dámaso Alonso calls *pluralidades* (an all-inclusive term for doublets, triads, synonymy, bifurcations, enumerations, and parallelistic syntactical constructions).[21] That this is one of the most obvious features of Valera's style, with examples on almost every page, has already been pointed out by Revuelta y Revuelta: "Otro aspecto característico es la preferencia que muestra por la expresión paralela de sinónimos verbales como apoyo o ritmo de frase, recurso que tiene su pujanza en el estilo del renacimiento español, pero que es connatural a Valera. . . ."[22] In regard to the reasons for Valera's use of *pluralidades*, she adds: "Esta agrupación es motivada unas veces por el concepto que del arte tiene Valera, el

Cf. also Cyrus C. DeCoster's useful study, "The Theory and Practice of the Novels of Valera: A Study in Techniques," Ph.D. Diss., Univ. of Chicago, 1951.

21 See Dámaso Alonso, "Sintagmas no progresivos y pluralidades: calillas en la prosa castellana," in *Seis calas en la expresión literatura española*, 2nd ed. (Madrid: Gredos, 1956), pp. 25–45, in which there are also essays by Carlos Bousoño. In this essay Alonso briefly studies the *pluralidades* and related features in the prose of Cervantes and other writers. The word *pluralidades* will be used here for lack of a precise English equivalent. For a treatment of similar problems in Italian and French literature, see Alfredo Schiaffini, *Tradizione e poesia nella prosa d'arte italiana dalla latinità medievale a G. Boccaccio*, 2nd ed. (Rome: Edizioni di "Storia e Letterature," 1943) and Sayce, *Style in French Prose*, pp. 73–80.

22 Luisa Revuelta y Revuelta, "Valera, estilista," *Boletín de la Real Academia de Ciencias, Bellas Letras y Nobles Artes de Córdoba*, XVII (1946), 39.

gusto por la armonía, el equilibrio clásico. Otras, ocasionado [*sic*] por la preocupación de una exactitud de juicio y de análisis que no logra expresar a su parecer con una palabra . . . ."[23] Valera's interest in balance and precision are valid reasons, but there are other important ones as well.

The liking for *pluralidades* and enumerations has frequently been singled out as a main feature of *Siglo de Oro* style. Menéndez Pidal even went so far as to say: "Este curso lento de la palabra, este deleite moroso que se entretiene a cada paso en la yuxtaposición de sinónimos, es, sin duda, el carácter más saliente de la lengua de casi todo el siglo XVI."[24] Dámaso Alonso has shown that in poetry this phenomenon goes back to Petrarch[25] and has intimated that it had already begun in Spanish prose of the Middle Ages;[26] Margherita Morreale has indicated that the use of doublets was one of the ways in which Boscán avoided a literal translation of the Italian absolute superlative in his *El cortesano*, a practice which indicates both the expressiveness and popularity of doublets;[27] Rebecca Switzer has pointed out that the enumerations and accumulations used by Fray Luis de Granada were primarily due to a Ciceronian influence;[28] and Helmut Hatzfeld has studied the accumulations in the *Quijote*.[29] Hatzfeld has likewise investigated what is, in essence, another manifestation of the same phenomenon in the prose of San Juan de la Cruz, namely, bipartite and tripartite rhythm, Biblical parallelism, and what he terms ". . . el estilo tradicional isidoriano español en busca de *similiter cadentia*, *similiter desinentia*, *figurae etymologicae*, juegos de palabras antitéticas, anáforas, epíforas, etc."[30] Leo Spitzer

23 *Ibid.*, p. 46.

24 Ramón Menéndez Pidal, *La lengua de Cristóbal Colón* (Buenos Aires: Espasa-Calpe Argentina, 1942), p. 70.

25 D. Alonso, *Seis calas*, p. 89.

26 *Ibid.*, p. 36.

27 Margherita Morreale, "El superlativo en *issimo* y la versión castellana del *Cortesano*," *Revista de Filología Española*, XXXIX (1955), 46–60; especially pp. 52–53 and 55.

28 Rebecca Switzer, *The Ciceronian Style in Fr. Luis de Granada* (New York: Instituto de las Españas, 1927), pp. 42–45 and 118–127.

29 Hatzfeld, *El "Quijote" como obra de arte*, pp. 284–292 and pp. 349–357.

30 Helmut Hatzfeld, *Estudios literarios sobre mística española* (Madrid: Gredos, 1955), p. 366. See also pp. 367–376.

has studied the closely related problem of the chaotic enumerations in the *Siglo de Oro*, especially those of Calderón and of Quevedo.[31] But even these extreme cases are usually mitigated, as Spitzer shows: in Calderón and in Cervantes by summation phrases and by the use of *todo*; in Quevedo (only rarely) by the following of an established order.

This vast and important stylistic phenomenon is evidently one to which the critics have devoted a great deal of attention and one which, from Biblical, Latin, and Italian sources, and by the unique combination of historical events, became an outstanding feature of *Siglo de Oro* style. In spite of the fact that *pluralidades*, synonymy, enumerations, etc. may have a dynamic function, as is sometimes the case in Cervantes's prose and as is usually so in Quevedo's, their main function seems to be to provide, in addition to ornamentation, rhythmical, balanced periods which create a general tone of serenity, or *sosiego*.[32] I say this at the risk of oversimplification, since, while such a general trend may exist, it is still possible for different writers, or even the same writer, to use *pluralidades* for a variety of effects; but, to my mind, the main effect is one of mitigation. The use of *pluralidades* is only part of a greater tendency toward mitigation, for within the framework of Spanish history and literary traditions, there appears to be in the *Siglo de Oro* a real effort to attenuate the baroque movement; in other words, although not so strong, there existed in Spain the Spanish equivalent of French classical mitigation.[33]

A. *Classical Stylistic Expressions of Mitigation and Their Use in* Pepita Jiménez

The modes and devices by which mitigation was achieved in the *Siglo de Oro* and which Valera also utilized include *pluralidades*,

[31] Leo Spitzer, *La enumeración caótica en la poesía moderna* (Buenos Aires: Instituto de Filología, 1945), especially pp. 39–43 and 47–55.

[32] According to Dámaso Alonso, *Seis calas*, p. 36.

[33] Similar to what Leo Spitzer terms "*Klassische Dämpfung*: a continuous repression of the emotional by the intellectual." "The 'Récit de Théramène,'" in *Linguistics and Literary History* (Princeton: Princeton Univ. Press, 1948), p. 110.

summation phrases, traditional descriptions, and miscellaneous devices and formulas, like the use of euphemisms, litotes, round numbers, restrictive clauses, *tal vez*, and *no parecer sino*. In this wise, it is justifiable to group together stylistic devices which, although used desultorily in almost all periods, form a constellation of elements that occur with significant frequency and with the same essential but not unique purpose of mitigation in both *Pepita Jiménez* and classical prose. Thus we may speak of Valera's assimilated rather than servile imitation of *Siglo de Oro* forms of expression on a truly stylistic level. From the outset, I must plainly state that in the study of these various features of classical Spanish prose writers I lay no claim to comprehensiveness. Indeed, my attention is constantly directed toward *Pepita Jiménez* and my choice of passages from the *Siglo de Oro* is very selective. Nevertheless, I consider the points made to be valid and the examples very representative ones.

1. PLURALIDADES AND REPETITIVE FIGURES. Fray Luis de Granada's "Ciceronian" use of *pluralidades* and anaphorical parallelism is highly oratorical and ornamental, as in the following passage: "En ti nunca se veen tinieblas, *ni* noche, *ni* mudanza de tiempos. La luz que te alumbra *ni* es de lámpara, *ni* de luna, *ni* de lúcidas estrellas; sino Dios que procede de Dios, y luz que mana de luz es el que te da claridad. . . . *Allí* los ángeles a coros le dan música muy suave. *Allí* se goza la hermandad de aquellos nobles ciudadanos. *Allí* se celebran una perpetua solemnidad y fiesta con cada uno de los que entran desta peregrinación."[34] He goes on to begin sentences with "allí," with occasional doublets, a total of eleven times. One of his favorite rhetorical devices, also much used by Valera, is amplification: "Allí hallan a sus amigos, conocen a sus maestros, reconocen a sus padres, abrázanse y dánse *dulce paz* y reciben la norabuena de tal entrada y tal gloria. . . . Dulce es la sombra después del resistidero del mediodía; *dulce* la fuente al caminante cansado; *dulce* el sueño y reposo al siervo trabajador; *pero muy más dulce es* a los sanctos *la paz* después de la guerra, *la seguridad* después del peligro, y *el descanso*

[34] Fray Luis de Granada, *Guía de pecadores*, ed. Matías Martínez Burgos, "Clásicos Castellanos" (Madrid: Ediciones de "La Lectura," 1929), p. 59.

perdurable después de la fatiga de los trabajos pasados."[35] The ternary structure is amplified by the enhancing "pero muy más dulce es," followed by three objects, the last of which is the longest.

Fray Luis de León often employs a combination of bipartite and tripartite phrases that are well balanced, though not strictly so:

Porque assí como en el árbol la rays no se hizo para sí, ni menos el tronco, que nasce y se sustenta sobre ella, sino lo uno y lo otro juntamente con las ramas y la flor y la hoja y *todo lo demás* que el árbol produze, se ordena y endereça para el fructo que dél sale, que es el fin y como remate suyo; assí por la misma manera estos cielos estendidos que vemos, y las estrellas que en ellos dan resplandor, y entre *todas* ellas esta fuente de claridad y de luz, que *todo* lo alumbra, redonda y bellíssima; la tierra pintada con flores y las aguas pobladas de peces; los animales y los hombres, y este universo *todo*, cuán grande y cuán hermoso es, lo hizo Dios para fin de hazer hombre a su Hijo, y para producir á luz este único y divino fructo, que es Cristo, que con verdad le podemos llamar el parto común y general de *todas* las cosas.[36]

The word *todo* in this and similar cases, even when required by the thought, has a logical, didactic effect and at the same time tempers and justifies the use of doublets and triads. It is a minor indication of Luis de Leon's true classical balance and restraint. Sometimes he moderately engages in word play, while still employing the slightly asymmetrical binary and ternary forms: "*Luze*, pues, ¡o *solo* verdadero *sol*! en mi alma y *luze* con tan grande abundancia de *luz*, que con el rayo della juntamente y mi voluntad encendida te ame, y mi entendimiento esclarescido te vea, y enriquecida mi boca te hable y pregone, si no como eres del todo, á lo menos como puedes de nosotros ser entendido, y sólo á fin de que tú seas glorioso y ensalçado en todo tiempo y de todos."[37]

[35] *Ibid.*, p. 63.

[36] Fray Luis de León, *De los nombres de Cristo*, 3 vols., "Clásicos Castellanos" (Madrid: Espasa-Calpe, I, 1938), I, 66. In a book which, though otherwise informative, in effect ignores related studies on Spanish literature of the Golden Age and fails to establish the relationships between attitudes and form or to give a complete aesthetic and stylistic evaluation, Helen Dill Goode has recently studied what she prefers to call Fray Luis de León's rhetorical style, especially in ch. iii. See her *La prosa retórica de Fray Luis de León en "Los nombres de Cristo"* (Madrid: Gredos, 1969).

[37] León, *De los nombres de Cristo*, I, 26–27.

Closely related to the use of *pluralidades* is repetition, as in San Juan de la Cruz's

Por tanto, en este *camino*, el *entrar* en *camino* es *dejar* su *camino*, o, por mejor decir, es pasar al término, y *dejar* su *modo* es *entrar* en lo que no tiene *modo*, que es Dios. Porque el alma que a este estado llega, ya no tiene *modos* ni maneras, ni menos se *ase* ni puede *asir* a ellos. Digo *modos* de entender, ni de gustar, ni de sentir, aunque en sí encierra *todos los modos, al modo* del que no tiene nada, que lo tiene *todo*. Porque, *teniendo* ánimo para pasar de su *limitado natural* interior y exteriormente, entra en *límite sobrenatural* que no *tiene modo* alguno, *teniendo* en sustancia *todos los modos*.[38]

This deliberate repetition, here used in paradoxical statements, is often a didactic figure; but it also exemplifies a general characteristic of the *Siglo de Oro*, namely, the complete lack of the modern aversion to repetition.[39] The last two examples hint that the use of repetition and *pluralidades* both occasions and serves as a vehicle for the age's predominant fondness for word play, echo sounds, and paradoxical constructions.[40]

All the preceding examples are from works that are fundamentally didactic; a few passages from Cervantes will show that in fiction the purposes and effects are more varied. Don Quijote is characterized by his artificial use of near-synonymic doublets: "Bien te puedes llamar dichosa sobre cuantas hoy viven sobre la tierra. ¡Oh sobre las bellas bella Dulcinea del Toboso! pues te cupo en suerte tener *sujeto y rendido* á toda tu *voluntad é talante* á un *tan valiente y tan nombrado* caballero como *lo es y será* don Quijote de la Mancha; el cual, como todo el mundo sabe, ayer recibió la orden de caballería, y hoy

38 San Juan de la Cruz, *Obras*, p. 609 ("Noche activa del espíritu," ch. 4).

39 For a treatment of the lack of the *horror aequi*, see Gustav Siebenmann, *Über Sprache und Stil im Lazarillo de Tormes* (Bern: A. Francke, 1953), pp. 82–83. Also of interest for our purposes is Siebenmann's discussion of rhythm, sound patterns, word play, doublets, etc. in the *Lazarillo* (pp. 80–98).

40 Cf. Helmut Hatzfeld, "A Clarification of the Baroque Problem in the Romance Literatures," *Comparative Literature*, I (1949), 113–139, especially p. 129, where he says: "If, then, the traditional figures of speech called anaphora, figura etymologica, word play, annominatio, parechesis, paronomasia, paronymia enjoy something like a second springtime after having been the great style of the hymns and sequences of the Middle Ages, it is certainly because of their echo-like character."

ha desfecho el mayor *tuerto y agravio* que *formó la sinrazón y cometió la crueldad*: hoy quitó el látigo de la mano á aquel despiadado enemigo que tan sin ocasión vapulaba á aquel delicado infante" (*DQ* I, 123–124).[41] Cervantes often avoids rigid symmetry by interjecting single terms in a combination of binary and ternary phrases:

Y *estando* un día á la mesa con los Duques, y *comenzando* á *poner en obra su intención y pedir la licencia*, veis aquí á deshora entrar por la puerta de la gran sala dos mujeres (como después pareció), cubiertas de luto de los pies á la cabeza, y la una dellas, llegándose á don Quijote, se le echó á los pies tendida de largo a largo, la boca cosida con los pies de don Quijote, y daba unos gemidos *tan tristes, y tan profundos, y tan dolorosos*, que puso en confusión á todos los que la *oían y miraban*; y aunque los Duques pensaron que sería alguna burla que sus criados querían hacer á don Quijote, todavía, viendo con el ahinco que la mujer *suspiraba, gemía y lloraba*, los tuvo dudosos y suspensos, hasta que don Quijote, compasivo, la levantó del suelo y *hizo que se descubriese y quitase* el manto de sobre la faz llorosa. (*DQ* VII, 291–292)

Sometimes the long ceremonious speeches of Cervantes's characters in the *Quijote* and elsewhere take on an oratorical note, with a more complicated use of *pluralidades*.[42]

In Valera's novel, Luis often employs *pluralidades*, especially doublets and triads, in tightly organized periods which attenuate his emotional or guilt-ridden thoughts, thus masking his true nature under a balanced, formalized exterior. While leading up to his adolescent conjecture about whether Pepita had become aware of the "mysteries" of married life, he says: "Tal vez entendió que casarse con aquel viejo era consagrar su vida *a cuidarle, a ser su enfermera, a dulcificar* los últimos años de su vida, *a no dejarle* en

[41] Cf. Hatzfeld, *El "Quijote" como obra de arte*, p. 284, and D. Alonso, *Seis calas*, p. 36, note 11. Valera, in a similar way, uses *pluralidades* to characterize Luis.

[42] See, for instance, Don Quijote's speeches on the Golden Age (*DQ* I, 249–254), on the comparison of the life of the monk with that of the knight-errant (*DQ* I, 290–292), and on the comparison of his epoch with that of chivalry, in which he begins fourteen rhetorical questions with "¿Quién más . . . ?," although the device is justified and assuaged, as it were, by the summation phrase: "Todos estos caballeros, y otros muchos que pudiera decir . . ." (*DQ* V, 40–42). Also see the old gypsy's speech in "La gitanilla," *Novelas ejemplares*, 2 vols., "Clásicos Castellanos" (Madrid: Espasa-Calpe, I, 1948), I, 66–70.

soledad y abandono, cercado sólo de achaques y asistido por manos mercenarias, y *a iluminar y dorar, por último*, sus postrimerías con el rayo esplendente y suave de su hermosura y de su juventud, como ángel que toma forma humana. *Si algo de esto o todo esto* pensó la muchacha, y en su inocencia *no penetró en otros misterios*, salva queda la bondad de lo que hizo" (12–13). The bifurcations serve to amplify the five graded infinitive phrases, of which the last is the most important and the most stilted, with its near-synonymic pair of infinitives, the subsequent doublets, the rare adjective "esplendente," the didactic "por último," and the clichéd simile. What he says is simply a façade for the idea he has in mind, which is almost buried in the second conditional clause (significantly without the *si*), "no penetró en otros misterios," and which is dependent on the formal "*Si* algo de esto o todo esto . . ."; his real thought is: "Si . . . no penetró en otros misterios, salva queda la bondad de lo que hizo." In a formalized binary sentence he makes similar conjectures, this time hiding his identity in the euphemism, "alguien": "*Tal vez alguien presume o sospecha* que la soberbia de Pepita y el conocimiento cierto que tiene hoy de los pocos poéticos medios con que se ha hecho rica, traen su conciencia alterada y más que escrupulosa; y que, avergonzada a sus propios ojos y a los de los hombres, busca en la austeridad y en el retiro consuelo y reparo a la herida de su corazón" (13). The "Tal vez" itself is partially negated by the use of the present indicative rather than the subjunctive in "presume o sospecha."

After a brief, pseudo-philosophical digression, Luis gets around to discussing the situation between Pepita and his father, expressing his curiosity to meet her:

No creo que mi curiosidad carezca de fundamento, tenga nada de vano ni de pecaminoso; *yo mismo siento* lo que dice Pepita; *yo mismo deseo* que mi padre, en su edad provecta, venga a mejor vida, olvide y no renueve las agitaciones y pasiones de su mocedad, y llegue a una vejez tranquila, dichosa y honrada. Sólo difiero del sentir de Pepita en una cosa: en creer que mi padre mejor que quedándose soltero, conseguiría esto casándose con una mujer digna, buena y que le quisiese. *Por esto mismo deseo* conocer a Pepita y ver si ella puede ser esta mujer, pesándome ya algo, y *tal vez entre en esto cierto orgullo de familia*, que *si es malo* quisiera desechar, los desdenes, aunque melifluos y afectuosos, de la mencionada joven viuda. (14–15)

Here the binary and ternary phrases are skillfully interwoven, particularly in the first sentence, although exact symmetry is circumvented by small touches such as the slightly imperfect amplification. The first phrase beginning with "yo mismo" is much shorter than the second, but in the second the amplification is apparent: ". . . yo mismo deseo que mi padre, . . . (A_1) venga a mejor vida, (A_2) olvide y no renueve las (B_1) agitaciones y (B_2) pasiones de su mocedad, y (A_3) llegue a una vejez (B_1) tranquila, (B_2) dichosa y (B_3) honrada."[43] Although the verb pair, "olvide y no renueve," partly upsets the balance, it is obvious that the phrase is intellectually organized, setting the stage for Luis's seeming recognition of his pride, which is itself a false reason for wanting to meet Pepita and which he doubly invalidates, first by "tal vez" plus the subjunctive and then by the qualification, "si es malo." His stiltedness is further reflected in the preciosity of "desdenes, . . . melifluos y afectuosos" and in the legal-sounding "la mencionada joven viuda." Later, formally phrasing one thought with doublets and triads, Luis is really expressing a semiadmission of the opposite: "Siento un gran consuelo, una gran tranquilidad en mi conciencia, y doy por ello las más fervientes gracias a Dios, cuando advierto y noto que la fuerza de la sangre, el vínculo de la naturaleza, ese misterioso lazo que nos une, me lleva, sin ninguna consideración del deber, a amar a mi padre y a reverenciarle. Sería horrible no amarle así, y esforzarse por amarle para cumplir con un mandamiento divino. Sin embargo . . ." (18). The mere expression of these ideas hints that he must have had such thoughts, which is made clear by the comments following "Sin embargo."

In many of the deceptively smooth, well-organized sentences, there occurs an especially effective psychological artifice: the use of concessive clauses or similar qualifying remarks which serve as

[43] The capital letter indicates the genus and the subnumeral the number of occurrence. These signs will be used only when it is felt that they clarify the use of *pluralidades*.

escape valves for Luis's true feelings and motives and which lay bare his real critical attitude toward those around him. Speaking of the relations between Pepita and the Vicar, he makes a few humorous thrusts at the latter's ignorance:

No sé qué libros habrá leído Pepita Jiménez, ni qué instrucción tendrá; pero de lo que cuenta el señor Vicario se colige que está dotada de un espíritu inquieto e investigador, donde se ofrecen infinitas cuestiones y problemas que anhela delucidar y resolver, presentándolos para ello al señor Vicario, a quien deja agradablemente confuso. Este hombre, *educado a la rústica, clérigo de misa y olla* como vulgarmente suele decirse, tiene el entendimiento abierto a toda luz de verdad, *aunque carece de iniciativa*, y, por lo visto, los problemas y cuestiones que Pepita le presenta le abren nuevos horizontes y nuevos caminos, *aunque nebulosos y mal determinados*, que él no presumía siquiera, que no acierta a trazar con exactitud, pero cuya vaguedad, novedad y misterio le encantan. (45)

His ironical-critical attitude (and Valera's) is likewise disclosed by the phrases, "educado a la rústica, clérigo de misa y olla . . . ," and by a subsequent remark: ". . . distando mucho de ser un gran teólogo, sabe su catecismo al dedillo . . ." (45). Similar critical remarks are made in reference to Don Pedro and Pepita: "*Con los cincuenta y cinco años que tiene*, creo que está enamorado, y Pepita, *aunque buena por reflexión*, puede, *sin premeditarlo ni calcularlo*, ser un instrumento del espíritu del mal; puede tener una coquetería irreflexiva e instintiva, más invencible, eficaz y funesta aún que la que procede de premeditación, cálculo y discurso" (47). The pseudo-spiritual phraseology, dressed in binary and ternary form, fails to conceal Luis's ironical-critical feelings.

Since Luis is reporting remembered events in his letters, at the moment of writing each letter he has had time to reflect upon and analyze what he is relating, and is able to embellish and veil his thoughts. So it often happens that a descriptive, philosophical, or pseudo-spiritual passage, which is expressed in primarily bipartite and tripartite sentence structure, is given as a mitigating, self-deceiving prelude to the main statement, whereas the statement itself may be given in a more direct style. Such is the case when Luis describes the Pozo de la Solana before telling of Pepita's "apparition":

Siguiendo el curso del arroyo, y sobre todo en las hondonadas, hay muchos álamos y otros árboles altos que, con las matas y hierbas, crean un intrincado laberinto y una sombría espesura. Mil plantas silvestres y olorosas crecen allí de un modo espontáneo, y por cierto que es difícil imaginar nada más esquivo, agreste y verdaderamente solitario, apacible y silencioso que aquellos lugares. Se concibe allí en el fervor del mediodía, cuando el sol vierte a torrentes la luz desde un cielo sin nubes, en las calurosas y reposadas siestas, el mismo terror misterioso de las horas nocturnas. Se concibe allí la vida de los antiguos patriarcas y de los primitivos héroes y pastores, y las apariciones y visiones que tenían de ninfas, de deidades y de ángeles en medio de la claridad meridiana. (61–62)

As early as in the first letter, even though the emotions have not yet reached their peak, the same device is used twice by Luis to conceal his motives. First, in order to serve as a bridge between his suppositions concerning Pepita's unconsummated marriage to Don Gumersindo and her relations with his father, he gives a stilted statement, filled with commonplaces, about the different attitudes toward money of people in small towns and in big cities:

Aquí, como en todas partes, la gente es muy aficionada al dinero. Y digo mal *como en todas partes*: en las ciudades populosas, en los grandes centros de civiliza*ción*, hay otras distin*ciones* que se ambi*cion*an tanto o más que el dinero, porque abren camino y dan crédito y considera-*ción* en el mundo; pero en los pueblos pequeños, donde ni la gloria literaria o científica, ni tal vez la distin*ción* en los modales, ni la elegancia, ni la discre*ción* y amenidad en el trato, suelen estimarse ni comprenderse, no hay otros grados que marquen la jerarquía social sino el tener más o menos dinero o cosa que lo valga. *Pepita, pues, con dinero* y *siendo* además hermosa, y *haciendo*, como dicen todos, buen uso de su riqueza, se ve en el día *considerada y respetada extraordinariamente*. De este pueblo y de todos los de las cercanías han acudido a pretenderla los más brillantes partidos, los mozos mejor acomodados. Pero, a lo que parece, ella los desdeña a todos con extremada dulzura, procurando no hacerse ningún enemigo, y se supone que tiene llena el alma de la más ardiente devoción, y que su constante pensamiento es consagrar su vida a ejercicios de *caridad* y de *piedad* religiosa. (13–14)

This passage's similarity to *Siglo de Oro* style is due not only to the use of bifurcations, but also to the echo sounds in the abstract nouns ending in *-ción* and in the word pairs, "siendo . . . haciendo," "considerada y respetada," and "de caridad y de piedad," and to the rhythmical use of the conjunction "pues" after an introductory noun, participle, or adjective, as in "Pepita, pues, con dinero. . . ." That the last device was common in the *Quijote* is well known; every reader is familiar with such phrases as "Limpias, pues, sus armas . . ." (*DQ* I, 63). The reader may recall the similar situation of a rich, beautiful girl whose hand is sought by the most eligible suitors in the case of Marcela: ". . . la fama de su mucha hermosura se extendió de manera, que así por ella como por sus muchas riquezas, no solamente de los de nuestro pueblo, sino los de *muchas leguas a la redonda*, y de los mejores dellos, era rogado, solicitado e importunado su tío se la diese por mujer" (*DQ* I, 270–271). The similarity in content is reinforced by the italicized phrase, which had been said about Don Gumersindo only a few pages before the passage cited above: ". . . era el viejo más amigo de requebrar a las muchachas y que más las hiciese reír que había en *diez leguas a la redonda*" (10). Thus the balanced phrases, the *Siglo de Oro* style traits, and the literary reminiscence formalize the whole passage and, at the same time, reveal Luis's stiltedness.

The second major instance in which the attenuating digression appears in the first letter is between the introductory remarks to and the final broaching of the topic of illegitimacy. In spite of the fact that he is discussing two methods of education, thus necessitating some usage of binary phrases, the bifurcations are evidently artificially arranged by Luis: "He pensado muchas veces sobre dos métodos opuestos de educación: el de aquellos que procuran conservar la inocencia, confundiendo la inocencia con la ignorancia y creyendo que el mal no conocido se evita mejor que el conocido, y el de aquellos que, valerosamente y no bien llegado el discípulo a la edad de razón, y salva la delicadeza del pudor, le muestran el mal en toda su fealdad horrible y en toda su espantosa desnudez, a fin de que le aborrezca y le evite" (18). The rest of the passage, which is also stilted, contains more varied *pluralidades*. Then Luis indirectly bolsters his ego by thanking the Dean for the "tolerance" he has taught him, in a studiedly binary sentence: "Otra cosa que me considero obligado a agradecer a usted es la indulgencia, la tolerancia, aunque no complaciente y relajada, sino severa y grave, que ha sabido usted inspirarme para con las faltas y pecados del prójimo" (17). The next sentence clarifies the mitigating, rationalizing nature of this digression: "*Digo todo esto* porque quiero hablar a usted de un asunto tan delicado, tan vidrioso, que apenas hallo términos con que expresarle" (17). In all the last pages of the first letter (13–19), there are similar self-deluding, attenuating, and formalized digressions, the most important of which, other than those mentioned, is the ceremonious statement Luis makes about his calling (15–16). To such an extent is the device used, here and in other letters, that the result is often a wave-movement of tightly organized *pluralidades*, particularly of binary and ternary constructions, directly related to Luis's approach to and expression of his true motives and emotions, which constitutes, in conjunction with other methods of attenuation, an overall mitigating stiltedness.

Similar uses are made of *pluralidades* on a larger scale, as when Luis hypocritically says: "Para (A_1) adularme y (A_2) adular a mi padre, dicen (B_1) hombres y (B_2) mujeres (C_1) que soy (D_1) un real mozo, (D_2) muy salado, (C_2) que tengo mucho ángel, (C_3) que mis ojos son muy pícaros y (C_4) otras sandeces que me (E_1) afligen, (E_2) disgustan y (E_3) avergüenzan, a *pesar de que* (F_1) no soy tímido y (F_2) conozco las (G_1) miserias y (G_2) locuras de esta vida, *para* (A_3) no escandalizarme (A_4) ni asustarme de nada" (7). The following schema of the *pluralidades* shows that the apparent symmetry of the sentence masks an involved verbal evasion which is set in relief by "a pesar de que" and the peculiar conclusion of the sentence in the same form, outwardly, as the beginning, with a pair of infinitives dependent on "para," although this time with a different subject and in the negative. Luis is half aware of his self-deception and of the fact that he is really not so displeased by the townspeople's remarks.[44]

[44] For the apparently symmetrical expression of other involved thought processes, see p. 15, line 28, to p. 16, line 6, and p. 28, lines 21–30, both of which sentences have already been cited in other connections.

Longer sentences, occurring in the oratorical passages of the letters or in Valera's representation of his character's long and purposely formal speeches, are, of course, more complicated, as in Luis's pronouncement on Pepita's conscience:

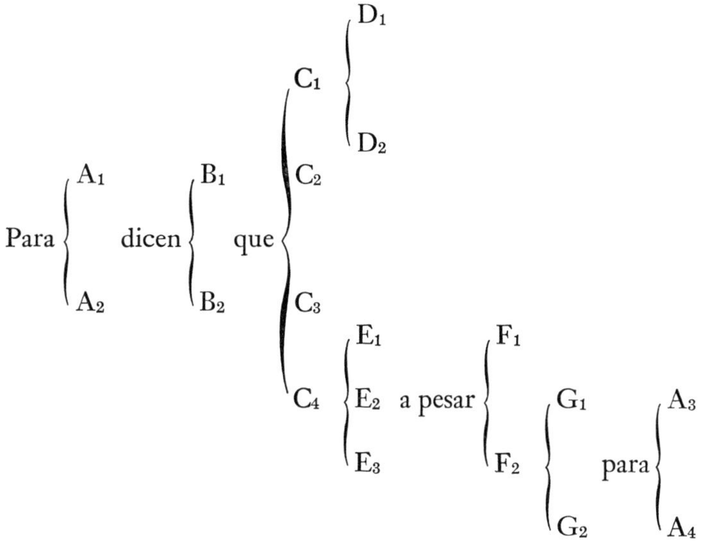

Para { A_1 / A_2 } dicen { B_1 / B_2 } que { C_1 { D_1 / D_2 } / C_2 / C_3 / C_4 { E_1 / E_2 / E_3 } a pesar { F_1 / F_2 } { G_1 / G_2 } para { A_3 / A_4 } }

(A_1) Realzado así cuanto nos rodea, (A_2) amando y estimando a las criaturas (B_1) por lo que son y (B_2) por más de lo que son, (A_3) procurando no tenerse superior a ellas en nada, antes bien, (A_4) profundizando con valor en el fondo de nuestra conciencia para descubrir todas nuestras (C_1) faltas y (C_2) pecados, y (A_5) adquiriendo (D_1) la santa humildad y (D_2) el menosprecio de uno mismo, el corazón (E_1) se sentirá lleno de afectos humanos, y (E_2) no despreciará, sino (E_3) valuará en mucho el mérito (F_1) de las cosas y (F_2) de las personas; *de modo que*, *si* sobre este fundamento (G_1) descuella luego y (G_2) se levanta el amor divino con invencible pujanza, y [*sic*; delete "y"] (H_1) no hay ya miedo de que (I_1) pueda nacer este amor (J_1) de una exagerada estimación propia, (J_2) del orgullo o (J_3) de un desdén injusto del prójimo sino que (I_2) nacerá de la (K_1) pura y (K_2) santa (J_4) consideración (L_1) de la hermosura y (L_2) de la bondad infinitas. (28)

The highly intellectual organization of this period and the complex syntactical relationships can best be seen in a diagram:

A_1
A_2 { B_1, B_2 }
A_3
A_4 { C_1, C_2 }
A_5 { D_1, D_2 }
corazón { E_1, E_2 de modo que, E_3 }
{ F_1, F_2 }
si { G_1, G_2 }
H_1 no hay { I_1 { J_1, J_2, J_3 }, I_2 }
{ K_1, K_2 }
—J_4 { L_1, L_2 }

The five introductory participial phrases, especially the first one which is used absolutely (all dependent, oddly enough, on "el corazón"), the affected "invencible pujanza," and the tautology of "*valuará en mucho el mérito de las cosas* y de las personas" contribute to the stiltedness of Luis's speech.

In the rhetorical periods of their long dialogue, *pluralidades* are used by both Luis and Pepita in a vain effort to hide from themselves, as well as from each other, the essentially erotic gist of their conversation. Luis's long periods, some of which have already been cited, could be compared favorably to the masterful rhetoric of Fray Luis de Granada or Fray Luis de León. The oratorical nature of the following sentence is too obvious to merit close analysis:

Yo las coronaba en mi mente con diademas y mitras orientales, y las envolvía en mantos de púrpura y de oro, y las rodeaba de pompa regia, como a Ester y a Vasti; *yo les prestaba* la sencillez bucólica de la edad patriarcal, como a Rebeca y a la Sulamita; *yo les daba* la dulce humildad y la devoción de Ruth; *yo las oía* discurrir como Aspasia o Hipatia, maestras de elocuencia; yo las encumbraba en estrados riquísimos y ponía en ellas reflejos gloriosos de clara sangre y de ilustre prosapia, como si fuesen las matronas patricias más orgullosas y nobles de la antigua Roma; *yo las veía* ligeras, coquetas, alegres, llenas de aristocrática desenvoltura, como las damas del tiempo de Luis XIV en Versalles, *y yo las adornaba, ya con* púdicas estolas, que infundían veneración y respeto, *ya con* túnicas y peplos sutiles, por entre cuyos pliegues airosos se dibujaba toda la perfección plástica de las gallardas formas; *ya con* la *coa* transparente de las bellas cortesanas de Atenas y Corinto, para que reluciese, bajo la nebulosa velatura, lo blanco y sonrosado del bien torneado cuerpo. (162–163)

Here the primary rhetorical device is the anaphorical parallelism of "yo las" plus a verb in the imperfect indicative (seven times), and of "ya con" (three times), with the accompanying doublets. It is easy to see through Luis's rationalizing effort to invalidate his love for Pepita; the sensuality of everything he says is apparent.

Pepita also uses *pluralidades*, although to a lesser degree. But in the following example, rather than a mitigation of her eroticism, there is actually an accumulative effect:

Yo ni siquiera concibo a V. sin usted. Para mí es V. su boca, sus ojos, sus negros cabellos, que deseo acariciar con mis manos; su dulce voz y el regalado acento de sus palabras, que hieren y encantan materialmente mis oídos; *toda su forma corporal, en suma*, que me enamora y seduce, y *al través de la cual, y sólo al través de la cual* se me muestra el espíritu invisible, vago y lleno de misterios. . . . *Máteme V. antes* para que nos amemos así; *máteme usted antes*, y, ya libre mi espíritu, le seguirá por todas las regiones y peregrinará invisible al lado de V., velando su sueño, contemplándole con arrobo, penetrando sus pensamientos más ocultos, viendo en realidad su alma, sin el intermedio de los sentidos. Pero viva no puede ser. Yo amo en usted, no ya sólo el alma; sino el cuerpo, y la sombra del cuerpo, y el reflejo del cuerpo en los espejos y en el agua, y el nombre y el apellido, y la sangre, y todo aquello que le determina como tal don Luis de Vargas; el metal de la voz, el gesto, el modo de andar y no sé qué más diga. *Repito que es menester matarme. Máteme V. sin compasión.* No; yo no soy cristiana, sino idólatra materialista. (168–169)

The *pluralidades* used here are mostly composed of two and three members, with a didactic summation phrase in the first long sentence, "toda su forma corporal, en suma. . . ." This is reinforced by the legal sounding "al través de la cual, y sólo al través de la cual. . . ." The seven members of the enumeration beginning with "Yo amo en usted . . ." are similarly summed up by "todo aquello." The logical hammering of "máteme V.," the summation phrases, and the balanced use of *pluralidades* indicate that Pepita is making a guilty attempt to assuage what she is truly saying: that she will do anything to gain Luis's love.

The preceding passages illustrate that *pluralidades* are used for both characterization and mitigation. Valera shows a marked predilection for them and often employs them, more moderately, to be sure, in narrative text. When they occur in enumerative, descriptive passages, they have little or no particular stylistic effect in themselves, although what is said may have. Without treating the instances in which *pluralidades* are more or less normal in accordance with the thought, and without analyzing in detail the functions of each example, I shall give a few of their formal characteristics.

In several cases, attention has already been drawn to one of the most common rhetorical figures in the novel, amplification, of which an additional striking example is:

> *No quiero* yo que en mí el espíritu peque contra la carne; pero *no quiero* tampoco *que* la hermosura de la materia, que sus deleites, *aun* los que más bien por el espíritu que por el cuerpo se perciben, *como* el silbo delgado del aire fresco cargado de aromas campesinos, *como* el canto de las aves, *como* el majestuoso y reposado silencio de las horas nocturnas, en estos jardines y huertas, me distraigan de la contemplación de la superior hermosura, y entibien ni por un momento mi amor hacia quien ha creado *esta armoniosa fábrica del mundo.* (31–32)[45]

Amplification appears in another place with the ironical use of "hasta": "Por lo dicho se explican las visitas de Antoñona a D. Luis, sus palabras *y hasta* los feroces, poco respetuosos y mal colocados pellizcos, con que maceró sus carnes y atormentó su dignidad la última vez que estuvo a verle" (103).

The last citation brings up what appears to be Valera's borrowing

[45] The phrase, "esta armoniosa fábrica del mundo," incidentally, is like similar ones of Fray Luis de León: ". . . toda aquesta máquina del universo . . ." (*De los nombres de Cristo*, I, 28). For additional examples of amplification in *Pepita Jiménez*, see p. 10, lines 15–20; p. 14, lines 24–27; p. 18, lines 8–11; p. 21, lines 23–32; p. 32, lines 15–20; p. 32, line 27, to p. 33, line 19; p. 125, lines 28–29; and p. 127, lines 1–4.

of a particularly Cervantine device: the use of *hasta* or *aun* (corresponding to the more modern *incluso*) before the mildly surprising or comical last element in a short accumulation. It occurs again in Valera's remarks: "No se puede negar que Antoñona estuvo discretísima en esta ocasión, *y hasta* su lenguaje fué tan digno y urbano . . ." (138). In the *Quijote* one often encounters this formula with *aun*: ". . . trújole su locura á la memoria aquel [paso] de Valdovinos y del Marqués de Mantua, cuando Carloto le dejó herido en la montaña, historia sabida de los niños, no ignorada de los mozos, celebrada y *aún creída* de los viejos . . ." (*DQ* I, 133). Of course, the device cannot be limited to Cervantes; it is a favorite ironical resource, as in the following sentences from the *Lazarillo: "Yo pensaua, y aun desseaua*, que allí me quería cargar de lo que se vendía . . ." (149); and "Bien consideré que deuia ser hombre mi nueuo amo, que se proueya en junto y que ya la comida estaria a punto y tal como yo la deseaua *y aun la auia menester*" (150). Sometimes *hasta* or *aun* is used before the third member of a tripartite construction for rhythm instead of for humor: "Más bien hubieran podido extrañarse la vida alegre, las tertulias diarias *y hasta* los paseos campestres de Pepita durante algún tiempo" (102). An example from Cervantes: ". . . me está diciendo, persuadiendo, *y aun* forzando . . ." (*DQ* II, 219).

Quite similar to amplification is gradation, which frequently appears in triads, as when Luis says about his father: "Tiene además el atractivo poderoso, irresistible para algunas mujeres, de sus pasadas conquistas, de su celebridad, de haber sido una especie de Don Juan Tenorio" (7–8). Additional cases, most of which occur in an ironical context, are: ". . . la linda, elegante, esquiva y zahareña viudita" (103); ". . . le veneraba, le admiraba y formaba de él un concepto sobrehumano . . ." (125); "Así es que estoy rendida y vencida y aniquilada desde el primer día" (166); "Dejo al creador por la criatura, destruyo la obra de mi constante voluntad, rompo la imagen de Cristo, que estaban en mi pecho . . ." (167); and "¿Por qué no nos amamos entonces sin vergüenza y sin pecado y sin mancha?" (167). The relationship between gradation, the ternary movement, and irony or criticism is more evident in extended passages, especially in the delightfully humorous description of Don

Gumersindo and of Pepita's family (9–10). For instance, Luis reports what he must have heard from the servants: "La madre de ella era una mujer *vulgar, de cortas luces y de instintos groseros.* Adoraba a su hija pero continuamente y con honda amargura se lamentaba *de los sacrificios* que por ella hacía, *de las privaciones* que sufría y *de la desconsolada vejez y triste muerte* que iba a tener en medio de tanta pobreza" (10).

Later Valera makes fun of Luis in a sentence arranged in two ternary constructions: "El propósito de toda su vida, lo que había sostenido y declarado ante cuantas personas le trataban, su figura moral, en una palabra, que era ya la de un aspirante a santo, la de un hombre consagrado a Dios, la de un *sujeto imbuído en las más sublimes filosofías religiosas,* todo esto no podía caer por tierra sin gran mengua de D. Luis, como caería, si se dejase llevar del amor de Pepita Jiménez" (122–123). In addition to the phrase "un aspirante a santo," the incongruous use of the informal and sometimes derogatory "sujeto" in connection with "las más sublimes filosofías" particularly reveals Valera's humorous mocking of his protagonist. Literally dozens of cases occur in which the tripartite structure softens the author's criticism of his characters, as if he were mitigating the irony by elevating it to a refined and objective level of understanding. He is able to present the foibles of his characters without resorting to harsh invective because, even though his approach is a pseudo-objective one, he nevertheless realizes that his characters are products of the society in which they live.

The ternary movement becomes so conspicuous in many parts of the novel that it certainly constitutes a dominant.[46] It occurs with such frequency in the pseudo-spiritual passages, especially in the dialogue between Pepita and Luis, that it appears to assume even parodistic proportions. As is well known, many writers of mystical

[46] For additional ternary phrases, see: p. 9, lines 9–12; p. 13, lines 15–16; p. 18, lines 8–11; p. 31, lines 13–17; p. 90, lines 9–16; p. 105, line 1; p. 123, lines 15–18; p. 128, lines 23–24; p. 129, lines 6–7, 15–16, and 22–23; p. 159, lines 6–7; p. 160, lines 9–10 and 21–22; p. 163, lines 30 and 32–33; p. 165, line 7; p. 167, line 17; p. 194, lines 10–11 and 18–19; p. 198, lines 13–14; p. 204, lines 6–7 and 26–31; and p. 213, line 6. Many of these examples express irony, which, it seems, is attenuated and refined by the elegant form.

and ascetical literature (such as Raymond Lully) were motivated to use ternary constructions in order to relate their work to the Holy Trinity. This also seems to be true of Fray Luis de León and San Juan de la Cruz. About the latter, Hatzfeld says: "Estos modelos en grupos de tres participios, tres substantivos y tres adjetivos se extienden copiosamente en el comentario de la *Llama.* Nunca poseen un carácter de gradación, pero reflejan como una resonancia prolongada el tema de la Santísima Trinidad. . . ."[47] Valera may have noted an unusually high frequency of tripartite constructions in the works of these writers, as well as in other spiritual literature and sermons, and may therefore have been led to use them often. He probably also liked their general rhythmical effect and literary quality. At any rate, Valera's use of triads may be related either to irony, to mitigation, or to a combination of the two, though his desire to write rhythmical prose must also be considered.

These points become obvious on examining representative selections. At one point, Luis remarks: "Para hacer de Pepita ese símbolo, esa vaporosa y etérea imagen, esa cifra y resumen de cuanto puedo amar por bajo de Dios, en Dios y subordinándolo a Dios, me la finjo muerta, como Beatriz estaba muerta cuando Dante la cantaba" (93–94). But it is in the dialogue between the two lovers that the ternary movement is most used, so much so, in fact, that many of the phrases appear mannered. This is an indication of an attempted intellectual masking of eroticism by the characters. The triads here occur in both polysyndetic and asyndetic phrases, in isolation, and in combination with doublets or other *pluralidades*. Some examples from this passage follow:

> Llena está mi alma, sin embargo, de piedad religiosa, y conozco y amo y adoro a Dios; pero. . . . (165–166)

> ¿O es acaso que para avasallar y rendir un alma pequeña, cuitada y débil como la mía, basta un pequeño amor, y para avasallar la de V., cuando tan altos y fuertes pensamientos la velan y custodian, se necesita amor más poderoso, *que yo no soy digna de inspirar, ni capaz de compartir, ni hábil para comprender siquiera?* (167)

[47] Hatzfeld, *Estudios literarios sobre mística española*, p. 375.

. . . mas para ello es fuerza que nuestros cuerpos se separen; que yo vaya adonde me llama mi deber, mi promesa y la voz del Altísimo, que dispone de su siervo y lo destina al culto de sus altares. (168)

Mira, no pienses que ha habido en mí artificio, ni cálculo, ni plan para perderte. . . . No es en ti el pecado sino muy leve. En mí es grave, horrible, vergonzoso. . . . Vete: . . . Vete: . . . Vete: . . . Básteme el haber hecho caer por sorpresa al lucero de la mañana; no quiero, ni debo, ni puedo retenerlo cautivo. Lo adivino, lo infiero de tu ademán, lo veo con evidencia; ahora me desprecias más que antes, y tienes razón en despreciarme. No hay honra, ni virtud, ni vergüenza en mí. (171)

A pesar de toda tu hermosura, a pesar de tu talento, a pesar de tu amor hacia mí, yo no hubiera caído, si en realidad hubiera sido virtuoso, si hubiera tenido una vocación verdadera. (173)

A too constant appearance of triads would be wearisome; consequently Valera often counterbalances or mixes them with doublets. The functions are, of course, the same as those of triads alone and of *pluralidades* in general. Two passages without comment will serve to show how doublets and triads are mixed:

En fin, querido tío, menester es tener la gran confianza que tengo yo con V. para contarle estas muestras de sentimiento extraviado y vago, y hacerle ver con ellas que necesito volver a mi antigua vida, a mis estudios, a mis altas especulaciones, y acabar por ser sacerdote para dar al fuego que devora mi alma el alimento santo y bueno que debe tener. (42)

A las personas recogidas, que no asisten a reuniones de hombres solos, escandalizará sin duda este lenguaje, les parecerá desbocado y brutal hasta la inverosimilitud; pero los que conocen el mundo confesarán que este lenguaje es muy usado en él, y que las damas más bonitas, las más agradables mujeres, las más honradas matronas suelen ser blanco de tiros no menos infames y soeces, si tienen un enemigo, y aun sin tenerlo, porque a menudo se murmura, o mejor dicho, se injuria y se deshonra a voces para mostrar chiste y desenfado. (129)

The number of sentences in which there are bifurcations and doublets is very great; but the only new thing that I should like to point out about them is that doublets, especially verb pairs, bear a marked resemblance to many similar ones of the *Quijote*. One almost invariably recalls the *Quijote* upon encountering such pairs as: "le promueva y excite" (26), "Yo no he tenido ni tengo" (39), "después de mil vueltas y rodeos" (44), "Quiero y debo" (80), "puede y debe" (160), "me pica y enoja" (82), "He pasado y paso en vela" (91), "puedo y quiero" (92), "con aplomo y descaro" (135), "yo la amaba y la amo aún" (135), and "dando lugar y abriendo paso a" (163). Or it may be that three verbs are used, as in: "¿Te imaginas que no es, que no está siendo, que no será inmenso el sacrificio que hago?" (136); and "Supongo, pues, y creo, y tengo por cierto . . ." (162).[48] Many of these doublets have become literary conventions and thus contribute a mitigating effect quite like that caused by stereotyped phrases in general, but with the added distinctions of the literary reminiscence, the humorous tautology, and the rhythm.

The enumerations in *Pepita Jiménez* are arranged in an ordered fashion and rarely exceed five members, thus keeping the items listed within immediate comprehension. Such logical arrangement, which is often reinforced by a summation phrase, points out that enumeration in Valera is more didactic-planned than affective-chaotic. No matter how tense the situation, the intellect is ever at work to repress the emotion; but even where there is no emotion present, at least not on the surface, didactic enumerations tend to formalize the characters' speech and may reveal more subtle shades of stiltedness, which in itself must ultimately be considered a mode of attenuating the self-deluding rationalizations. In a passage that is generally oratorical, Luis says of Pepita, for instance: ". . . debe esforzarse por ver en cada ser humano un objeto digno de amor, un verdadero prójimo, un igual suyo, un alma en cuyo fondo hay un tesoro de excelentes prendas y virtudes, un ser hecho, *en suma*, a imagen y semejanza de Dios" (27–28). Five predicate nominatives, employed after four stilted vocatives, occur in an ironical context: "—Alma mía . . . , vida de mi alma, prenda querida de mi corazón, luz de mis ojos, levanta la abatida frente y no te prosternes más delante de mí.

48 See Hatzfeld, *El "Quijote" como obra de arte*, pp. 284–294, for examples from the *Quijote*.

El pecador, el flaco de voluntad, el miserable, el sandio y el ridículo soy yo, que no tú" (172). Five active forms, one of which is a doublet, are used in the following: "Esta, creyéndola dormida, o deseando que durmiera, se inclinó hacia Pepita, puso con lentitud y suavidad un beso sobre su blanca frente, le arregló y plegó el vestido sobre el cuerpo, entornó las ventanas para dejar el cuarto a media luz, y se salió de puntillas, cerrando la puerta sin hacer el menor ruido" (121). It is curious to note that Valera encloses the active verbs with participial phrases which lend continuity to the sentence. At the same time, he may have purposely avoided going beyond the number five by putting the last action in a participle, "cerrando la puerta," instead of saying "y cerró la puerta."

Enumerations of six, seven, or eight members are also toned down by logical sequence and by summation phrases. Telling his uncle of what in reality are the inceptive feelings of love, Luis employs six infinitive phrases, of which the last two are so related in meaning that they practically form a doublet:

> . . . no sé qué extraño temor, qué singular *escrúpulo*, que apenas perceptible e indeterminado *remordimiento* me atormenta ahora, cuando tengo, como antes, como en otros días de mi juventud, como en la misma niñez, alguna efusión de ternura, algún rapto de entusiasmo, *al penetrar* en una enramada frondosa, *al oír* el canto del ruiseñor en el silencio de la noche, *al escuchar* el pío de las golondrinas, *al sentir* el arrullo enamorado de la tórtola, *al ver* las flores o *al mirar* las estrellas. Se me figura a veces que *hay en todo esto algo* de delectación sensual. . . . (31)

Luis is aware that these strange new feelings, those originating in the senses of hearing and sight, are contrary to the calling he has chosen to follow and mitigates the expression of them, as well as the complaints of his conscience, by the intellectual organization of the period. This general impression is corroborated by the use of "todo esto." In another passage there is an enumeration of six epithets: ". . . me parece la esposa del *Cantar de los Cantares*, y la llamo con voz interior, y la bendigo, y la juzgo fuente sellada, huerto cerrado, flor del valle, lirio de los campos, paloma mía y hermana" (90). Don Pedro employs a polysyndetic enumeration of six members in writing the Dean about his possible grandchildren: ". . . me olerían a rosas del paraíso, y vendrían a ponerse sobre mis rodillas, y jugarían conmigo, y me besarían, y me llamarían abuelito, y me darían palmaditas en la calva que ya voy teniendo" (201–202).

There are seven members linked by *ni*, with an antithetical eighth member, in the following enumeration: ". . . no ha sido hombre mortal, ni capricho del voluble y servil populacho, ni irrupción o avenida de gente bárbara, ni violencia de amotinadas huestes movidas de la codicia, ni ángel, ni arcángel, ni potestad criada, sino el mismo Paráclito quien la ha fundado" (124). Directly after this passage is another enumeration of seven members: ". . . atando y desatando . . . perdonando . . . regenerando . . ." etc. (124–125). In descriptions, where enumerations are often used by all writers, Valera seldom uses more than from five to seven members, as is exemplified in the description of the Casino: "El centro de la concurrencia era el patio, enlosado de mármol, con fuente y surtidor en medio y muchas macetas de don-pedros, gala-de-Francia, rosas, claveles y albahaca. Un toldo de lona doble cubría el patio, preservándole del sol. Un corredor o galería, sostenida por columnas de mármol, le circundaba, y así en la galería, como en varias salas a que la galería daba paso, había mesas de tresillo, otras con periódicos, otras para tomar café o refrescos, y, por último, sillas, banquillos y algunas butacas" (127). The first enumeration contains five members and the second, although apparently composed of seven, could be reduced to four in view of the fact that the two phrases beginning with "otras" actually refer to "mesas." The placing of "por último" between the first three members and the last four likewise produces a logical effect. Listing the food served at the wedding, Valera writes: "Hubo hojuelas, pestiños, gajorros, rosquillas, mostachones, bizcotelas y mucho vino para la gente menuda. El señorío se regaló con almíbares, chocolate, miel de azahar y miel de prima, y varios rosolis y mistelas aromáticas y refinadísimas" (204). In the first enumeration there are seven nouns and in the second there are only six, four of which are arranged in pairs.

Valera's limited use of enumerations, even in descriptions, shows how different he is from other writers of his generation. José María de Pereda, for instance, is given to long enumerations. At the beginning of the third chapter of *Peñas arriba* there occurs one of his typical enumerations: a cataloging of the impressions received by Marcelo upon his arrival in the mountain village. Seventeen different impressions are simply listed, many of which are explained or commented on, with no attempt at intellectual organization other than the systematic order. It seems that Pereda wishes to give a total effect, which he sums up with: "A esto se reducen todos los recuerdos que conservo de mi llegada al 'solar de mis mayores.' "[49] Two conclusions may be drawn from this comparison. First, that Valera is not primarily a descriptive writer, but rather one who, like his *Siglo de Oro* models, uses evocative descriptions somewhat perfunctorily. Second, that Valera employs enumerations sparingly and with restraint, a practice which is in keeping with the general mitigating nature of his style. In *Pepita Jiménez*, at least, he avoids using more than seven or eight members (which even then are attenuated by their shortness, by quasi-synonymous pairs, by the logical organization, or by summation phrases) and ordinarily stops at five. While the restrained use of enumerations is not exactly the same as the deliberately formal expression of emotion, it is nevertheless an integral part of the novel's "classical mitigation."

Of the repetitive figures, the one most closely related to *pluralidades* is anaphora, which by its very nature usually appears in parallelistic constructions. Being a favorite oratorical figure, it is used frequently in the rhetorical speeches, as when Luis says, just before mentioning his new feelings of love: "*Aunque* con poco aprovechamiento en la virtud, *aunque* nunca libre mi espíritu de los fantasmas de la imaginación, *aunque* no exento en mí el hombre interior de las impresiones exteriores y del fatigoso método discursivo, *aunque* incapaz de reconcentrarme por un esfuerzo de amor en el centro mismo de la simple inteligencia . . ." (30). Anaphora occurs again shortly afterwards: "*Harto sé que* los impíos del día presente acusan, . . . *Harto sé que* no es así, que no es ésta la verdadera doctrina, . . . *Harto sé que* no peco amando las cosas por el amor de Dios . . ." (30–

[49] José María de Pereda, *Peñas arriba*, 3rd ed. (Buenos Aires: Sopena Argentina, 1945), p. 22.

31). The rhetorical nature of these passages is as noticeable as if Luis were writing a sermon; yet the pseudo-spiritual thoughts are merely expressed, in this lofty style, to conceal from his uncle (or at least prepare him for the shock of) the unpriest-like, sensuous feelings he has experienced. That he himself is aware of this comes out in the last sentence of the same letter: "Dígame usted qué piensa de estas cosas; *si hay algo de enfermizo* en esta disposición de mi ánimo" (33). He knows that there is something "enfermizo" in this, and has used rhetoric and false spirituality to alleviate his guilt.

Of Pepita's image, Luis states: "*Entre* el Crucifijo *y yo se interpone*, *entre* la imagen devotísima de la Virgen *y yo se interpone*, *sobre* la página del libro espiritual que leo también *viene a interponerse*" (76). Precise anaphora is broken in the last member of the sentence, although the parallelism is still apparent. Another case of anaphora, strengthened by the repetition of "todo," is particularly reminiscent of Biblical antitheses: "Ante este bien todo es miseria; ante esta hermosura es fealdad todo; ante esta felicidad todo es infortunio; ante esta altura todo es bajeza" (99). In a more oratorical vein, the seminarian ceremoniously says to Pepita: "*Yo conocía*, pues, el precio del sacrificio que hacía, y hasta lo exageraba, cuando renuncié al amor de estas mujeres. . . . *Harto conocía yo*. . . . *Harto conocía yo también* . . ." (160). Pepita also makes use of rhetoric to express herself, which is perhaps another indication of the influence exercised upon her speech habits by the cant she hears from Luis and the Vicar (one thinks of the *quijotización* of Sancho):[50]

> *Si amor es lo que V.* dice, si es morir en sí para vivir en el amado, verdadero y legítimo amor es el mío, porque he muerto en mí y sólo vivo en V. y para V. *He deseado* desechar de mí este amor, creyéndole mal pagado, y *no me ha sido posible. He pedido* a Dios con mucho fervor que me quite el amor o me mate, *y Dios no ha querido oírme. He rezado* a María Santísima para que borre del alma la imagen de V., *y el rezo ha sido inútil. He hecho promesas* al santo de mi nombre para no pensar en V. sino como él pensaba en su bendita Esposa, y *el santo no me ha socorrido*.

[50] Everyone knows the influence of Don Quijote's speech on Sancho's, perhaps best exemplified in V, ch. x. Cf. Erich Auerbach, "The Enchanted Dulcinea," in *Mimesis: The Representation of Reality in Western Literature*, trans. Willard Trask (Garden City, N.Y.: Doubleday, 1957), pp. 293–315, especially p. 298.

Viendo esto, he tenido la audacia de pedirle al cielo que V. se deje vencer, que V. deje de ser clérigo, que nazca en su corazón de V. un amor tan profundo como el que hay en mi corazón. Don Luis, dígamelo V. con franqueza: ¿ha sido también sordo el cielo a esta última súplica? (166–167)

The first phrase indicates that she, a clever dialectician, has picked up her opponent's phrases in order to fight him with his own arms, a tactic which is common in all of her long speeches. In the parallelistic phrases, she states that she has exhausted, in her opinion, all possible sources for help in overcoming her love, and since she has had no answer, she has switched the responsibility for the solution to Luis. Thus, by specious reasoning, she has asked Heaven to help her win Luis's love. Ironically, her effort to attenuate what she must realize are unchristian attitudes is expressed in antithetical parallelism like that of the Bible. Another detail hinting at an attempted mitigation is the causal phrase, "viendo esto," which is used here to express a false consequence.

As a result of the investigation of the *pluralidades* in *Pepita Jiménez*, several conclusions have come to the fore. First of all, that from the vantage point of characterization, they are used for the guilt-instigated concealment of true motives and emotions behind an apparently symmetrical exterior, which is none the less sometimes broken through by a revealing clause that serves as an escape valve for the repressed emotions. Second, that the mitigating stiltedness of the sentence structure may also be related to the parodistic and ironical purposes of the author. Third, that Valera, with his classical taste, exhibits a marked predilection for binary and ternary phrases, controlled enumerations, and logical summation phrases. And finally, that anaphora and parallelism, the same as any other rhetorical figure used to formalize speech in crucial moments, likewise contribute to the stiltedness and to the mitigation.

2. SUMMATION AND LINKING PHRASES. In a broad sense, summation phrases like *en resolución*, *en suma*, and *todo esto* (or *eso*) are didactic; but since they are often used by the speakers to sum up their oratorical statements and since, as has been seen, they serve to

attenuate enumerations, they too are among the devices used for mitigation. In the final analysis, anything which formalizes or gives an intellectual coating to the expression of emotion and to rationalizing thought processes is a reflection of "classical mitigation": the control, or attempted control, of emotion and passion by the intellect. The summation phrase ordinarily comes at the end of a passage; but there is a closely allied device which occurs at the beginning to connect the new passage with the preceding one, namely, "linking" phrases like *En esto*, *Estando en esto*, *Viendo esto*, *Visto esto*, and absolute participial and adjectival phrases used in much the same way. Without forgetting that they often had a causal force, it seems that linking phrases were widely used in *Siglo de Oro* prose in a twin function: for dynamism and movement, on the one hand; and on the other, to give a smooth, rhythmical introduction to the sentence, thus providing an attenuating effect. Such linking phrases occur most naturally and frequently in works where there is much action, to mark the transition from one action or situation to another. The remarkable thing is that in Valera's novel, in two-thirds of which there is little action, linking phrases are so common. This unexpected frequency suggests that Valera used them primarily for their rhythmical, ironical, and evocative qualities.

As was noted above, the word *todo*, either alone or in the combinations (*con*) *todo esto* (*eso*), was used in the *Siglo de Oro* and in *Pepita Jiménez* to summarize enumerations.[51] In addition to phrases with *todo*, Valera has recourse to *en resolución* and *en suma*, both of which are often encountered in the *Siglo de Oro*.[52] The first of these, although not so frequent, is the most interesting because it "sums up" a psychological struggle; the speaker comes to a decision, at least apparently, as when Luis says after much delaying: "*Digo todo esto* porque quiero hablar a usted de un asunto tan delicado, tan vidrioso, que apenas hallo términos con que expresarle. *En resolución*, yo me pregunto a veces: este propósito mío, ¿tendrá por fundamento, en parte, al menos, el carácter de mis relaciones con mi padre?" (17).

[51] For examples, see *Pepita Jiménez*, p. 31, line 24; p. 39, line 29; p. 55, line 12; p. 123, line 3; and p. 160, line 26.

[52] Examples from *Don Quijote*: I, 27, line 7; I, 56, line 9; II, 26, line 15; and II, 57, line 4.

The same expression appears in Pepita's remark: "—No, Antoñona. Veo que mi locura es contagiosa y que tú deliras también. *En resolución*, no hay más recurso que hacer lo que me aconseja el padre Vicario. Lo haré aunque me cueste la vida" (120–121). The frequent use of *en suma* and of *por último* is, of course, typical of didactic prose. Both are used in the novel as summation phrases and as an indication of the characters' formality. Although neither of them demands special treatment, their role in depicting the dialectical nature of Luis's speech is prominent in one passage. About his father, Luis states:

> Me aseguró, *por último*, que en dos o tres semanas haría de mí el mejor caballista de toda Andalucía; capaz de ir a Gibraltar por contrabando y de volver de allí, burlando al resguardo, con una coracha de tabaco y con un buen alijo de algodones: apto, *en suma*, para pasmar a todos los jinetes que se lucen en las ferias de Sevilla y Mairena, y para oprimir los lomos de *Babieca*, y de *Bucéfalo*, y aún de los propios caballos del Sol, si por acaso bajaban a la tierra y podía yo asirlos de la brida.
>
> Ignoro qué pensará usted de este arte de la equitación que estoy aprendiendo; pero presumo que no le tendrá por malo. (67)

Here we witness, on a small scale, the attempted mitigation in the didactic phrases, "por último" and "en suma." Luis is reporting his father's statements which, as usual, are ironical, but the two summation phrases are probably his own. As the last sentence intimates, he knows that his decision to learn to ride a horse is motivated by his wounded self-esteem and by the desire to appear manly in the eyes of Pepita. Other occurrences of the two phrases within a few pages verify the assertion that Luis, even though unconsciously, uses them in this passage as a mitigating device. Of his father Luis says: ". . . cita ejemplos en apoyo de su opinión. Cita en primer lugar a Santiago . . .; cita a un señor de la Vera . . .; y cita, *por último*, al hidalgo vizcaíno D. Iñigo de Loyola . . ." (69). These remarks, of course, are purely polemical and seem to be Luis's way of phrasing the statements of Don Pedro, who, as is shown by his letters, does not speak in precisely this manner. Other examples in the same passage are: "Y, *por último*, presumiendo también mi padre de manejar como nadie una navaja . . ." (68–69); and "*En suma*, yo me defiendo como puedo de las bromas de mi padre . . ." (70).[53]

In the *Siglo de Oro* there was undoubtedy an inner need to unify as much as possible the component parts of works of literature. One of the means of satisfying this need in prose was to employ phrases for summation and linking, which provided continuity. In the *Lazarillo* one encounters phrases like: "Visto esto y las malas burlas . . ." (103); "Pues estando en tal aflicción . . ." (122); and "Pues, estando en esto . . ." (195). Even in didactic prose one finds similar expressions: "Mas, tornando á lo que dezía . . ." and "Pues viniendo á lo que pedís . . . ."[54] They are much more numerous in the narration of action, however; hence the many phrases in the *Quijote* such as: "Y en diciendo esto . . ." (*DQ* I, 122 and 129), "En esto . . ." (*DQ* I, 124), and "Estando en esto . . ." (*DQ* I, 261). An indication of their unifying force is that the last phrase cited begins a chapter; the others begin paragraphs.[55]

When used in *Pepita Jiménez*, linking phrases have a mitigating force, the same as most other conventional devices and phrases. In the representation of the meeting between Pepita and himself at the Pozo de la Solana, Luis writes:

En la primera nueva expedición que hagamos–le dije–, he de ir en el caballo más fogoso de mi padre, y no en la mulita de paso en que voy ahora. –Mucho me alegraré–replicó Pepita con una sonrisa de indecible suavidad. *En esto* llegaron todos al sitio en que estábamos, y yo me alegré en mis adentros, no por otra cosa, sino por temor de no acertar a sostener la conversación, y de salir con *doscientas mil simplicidades* por mi poca o ninguna práctica de hablar con mujeres.

Después del paseo, sobre la *fresca hierba* y en el más *lindo sitio* junto al

[53] Other examples of *en suma* in *Pepita Jiménez*, p. 28, line 3; p. 110, line 24; p. 142, line 5; p. 152, line 14; p. 168, line 30. Of *por último*: p. 55, line 10; p. 100, line 20; p. 111, line 26; p. 131, line 32; p. 143, line 20; p. 152, line 27; p. 180, line 27; and p. 185, line 7.

[54] León, *De los nombres de Cristo*, I, 38 and 75 respectively. Such phrases also occur in the works of Santa Teresa and of San Juan de la Cruz.

[55] For other examples and a complete treatment of unifying and linking phrases in the *Quijote*, see Hatzfeld, *El "Quijote" como obra de arte*, pp. 165–175, and Raymond S. Willis, *The Phantom Chapters of the Quijote* (New York: Hispanic Institute, 1953).

arroyo, nos sirvieron los criados de mi padre una rústica y abundante merienda. (65)

It would seem, in the reporting of this tense moment, that the phrase "En esto . . . ," along with the italicized conventional devices (the use of round numbers and of stereotyped adjective-substantive combinations), attenuates the emotion.

On a lower, farcical level "Dicho esto" occurs: "*Dicho esto*, la endiablada mujer me aplicó, . . . seis o siete feroces pellizcos . . ." (100). Here, as in other places (113, line 32, and 169, line 33), the past participle of *decir* is used in absolute phrases, not for attenuation, but as a conventional literary device. More interesting and more like *Siglo de Oro* linking phrases are two locutions with *en* plus the demonstrative adjective and a noun. The Count is criticizing Pepita when we are told: "*En este ameno ejercicio* se hallaba el Conde cuando *quiso la mala ventura* que D. Luis y Currito llegasen y se metiesen en el corro, que se abrió para recibirlos, de los que oían el *extraño sermón de honras*" (128). The irony of the whole passage is due to the traditional introductory phrase as well as to the adjective "ameno," to the phrase "quiso la mala ventura,"[56] and to the already mentioned "sermón de honras." A similar construction with a particularly Cervantine ring to it is used to sum up Luis's rationalizing paraphrase of the Sermon on the Mount: "*En estas y otras meditaciones por el estilo* transcurrieron las horas hasta que dieron las tres . . ." (133).[57]

Past participial and adjectival phrases which are even more effective in making smooth introductions call to mind similar phrases of *Siglo de Oro* prose.[58] At times the phrases are absolute, as in the following:

Oído el señor Vicario, y *fiándome* en su juicio, ya no puedo menos de desear que mi padre se case con la Pepita. (24)

[56] Without suggesting a direct parallel, of course, we may recall such Cervantine phrases as: "Quiso la mala suerte . . ." (*DQ* II, 64).

[57] Cf. *DQ* II, 103: "En estas y otras pláticas les tomó la noche en mitad del camino."

[58] Cf., for instance, Siebenmann, *Über Sprache und Stil*, pp. 68–69.

Hecho el anuncio con la formalidad debida, la discreta Antoñona se retiró de la sala, *dejando* a sus anchas al visitante y a la niña, y *volviendo* a cerrar la puerta. (150)

Terminados estos preparativos, que nos será lícito clasificar y dividir en *cosméticos*, indumentarios y religiosos, Pepita se instaló en el despacho, *aguardando* la venida de D. Luis con febril impaciencia. (153)

Así es que, *vencidos los obstáculos que se oponían a su dicha*, *viendo* ya rendido a D. Luis, *teniendo* su promesa espontánea de que la tomaría por mujer legítima, y *creyéndose* con razón amada, adorada, de aquel a quien amaba y adoraba tanto, brincaba y reía y daba otras muestras de júbilo, que, en medio de todo, tenían mucho de infantil y de inocente. (174–175)

Pero ahorcados ya los hábitos y teniendo que declarar en seguida que Pepita era su novia y que iba a casarse con ella, D. Luis, a pesar de su carácter pacífico. . . . (185)

Decidido, *pues*, *al lance*, resolvió llevarlo a cabo en seguida. Y *pareciéndole* feo y ridículo enviar padrinos y hacer que trajesen en boca el honor de Pepita, halló lo más razonable buscar camorra con cualquier otro pretexto. (186)

Aside from the smooth, attenuating note of these introductory phrases, it is noteworthy that they all take place in an ironical context, which is in turn augmented by the conventional nature of the phrases themselves, and that they are followed by present participial phrases. Characteristic of the way Valera uses present participial phrases, of which he is very fond, is that he generally avoids beginning sentences with them, as Revuelta y Revuelta has remarked: ". . . Valera evita comenzar la frase después del punto y seguido por un gerundio y utiliza un participio para abrir el período, pero continúa la relación de acciones en gerundio."[59]

The last example cited also brings up a rhythmical device which Valera took from the *Siglo de Oro*: the use of *pues* after the first word in a sentence. Thus when Luis writes: "*Pepita, pues, con dinero y siendo* además hermosa, y *haciendo*, como dicen todos, buen uso de su riqueza, se ve en el día *considerada y respetada extraordinaria-*

[59] Revuelta y Revuelta, "Valera, estilista," p. 49.

mente" (14), we may remember one of the many such phrases by Cervantes as: "*Llegado, pues, el temeroso día*, y habiendo mandado el Duque que delante de la plaza del castillo se hiciese un espacioso cadahalso . . ." (*DQ* VIII, 24). Although this is not always the case, we again see in the first example the use of present participial phrases after the introductory adjectival phrase and that the passage is ironical, an effect which is emphasized by the rhyme in the doublet, "considerada y respetada," and by the termination of the sentence in the long adverb, "extraordinariamente." Other introductory phrases with *pues* follow:

Pepita, pues, se me mostraba en los ojos . . . de un modo ideal y etéreo. . . . (66)

Poco tuvo, pues, la señora que confiar a una criada tan zahorí de cuanto pasaba en lo más escondido de su pecho. (104)

Volvió, pues, Antoñona a casa de se dueño. . . (138)

Encomendóse, pues, de todo corazón a la Virgen para que la perdonase. . . . (176)

Pues, as employed here, while not at all unusual, is another indication of Valera's concern to begin sentences smoothly and rhythmically.

The smoothness is also achieved by adjectival and past participial phrases which are equally useful for their descriptive precision. Many of them begin paragraphs and are excellent modes of transition, as in:

Solo ya D. Luis, dejó el comedor para no ver a nadie, y volvió al retiro de su estancia para *abismarse* más profundamente *en sus ideas*.

Abismado en ellas estaba hacía largo rato. . . . (134)

Impulsado por tales razones, lo primero que pensó D. Luis fué faltar a la cita. . . . (141)

Aguijoneado de esta necesidad, tomó su sombrero y su bastón y se fué a la calle. (143)

Embelesado en estos discursos, retardaba D. Luis su vuelta. . . . (147)

Arrastrado D. Luis como por un poder sobrehumano, *impulsado* como por una mano invisible, penetró en pos de Pepita en la estancia sombría. (170)

Temeroso el señor Deán de que su hermano le embromase demasiado . . . , y *conociendo*. . . . (203)

Fiada, sin embargo, en esta semipromesa, Antoñona ha consentido en volver bajo el techo conyugal. (207)

From the examination of the above examples, it is apparent that Valera has a definite tendency to introduce sentences, especially at the beginning of a paragraph, with a logical and yet rhythmical phrase that both sums up the preceding statements and sets the stage for the new development of thought or activity.[60] Frequently the linking phrases recall similar ones of the *Siglo de Oro* and occur in an ironical context. Furthermore, it often happens that the introductory phrases lead into the use of present participles before the active verb form appears, or the present participles may be interspersed with active verb forms. Revuelta y Revuelta makes the claim, seemingly correct, that the past participle gives the idea of *sosiego* or inactivity, whereas the present participle often has the force of an extended and active present.[61] At any rate, Valera also skillfully blends linking phrases with present participles and active verb forms, thus avoiding abrupt transitions.

3. TRADITION AND EVOCATIVENESS IN DESCRIPTIONS. Valera, who rejected documentary realism in favor of evocative descriptions, follows to such an extent established literary traditions in the depiction of landscapes and characters that the reader is constantly reminded of *Siglo de Oro* descriptive phrases and techniques. Thus his landscapes are orderly, serene, and pleasant, or as Revuelta y Revuelta puts it: "Ante la naturaleza, Valera presenta por inclina-

[60] Other favorite ways of introducing the paragraph are: *al* plus the infinitive (p. 64, line 12; p. 85, line 16; p. 86, line 6; p. 97, line 25; p. 141, line 6; p. 144, line 18; p. 150, line 10; p. 171, line 31; p. 176, line 13); *cuando* (p. 24, line 18; p. 41, line 9; p. 85, line 24; p. 87, line 14; p. 89, line 23; p. 90, line 20; p. 104, line 5; p. 125, line 12; p. 134, line 26; p. 175, line 13); and *mientras* (p. 76, line 15; p. 122, line 1; p. 140, line 25; p. 149, line 19; p. 176, line 13).

[61] Revuelta y Revuelta, "Valera, estilista," p. 48.

ción natural una elegante serenidad objetiva de procedencia clásica. . . . En los paisajes de Valera dominan la serenidad, la nitidez, la frescura incólume, la gracia. . . . Su contemplación es un suave y sereno placer de los sentidos." Rather than describe, Valera often depends on the names of flora to evoke the scene: "La sola presencia del nombre de un arbusto, un árbol o una flor con sencillo adjetivo o sin él, evocan el paisaje."[62] By using conventional epithets, often placed before the noun, he deliberately avoids any attempt at originality, but nevertheless creates an atmosphere well in keeping with the general tone of the novel. Montesinos also speaks of the classical evocativeness and unusual effectiveness of Valera's treatment of nature in *Pepita Jiménez*: "La sugestión del ambiente está lograda con parcos toques. Valera, formado en el gusto clásico, no gustaba de las descripciones a la moda, y, como los clásicos, indica los lugares y sus accidentes por menciones o alusiones ocasionales de lo que es preciso tener en cuenta. . . . Y es que la naturaleza que en *Pepita* se sugiere, ni bravía ni remota, los inmediatos aledaños de un pueblo agrícola, sus huertas, sus sembrados, en este tiempo vernal que D. Luis vive, se diría que, por primera vez, interviene tanto en el desarrollo de la novela que es casi uno de los protagonistas."[63]

The progression of nature from spring to St. John's Eve closely corresponds to Luis's developing love for Pepita. Luis is perhaps only half aware of his heightened sensibility, of his sense of joy at his newly found freedom, now that he is out of the seminary, when he writes:

Lo que ahora comprendo y estimo mejor es el campo de por aquí. Las huertas, sobre todo, son deliciosas. ¡Qué sendas tan lindas hay entre ellas! A un lado, y tal vez a ambos, corre el *agua cristalina* con *grato murmullo*. Las orillas de las acequias están cubiertas de *hierbas olorosas* y de *flores de mil clases*. En un instante puede uno coger un gran ramo de violetas. Dan sombra a estas sendas *pomposos y gigantescos nogales*, higueras y *otros árboles*, y forman los vallados la zarzamora, el rosal, el granado y la madreselva.

[62] *Ibid.*, p. 58, and, in general, pp. 58–63. For character portrayal, see pp. 51–58.

[63] José F. Montesinos, *Valera o la ficción libre* (Madrid: Gredos, 1957), pp. 108–109.

Es portentosa la *multitud de pajarillos* que alegran estos campos y alamedas.

Yo estoy encantado con las huertas, y todas las tardes me paseo por ellas un par de horas. (5–6)

We may conjecture that Luis understands and values the country more because of his new sense of awareness and because of his reading, which he may be imitating in the description he gives. In addition to the traditional adjective-substantive combinations, the phrase, "tal vez," meaning "at times" ("A un lado, y *tal vez* a ambos . . ."), in the midst of a descriptive passage, is typical of the *Siglo de Oro*, as may be seen by comparing it to a phrase by Quevedo: "Halléme en un lugar favorecido de naturaleza por el sosiego amable, donde, *sin malicia*, la hermosura entretenía la vista; muda recreación y sin respuesta humana, platicaban las fuentes entre las guijas y los árboles por las hojas, *tal vez cantaba el pájaro*, *ni sé determinadamente* si en competencia suya o agradeciéndoles su armonía."[64] The phrases, "sin malicia" and "ni sé . . . ," are of the same kind; they indicate an intellectual and moral toning-down of Renaissance nature descriptions, akin to the ironical treatment of mythological subjects in the *Quijote*.[65] Cervantes similarly attenuates descriptions: "El mar alegre, la tierra jocunda, el aire claro, sólo *tal vez* turbio el humo de la artillería, *parece* que iba infundiendo y engendrando gusto súbito en todas las gentes" (*DQ* VIII, 129); ". . . no había otra cosa de adorno que una mesa, *al parecer*, de jaspe, que sobre un pie de lo mesmo se sostenía, sobre la cual estaba puesta, al modo de las cabezas de los emperadores romanos, de los pechos arriba, una que semejaba ser de bronce" (*DQ* VIII, 137).[66]

The resemblance in tone between another descriptive passage from *Pepita Jiménez* (as well as the previously cited one) and classical description will be more apparent by placing it and one

64 Francisco de Quevedo Villegas, *Los sueños*, ed. Julio Cejador y Frauca, 2 vols., "Clásicos Castellanos" (Madrid: Espasa-Calpe, I, 1954), I, 95–96.

65 See Hatzfeld, *El "Quijote" como obra de arte*, pp. 372–377 and pp. 356–357, for this and other characteristics of descriptions in the *Quijote*.

66 The use of *tal vez*, *parecer*, *al parecer*, etc. may be related also to Cervantes's "baroque impressionism." Cf. Helmut Hatzfeld, "Artistic Parallels in Cervantes and Velazquez," *Estudios dedicados a Menéndez Pidal*, III (1952), 265–297, especially pp. 267–268 and pp. 278–283.

from Fray Luis de León in parallel columns. In Valera, as among the Spanish classics, meadow or orchard, complemented by running water and trees, produces a delightful if slightly disordered sense of *deleite* and *sosiego*.

Pepita Jiménez (34–35)

Sea como sea, anteayer tarde fuimos a la huerta de Pepita. *Es hermoso sitio, de lo más ameno y pintoresco que puede imaginarse.* El riachuelo que riega casi todas estas huertas, sangrado por *mil acequias*, pasa al lado de la que visitamos; se forma allí una presa, y cuando se suelta el agua sobrante del riego, cae en un hondo barranco poblado en ambas márgenes de álamos blancos y negros, mimbrones, adelfas floridas y *otros árboles frondosos.* La cascada, de agua limpia y transparente, se derrama en el fondo, formando espuma, y luego sigue su curso tortuoso por un cauce que la naturaleza misma ha abierto, esmaltando sus orillas de *mil hierbas y flores*, y cubriéndolas ahora de *multitud de violetas.* Las laderas que hay en un extremo de la huerta están llenas de nogales, higueras, avellanos *y otros árboles de fruta.*

De los nombres de Cristo (I, 20–22)

Es la huerta grande, y estaba entonces bien poblada de *árboles, aunque puesto sin orden*; *mas esso mismo hazía deleyte* en la vista, y sobre todo, la hora y la sazón. Pues entrados en ella, primero, y por un espacio pequeño, se anduvieron paseando y gozando del *frescor*, y después se sentaron juntos, á la sombra de unas parras y junto á la corriente de una pequeña fuente, en ciertos assientos. Nasce la fuente de la cuesta que tiene la casa á las espaldas, y entrava en la huerta por aquella parte, y *corriendo y estropeando*, *parecía reyrse.* Tenían también delante de los ojos y cerca dellos *una alta y hermosa alameda.* Y más adelante, y no muy lexos, se veya el río Tormes, que aun en aquel tiempo, hinchiendo bien sus riberas, iva torciendo el passo por aquella vega. El día era *sossegado* y puríssimo, y la hora muy fresca.[67]

Fray Luis de León's description is even more restrained than Valera's; his aim is primarily to evoke a calm, cool, and amenable atmosphere, appropriate for tranquil and fruitful conversation. Thus, instead of listing different kinds of trees or plants, he merely says "árboles" and "una alta y hermosa alameda." The phrase, "y más adelante, y no muy lexos," appears to be of the same order as the mitigating insertions mentioned above, although its functions are

[67] Cf. also Fray Luis de León's famous poem, "¡Qué descansada vida!" Of course, Valera could have acquired these descriptive phrases, in both poetry and prose, anywhere from Garcilaso de la Vega and Montemayor on.

also rhythmical and descriptive, since it locates the river. Valera more specifically names several trees but stops far short of a realistic enumeration by saying "y otros árboles." In the same vein are the traditional modes of indicating quantity, "mil" and "multitud."[68] We may also notice that Valera subordinates the description to the imaginative power and memory of the human mind when he states at the outset that "Es hermoso sitio, de lo más ameno y pintoresco *que puede imaginarse.*" The same thing occurs later: "Mil plantas silvestres y olorosas crecen allí de un modo espontáneo, *y por cierto que es difícil imaginar nada más esquivo . . .*" (61).

The truly interesting fact about this descriptive passage (34–35) is that it is a mitigating device placed in an only partly veiled sensual narration of the trip to Pepita's *huerta*. Indicative of Luis's emotion is the fact that, contrary to normal usage, he terminates several sentences in an active verb form both before and after the nature description. The symbolically erotic implications of "fresas" and "leche de cabras" likewise contribute to the impression of sensuality: ". . . nos agasajó Pepita con una espléndida merienda, a la cual dió pretexto el comer *las fresas*, que era el principal objeto que allí nos llevaba. La cantidad de fresas fué asombrosa para lo temprano de la estación, y nos fueron servidas con *leche de algunas cabras* que Pepita también posee" (35). As has been remarked, the description in the seventh letter is also given by Luis as an attenuating device.

The remaining important descriptive pages of the novel are those that form the poetic prelude to Luis's visit to Pepita's home on St. John's Eve; it is here that nature becomes a protagonist, aiding the activities of Don Pedro, Antoñona, and even the Vicar in bringing the incipient love to a climax and providing the last spark which causes Luis to yield to the demands of his sensuality. In spite of this cohesion between the plot development and the atmosphere, the description is still primarily conventional:

[68] Cf. "En esto, ya comenzaban á gorjear en los árboles *mil suertes de pintados pajarillos*, y en sus diversos y alegres cantos parecía que daban la norabuena y saludaban á la fresca aurora, que ya las puertas y balcones del Oriente iba descubriendo la hermosura de su rostro, sacudiendo de sus cabellos un *número infinito* de líquidas perlas . . ." (*DQ* V, 258).

La bóveda azul no trocó en negro su color azulado; conservó su azul, aunque lo hizo más oscuro. El aire era tan diáfano y tan sutil que se veían *millares y millares de estrellas* fulgurando en el éter sin términos. *La luna plateaba las copas* de los árboles y se reflejaba en la corriente de los arroyos, que parecían de un *líquido luminoso y transparente*, donde se formaban *iris* y cambiantes como el *ópalo*. Entre la espesura de la arboleda cantaban los ruiseñores. Las hierbas y flores vertían más generoso perfume. Por las orillas de las acequias, entre la *hierba menuda* y las *flores silvestres*, relucían como diamantes o carbunclos los gusanillos de luz en *multitud innumerable*. . . . Muchos árboles frutales, en flor todavía; muchas acacias y rosales *sin cuento* embalsamaban el ambiente, impregnándole de suave fragancia.

Don Luis se sintió dominado, seducido, vencido por aquella voluptuosa *naturaleza*, y dudó de sí. (146)

The italicized phrases point out the easily recognizable traditional elements in this description. Nevertheless, the total effect, one that incites Luis to love, is modern, romantic, and semipantheistic, and thus basically unlike *Siglo de Oro* nature descriptions.[69] Such descriptions are rather the exception in Valera, however. He more usually keeps his intellect between the scene and the literary reproduction of it, as when he says, with another mitigating insertion: "El sol acababa de ocultarse detrás de los picos gigantescos de las sierras cercanas, haciendo que las pirámides, agujas y rotos obeliscos de la cumbre se destacasen sobre un fondo de púrpura y topacio, *que tal parecía el cielo*, dorado por el sol poniente" (145).

The characters are portrayed in the classical manner too. Valera follows Cervantes's lead in giving both physical and moral (or psychological) traits without indulging in long, detailed descriptions. The most typically Cervantine modes of characterization to be found in Valera are ironical; these I shall take up later. For the

[69] The romantic nature of these pages in *Pepita Jiménez* (145–147) may be apprehended by comparing them to similar though much more exaggerated passages at the end of Gustavo A. Bécquer's *El Miserere*, in his *Obras completas*, 2nd ed. (Buenos Aires: Joaquín Gil-Editor, 1944), pp. 388–391. Rosa Seeleman, who says that landscapes did not really become popular in Spain until the Generation of 1898, has pointed out the pantheistic characteristics of nature descriptions in the nineteenth century. "The Treatment of Landscape in the Novelists of the Generation of 1898," *Hispanic Review*, IV (1936), 226–238.

moment, I should like merely to present a few examples of character descriptions that are in the *Siglo de Oro* tradition. One of them is an important subterfuge used by Luis to express in an indirect and self-deluding way his admiration for Pepita's beauty. To conceal his admiration from himself and from his uncle, he first describes Pepita's two servants, and only then does he reveal the prime object of this scrutiny by comparing Pepita to her servants, a euphemistic trick that allays the pangs of his conscience:

> Por un refinamiento algo sibarítico, no fué el hortelano, ni su mujer, ni el chiquillo del hortelano, ni ningún otro campesino quien nos sirvió la merienda, sino dos lindas muchachas, criadas y como confidentas de Pepita, vestidas a lo rústico, si bien con suma pulcritud y elegancia. Llevaban trajes de percal de vistosos colores, *cortos y ceñidos al cuerpo*, pañuelo de seda cubriendo las espaldas y descubierta la cabeza, donde lucían abundantes y lustrosos cabellos negros, trenzados y atados luego, formando un moño en figura de martillo, y por delante rizos sujetos con sendas horquillas, por acá llamados caracoles. Sobre el moño o castaña ostentaba cada una de estas doncellas un ramo de frescas rosas.
>
> *Salva la superior riqueza de la tela* y su color negro, *no era más cortesano el traje de Pepita*. Su vestido de merino tenía la *misma* forma que el de las criadas, y, sin ser muy corto, no arrastraba ni recogía suciamente el polvo del camino. Un modesto pañolito de seda negra cubría *también*, al uso del lugar, su espalda y su pecho, y en la cabeza *no* ostentaba tocado, *ni* flor, *ni* joya, *ni* más adorno que el de sus propios cabellos rubios. (35–36)

From the outset one detects the elegant, rather rococo playfulness of "refinamiento algo sibarítico" and of the first sentence, in which the author creates a note of teasing suspense by listing negative phrases before giving the truth: ". . . *no* fué el hortelano, *ni* su mujer, *ni* el chiquillo del hortelano, *ni* ningún otro . . . , *sino dos lindas muchachas*, criadas y *como confidentas* de Pepita. . . ." We do not learn who is involved until we reach the word "criadas," which is followed by "como confidentas," as if Pepita were an aristocratic lady who engaged in all sorts of romantic intrigues. Luis carefully notes the details of the servants' dresses and coiffures. Then he gives the description of Pepita, based on that of the servants, as is indicated by the phrases "*Salva* la superior riqueza . . . ," "*no* era *más* cortesano el traje de Pepita," "Su vestido . . . tenía la *misma* forma . . . ," and "Un modesto pañolito de seda negra cubría *también*, . . . su espalda y su pecho. . . ." Contrary to the "ramo de frescas rosas" worn by the servants, the only adornment Pepita needed was her blond hair. This detail is given only after a series of "teasing" negatives, like those at the beginning of the passage. The essentially erotic description of Pepita, even though refined and playful, is impersonalized and mitigated by the indirect subterfuge.

That Valera could employ conventionally Spanish descriptive phrases and yet attain an effect that is more in accord with eighteenth-century France than with the *Siglo de Oro* tradition may be seen by comparing the above passage with one of Cervantes's descriptions of two younger girls:

> También le pareció bien otra que entró de doncellas hermosísimas, tan mozas, que, al parecer, ninguna bajaba de catorce ni llegaba á diez y ocho años, *vestidas todas de palmilla verde, los cabellos parte trenzados y parte sueltos*; pero todos *tan rubios, que con los del sol podían tener competencia*; sobre los cuales traían *guirnaldas de jazmines, rosas, amaranto y madreselva compuestas.* Guiábalas un venerable viejo y una anciana matrona; pero más ligeros y sueltos que sus años prometían. Hacíales el son una gaita zamorana, y ellas, llevando en *los rostros y en los ojos á la honestidad y en los pies á la ligereza*, se mostraban las mejores bailadoras del mundo. (*DQ* VI, 36)

The dress of these girls is only briefly mentioned, but the hair and garlands of flowers are equally stressed. The delightful phrase, ". . . llevando en los rostros y en los ojos á la *honestidad* y en los pies á la ligereza," shows that Cervantes's girls can be gay and festive without being any the less pure, for Cervantes could not stress such implications as "trajes cortos y ceñidos al cuerpo" in the description of his *honestas bailadoras.* This comparison illustrates the vast and fundamental difference between the two descriptions, despite the similarity of descriptive techniques.

Pepita's description is given piecemeal in scattered allusions, with the attention centered on her eyes (already discussed) and hands.

In the same passage cited above, Luis describes Pepita's hands, again departing from a brief allusion to the servants and "usos aldeanos": "En la única cosa que noté por parte de Pepita cierto esmero, en que *se apartaba de los usos aldeanos*, era en llevar guantes. Se conoce que cuida mucho sus manos y que *tal vez* pone alguna vanidad en tenerlas muy blancas y bonitas; con unas *uñas lustrosas y sonrosadas* . . ." (36). He goes on to say that Santa Teresa had a similar vanity when young, and then: "¡Es tan distinguido, tan *aristocrático*, tener una linda mano! Hasta se me figura, a veces, que tiene algo de simbólico." After a momentary pseudo-philosophical digression, much like the ones pointed out previously, he resumes, beginning with the curious use of the depreciative "esta," even while paying compliments to Pepita:

En cambio, las manos de *esta* Pepita, que parecen *casi diáfanas como el alabastro*, si bien con *leves tintas rosadas*, donde *cree uno ver circular la sangre pura y sutil*, que da a sus venas un *ligero viso azul*; estas manos, digo, de dedos afilados y *de sin par corrección* de dibujo, parecen el símbolo del imperio mágico, del dominio misterioso. . . . Imposible parece que *el que* tiene manos como Pepita tenga pensamiento impuro, ni idea grosera, ni proyecto ruín que esté en discordancia con las limpias manos que deben ejecutarle. (37)[70]

It is interesting to note, in addition to "esta," several attenuating devices which are concessions to his sense of guilt for having these thoughts: first, in the "*casa* diáfanas . . ." and in the *Siglo de Oro*–type closed phrase, "de *sin par* corrección"; second, the identity-hiding euphemisms of "cree uno" (equaling Luis) and "el que" (equaling Pepita). The stuttering dentals of "digo, de dedos afilados" etc. betray Luis's emotion. We have seen that there are ironical overtones in a subsequent mention of Pepita's hands (112), and apparently the same is true of the following remarks: "El padre Vicario . . . ha

[70] Cf. Lope de Vega's description of a lady's hands: "Si yo pudiera hacer al guante engaste/ No de las piedras que al presente aplico/ Sino de las estrellas de los cielos,/ Rotos dejara sus *azules velos*./ ¡Oh mano de cristal! ¿Qué nieve pura/ En las cumbres del alto Pirineo/ Más intacta se vió, pues fuera obscura/ Con los marfiles que en tus manos veo?" (*¡Si no vieran las mujeres!*, III), cited by Myron A. Peyton, "Lope de Vega and his Styles," *The Romanic Review*, XLVIII (October, 1957), 161–184, 167.

pasado a mejor vida. Pepita . . . le ha cerrado la entreabierta boca con sus hermosas manos" (208).

The physical portrayal of Luis is also deliberately formalized:

> Poco hemos dicho hasta ahora de la figura de D. Luis. Sépase, pues, que era un buen mozo en toda la extensión de la palabra: alto, ligero, bien formado, cabello negro, ojos negros también y llenos de fuego y de dulzura. La color trigueña, la dentadura blanca, los labios finos, aunque relevados, lo cual le daba un aspecto desdeñoso; y algo de atrevido y varonil en todo el ademán, a pesar del recogimiento y de la mansedumbre clericales. Había, por último, en el porte y continente de D. Luis aquel indescriptible sello de distinción y de hidalguía que parece, aunque no lo sea siempre, privativa calidad y exclusivo privilegio de las familias aristocráticas.
>
> Al ver a D. Luis, era menester confesar que Pepita Jiménez sabía de estética por instinto. (144)

In spite of the conventionality of the phraseology, Valera adds two personal touches: the aristocratic ideal expressed and the irony of the aside, "a pesar del recogimiento y de la mansedumbre clericales," and of the final sentence.

Much of the traditional tone of descriptive phrases in the novel is imparted by the pre-position of the adjective in adjective-substantive combinations, of which, although occasional nuances of meaning may thus be rendered, the ordinary effect is one of rapid evocation, which again means mitigation, if compared to lengthy descriptions.[71] These characteristics have been noted in some of the passages cited and are readily visible in the selected list of examples which follows: "serenas noches" (29), "verdes sembrados" (29, 34), "lindas y sombrías alamedas" (29), "mansos arroyos" (29), "majestuoso y reposado silencio" (31), "fría indiferencia" (38), "serena y tranquila mirada" (38), "nobles y desinteresados deseos" (39), "sombría espesura" (61), "verde enramada" (66), "tímida gacela" (113), "iracunda leona" (113), "inmundo lodo" (129), "vacilante admirador" (150–151), "mullidas alfombras" (157), "cándida y bien formada garganta" (157), "plebeyo y modesto pañolito" (157),

[71] For a treatment of this practice, see Gonzalo Sobejano, *El epíteto en la lírica española* (Madrid: Gredos, 1956), especially ch. xi on Meléndez Valdés.

"áureos salones" (158), "voluptuosos gabinetes" (158), "zafia aldeana" (158), "cultivado y sublime espíritu" (159), "terrenal afecto" (159), "florecientes ciudades" (160), "exquisito ornato" (162), "dulce humildad" (162), "clara sangre" (163), "ilustre prosapia" (163), "aristocrática desenvoltura" (163), "púdicas estolas" (163), "gallardas formas" (163), "ingentes peñascos" (163), "subidísimo deleite" (164), "encumbradas esferas" (165), "infames cadenas" (169), "negros rizos" (178), "poderoso esfuerzo y costoso sacrificio" (182), "suavísimo y perpetuo idilio" (183), "lasciva señora" (183), "vicioso jugador" (186), "dulce coloquios" (196), and "fresca y lozana hiedra" (201). These combinations, most of which are stereotyped, tend to reflect, especially in passages like the dialogue between Luis and Pepita, the speakers' stiltedness and are often evocative of persons, costume, or landscape.

The occasional closed phrases (*frases cerradas*) of *Pepita Jiménez* seem to provide humor and faint irony, and to evoke the much more emphatic ones of the *Quijote*, which were used to parody the style of novels of chivalry.[72] A few examples are: "los en verdad atrevidos pensamientos de D. Gumersindo" (11), "una fea y no pensada caída" (49), "de lo caprichoso y no esperado de la suerte" (123), "la antigua y ya suprimida o suspendida tertulia" (138), "para la solemnidad, trascendencia y no turbado sosiego" (140), and "Será efecto de mi no domada soberbia" (164). Of course, these phrases are quite within the range of ordinary usage and are not surprising in themselves; nevertheless, they and the other means pointed out are illustrative of Valera's utilization of conventional descriptive means, many of which may be traced back to the *Siglo de Oro* (or even earlier), and which may have an attenuating effect in relation to the rationalizing, stilted self-expression of the characters as well as in the creation of a general tone of elegant restraint.

4. EUPHEMISMS. Various other means of attenuation occur in the novel, of which euphemism is by far the most important and the most interesting. It will be remembered that Santa Teresa, in her humility, called her autobiography *El libro de su* [not *mi*] *vida*, and

[72] See Hatzfeld, *El "Quijote" como obra de arte*, pp. 371–372.

that she often referred to herself in the third person, as *una persona*. By Cervantes's time, euphemisms were a significant part of baroque metonymic and periphrastic expressions of grandeur, and certainly were used for mitigation, irony, and humor in the *Quijote*.[73] We have seen the euphemistic devices found in Luis's description of Pepita and the uses to which they are put. We might add as a significant example the hypothetical case of conscience concerning Pepita. By means of it Luis reduces the emotional relationships to the relative anonymity of the third person, thus attaining a pseudo-objective point of view from which he can at once give vent to his ill-founded suppositions and assuage his critical remarks, in much the same fashion that the author softens his criticism by refined irony and by the use of traditional forms of expression. Valera gives us a hint of this procedure when he says of the Dean, whom he pretends is the "author" of the novel: "Tampoco hizo mal, en mi sentir, en ocultar su personalidad y en no mentar su yo, lo cual no sólo demuestra su humildad y modestia, sino buen gusto literario, porque los poetas épicos y los historiadores, que deben servir de modelo, no dicen yo aunque hablen de ellos mismos y ellos mismos sean héroes y actores de los casos que cuentan. Jenofonte Ateniense, pongo por caso, no dice yo en su *Anábasis*, sino se nombra en tercera persona, cuando es menester, como si fuera uno el que escribió y otro el que ejecutó aquellas hazañas" (180).

As has been seen, identity-concealing euphemisms are used by Luis on a small scale in the words "alguien" (13, line 18; 80, line 23), "uno" (37, line 10), and "el que" (52, line 8); this is also the case with "prójimo" in the following: "Sus ojos están llenos de caridad y dulzura. Se posan con afecto en un rayo de luz, en una flor, hasta en cualquier objeto inanimado; pero con más afecto aún, con muestras de sentir más blando, humano y benigno, se posan en *el prójimo, sin que el prójimo, por joven, gallardo y presumido que sea*, se atreva a suponer nada más que caridad y amor al prójimo, y cuando más, predilección amistosa en aquella serena y tranquila mirada" (38). The "prójimo" is no doubt Luis himself; he has felt

[73] See *ibid.*, pp. 225–233, for the role of euphemisms in *Don Quijote*.

Pepita's glances, and we may legitimately assume that, at least subconsciously, he could even be adding "como yo" to the phrase, "el prójimo, por joven, gallardo y presumido que sea." The same could be said of the "yo" (in which Luis actually replaces his father) and of the "mortal dichoso" mentioned earlier (25, line 32).

It seems that the demonstrative adjective sometimes has an attenuating value rather than a depreciative one, as when Luis continues with: "La misma naturaleza, pues, es la que guía y sirve de norma a *esta* mirada y a *estos* ojos" (38); for, by saying "esta" and "estos" instead of using the possessive adjectives, he makes the remark more distant, more objective. Quite similar to these cases are the various passages in which Luis calls Pepita a *maga*, an *ángel*, or in which he compares her to famous women of history, trying not only to mitigate his interest in her but also to remove her from his conscious mind, thus enabling his unconscious mind to identify her with both his mother and the ideal creation of his adolescent daydreams.

Scattered statements throughout the novel and the repeated use of *mitigar*, *disimular*, *pretextar*, and their synonyms reveal that Luis and Pepita are partially cognizant of their efforts to subdue their emotions. For instance, in the sentence: "Viendo D. Luis que no había remedio, mitigó el enojo, se armó de paciencia, y, ya con acento menos cruel, exclamó . . ." (135). Pepita tells the Vicar that Luis is trying to repress his love: ". . . él me quiere también, *aunque lucha por sofocar su amor* y tal vez lo consiga . . ." (109). Valera gives us another clue to the mitigating speech of his characters when he states:

Los respetos sociales, *la inveterada costumbre de disimular y de velar los sentimientos*, que se adquiere en el gran mundo, y que *pone dique a los arrebatos de la pasión y envuelve en gasas y cendales y disuelve en perífrasis y frases ambiguas* la más enérgica explosión de *los mal reprimidos afectos*, nada podían con Pepita. . . . Así es que Pepita habló en aquella ocasión y se mostró tal como era. Su alma, con cuanto había en ella de apasionado, tomó forma sensible en sus palabras, y sus palabras no sirvieron para envolver su pensar y su sentir, sino para darle cuerpo. *No habló* como hubiera hablado una dama de nuestros salones, *con ciertas plegue-*

rías y atenuaciones en la expresión, sino con la desnudez idílica con que Cloe hablaba a Dafnis y con la humildad y el abandono completo con que se ofreció a Booz la nuera de Noemi. (156–157)

This is one of Valera's typical extended litotes, because Pepita immediately begins to speak in the way he says she will not, with ambiguity, euphemisms, and strategic skill, or, in Valera's words, "con ciertas pleguerías y atenuaciones en la expresión." When Valera speaks of "la inveterada costumbre de disimular y de velar los sentimientos, . . . que pone dique a los arrebatos de la pasión," etc., he is revealing the secret of his own refined and elegant style which, in general, conceals "en perífrasis y frases ambiguas" the repressed emotions of his characters. His use of *palabras castizas*, conventional language, and *Siglo de Oro* expressions is at once a mitigation of his critical parody and an elegant exterior which has perhaps prevented the critics from realizing how remarkably close to modern psychology he was, although the critics, vaguely aware of this, have often called *Pepita Jiménez* the best Spanish psychological novel of Valera's time.

Both Pepita's and Luis's speech is characterized by the stated qualities throughout their decisive dialogue. It is here that euphemisms are employed on a grand scale by the two lovers in order to veil their identity in what is primarily an attempt to alleviate the guilt aroused by their inhibited love. Pepita begins formally:

Señor D. Luis, voy a hacer un esfuerzo; voy a olvidar por un instante que soy una ruda muchacha; voy a prescindir de todo sentimiento, y *voy a discurrir con frialdad*, como si se tratase del asunto que me fuese más extraño. Aquí hay hechos que se pueden comentar de dos modos. Con ambos comentarios queda usted mal. Expondré mi pensamiento. Si *la mujer* que con sus coqueterías, no por cierto muy desenvueltas, casi sin hablar a V. palabra, a los pocos días de verle y tratarle, ha conseguido provocar a V., moverle a que la mire con miradas que auguraban amor profano, y hasta ha logrado que le dé V. una muestra de cariño, que es una falta, un pecado en cualquiera, y más en un sacerdote; si *esta mujer* es, como lo es en realidad, *una lugareña ordinaria*, sin instrucción, sin talento y sin elegancia, ¿qué no se debe temer de V. cuando trate y vea y visite en las grandes ciudades a otras mujeres mil veces más peligrosas? Usted se volverá loco cuando vea y trate a las grandes damas que habitan palacios.... (157)

Pepita, in her subterfuge, partially mitigates her role in their love by referring to herself in the third person as "la mujer," "esta mujer," and, with rhetorical self-depreciation, "una lugareña ordinaria." Furthermore, she specifically states that she is going to speak formally, logically ("discurrir con frialdad"), as if discussing a matter completely indifferent to her. We also note that she uses dialectical terminology: ". . . comentar de dos modos. Con ambos comentarios queda usted mal. Expondré mi pensamiento." Other rhetorical devices in the passage, the parallelistic anaphora of the four phrases beginning with "voy a," the repetition of "ver" and "tratar," along with the attenuation of "como lo es en realidad," further formalize her speech.

Pepita resorts to stylized euphemistic, polemical, and rhetorical means of expression in the whole dialogue, as does Luis. While bearing this in mind, I should like to treat other euphemisms in the passage. Pepita continues to refer to herself in the third person, as "una zafia aldeana," "una mujer," and "esa mujer" (158–159), before universalizing their relationship: "Pues qué, cuando *el amor* es grande, elevado y violento, ¿deja nunca de imponerse? ¿No tiraniza y subyuga al *objeto amado* de un modo irresistible? Por los grados y quilates de su amor debe usted medir el de *su amada.* ¿Y cómo no temer por ella si V. *la* abandona?" (159). But the most significant euphemism occurs in the following: "Si V. ha estrechado las manos con el ahinco y la ternura del más frenético amante; si V. ha mirado con miradas que prometían un cielo, una eternidad de amor, y si V. ha . . . *besado a una mujer que nada le inspiraba sino algo que para mí no tiene nombre*, vaya V. con Dios, y no se case V. con esa mujer" (158). Her momentary suspension in the crucial part of her statement reveals her emotional intensity and, at the same time, shows that she suddenly becomes aware of what she is about to say, which she then attenuates by referring to herself in the third person and by the euphemism for sex, "algo que para mí no tiene nombre." It is evident that, despite these inhibitions, she intends to use all possible means to win Luis's love.

Luis begins his defense in a polemical, mitigating vein, trying to hide his emotion:

> –Señora–contestó D. Luis, haciendo un esfuerzo para *disimular su emoción* y para que no se conociese lo turbado que estaba en lo trémulo y balbuciente de la voz–: Señora, yo también *tengo que dominarme* mucho para contestar a V. *con la frialdad* de quien opone argumentos a argumentos *como en una controversia*; pero la acusación de usted viene tan *razonada* (y V. perdone que se lo diga), as tan hábilmente *sofística*, que me fuerza a desvanecerla con *razones*. No pensaba yo tener que *disertar* aquí y que *aguzar mi corto ingenio*; pero V. me condena a ello, si no quiero pasar por un monstruo. (159)

From Luis's emotion we can see that he has already lost the battle; it is only a question of how long he can resist Pepita's charms and the demands of his sensuality. The phraseology employed illustrates a characteristic that will be taken up later: the fact that the long speeches of Valera's characters, all of whom are experts in the dialectical art, actually constitute stylized debates. We shall also see that Luis, although better trained, will be out-maneuvered by his opponents, as he is by Pepita in the present contest.

The dialectical elements are an integral part of the oratorical, euphemistic mitigation of this dialogue. Pepita cunningly invalidates Luis's assertion that the ideal women of his fantasies are more beautiful than real women with the logical reply that they also have less "eficacia seductora" and cannot compete with what affects the senses: "¿Cómo negar a V. que lo que V. se pinta en la imaginación es más hermoso que lo que existe realmente? Pero ¿cómo negar tampoco que lo real tiene más eficacia seductora que lo imaginado y soñado? Lo vago y aéreo de un fantasma, por bello que sea, no compite con lo que mueve materialmente los sentidos. Contra los ensueños mundanos comprendo que venciesen en su alma de usted las imágenes devotas; pero temo que las imágenes devotas no habían de vencer a las mundanas realidades" (161). Also noteworthy is the rhetorical trick (a disguised chiasmus) used to heighten the meaning of the adjective "mundanas" in the pre-position ("mundanas realidades"), while in the first usage it has the weaker position ("ensueños mundanos"). After Luis says: "Se diría que hubo en esto algo de fatídico; que estaba escrito; que era una predestinación," Pepita annihilates his weak defenses with a devastating repartee: "—Y si es una predestinación, si estaba escrito—interrumpió Pepita—, ¿por qué no someterse, por qué resistirse todavía? Sacrifique V. sus propósitos a nuestro amor. ¿Acaso no he sacrificado yo mucho? Ahora mismo, al rogar, al esforzarme por vencer los desdenes de V., ¿no sacrifico mi orgullo, mi decoro y mi recato?" (165). Throughout the dialogue she takes up his arguments almost point by point and refutes them in what is essentially a rebuttal technique. She finally subdues him completely by proclaiming her unworthiness and by saying that his scorn will kill her, before breaking into tears and leaving the room (168–170).

But before this happens, Luis resorts to an intellectual euphemism when he attempts to elevate Pepita to a philosophical abstraction, the idea he has formed of her (this was discussed previously), which is also expressed in neuter pronouns, "todo esto," "eso," etc. (160–162). There is a change in Pepita's tactics when she refers to Luis as "alguien" (162), although the euphemism no longer mitigates; it is rather a means of flirtation: "*Con alguien*, no obstante, más bello, entendido, poético y amoroso que los hombres que me han pretendido hasta ahora; *con un amante más distinguido* y cabal que todos mis adoradores de este lugar y de los lugares vecinos, soñaba yo para que me amara y para que yo le amase y le rindiese mi albedrío. Ese alguien era V." (166). We see that Luis and Pepita have recourse to euphemisms in order to objectify and attenuate their emotional relationships and to engage in playful flirtations with erotic overtones, although on a refined level. In his utilization of euphemisms, then, we may conclude that Valera is more in the spirit of the French rococo tradition of playful frivolity than in the Spanish, Cervantine tradition, which has only very slight elements of this nature.[74]

[74] Hatzfeld (*ibid.*, p. 229) says: "De esta tradición antigua española, grosera pero sana, se separa la francesa, eufemístico-frívola." After giving examples he says of the few similarly frivolous passages in the *Quijote*: "Tales frívolas sutilezas son, para Cervantes, objeto de sátira, no temas de imitación. . . . El eufemismo de lo conveniente, o decente, tiene, para Cervantes, una raíz de humor más sano."

5. MITIGATING DEVICES AND PHRASES. Another mitigating figure, closely connected to euphemisms and irony, is litotes, employed by Valera for direct humor or to show indirectly the self-delusion of the characters.[75] Of Don Gumersindo, for instance, we are told: "Nadie por aquí le critica de usurero, antes bien le califican de caritativo, porque *siendo moderado en todo, hasta en la usura lo era*, y no solía llevar más de un 10 por 100 al año, mientras que en toda esta comarca llevan un 20 y hasta un 30 por 100, y aun parece poco" (9). Ten percent, naturally, is a high rate of interest and it is impossible to be moderate in usury; thus it is certain that he is not called "caritativo." Subsequent comments on Don Gumersindo are similar in tone: "Don Gumersindo, muy aseado y *cuidadoso* de su persona, *era un viejo que no inspiraba repugnancia*" (9). Then we discover that he is moderate and careful about things only because of his avarice. As if Valera wants to be sure that the reader understands the truth, two later statements completely reverse the surface meaning of these statements. First, in a passage which is itself a hyperbolic depiction of the great esteem Pepita enjoys in the village: "Pepita Jiménez, a quien muchos han visto nacer, a quien vieron todos en la miseria, viviendo con su madre, a quien han visto después casada con *el decrépito y avaro D. Gumersindo*, hace olvidar todo esto, y aparece como un ser peregrino, venido de alguna tierra lejana, de alguna esfera superior, pura y radiante, y obliga y mueve al acatamiento afectuoso, a *algo como admiración amantísima* a todos sus compatriotas" (48). It is typical of Valera's irony that Luis is allowed to correct a previous evaluation of a character while presenting an exaggerated evaluation of another. It is obvious that the villagers do not feel for Pepita "algo como admiración amantísima" and that Luis's previous remark does not give the whole truth about their attitudes: "Los niños pequeñuelos acuden a verla las pocas veces que sale a la calle y quieren besarle la mano; las mozuelas le sonríen y la saludan con amor; los hombres todos se quitan el sombrero a su paso y se inclinan con la más espontánea reverencia y con la más sencilla y natural simpatía" (47–48).

The second correction of the original impression of Don Gumer-

[75] See *ibid.*, pp. 225–226, for examples in the *Quijote*.

sindo is given by the Count and, even though he is bitter at having been rejected, it may be that his statements about Pepita are more in accord with the true opinions of the townspeople:

—No es mala pécora la tal Pepita Jiménez. Con más fantasía y más humos que la infanta Micomicona, quiere hacernos olvidar que nació y *vivió en la miseria hasta que se casó con aquel pelele, con aquel vejestorio, con aquel maldito usurero*, y le cogió los ochavos. La única cosa buena que ha hecho en su vida la tal viuda es concertarse con Satanás para enviar pronto al infierno a su *galopín de marido*, y librar la tierra de *tanta infección y de tanta peste*. Ahora le ha dado a Pepita por la virtud y por la castidad. ¡Bueno estará todo ello! Sabe Dios si estará enredada de ocultis con algún gañán, y burlándose del mundo como si fuese la reina Artemisa. (128)

It is significant that no sign of protest is made by the listeners, an indication of their agreement or indifference, and that the information reported by Luis in the first letter, not entirely favorable to Pepita, had its source in the gossip of the servants and of others, which also discloses the real popular conception of her.

Luis, in the following negative statement, actually stresses the opposite: "¿Había de decirle que yo soy quien está enamorado de Pepita, que yo codicio el tesoro que ya él tiene por suyo? Esto no es verdad; y sobre todo, ¿cómo declarar esto a mi padre, *aunque fuera verdad*, por mi desgracia y por mi culpa?" (83). By putting the positive statement in a pretended indignant question, Luis is deceiving himself and his uncle; even so, the truth comes out in the concessive clause, "aunque fuera verdad." This type of litotes in an extended sense is employed for characterization; but humorous ones are found too, like Antoñona's reply when Pepita says, after a blasphemous remark: "—¡ . . . estoy loca . . . , no sé lo que digo y blasfemo!—Sí, hija mía, ¡estás algo empecatada!" (120). A similar humorous litotes occurs when the Dean writes that Pepita's only fault was to have fallen in love with Luis "como una loca con un candor y un ímpetu selváticos" (183).

Valera makes use of two mitigating devices, the enhancing adverb, *tan*, and the formula, *no . . . sino*, that were also used in the *Siglo de*

Oro for attenuation, as is shown by the following comment about Cervantes: "His dignified superlatives are no less mitigated . . . than the Racinian ones, when he speaks of: 'un *tan* valiente y *tan* nombrado caballero' (I, 9), or 'estos *tan* calamitosos tiempos' (I, 9)." As in Racine, majestic dignity, albeit mock-heroic, inheres in his imposing imperatives expressed by rare, urbane, smooth subjunctive forms: " 'No quiero otra cosa sino que volváis al Toboso y que . . . os presentéis ante esta señora . . . y le digáis lo que . . . he fecho' (I, 8)."[76] To be sure, these are not utilized for the same purposes, although they do have a mitigating effect, nor are they necessarily derived from Cervantes. In fact they have long been favorite ironical devices, as may be seen in the following remark from the *Lazarillo*: " 'Lázaro, de oy mas eres tuyo y no mio. Busca amo y vete con Dios. Que yo no quiero en mi compañia *tan diligente servidor. No* es posible *sino* que ayas sido moço de ciego' " (145).

A note of irony is likewise detectable in the adverb *tan* as it appears in *Pepita Jiménez*; but it nevertheless may indicate mitigation in the semidetached avoidance of more direct comparison or description. A few illustrations of the ironical usage of *tan* are: "El padre Vicario era *tan bueno* y *tan humilde* . . ." (110); ". . . rompió Pepita en lastimeros gemidos, . . . y dió con su cuerpo, *tan lindo y delicado*, sobre las losas frías del pavimento" (117); ". . . Pepita, que era *tan buena* . . ." (142); ". . . Pepita era *tan* simpática y D. Pedro *tan* venerado y D. Luis *tan* querido, que no hubo cencerros . . ." (205); and ". . . otra representaba a Cloe cuando la cigarra fugitiva se le mete en el pecho, donde, creyéndose segura, y a *tan grata sombra*, mientras que Dafnis procura sacarla de allí" (214).

Another important function of *tan*, a characterizing psychological one, is to provide a starting point from which evaluations, good or bad, may be made of a character, as in the following case: "Este antojo de Pepita de obsequiar tanto a mi padre, quien la pretende y a quien desdeña, me parece a menudo que tiene su poco de *coquetería*, digna de reprobación; *pero* cuando veo a Pepita después, y la hallo *tan natural*, *tan fresca y tan sencilla*, se me pasa el mal pensamiento e *imagino que todo lo hace candorosamente* y que no la lleva

[76] Hatzfeld, "A Clarification of the Baroque Problem," p. 135.

otro fin que el de conservar la buena amistad que con mi familia la *liga*" (34)[77] Here *tan*, plus the adjectives, serves as a link between critical suppositions and complimentary ones; but the phrase, "Sea como sea . . .," at the beginning of the next sentence reveals that this change is not final either. Incidentally, we may notice the termination of this sentence with a finite verb, "liga," deliberately arranged by the inversion of "con mi familia." Several explanations suggest themselves: a betrayal of emotion; a stressing of the verb *ligar*, which shows that Luis may already have in his unconscious mind the desire for Pepita to be *ligada* to his family through himself, not through his father; or simply that Valera occasionally followed a *Siglo de Oro* latinizing practice in placing the verb at the end of the sentence. Whatever may have motivated Valera to do so does not change the stress thus given the verb for the modern reader and the ensuing complication for a precise comprehension of what Luis is truly saying or thinking.

The adverb *tan* appears in an attenuated comparison when Luis says of Pepita: "Como esta mujer *vive tan retirada*, no la conocí hasta el día del convite; *me pareció, en efecto, tan bonita como dice la fama*, y advertí que tiene con mi padre una *afabilidad tan grande*, que le da alguna esperanza, *al menos* miradas las cosas someramente, de que al cabo ceda y acepte su mano" (21). By saying merely that Pepita is "tan bonita como dice la fama," Luis euphemistically mitigates the strong impression she must have really made in his mind. The other curious things are that Luis uses *tan* three times in a short sentence and that the qualification beginning with "al menos" reduces his father's hope to a minimum, perhaps denoting that, unconsciously, Luis is already a rival of his father. Another mitigating comparison is used in the description of Pepita's hands: "Las manos eran, *en efecto, tan bellas, más bellas* que lo que D. Luis había dicho en sus cartas" (112). This is like the first example, the comparison of someone or something to a pre-established evaluation, but a new problem is that of cross-reference. Although Valera pretends that the Dean wrote the second part of the novel, the *Paralipómenos*, this

[77] About the role of *expresiones ponderativas* in Valera's works, see Revuelta y Revuelta, "Valera, estilista," pp. 41–43.

cannot be accepted as valid for the interpretation of what is said. A later detailed treatment may explain the significance of such cross-references throughout the novel; here the explanation seems to be that of mitigation and gentle irony. Also noteworthy is the fact that in each of these comparisons the prosaic "en efecto" occurs.

No . . . sino is used not as an attenuated imperative but in attenuated comparisons in the formula, *no parecer sino*. Though common in all epochs, the phrase seems to be especially prominent as a mitigating device in the *Siglo de Oro* and in *Pepita Jiménez*. It is an elegant way to introduce a comparison, metaphor, or statement, as in the following examples from Cervantes: "¿ . . . aquella tez de rostro, que *no parece sino* de una espada acicalada y tersa, aquellas dos mejillas de leche y de carmín, que en la una tiene el sol y en la otra la luna, y aquella gallardía con que va pisando y aun despreciando el suelo, que *no parece sino* que va derramando salud donde pasa?" (*DQ* VII, 222); ". . . eran tales [los pies de Dorotea], que *no parecían sino* dos pedazos de blanco cristal que entre las otras piedras del arroyo se habían nacido" (*DQ* III, 47); and ". . . *no parece sino* que el jumento entendió lo que Sancho dijo . . ." (*DQ* VIII, 16). With a slight variation, the same formula occurs before an image in Valera's novel: "*No parecía ya* tímida gacela, *sino* iracunda leona" (113). However, it is more frequently employed to mitigate ordinary statements: "*No parece sino* que la excesiva indulgencia de usted para conmigo ha hecho cundir aquí mi fama de hombre de consejo . . ." (26); "*No parece sino* que para ellos el estudio de la teología, a que me he dedicado, es contrario del todo al conocimiento de las cosas naturales" (33); ". . . *no parece sino* que ella no lo sabe . . ." (38). All of these are used by Luis and, along with other mitigating means, appear in stilted or self-deceiving contexts.

There are several miscellaneous stylistic devices which also serve important functions in the overall expression of mitigation. Round numbers as a conventional method of intensification have become fixed into the language and seem to have an attenuating effect, like that of stock phrases. Attention has been drawn on several occasions to this function, of which two additional examples are: ". . . me veo . . . distraído de mis estudios, meditaciones y oraciones por *mil* objetos profanos" (49), and ". . . la tal Antoñona, . . . tan parlanchina como la tía Casilda, pero *cien mil* veces más discreta" (60). A particularly subtle manner of qualifying and of attenuating statements, and a smooth way of expressing doubt in many cases, is the frequent use of *tal vez*. A few new examples of this are: ". . . ¿cómo penetrar en lo íntimo del corazón, . . . de una doncella, criada *tal vez* con recogimiento exquisito e ignorante de todo, y saber qué idea podía ella formarse del matrimonio? *Tal vez* entendió que . . ." (12); and "*Tal vez* soy yo mismo quien provoca las miradas si tardan en llegar. La miro con insano ahinco . . ." (86). The few occurrences of the restrictive Gongorine formula, *si no A, B*, apparently formalize and mitigate the statement, as when Luis says that by going to distant lands as a missionary he would leave behind ". . . a tanto compatriota, *si no* perdido, algo pervertido" (20); or as when he says of his father: ". . . éste sería el único modo de que cambiase su vida, tan agitada y tempestuosa hasta aquí, y de que viniese a parar a un término, *si no* ejemplar, ordenado y pacífico" (24). To these devices may be added the deliberately formal phrases which produce attenuation because they reveal the omnipresent author who inserts them for no visible reason and who, for all his pretended detachment, is always between the characters and the reader. Several times statements are logically reinforced or clarified by *como*, which in this use is typical of didactic prose, as is "ahora bien" in the first example: "*Ahora bien*, si esto es así, *como lo es* . . ." (51); ". . . siendo grande el cuarto, *como lo era* . . ." (154); and ". . . si esta mujer es, *como lo es en realidad*, una lugareña ordinaria . . ." (157). A few examples of the same thing in *Siglo de Oro* prose: "Pues si esto es, *como lo es* . . .";[78] "Siendo, pues, esto ansí, *como lo es* . . ." (*DQ* II, 289); and "Si esto es verdad, *como lo es* . . ." (*DQ* II, 326). Similar phrases are: "Aquella sala *era y se llamaba* el despacho" (105); ". . . criando a sus hijos, *pues ya los deseaba* . . ." (179); and ". . . sólo en aquel instante, *digo, y no de antemano* . . ." (180–181). At times, the effect is achieved by negative periphrasis: "Antoñona *no calló* a Pepita *su descubrimiento* y Pepita *no acertó a negar la verdad* a aquella mujer . . ." (103).

[78] Santa Teresa de Jesús, *Moradas primeras*, ch. 1, p. 6.

While it is obvious that Valera had recourse to means of attenuation which, as a rule, were prominent in the *Siglo de Oro*, it is unnecessary to think that he consciously borrowed them or that the *Siglo de Oro* was his only source, since, in varying degrees, they may be used in all periods. Nevertheless, the expressions treated are sufficiently close in form and function to allow us to maintain that in *Pepita Jiménez* the skillful, aesthetically pleasing, and well-assimilated utilization of classical mitigating devices was a prime factor in the psychologically valid representation of the repressed desires and emotions, inhibited love, rationalizations, interior contradictions, and stiltedness of Luis and, to a lesser degree, of Pepita. Classical mitigating forms also contribute to a tone of elegant restraint in description and to general evocativeness, as was the custom in *Siglo de Oro* style.

B. *Rhythm, Repetition, and Word Order*

Without treating in detail all aspects of these three elements in *Pepita Jiménez*, we may point out those characteristics of them which approximate Valera's prose style to that of the *Siglo de Oro*. Although no complete study of these features of modern Spanish is available, a comparison of Valera's prose with that of other nineteenth-century writers indicates that he distinguishes himself from them by a greater predilection for perceptible *clausulae*, for repetition, and for the final latinizing position of the finite verb.

1. RHYTHM AND SOUND PATTERNS. Valera was drawn into the use of the *cursus tardus*, it seems, by his subtle parody of ascetical-mystical langauge, which contains many proparoxytones and absolute superlatives, both mostly *cultismos*, as well as by his recognition of the rhythmic possibilities of this *cursus* in alternation with more normal ones. Futhermore, without considering his knowledge of Latin and Italian literature, he must have been aware of its poetic and ironical values from the way it was used in the *Siglo de Oro*.[79] The

[79] On the *cursus* and rhythm of ascetical-mystical writers of the *Siglo de Oro*, see Sister Rosa María Icaza, *The Stylistic Relationship between Poetry and Prose*

ironical use of the *cursus tardus* in *Pepita Jiménez* depends primarily on proparoxytones taken from spiritual language. In this new connection, we may recall the frequency of words like *clérigo, escrúpulo, prójimo,* and *teólogo* that greatly facilitate this *cursus tardus.* The most striking examples merit repeating: ". . . una ambición hipócrita, sacrílega, simoníaca" (173), and "un varón místico, extático y apostólico" (213). Strictly speaking, these proparoxytones are not perfect cases of the *cursus tardus,* in which the stress falls on the third and sixth syllables from the last, but they produce the same rhythmic effect.

Only two percent of the interior and final *cola* in the first letter are the *cursus tardus,* but even such a low percentage is greater than that of ordinary prose. The *cursus tardus* is effective because it occurs throughout the novel in clusters, usually in proportion to the pseudo-spiritual or poetic nature of the passage. The importance of the *cursus tardus* may be seen in the following examples, allowing for synalepha or syneresis in some cases: "sirve de epígrafe . . ." (3), "el título bíblico de Paralipómenos" (4), "me ha embargado el ánimo . . ." (5), "paciencia poco evangélica . . ." (10), "poca mella en mi ánimo" (15), "bondad del Altísimo . . ." (16), "valle de lágrimas . . ." (17), "pecados del prójimo" (17), "vuelve mi escrúpulo . . ." (18), "sutiles y aéreos . . ." (31), "pensamientos artísticos . . ." (37), "educado a la rústica . . ." (45), "de corrupción y de escándalo" (57), "de un modo espontáneo . . ." (61), "¡. . . cómo se deleita enseñándome!" (68), "un espectáculo sencillo y poético . . ." (70), "la verdad caduca y efímera . . ." (75), "tan agudo filósofo . . ." (82), "quedarme muerto mirándola . . ." (87), "por arte diabólico . . ." (89), "cedro de Líbano . . ." (91), "secuaces fanáticos . . ." (132), "culta, elegante e idónea . . ." (134), "elegante y poética" (142), "muestras de júbilo . . ." (175), and "lo pequeño y doméstico . . ." (183). Two additional cases of proparoxytones, both interesting

---

in the "Cántico espiritual" of San Juan de la Cruz (Washington: Catholic Univ. of America Press, 1957), pp. 158–161. See also Hatzfeld, *Estudios literarios sobre mística española,* pp. 370–374, on the rhythm of San Juan de la Cruz's prose, and *El "Quijote" como obra de arte,* pp. 377–384, for similar problems in the *Quijote.* For a treatment of *cursus* and *cola* in Fray Luis de León, see Helen Dill Goode, *La prosa retórica de Fray Luis de León en "Los nombres de Cristo,"* pp. 49–66.

because of their ironical connotations, are: "fatídicos pronósticos" (54) and "el método homeopático . . ." (207).

The absolute superlative is sometimes used to form the *cursus tardus* too: "Mi padre estuvo finísimo . . ." (23), "debió de ser hermosísima . . ." (57), "un yugo dulcísimo" (90), "un azote durísimo . . ." (99), "estrados riquísimos . . ." (163), "angustia grandísima . . ." (194), and "un jardín amenísimo . . ." (213).

Traditionally the absolute superlative has been used for irony. At the beginning of the sixteenth century, it was so rare that Juan Boscán often avoided a direct translation of it in *El cortesano*, and it was still used sparingly by Alfonso de Valdés and Cristóbal de Villalón.[80] Although the absolute superlative does not appear often in the *Lazarillo*, there is a significant example of its ironical use: ". . . con el destiento de la cumplidissima nariz, medio quasi ahogandome . . ." (99). By the time of Cervantes and Quevedo, as is well known, it was more frequently used for irony and humor; every reader will recall, for instance, the following remarks of the Countess Trifaldi and Sancho:

> —Confiada estoy, señor poderosísimo, hermosísima señora y discretísimos circunstantes, que ha de hallar mi cuitísima en vuestros valerosísimos pechos acogimiento, . . . quisiera que me hicieran sabidora si está . . . el acendradísimo caballero don Quijote de la Manchísima, y su escuderísimo Panza.
>
> —El Panza . . . aquí está, y el don Quijotísimo asimismo; y así, podréis, dolorosísima dueñísima, decir lo que quisierdísimis; que todos estamos prontos y aparejadísimos á ser vuestros servidorísimos. (*DQ* VII, 32)

Such an obvious and exaggerated parody of speech never appears in *Pepita Jiménez*; it is always more refined, on the borderline between sincerity and irony. Also, Valera, who takes no linguistic liberties, is content to avail himself of those superlatives consecrated by usage. Thus in the following cases subtle shades of irony or stiltedness are discernible: "mezquinísimo mayorazgo" (8), "finísi-

[80] See Margherita Morreale, "El superlativo en *issimo* y la versión castellana del *Cortesano*," pp. 55–58.

The absolute superlative was abused by the Spanish romantics, as is seen in Ramón de Mesonero Romanos's parody, "El romanticismo y los románticos."

mo" (23), "bellísimas flores" (44), "admiración amantísima" (48), "mujer peligrosísima" (84), "sutilísima fragancia" (86), "naturalísimo" (102), "fuego purísimo" (168), "toque delicadísimo" (178), "coquetísima" (198), "criatura remonísima" (200), and "soplete utilísimo" (202).

The frequent use of rhyme, assonance, and alliteration, particularly manifested in word pairs, is another characteristic by which Valera's style may be closely related to that of the *Siglo de Oro*. Rhyme and assonance in verb doublets produce euphony and rhythm: "le cuidaba y regalaba . . . , le atendió y veló" (13), "suavizarlas y humanarlas" (20), "a enseñar y a moralizar" (20), "se turbaría y se empeñaría" (27), "analizar y desentrañar" (27), "amarlos y estimarlos" (27), "se conformará y contentará" (28), "pensar y meditar" (29), "excitándole y sublimándole" (30), "trenzados y atados" (36), "decantándolos y ensalzándolos" (44), "sin premeditarlo ni calcularlo" (47), "embromarme y atormentarme" (60), "Me complacía y me afligía" (63), "regalados y agasajados" (71), "lucharía y vencería" (76), "nos veremos y abrazaremos" (101), "a exornarle y bordarle" (51), "cohonestarle y disculparle" (184), "marchitarse y deshojarse" (187), and "acompañándole y mimándole" (195). This partial list gives an idea of how very much Valera used rhyme and assonance in verb pairs, a practice that is ordinarily shunned by modern writers, unless they are imitating traditional language for ironical or pseudo-naïve effects.

The same features occur in noun doublets and in other combinations, sometimes with alliteration. The euphonic effect is more pronounced in those places where there is a concentration of significant sound patterns, as at the beginning of the first letter: "Yo estoy encan*t*a*d*o con las huertas, y *t*o*d*as las *t*ar*d*es me *p*aseo *p*or ellas un *p*ar de horas. Mi *padre* quiere *llevarme* a ver sus *olivares* . . ." (6). Here the alliteration of dentals and labials, as well as the assonance in *a-e* of the second sentence, is noticeable. Shortly afterwards we find: "Hasta cinco *mujeres* han venido a *verme*, que todas han sido mis amas y me *han abrazado y besado*" (6). The impression of euphony is strengthened by the natural division of the first part into two heptasyllabic phrases. Additional examples of these sound patterns are “las agitaciones y pasiones” (15), “*Varios canarios* en jaulas dor*adas* an*i*man con sus tr*i*nos toda la *casa*” (22), “las preocupaciones y ocupaciones” (26), “irreflexiva e instintiva” (47), “meditaciones y oraciones” (49), “sin andar antes *paso* a *paso* el *áspero* camino” (49), “volar a librar” (137), “Aunque me he *criado* al *lado* de mi tío . . .” (16), “Yo conoc*ía*, *pues*, el *precio* del sacrific*io* que *hacía* . . .” (160), “la publicación y divulgación . . . , reflexiones y aclaraciones” (179), “mi mortificación y mi aflicción” (199), and “vertía un ch*orro* de sud*or por* cada *poro*” (204).

2. REPETITION. Like writers of the *Siglo de Oro*, Valera does not share the modern antipathy for repetition; rather, he deliberately repeats words and phrases, as may be seen in the following examples from the first few pages of the novel: “. . . empezó D. Gumersindo . . . a *requebrar* a Pepita con más ahinco y persistencia que solía *requebrar* a otras” (11); “. . . aunque la pregunta venía después de *broma* y pudiera tomarse por *broma* . . .” (11); “. . . me *interesa* y supongo que debe *interesarle* . . .” (12); “. . . no *perdona* lo que mi madre *perdonó* . . .” (19); “. . . hay multitud de *flores y plantas*. No tiene, en verdad, ninguna *planta* rara ni ninguna *flor* exótica; pero sus *plantas* y sus *flores* . . .” (22); and “. . . tiene *los gatos*, *los canarios*, las flores y al propio Niño Jesús, que en el fondo de su alma tal vez no esté muy por cima de *los canarios* y de *los gatos*” (23). Repetition is even more striking in Luis's oratorical speeches: “. . . yo lo despreciaría todo por el amor de Dios: *la fama*, *la honra*, *el poder y el imperio* . . . si el enemigo tentador . . . me ofreciese *todos los reinos de la tierra* porque *doblase* ante él la rodilla, yo no la *doblaría*; pero cuando me ofrece a *esta mujer*, vacilo. . . . ¿Vale más *esta mujer* a mis ojos que *todos los reinos de la tierra*; más que *la fama*, *la honra*, *el poder y el imperio*?” (92); “Estas almas se *aman* y se *gozan* entonces, como si *amaran y gozaran* a Dios, *amándole y gozándole*, porque Dios son ellas” (168). Repetition also occurs in expository material and in the speech of the other characters: “Apenas empezó Pepita a lanzar sobre él aquellas . . . *miradas* . . . , *miradas* que nadie sorprendió de los que estaban presentes, Antoñona, que no lo estaba, habló a Pepita de las *miradas*” (104); “He estado

engañando a V., *engañándome* a mí misma, queriendo *engañar* a Dios" (107); and "Cuando *acude* la buena dicha, *acude* para todo, y lo mismo cuando la desdicha *acude*" (189).

3. WORD ORDER. As may be seen in the last example cited above, and as I have mentioned before, one of the strange things about the word order in *Pepita Jiménez*, from the viewpoint of modern usage, is that the sentence often ends in a finite verb. Lapesa, among others, has commented that this was one of the distinguishing characteristics of *Siglo de Oro* prose: "Las mayores diferencias entre el orden de palabras usual en la época clásica y el de la sintaxis moderna consisten en la colocación del verbo. . . . Los autores de gusto más latinizante, sobre todo en el siglo XVI, tendían a situar el verbo al final de la frase. . . ." [81] As a general rule, the placing of the verb at the end of the sentence, or even at the end of a clause within a sentence, in *Pepita Jiménez* is related to the speaker's emotionalism or stiltedness. The final position of the verb is natural when the subject is understood or in relative clauses, as in the first sentence of the novel: ". . . sin que . . . se haya perdido uno solo de los documentos de que *constaba*" (3).[82] But when the subject is expressed, the position is more striking: ". . . a fin de completar el cuadro con sucesos que *las cartas no refieren*" (4).

The most remarkable occurrence of this phenomenon is in Luis's self-deluding narration of the trip to the Pozo de la Solana. In little more than one page of text, Luis reveals his emotion, it seems, by placing the verb in the end-position five times: ". . . comer las fresas tempranas que en ella *se crían*" (34); ". . . conservar la buena amistad que con mi familia la *liga*" (34); ". . . las que por aquí más comúnmente *se crían*" (35); ". . . era el principal objeto que allí nos *llevaba*" (35); and ". . . leche de algunas cabras que Pepita también *posee*" (35). In each of these cases, even where the direct object is a pronoun, it would have been easy to avoid placing the verb in the final position. The same is true of the following phrases: ". . . por más

[81] Rafael Lapesa, *Historia de la lengua española*, p. 254.

[82] See Daniel M. Crabb, *A Comparative Study of Word Order in Old Spanish and Old French Prose Works* (Washington: Catholic Univ. of America Press, 1955), especially pp. xii–xiii.

que con modestia lo *disimule* . . ." (25); ". . . las cosas visibles . . . que por medio del hombre Dios *completa y mejora*" (37); ". . . con un cariño más filial de lo que mi padre *quisiera*" (37); ". . . en quien el esposo *se complace*" (50); ". . . nada descubro que me haga temer lo que V. *teme*" (51); ". . . casi me ha llevado por un instante a que yo mismo *sospeche*" (51); ". . . que yo de todo corazón le *agradezco*" (54); "Mi padre no me deja parar y las visitas me *asedian*" (54); ". . . fragancia que su limpio cuerpo *despide*, . . . que supera al aroma silvestre del tomillo que en los montes *se cría*" (86); ". . . cuando Dante la *cantaba*" (94); ". . . que allí nuestros espíritus *se amen y se confundan*" (121); ". . . cuando el villano las *pisa*" (133). Sometimes normal end-position of the verb is still striking because of the frequency with which it occurs within a passage: ". . . se cantan canciones que no hay voz que *exprese* ni acordada cítara que *module*"; ". . . siento que *me resbalo* y que *me hundo*"; "Pero esta consideración y esta meditación ni *me atemorizan* ni *me arredran*"; ". . . quedarme muerto mirándola, aunque *me condene*" (all on page 87). In most of the cases listed the verbs end the sentences, thus drawing special attention to themselves. Other interesting aspects of the word order in *Pepita Jiménez* are evidently dependent on Valera's stylistic choice and not on any possible *Siglo de Oro* influence.

III. STRUCTURAL COMPARISONS BETWEEN *PEPITA JIMÉNEZ* AND *DON QUIJOTE*

Not only did Valera adapt to his purposes various stylistic resources from *Siglo de Oro* writings, mainly the *Quijote*; but he also succeeded in writing an excellent psychological novel which, structurally and thematically, is much closer to the *Quijote* than the great difference in subject matter and scope might indicate. What Valera learned from Cervantes, broadly speaking, were techniques of parody, irony, and the representation of the reality problem and ways to depict Luis's quixotic mind, which confuses natural sensuality with the mystical love about which he had read in the books at the seminary. Everything is assimilated and toned down to match

Valera's more restrained and sophisticated style. In other words, Valera could not go to extremes in his parody without disrupting the carefully arranged balance between sincerity and irony and without incurring in artificiality, for the drastic parodistic measures used in *Don Quijote* that were in keeping with its larger purposes and with its greater opportunities for the correction of exaggerations would have been out of place in Valera's more modest effort. Following Cervantes's own dictum, expressed by Maese Pedro, that ". . . toda afectación es mala" (*DQ* VI, 164), Valera refused to fall into an easy imitation of Cervantes by interspersing his novel with obviously Cervantine phrases, as Galdós, for instance, sometimes did.[83] What we see in *Pepita Jiménez* is a thoroughly assimilated utilization rather than a direct imitation of Cervantine resources and techniques.

A. *Parodistic Purposes and the Problem of Reality*

At the risk of incompleteness, we may reduce the common purposes of Cervantes and Valera to those of parody and the treatment of the reality problem. Don Quijote, from having read novels of chivalry, imitates them anachronistically in word and deed; Luis, from his reading of mystical-spiritual writings and of literature in general, imitates the mystics without the proper ascetical preparation and mimics spiritual language, while also reflecting his literary acquisitions. Thus both protagonists are characterized by stilted speech—Don Quijote, markedly; Luis, subtly—and both interpret reality, especially when placed in new situations, according to their readings. Each author exemplified in one man what he considered to be a common folly of his age, thus universalizing the implied criticism. But, from the outset, there are essential differences in the two parodies: Cervantes's is of the obviously untrue novel of chivalry

[83] J. Chalmers Herman, "Quotations and Locutions from *Don Quijote* in Galdós's Novels," *Hispania,* XXXVI (1953), 177–181. Herman has sorted out Cervantine locutions used by Galdós such as: "Una olla de algo más vaca que carnero," "la razón de la sin razón," "enderezar tuertos," and "¿Leoncitos a mí?" Such phrases, of course, can have an important characterizing function.

This section of my study served as a basis for an article, "*Pepita Jiménez* and *Don Quijote*: A Structural Comparison," *Hispania,* XLV (1962), 395–401.

and is (according to some interpreters) in the Catholic tradition; Valera's is undoubtedly anticlerical and anti-Catholic, for it is primarily of the selection and training of candidates for the priesthood and secondarily of mysticism in general. Even so, there is perhaps in each writer a common note of regret, of reluctant admiration for a world of lost ideals, and, what is of greater importance, each is carried far beyond the original parodistic purpose of the novel: Cervantes to ". . . the modern genre of the critical novel . . . a new integration of the critical and the imaginative . . .";[84] Valera to a new synthesis of *Siglo de Oro* traditions and stylistic expressions, refined by nineteenth-century sophistication and critical empathy in his formulation of the modern psychological novel. Finally, the parody in each case is mitigated by the author's sympathy for the protagonist, even though the latter has deviated from what the author believes is right behavior.

That the problem of reality versus illusion is a central one in *Don Quijote* is too well known to merit comment; less apparently, the same is true of *Pepita Jiménez.* The whole novel hinges on Luis's forced reactions and adjustments to reality, which he constantly misinterprets in his attempt to provide a protective covering for his sensual, nonpriestly nature. Thus, unlike Don Quijote, who in his monomania does not realize that he is falsifying reality, Luis is half-aware of his self-delusion all the time, which makes the psychological problem more complex and more interesting. From the very beginning, Luis is placed in a new world, the world outside the seminary where he had spent ten years without returning home; everything is new and attractive to him: the flattering attention and remarks of so many people, especially women; the local forms of amusement—the food, the excursions, the visits to the Casino, and Pepita's *tertulia*; and above all, the fascinating young widow herself. He even takes delight in local gossip and the colloquial way in which it is expressed, for he apparently enjoys quoting or reporting in his letters the phraseology of the townspeople. Although he was not completely isolated in the seminary, since leaving it he has

[84] Leo Spitzer, "Linguistic Perspectivism in the *Don Quijote,*" in *Linguistics and Literary History*, p. 68.

become more fully aware of the difference between the speech of theologians and that of his father, of Antoñona, and of most of the townspeople, and perhaps took secret pleasure in citing their ironical or even irreverent comments, being sure to include some such phrase as *como dicen*, *como dice mi padre*, etc., with which he justifies having made the remark at all. But his interior struggle begins at once also; he knows that he should not be attracted by these worldly pleasures and seeks not so much to overcome this tendency as to conceal and rationalize it. Thus it is the inward twisting and coloring of reality rather than the outward misinterpretation of it that is seen in *Pepita Jiménez.*

To Américo Castro idealism and reality in the Quijote are not in conflict but in harmony; there is a mutual interpenetration of character traits between Don Quijote and Sancho Panza.[85] Since, however, the harmonization of the antithesis is a gradual process, many have considered the illusion-reality antithesis an essential element of the *Quijote.*[86] In *Pepita Jiménez*, as in other nineteenth-century novels, the problem of reality versus illusion is a central one. We may contrast the comic, epico-heroic treatment of illusion and reality in *Don Quijote* with Valera's ironical-critical treatment of Luis's forced rejection of false illusion (spurious mysticism and false vocation) and acceptance of his natural being.

The characters of the *Quijote* are too complex to permit a categorical treatment of them as typical idealists or realists. They are not static but dynamic, evolving characters whose behavior reflects many gradations of idealistic and realistic attitudes and whose interpretations of reality are dependent on their own weaknesses and illusions. Nevertheless, some of them (Sancho, Andrés, Don Diego, Teresa, and Roque Guinart) are more clearly or usually exponents of a correct, factual interpretation of reality.

In *Pepita Jiménez* the characters may easily be divided into those who are idealistic and those who are not. Those who do not accept

[85] Américo Castro, "La estructura del *Quijote*," in *Semblanzas y estudios españoles* (Princeton: Princeton Univ. Press, 1956), pp. 232 ff. Cf. also Joaquín Casalduero, *Sentido y forma del "Quijote"* (Madrid: Insula, 1949), p. 47.

[86] For instance, most of Richard L. Predmore's *El mundo del Quijote* (Madrid: Insula, 1958), concerns various aspects of the reality problem and related matters.

the truth of Luis's nature and of his love for Pepita are Luis himself, the Vicar, and the Dean, all of whom, significantly, have had theological training. Those who represent natural reason, and what the author considers reality, are Don Pedro, Antoñona, Pepita, and all the secondary characters. Pepita, however, has misgivings of her own about what should be done and, being impressionable, reflects the attitudes of the other group, though more in speech than in action, for she uses all means at her disposal to win Luis. Yet there is an essential difference in the two presentations of the reality problem: Cervantes's is from a vantage point sufficiently perspectivistic to divide the critics into opposing camps; Valera's position is so evident that few critics have failed to detect it.[87]

Another essential difference is that whereas Don Quijote (although he briefly harbors the substitutionary illusion of becoming a shepherd) recovers his sanity and, before dying, renounces novels of chivalry and all he had done, Luis goes from one self-delusion to another. After his *caída* he recognizes his original error:

Jamás hubo en mí virtud sólida, sino hojarasca y pedantería de colegial, que había leído los libros de votos [*sic*, devotos] como quien lee novelas, y con ellos se había forjado su novela necia de misiones y contemplaciones. *Si hubiera habido virtud sólida en mí*, con tiempo te hubiera desengañado y no hubiéramos pecado ni tú ni yo. La verdadera virtud no cae tan fácilmente. A pesar de toda tu hermosura, a pesar de tu talento, a pesar de tu amor hacia mí, *yo no hubiera caído, si en realidad hubiera sido virtuoso*, si hubiera tenido una vocación verdadera. *Dios*, que todo lo puede, *me hubiera dado su gracia. Un milagro*, sin duda, *algo de sobrenatural* se requería para resistir a tu amor; *pero Dios hubiera hecho el milagro* si yo hubiera sido digno objeto y bastante razón para que lo hiciera. (172–173)

It is significant that at this crucial moment of self-recognition and of the acceptance of reality in the author's terms Luis expresses himself in contrary-to-fact conditional sentences, one of Cervantes's most

[87] Unfortunately, Revuelta y Revuelta, in spite of her excellent descriptive study of Valera's style, does not detect his critical irony and says of him: ". . . la espiritualidad, la dulzura de afectos, propia de su concepción cristiana" ("Valera, estilista," p. 54).

important means of treating the reality problem.[88] Even in the midst of self-recognition Luis begins the process of rationalization and subsequent self-delusion by saying that something miraculous was the only thing that could have enabled him to resist Pepita, thus half freeing himself from blame. The author's comment on Luis's new orientation shows that Luis has simply amalgamated sensuality and spirituality as incarnated in Pepita: "Su resolución estaba tomada, y todo acudía a su mente a confirmar su resolución. La sinceridad y el ardor de la pasión que había inspirado a Pepita; su hermosura; la gracia juvenil de su cuerpo y la lozanía primaveral de su alma, se le presentaban en la imaginación y le hacían dichoso" (177). There follows the ironical admission of false mysticism and the expression of his new ideal (in which the humor is noticeable even in the rhythm), namely, to be "... un buen lugareño cualquiera, ... siendo modelo de maridos al lado de su Pepita" (179).

Valera invites us to compare Luis's position with Don Quijote's when he says, after telling us how Luis rationalized his failure to emulate St. Edward and St. Vincent:

Don Luis pensó desde luego en sustituir el antiguo y encumbrado ideal con otro más humilde y fácil. Y si bien recordó a D. Quijote, cuando, vencido por el caballero de la Blanca Luna, decidió hacerse pastor, maldito el efecto que le hizo la burla, sino que *pensó en renovar con Pepita Jiménez*, en nuestra edad prosaica y descreída, la edad venturosa y *el piadosísimo ejemplo de Filemón y de Baucis*, tejiendo un dechado de vida patriarcal en aquellos campos amenos; fundando en el lugar que le vió nacer un hogar doméstico lleno de religión, que fuese a la vez asilo de menesterosos, centro de cultura y de amistosa convivencia, y limpio espejo donde pudieran mirarse las familias; y *uniendo*, por último, *el amor conyugal con el amor de Dios para que Dios santificase y visitase la morada de ellos, haciéndola como templo, donde los dos fuesen ministros y sacerdotes*, hasta que dispusiese el cielo llevárselos juntos a mejor vida. (184–185)

This passage shows that Luis is still unrealistic because, although the ideal itself is not wrong or absolutely unattainable, the contingent result of the union of conjugal love with the love of God, that their

[88] Cf. Hatzfeld, *El "Quijote" como obra de arte*, pp. 63–77.

home should be like a "templo, donde los dos fuesen ministros y sacerdotes," is childish. This illusion too is threatened with failure as a result of the duel and actually comes to have ". . . su poquito de paganismo, como poesía rústica amoroso-pastoril . . ." (213). Luis's inability to accept reality is also seen in his comical ideas about the method of curing an alcoholic, Antoñona's husband: ". . . habiendo oído afirmar que los confiteros aborrecen el dulce, ha inferido que los taberneros deben aborrecer el vino y el aguardiente, y ha enviado a Antoñona y a su marido a la capital de esta provincia, donde les ha puesto de su bolsillo una magnífica taberna" (207). Thus Valera never produces in Luis anything like Don Quijote's complete *desengaño*, but has him proceed from one rationalization and one illusion—or more frequently, self-delusion—to another.

To a great extent, the correct evaluation of the parody, reality problem, and ambiguity of each of the two novels is dependent upon the recognition of the author's irony, which in each case permeates the whole and provides unity. Cervantes's irony is an outgrowth of his sound humor and is essentially constructive: ". . . irradia la ironía desde el centro del humorismo cervantino a todas las partes y partículas del *Quijote* e informa todo el estilo."[89] Valera's skeptical and playful irony, though directed, at least in part, against the established order, is essentially aloof.

Another indication of Valera's relations with Cervantes is his use of Cervantine ironical techniques. Cervantes used concessive clauses or other qualifying remarks, as in the description of Sansón Carrasco, for characterizations: "Era el Bachiller, *aunque se llamaba Sansón*, no muy grande de cuerpo, *aunque muy gran socarrón;* de color macilenta, *pero de muy buen entendimiento*; tendría hasta veinticuatro años, carirredondo, de nariz chata y de boca grande, señales todas de ser de condición maliciosa y amigo de donaires y de burlas . . ." (*DQ* V, 67). Such qualifying remarks are antithetical and compensatory in nature and are usually humorous, like the first one, or psychological, like the other two.[90] Although one cannot be sure

[89] *Ibid.*, p. 249. See also, for the humor and irony in the *Quijote*, pp. 237–261, although discussion of them is not limited to these pages.

[90] Cf. *ibid.*, pp. 118–119.

that Valera learned this technique from Cervantes, his frequent use of it seems to be more than coincidental. The most ironical, the most delightful portrait in *Pepita Jiménez*, that of Don Gumersindo, begins with another characteristic of both Cervantes's and Valera's irony–humorous, erudite periphrasis: "No se podría decir que crease riqueza; *pero tenía una extraordinaria facultad de absorción con respecto a la de los otros*, y en punto a consumirla, será difícil hallar sobre la tierra persona alguna en cuyo mantenimiento, conservación y bienestar hayan tenido menos que afanarse la madre naturaleza y la industria humana" (8). The simple meaning is that he lived by usury and was so miserly that he spent almost nothing, all of which is said in the predominant *pero* clause. Three ironical observations occur shortly afterwards: "Con este arreglo, con esta industria y con el ánimo consagrado siempre a aumentar y a no disminuir sus bienes, *sin permitirse el lujo de casarse, ni de tener hijos, ni de fumar siquiera*, llegó D. Gumersindo a la edad que he dicho . . ." (9). The humorous asides become climactic in the following: "Con todos estos defectos, que aquí y en otras partes muchos consideran virtudes, *aunque virtudes exageradas*, D. Gumersindo *tenía excelentes cualidades*; era afable, servicial, compasivo, y se desvivía por complacer y ser *útil* a todo el mundo, aunque le costase trabajos, desvelos y fatigas, *con tal que no le costase un real.* Alegre y amigo de chanzas y de burlas, se hallaba en todas las reuniones y fiestas, *cuando no eran a escote*, y las regocijaba con la amenidad de su trato y con su discreta, *aunque poco ática*, conversación" (9–10). The whole passage is ironical. Virtues cannot be exaggerated, so they are not virtues; the "excelentes cualidades" are all subjected to being "useful" (i.e., to lend money); and in general, the old man's miserly nature is made clear.[91]

Although Don Quijote reflects his bookish learning in his speech (as does Luis), it seems that erudition and extended litotes as means of irony are used more by Valera than by Cervantes. This may be seen in the passage following the comment that Pepita and her

[91] As is true of many other aspects of *Pepita Jiménez*, this depiction of Don Gumersindo, though shorter, is virtually repeated in that of Don Acisclo at the beginning of *Doña Luz.*

mother had never imagined that Don Gumersindo might ask Pepita to marry him: ". . . ambas se quedaron *atónitas y pasmadas* cuando, después de varios requiebros, entre burlas y veras, D. Gumersindo *soltó con la mayor formalidad, y a boca de jarro*, la siguiente categórica pregunta: '—Muchacha, ¿quieres casarte conmigo?' Pepita, aunque la pregunta venía después de mucha broma y pudiera tomarse por broma, y aunque *inexperta* de las cosas del mundo, por *cierto instinto adivinatorio* que hay en las mujeres, y sobre todo en las mozas, por *cándidas* que sean, *conoció que aquello iba por lo serio* . . ." (11). Here the ironical litotes is extended, because Pepita's mother was no doubt trying to induce D. Gumersindo to marry Pepita and they would not, therefore, have been "atónitas y pasmadas." (Incidentally, these two adjectives and *suspenso* occur often in both novels.) Furthermore, the statement that introduces the question, with its combination of colloquialisms ("soltó . . . a boca de jarro") and erudition, indicates plainly that the question was quite serious, point-blank, and categorical. Consequently Pepita would not need a "cierto instinto adivinatorio" (erudition) to know that it was serious. The litotes appears on a third level if one considers that Pepita had spent her life in poverty and may not have been in fact so inexpert or candid. Such ironical techniques are still in the Cervantine tradition, for they are logical extensions of what Hatzfeld has called Cervantes's "enlaces abstractos-concretos" and "congruencia de lo incongruente."[92] This is not to discount the possibility that Valera was aware of Cervantes's litotes too, but in Cervantes the litotes and other means of irony are drastic and obvious. In Valera the irony is so refined and so subtle that an immediate distinction between it and sincerity is not always possible. The extended litotes, then, makes a statement, either positive or negative, that only discloses its true, opposite meaning on close examination; it is an important stylistic device which, in its subtlety, again points out the author's restraint.

Thus it is seen that Valera's irony, like Cervantes's, may juxtapose the abstract and the concrete or the learned and the popular for humorous effects. Another such juxtaposition is seen in the use of

[92] Hatzfeld, *El "Quijote" como obra de arte*, pp. 53–62.

the colloquialism, *llevar* (*dar*, etc.) *calabazas*, obviously a favorite with Valera, for he uses it three times in *Pepita Jiménez* and, indeed, frequently in his novels. Don Pedro has told Luis that all Pepita's suitors "... habían *llevado calabazas*," that he "... hasta cierto punto las había también llevado; pero se lisonjeaba de que no fuesen *definitivas* ..." (25). And about the Count of Genazahar we are told: "El Conde ... *había recibido las confitadas calabazas* que ella solía propinar a quienes la requebraban y aspiraban a su mano. *La herida que aquel duro y amargo confite* había abierto en su endiosado corazón no estaba cicatrizada todavía" (128).[93] We learn that Currito, in imitation of Luis and Pepita, "... se ha casado con la hija de un rico labrador de aquí, sana, *frescota, colorada como las amapolas, y que promete adquirir* en breve *un volumen y una densidad* superiores a los de su suegra doña Casilda" (208). Here refined erudition, the scientific phraseology, is humorously blended with popular elements, "frescota" and the comparison. From a slightly different perspective, there occurs the ironization of erudition in one of the facetious mentions of the lying preface technique, which pretends that someone else (the Dean) wrote this part of the novel and that the author is simply editing it (like Cide Hamete Benengeli and Cervantes): "Lo que sí hizo fué poner glosas y comentarios de provechosa edificación, cuando tal o cual pasaje lo requería; pero yo los suprimo aquí porque no están de moda las novelas anotadas o glosadas, y porque sería voluminosa esta obrilla si se imprimiese con los mencionados requisitos. Pondré, no obstante, en este lugar, como única excepción, e incluyéndola en el texto, la nota del señor Deán ..." (181).

Erudition and erudite periphrasis have an important characterizing function too: they help to portray Luis's stiltedness and hypocrisy. Conscious of his knowledge, Luis likes to display it before the townspeople: "¡Cuánto han admirado mi *erudición* ... ! ¡Cuánto han admirado también que en los verdes sembrados sepa yo distinguir la cebada del trigo y el anís de las habas; que conozca muchos árboles frutales y de sombra, y que, aun de las hierbas que nacen espontánea-

93 See also, *Pepita Jiménez*, p. 176, where Antoñona says, with no admixture of erudition: "... como la niña le ha dado mil veces calabazas, está que trina."

mente en el campo, acierte yo con varios nombres y refiera bastantes condiciones y virtudes!" (33–34). It is not difficult to imagine the condescending sort of admiration that Luis's "erudition" must have aroused, since any child of the town could distinguish barley from wheat, anise from beans, and would know fruit trees and shade trees. The same type of irony is found in Luis's stilted circumlocutions, which reveal the opposite of what they state: "No hallo motivo suficiente para variar de opinión respecto a lo que ya he dicho a V. contestando a sus recelos de que Pepita puede sentir cierta inclinación hacia mí" (80); "Lo rápido, lo fugitivo de la impresión, me induce a conjeturar que no ha tenido nunca realidad extrínseca; que ha sido un ensueño mío" (81); and "Pero, no: mi pecado no ha de traer como indefectible consecuencia otro pecado" (100). The irony is enhanced by the incongruity of the remark Luis makes about the Vicar: "Me encantan sobre todo, la sencillez, *la sobriedad en hiperbólicas manifestaciones de sentimentalismo*, la naturalidad . . ." (43).

Valera follows the lead of Cervantes and of countless others in the use of the narrative method which insists that the author is only an editor. This gives the author the opportunity to intervene at will, while remaining semidetached; in Valera's case it provides him with an excellent vantage point for his criticism, afterthoughts, and psychological probings. Of the two most prolonged occurrences of the device, the first is an ironization of the romantic novel. Valera lists less prosaic ways in which the crucial meeting between Luis and Pepita could have happened: they might have been forced by unlikely events to have spent the night in some abandoned castle, in a deserted cave, or on a remote desert island. But Valera rejects these measures and adds, not too seriously: ". . . no echemos la culpa al acaso, sino a los mismos personajes que en esta historia figuran y a las pasiones que sienten" (151). The second seems to be a burlesque of pedantic, overcautious writing in general and of Luis's self-contradictory, wavering style in particular (179–181).

Although Valera does not go so far as to leave two combatants with swords in midair during one of these "editorial" interventions, as Cervantes ironically did (*DQ* I, 210–223), he does similarly use them for irony and to create suspense.[94] Of the two examples cited, the first, which could be expanded to include the ironical description of Pepita's preparation for her visitor (150–153), provides a note of suspense, since Luis had already been presented by Antoñona. There may be seen in this and other passages phrases like: "Según hemos llegado a averiguar..." (152) and "Dejemos que ellos mismos se expliquen, y copiemos al pie de la letra sus palabras" (154), which recall similar ones from the *Quijote*: "Don Quijote, arrimado á un tronco de un haya, ó de un alcornoque (que Cide Hamete Benengeli no distingue el árbol que era) . . ." (*DQ* VIII, 241). This ironical narrative technique is related to mitigating phrases like *tal vez*. It too may have a mitigating function, since by using it the author removes himself one step farther from the characters, while enhancing his own role.

B. *Cervantine Style Reminiscences in* Pepita Jiménez

Not only are the fundamental purposes and informing principle—parody, the reality problem, and irony—modeled on those of *Don Quijote*—but one also finds devices, formulas, techniques, and situations which are broadly reminiscent of Cervantine ones. First of all, in addition to the previously treated motif of Luis's mission, comparable to Don Quijote's, there are at least two other leitmotifs in Valera's novel that have their parallels in the *Quijote*: the constant statements by Luis that he wishes to return to his old life, to the seminary, which is like the similar theme of Sancho's threats to abandon his master; and the frequent mentioning of demons and magic, which is analogous to Don Quijote's references to sorcerers and Sancho's mentions of devils.[95] We have seen that the theme of the priestly calling was used by Luis for mitigating and rationalizing purposes, unlike Don Quijote, who usually believed in his mission

[94] See Hatzfeld, *El "Quijote" como obra de arte*, pp. 133–134. For other means of maintaining interest, which will be briefly treated, see pp. 133–154.

[95] See *ibid.*, pp, 15–38, for leitmotifs in the *Quijote*. Similar parallels could be made with other motifs in the novel, namely, the praise of Dulcinea and the anger and folly of Don Quijote; but these would have naturally come out in *Pepita Jiménez* anyway, whereas the other three may represent Valera's deliberate choice of Cervantine themes.

and in enchantments. Similarly, the other motifs in *Pepita Jiménez* are used by Luis for rationalization and, to some extent, for mitigation. Luis's mission, of course, is closely related to the motif of returning to his uncle and to his studies.

Luis's return-motif takes on several aspects: the return itself, the fact that he is tired of being in the town, and the blaming of his father for keeping him there against his will. The last one has a double function because, while it is true that Don Pedro wants his son to stay and fall in love with Pepita, neither Luis nor the reader is aware of this until the end of the novel (202). Thus delightful ambiguity is created: what Luis says is true, but he says it as an excuse for staying and for participating in local diversions. (The same ambiguity occurs in Luis's repeated remarks about his father's insistence that he visit Pepita.) Especially at the beginning and at the end of the letters is this motif expressed:

> . . . necesito volver a mi antigua vida, a mis estudios, a mis altas especulaciones, y acabar por ser sacerdote. . . . (42)
>
> Tengo la esperanza de que lo más que mi padre me retendrá ya por aquí será todo este mes. En junio nos iremos juntos a esa ciudad, y ya V. verá cómo, libre de Pepita, que no piensa en mí ni se acordará de mí para malo ni para bueno, tendré el gusto de abrazar a V. y de lograr la dicha de ser sacerdote. (71–72)
>
> Me iré y la olvidaré. (76)
>
> Lo mejor es . . . tratar de abandonar cuanto antes este pueblo y de volverme con V. (83)
>
> No me queda más recurso que huir. Si en lo que falta para terminar el mes mi padre no me da su venia y no viene conmigo, me escapo como un ladrón; me fugo sin decir nada. (88)
>
> El 25 saldré de aquí sin falta. Pronto tendré el gusto de dar a V. un abrazo. (99)
>
> Adiós. Hasta dentro de pocos días, que nos veremos y abrazaremos. (101)

We see that the return-motif sometimes is one of flight, of escape from Pepita. On one occasion, it even becomes a frantic plea for help: "Sáqueme V. de aquí. Escriba V. a mi padre que me dé licencia para irme. Si es menester, dígaselo todo. ¡Socórrame V.! ¡Sea V. mi amparo!" (90). The other characteristics of the motif, boredom at being in the town and the blaming of Don Pedro, as well as Luis's obvious self-delusion, may be seen in the following:

> Me voy cansando de mi residencia en este lugar, y cada diá siento más deseo de volverme con usted, y de recibir las órdenes; pero mi padre ... exige de mí que permanezca aquí con él dos meses por lo menos. (19)

> La monotonía de mi vida en este lugar empieza a fastidiarme bastante.... (29)

> Sigo haciendo la misma vida de siempre y detenido aquí a ruegos de mi padre. (43)

> ¡Cuánto me pesa de haber venido por aquí y de permanecer aquí tan largo tiempo! (48)

> Extraño es que en tantos días yo no haya tenido tiempo para escribir a V.; pero tal es la verdad. Mi padre no me deja parar y las visitas me asedian. (54)

The least essential of the leitmotifs, regarding magic and the diabolical, points out Luis's romantic nature and his refusal to accept facts as they are. Some examples are: "¿Quién sabe, ... si ... no hay algo de *magia diabólica* en este prestigio de que se rodea y con el cual emboba a este cándido padre Vicario, y le lleva y le trae y le hace que no piense ni hable sino de ella a todo momento?" (47); "En la mano el látigo, que se me antojó como varita de virtudes, con que pudiera *hechizarme* aquella *maga*" (62); "Sus ojos están dotados de una atracción magnética inexplicable. Me atrae, me seduce, y se fijan en ella los míos" (85). An ironical twist is given this motif when Antoñona accuses Luis of being a *mago*: "La has hechizado; la has dado un bebedizo maligno" (135). The other aspect of the theme is that of the Devil and demons, which is more than a manner of speaking and is part of Luis's effort to attribute to supernatural causes what he himself is responsible for: "¿Será vanidad ridícula sugerida por el mismo *demonio*?" (81); "No logro enmendarme.

Lejos de dejar de ir a casa de Pepita, voy más temprano todas las noches. Se diría que los *demonios* me agarran de los pies y me llevan allá sin que yo quiera" (89); "Merezco que me *atenacen* los *demonios* con tenazas hechas ascua" (100); "Don Luis, como si el mismo *diablo* lo hubiera dispuesto, se encontró cara a cara con el Conde..." (128).

By the briefest of allusions, Valera evokes scenes or characters from *Don Quijote*. For instance, upon reading the narration of the humorous pinching scene of *Pepita Jiménez*, in which it is said of Antoñona: ". . . la endiablada mujer me aplicó, de una manera indecorosa y plebeya, por bajo de las espaldas, seis o siete feroces *pellizcos*, como si quisiera sacarme a túrdigas el pellejo. Después se largó echando chispas" (100), one recalls the scene of the *Quijote* in which the Duchess and Altisidora enter Don Quijote's room and pinch him: ". . . acudieron á Don Quijote y desenvolviéndole de la sábana y de la colcha, le *pellizcaron* tan a menudo y tan reciamente ..." (*DQ* VII, 233). Don Quijote thinks immediately of the "perverso encantador" who had done this, as Luis thinks of devils right away; also, the phrasing of Luis's thought is like a subsequent statement by Sancho: "Gatéenme el rostro, . . . *atenázenme los brazos con tenazas de fuego*; . . . pero que me toquen dueñas no lo consentiré si me llevase el diablo" (*DQ* VIII, 257). Thus the physical punishment inflicted upon the protagonist in this brief incident may evoke several scenes from the *Quijote*: the pinching scene itself and Sancho's remark, which occurs in a similar context and which mentions another burlesque happening, the *espanto cencerril y gatuno* of Don Quijote (*DQ* VII, 176–179). Valera, like Cervantes, has the habit of making subsequent references to such events: "Don Luis, aturdido, no sabía qué objetar a estos raciocinios de Antoñona, más atroces que sus pellizcos pasados" (136).

In other instances, the same type of situation or comment is used for comic effect in both novels, although the lack of close similarity indicates an assimilated or digested imitation rather than a direct one. The ludicrous dancing of Don Quijote (*DQ* VIII, 143–144) has its parallel in the description of Don Pedro at his son's wedding: "Bailó el fandango con Pepita, con sus más graciosas criadas y con otras seis o siete mozuelas. A cada una, al volverla a su asiento, cansada ya, le dió con efusión el correspondiente y prescrito abrazo, y a las menos serias, algunos pellizcos, aunque esto no forma parte del ceremonial. Don Pedro llevó su galantería hasta el extremo de sacar a bailar a Doña Casilda, que no pudo negarse, y que, con sus diez arrobas de humanidad y los calores de julio, vertía un chorro de sudor por cada poro" (204). Again a phrase, "con sus diez arrobas de humanidad . . . ," may bring to mind another scene from the *Quijote*, the one in which Sancho decides what should be done about the race between a man weighing only five *arrobas* and one weighing eleven (*DQ* VIII, 212–214). In each novel a character who ordinarily speaks in a very colloquial way attains a surprising degree of eloquence: "Todos los que conocían á Sancho Panza se admiraban oyéndole hablar tan elegantemente . . ." (*DQ* VII, 226); and ". . . Antoñona estuvo discretísima . . . , y hasta su lenguaje fué tan digno y urbano, que no faltaría quien le calificase de apócrifo . . ." (138). Both Valera and Cervantes humorously describe a female character as being unusually strong: Sancho says of Aldonza Lorenzo (Dulcinea): ". . . que tira tan bien una barra como el más *forzudo* zagal de todo el pueblo" (*DQ* II, 306); and Valera says: "Antoñona tendría cuarenta años, y era dura en el trabajo, briosa y más *forzuda* que muchos cavadores" (118).

Valera's adeptness at briefly depicting poses and gestures suggests that he may have gone to Cervantes for inspiration.[96] A few illustrations follow:

> Pepita, que se había levantado para despedir al padre Vicario, no bien volvió a cerrar la puerta y quedó sola, de pie, en medio de la estancia, permaneció un rato inmóvil, con la mirada fija, aunque sin fijarla en ningún objeto, y con los ojos sin lágrimas. (117)

> Abismado en ellas estaba hacía largo rato, sentado junto al bufete, los codos sobre él y en la derecha mano apoyada la mejilla, cuando sintió cerca ruido. (134)

> Cuando D. Luis vió a Antoñona arrugó el entrecejo, mostró bien en

[96] See *ibid.*, pp. 103–113, for examples in *Don Quijote.*

el gesto lo que le contrariaba aquella visita, y dijo con tono brusco. . . . (134)

Al decir esto, Pepita hincó en tierra ambas rodillas, y se inclinó luego hasta tocar con la frente el suelo del despacho. Don Luis siguió en la misma postura que antes tenía. Así estuvieron los dos algunos minutos en desesperado silencio. (171–172)

Although there is little action in the novel, Valera is quite capable of representing it in a few deft strokes: "Y Antoñona echó a correr, bajó la escalera de dos en dos escalones y se plantó en la calle" (138). In a longer passage Valera's skill in combining gestures, poses, and movement with an economy of means is seen, although the effectiveness of the representation is not thereby diminished:

Al cabo de un largo rato, D. Luis apareció de nuevo, saliendo de la obscuridad. En su rostro se veía pintado el terror; algo de la desesperación de Judas.

Se dejó caer en una silla; *puso ambos puños cerrados en su cara y en sus rodillas ambos codos*, y así permaneció más de media hora, sumido sin duda en un mar de reflexiones amargas.

Cualquiera, si le hubiera visto, hubiera sospechado que acababa de asesinar a Pepita.

Pepita, sin embargo, apareció después. *Con paso lento*, *con actitud de profunda melancolía*, *con el rostro y la mirada inclinados al suelo*, llegó hasta cerca de donde estaba D. Luis. . . . (170–171)

In addition to the remarkably well-suggested scene itself, two points are noteworthy: first, the light humor of "Cualquiera, . . . hubiera sospechado que acababa de asesinar a Pepita" and the following correction of this "misconception"; and second, the word "actitud," which is one of many indications that all the main characters of the novel are skilled actors: they are capable of feigning one attitude or emotion while actually experiencing another. Although these gestures, poses, and sketched actions are not of epic stature, as they are in the *Quijote*, they seem to be even more closely related to the characters and to their psychological situation. Valera (like Cervantes, Diderot, and Manzoni) is a precursor of the *modernistas* in the portrayal of gestures and poses, about which Amado Alonso said, speaking of Larreta and Valle-Inclán: "Ellos son los primeros en haber hecho estudios de gestos y también de ademanes, de movimientos corporales que reproducen y materializan los movimientos e intenciones del alma, con el enfocamiento de la atención a un reducido espacio, al rostro y aun a una parte del rostro, a las manos, a los pies de los personajes, para indicar al lector . . . que todo allí es intencional, tanto lo quieto como lo cambiante."[97] Although these descriptive techniques may have been more fully utilized by the *modernistas*, earlier writers were certainly aware of them. For instance, quite successful is the following cinematographic description of Pepita's instantaneous and fleeting transition from sadness to joy, in which the past participle, "contraída," depicts the past facial expression, while the present participles indicate the rapidity and simultaneity of the actions therein expressed, as dependent upon "se abrió" and "brilló": "Por entre las lágrimas que nublaban los hermosos ojos de Pepita *brilló* un alegre rayo de luz; su linda y fresca boca, *contraída* por la tristeza, *se abrió* con suavidad, *dejando ver* las perlas de sus dientes y *formando* una sonrisa" (108).

Valera's use of all stylistic resources is so natural and unobtrusive that their effectiveness is often overlooked. Such is the case with his methods of achieving suspense, which are also in the Cervantine tradition. We have already seen certain aspects of these methods in the "editorial" narrative intervention and in the protagonist's evasive digressions. On a small scale, Valera sometimes uses a moderate version of what Hatzfeld has called Cervantes's "oración consecutiva 'espectativa.' "[98] Something like this suspense, although playful, is seen in the sentence examined earlier: ". . . no fué el hortelano ni su mujer, ni . . . ," etc. (35). A better example occurs after the Vicar asks Pepita with whom she was in love: "Pepita se levantó de su asiento; fué hacia la puerta; la abrió; miró para ver si alguien escuchaba desde fuera; la volvió a cerrar; se acercó luego al padre Vicario, y toda acongojada, con voz trémula, con lágrimas en los ojos, dijo casi al oído del buen anciano . . ." (108). Three cases of suspense are of particular psychological interest because of Luis's reactions—

[97] Amado Alonso, *Ensayo sobre la novela histórica*, pp. 220–221.
[98] Hatzfeld, *El "Quijote" como obra de arte,* p. 149. See also pp. 149–154.

curious combinations of association of ideas and retrospective rationalizations. The three occasions are Luis's first private meeting with Pepita (62–63), the first time he touches her hand (78–79), and his first kiss (97). While Valera is quite conventional and brief in the depiction of these moments and does not attempt to represent Luis's thoughts faithfully, the conflicting feelings and impulses are all discernible under the smooth exterior. Hence these associative passages are of the same family as later, more complex, techniques used to describe psychic life. Again, as is usually the case, a device which Valera could have acquired from Cervantes is used in a modern way with psychological implications.

Cervantes often employed contrary-to-fact conditional sentences to show, humorously, idealism checked by realism.[99] In Valera this type of sentence sometimes has the serious purpose of providing for self-deception, as we saw in the passage beginning with "Si hubiera habido virtud sólida en mí . . ." (173). But ordinarily it is used for irony or humor, as in:

. . . D. Iñigo de Loyola . . . se fué sobre él espada en mano, y *si el moro no se salva por pies*, le infunde el convencimiento en el alma por estilo tremendo. (69)

Bien pudiera conversar con Dios con plena seguridad, *si* el enemigo no viniese a pelear contra mí en el mismo santuario. (74–75)

Así hubiera seguido largo tiempo *si* no llega Antoñona. (118)

. . . no faltaría quien le calificase de apócrifo, *si no se supiese* con la mayor evidencia *todo esto que aquí se refiere*, y *si no constasen*, además, los prodigios de que es capaz el ingénito despejo de una mujer. . . . (138)

¡Alabado sea Dios, que ha querido que el desengaño de Luisito llegue a tiempo! ¡Mal clérigo hubiera sido *si no acude* tan en sazón Pepita Jiménez! (182)

That the stylistic means treated above are taken by Valera from Cervantes is made more probable by other general Cervantine reminiscences in the novel. Apart from the direct mention of charac-

[99] Cf. *ibid.*, pp. 63–77.

ters—Micomicona (128), Don Quijote and the Caballero de la Blanca Luna (184)—other allusions or phrases are evocative of the *Quijote*: Amadís and Oriana (which also recalls *Amadís de Gaula*, of course) (37); "*Babieca*, . . . *Bucéfalo*, y . . . los propios caballos del Sol . . ." (67; cf. *DQ* VII, 59); ". . . mi padre . . . , ejerciendo mero y mixto imperio como cacique . . ." (41; cf. *DQ* VIII, 88); "¡ . . . esas majaderías que ahí estás ensartando!" (116; cf. *DQ* II, 286); ". . . la flor y nata de los elegantes . . ." (127); and ". . . con ojos de mochuelo . . ." (201; cf. *DQ* VI, 331). Although the phrases are only peripheral, since it is difficult to know how much they are a part of the language now, there can be little doubt that Valera was thoroughly familiar with Cervantes's great novel and that his debt to Cervantes is a significant one. The fact that Valera made use not of many obviously Cervantine phrases, but rather of important and well-assimilated devices and techniques, indicates his avoidance of artificiality.

In this chapter, I have pointed out the *Siglo de Oro* stylistic expressions utilized by Valera and shown how he used them. My guiding principle has been not merely to disclose sources, although that too is important for the historical derivation of the major forms of expression, but to arrive at a better understanding of the functional values of these forms and to attain a better aesthetic appreciation of the novel as a whole. In *Pepita Jiménez* there are many words and phrases that are evocative of the *Siglo de Oro* either because they are archaic, or near-archaic, or because they perceptibly belong to older language and style, but also because Valera shuns linguistic innovation and resorts to clichés, particularly manifested in stereotyped comparisons and epithet-substantive combinations, and to conventional descriptive methods. Yet Valera, who in his stylistic choice among synonymic possibilities is careful to avoid exaggeration, prefers to select words and locutions that are elegant and *castizos* in his desire to suggest or evoke an older, more classical style rather than to make a mannered imitation of it. The same is true of borrowed devices, formulas, and other means, many of which —the use of *pluralidades*, especially the binary and ternary constructions with frequent amplification, the controlled enumerations, the logical summation phrases, and the various attenuating phrases—may be grouped under the heading, "classical mitigation," as a result of their general though not exclusively mitigating functions in both Valera and in writers of the *Siglo de Oro.* As for other characteristics of *Siglo de Oro* prose style in Valera's novel, he shows, more than his contemporaries, a marked predilection for the *cursus tardus* and, in conjunction with it, proparoxytones and the absolute superlative, often used for irony; rhyme, assonance, and alliteration, especially in verb doublets; repetition in close proximity of the same word; and the end-position of the finite verb, often indicative of intense emotion. I also compared the subtle parody, the refined irony, and the treatment of the reality problem in *Pepita Jiménez* to the more drastic, more obvious parody and irony of *Don Quijote.* All these assimilated borrowings and influences, however, are subjected to Valera's avoidance of affectation, to his true classical restraint, and to his psychological and ironical-critical purposes.

The mitigating devices mentioned, along with playful or guilt-concealing euphemisms and attenuating digressions, are part of an interior stiltedness in Luis (and to a lesser degree, in Pepita) which is the result of an attempted concealment of true feelings and attitudes, almost all of which are closely related to Luis's inhibited love for Pepita or to his relations with his father. Hence the smooth, symmetrical exterior of the style, which veils the inner passion and which may be used for rationalization, contributes to the novel's ambiguity. Valera, in his avoidance of extremes, keeps things on the borderline of sincere representation and irony; thus the parody itself is such a subtle one that many of the pseudo-mystical or otherwise parodistic passages are only discernible as being so on close examination. To this essential ambiguity is attributable much of the novel's aesthetic value, just as the psychological validity of Luis's characterization is dependent upon the self-deluding, self-revealing manner in which he represents his contradictory emotions.

PART TWO

Adolescent Psychology through Critical Empathy

PREMISES

Although Valera often followed the *Siglo de Oro* tradition in his choice of expressions, he broke completely away from it in his treatment of youth and love, to which he imparted modern implications of eroticism, guilt, and inhibitions. According to Pfandl, the traditional love story in Spain was one of pure, innocent love, without the exclusion of the love of God and of one's neighbor, ". . . al servicio de altos ideales, lleno de alegre abnegación, para el cual ningún obstáculo era demasiado grande y ninguna empresa difícil. . . ."[1] Cervantes's foremost precursor in this tradition was Jerónimo de Contreras, whose *Selva de aventuras* relates the love of Luzmán and Arbolea which is renounced for divine love after the adventures and travails of Luzmán.[2] In this novel, as well as in Cervantes's *Persiles y Sigismunda*, there is an ascetical-mystical note, resulting from the subordination of pure and noble human love to divine love.[3] Pfandl's observations on the *Selva de aventuras* show by contrast how far Valera was from Contreras's concepts of human love and physical beauty: ". . . Luzmán es el símbolo del espíritu purificado del peso de la tierra por el sufrimiento de esta vida, al cual eleva hasta sí el amor celestial triunfando del terrenal. Depuración en el dolor para

[1] Ludwig Pfandl, *Historia de la literatura nacional española en la Edad de Oro*, trans. Jorge Rubió Balaguer, 2nd ed. (Barcelona: Gustavo Gili, 1952), p. 56.

[2] Jerónimo de Contreras, *Selva de aventuras*, in *Novelistas anteriores a Cervantes*, 2nd ed., "Biblioteca de Autores Españoles," vol. 3 (Madrid: Imprenta de la Publicidad, 1849), pp. 471–505.

[3] Pfandl, *Historia de la literatura*, p. 70.

alcanzar un mundo mejor, tal es el profundo sentido. . . . La belleza corporal se considera sólo como una imagen de la espiritual, de la del cielo, alejada de la tierra; el amor terreno sólo tiene valor y significación en sentido sobrenatural."[4]

Cervantes followed Contreras's pattern in *Persiles y Sigismunda*, but, under the influence of the Byzantine novel, he has the hero and heroine, who from all indications were going to renounce human love, marry at the last moment. This ending is considered a flaw by Pfandl, who believes that renunciation would have been the proper solution.[5] However, the characters in these novels are so symbolic and so idealized that relatively little psychological insight is attained. Probably the most psychologically accurate representation of youth and love in the *Siglo de Oro* takes place in *Don Quijote*.[6] The sanctity of young lovers' relations is maintained in the *Quijote*, but the characters are less ideal and more believable. The most charming depiction of young love in it is of Don Luis and Doña Clara, both of whom are adolescents, being sixteen or younger (*DQ* IV, chs. 42–44). It is interesting to note that, although there are other young couples presented in the novel—the captain and Zoraida, Don Gregorio and Ana Félix—in none of these cases is there more than a suggested depiction of adolescent love, since all the couples are represented as already being in love when they come on the scene. They report, usually in a rather formal way, how they came to fall in love; thus the treatment must be sketchy. True psychological depiction of adolescent love studies its inception.

The seventeenth-century love novel, with minor exceptions, follows Cervantes's models, notwithstanding an occasional element of coarse sensuality, as in the novels of María de Zayas y Sotomayor. The main trend, however, is better exemplified by Pérez de Montalbán's *La fuerza del desengaño*, a novel in which the *desengaño*, a revelation of the other life, causes the two lovers, according to

[4] *Ibid.*, p. 96. See also p. 281, where Pfandl says the same thing about the *Persiles*. Both of these "novelas simbólicas amorosas" are placed in the tradition of Heliodorus.

[5] *Ibid.*, pp. 284–285.

[6] Cf. Helmut Hatzfeld, *El "Quijote" como obra de arte del lenguaje* (Madrid: Patronato del IV Centenario del Nacimiento de Cervantes, 1949), pp. 387–393.

Contreras's pattern, to withdraw to the cloister.[7] The most significant novelists between the seventeenth century and Valera, Padre Isla and Fernán Caballero, do not take up the problem of young lovers, and the excellent psychology of Leandro Fernández de Moratín's plays, especially *El sí de las niñas*, is primarily one of the relations between youth and age.[8] Among Spanish romantics, depictions of young love stress the inevitability of love and the ill-fated circumstances surrounding it which drive the protagonists to a half-hearted rebelliousness. Psychological verisimilitude is not a primary concern.

It seems that the originality of the treatment of young love in *Pepita Jiménez* is in large measure achieved as a consequence of the very way in which Valera differs from the *Siglo de Oro* tradition—in his ironical-critical treatment of inhibited love, with erotic overtones, and in his ridiculing of the sublimation of human love. He scoffs at the idea that human love is sinful and must be rejected for divine love, though he read and grew to admire the mystics and the Spanish novel of the *Siglo de Oro*. Thus he makes the forces of nature work against what he would consider a sin against nature. Transcending the restricting possibilities of the *Siglo de Oro*, in which the treatment of psychological problems was usually awkward or exaggerated, as in the description of Don Quijote's monomania, Valera wrote the first modern psychological novel in Spanish literature. In this part, then, I shall try to show first what the novel's psychological validity consists of, how it is achieved, and what its aesthetic value is. Then I shall discuss other modern aspects of the novel and its author.

[7] On the love novel of the seventeenth century, see Pfandl, *Historia de la literatura*, pp. 354–375.

[8] We may note that Valera was also interested in this problem, which is alluded to in the case of Don Pedro and Pepita and in the story of Pepita's first marriage. But it is treated more fully in other novels by Valera.

CHAPTER III: *Psychology and Characterization*

If there was little to serve Valera as a guide for his psychological study among his Spanish predecessors, he was no doubt acquainted with foreign novelists highly proficient in psychological characterization, such as Manzoni, Benjamin Constant, Stendhal, and Flaubert, all of whom he mentioned often in his critical writings. In France, however, especially before Flaubert and the Goncourts, the emphasis was placed on the psychology of love, but not necessarily adolescent love. Justin O'Brien even says of nineteenth-century French literature that the child did not enter it until the romantic period, that little distinction was made between childhood and adolescence, and that no adequate representation of adolescent psychology appeared except three early, autobiographical, and, in his view, unsuccessful novels: Balzac's *Louis Lambert* (1832), Flaubert's *Novembre* (1842), and Taine's *Etienne Mayran* (1861–1862).[1] O'Brien continues to discuss briefly the beginnings of the novel of adolescence in other countries, for instance, in England with Dickens's *Oliver Twist* (1837) and *David Copperfield* (1849) and George Eliot's

[1] Justin O'Brien, *The Novel of Adolescence in France* (New York: Columbia Univ. Press, 1937), pp. 4–5. This excellent study, which concisely presents the principal characteristics of adolescence, is all the more valuable for our purposes because it deals with literature.

Mill on the Floss (1860), in Russia with Tolstoy and Dostoevsky. He concludes, nevertheless, that truly significant novels of adolescence were not written until the last decade of the nineteenth century and the first few decades of the twentieth. For Spanish literature he cites several works by Unamuno, Azorín, and others in the twentieth century, but nothing from the nineteenth. Hence, if it can be established that *Pepita Jiménez* is a valid and artistic novel of adolescence, Valera can be shown to have been well ahead of his time in Spain and among the first in Europe to depict adolescent psychology successfully.

Valera meets the qualifications for the psychological novelist because he is able to attain at least a semidetached point of view and to permit Luis to speak for himself. That this is a prime requisite may be witnessed by Flaubert's statement: "The artist ought to be in his work like God in creation, invisible and all-powerful; let him be felt everywhere but not seen."[2] Although it would be a mistake to equate Valera's and Flaubert's attitudes, one way in which Valera attains a degree of this pseudo- or quasi-objectivity is his ironical use of the traditional lying-preface technique, but a far more important one is the use of the epistolary method, which supposedly resulted in the accidental foundation of the psychological novel by Samuel Richardson.[3] Luis writes like a confused seminarian, not like Valera; thus the reader is in closer proximity to the character's thought processes and emotions.

I. A STUDY IN CHARACTERIZATION: LUIS DE VARGAS

A. *Luis the Adolescent*

José F. Montesinos remarks in passing that Luis's daydreams and ambitions are "... adolescencia pura, ensueños de pubertad casi. ..."[4]

[2] Quoted by Leon J. Edel, *The Psychological Novel: 1900–1950* (New York: J. B. Lippincott, 1955), p. 32.

[3] *Ibid.*, p. 39. This theory is subject to modifications, as will be seen later.

[4] José F. Montesinos, *Valera o la ficción libre* (Madrid: Gredos, 1957), p. 118.

Similar remarks are occasionally found among the critics, but no one has studied Luis as an adolescent. In order to determine to what extent Luis's behavior and attitudes are typically adolescent, I shall follow Justin O'Brien's major categories: the physical awakening, the sympathetic impulse, the egoistic impulse, and spiritual unrest and disillusion. As a rule, these characteristics form a composite drawn from many novels and novelists, and not all of them are to be found in each novel. Nor should one expect to find them all in *Pepita Jiménez*, not only for this reason but also because O'Brien's conclusions are based on the behavior of adolescents in French novels, and one may presuppose some national differences. Likewise, Luis is more than an adolescent; as an individual, there are other complicating factors in his makeup. In spite of these reservations, the similarities between Luis's behavior and the conclusions reached by O'Brien are remarkable.

O'Brien further defines the adolescent as follows: "He is torn between the need of recognizing authority, of conforming, and of imitating and the equally insistent need of throwing off authority and establishing his independence through solitude, flight into the world of the imagination, or open revolt. From this conflict of impulses, from this disequilibrium which in some cases may be resolved into some sort of stability at eighteen and in others not until after the twenty-first or even the twenty-fifth year, arise uncertainty, spiritual restlessness, and often great disillusion."[5] The fact that Luis is twenty-two years old does not prevent his still being an adolescent. Furthermore, the last twelve years that he has spent in the seclusion of the seminary and, mentally, in his dreamworld, have retarded his development; but as soon as he returns to his native town, his sensibility and awareness are heightened a hundredfold and his progression to maturity becomes rapid.

1. THE PHYSICAL AWAKENING. About this essential phase of adolescence, O'Brien tells us: "The greatest difficulty confronting an

See also p. 116 and p. 124, where Montesinos mentions the ". . . ensueños de una adolescencia morbosamente sobreexcitada. . . ."

[5] O'Brien, *The Novel of Adolescence*, p. 13.

author who chooses an adolescent hero was pointed out by Albert Thibaudet when he said that such a hero must feel and love as an adolescent, that the emphasis must be on the fact that he is *beginning* to feel and love."[6] There can be no doubt that the very beginnings of these feelings are depicted in Luis; from the first letter on he speaks of how much more he enjoys the beauty of the country around the town, the walks he takes, and the various outings. He also shows interest in the agricultural tasks connected with his father's farm and vineyard. In general, he evinces a new awareness of nature. He experiences a strange fear, an ill-defined sense of remorse because of his feelings of tenderness and enthusiasm on entering a leafy bower, on hearing the birds sing, or on seeing the flowers and stars, realizing that the result is an unaccustomed sensual pleasure (31).

At this stage, his poetic sensibility has not yet found an object; he has a feeling of lassitude, a loss of will, and is easily moved to tears, a fact which also frightens him (33). But these feelings are soon related to the awakening of eroticism, for ". . . in the maze of conflicting impulses . . . the adolescent encounters no greater problem than the one of adapting himself to his new sexual instinct."[7] After the visit to the Pozo de la Solana, during which he had observed so well the physical attractiveness of Pepita and her maids, Luis again mentions his new tenderness: ". . . la ternura de mi corazón, que no se fija en un objeto condigno, que no se emplea y consume en lo que debiera, brota y como que rebosa en ocasiones por objetos que tienen mucho de pueriles, que me parecen ridículos, y de los cuales me avergüenzo" (42). This passage illustrates the difference between Luis and the ordinary adolescent: because of his commitment to the priesthood and his training at the seminary, he is much more capable of self-criticism. Simultaneously, his keener sense of guilt produces interior conflicts. He is cognizant that his tender sentiments do not have a suitable object, as they should have; but he is more prone to rationalize and is less willing to admit that

[6] *Ibid.*, p. 116. O'Brien refers to Albert Thibaudet's article "Réflexions sur le roman," *La Nouvelle Revue Francaise*, VIII (1912), 213–220.

[7] O'Brien, *The Novel of Adolescence*, p. 143.

Pepita is becoming the object of his love. A further complexity is produced by his pride, for these things and others appear childish and ridiculous and make him ashamed. The rest of the passage is deeply significant in that, apart from becoming emotional upon hearing some lovesick peasant sing, he has begun to feel an "insane" compassion for such things as small birds taken from their nest or a calf with a broken leg.

Valera has Luis describe his love from the first moment; even before knowing her, Luis is filled with prurient curiosity about the attractive, wealthy young widow and her marital relations with Don Gumersindo. He feels vague longings and becomes the unconscious rival of his father before his awakened eroticism is progressively manifested in his visual perception of Pepita, in their first meeting alone, and in the exchange of ardent looks. Nor does Valera neglect the other senses in the representation of Luis's growing love: "No es ella grata a mis ojos solamente, sino que sus palabras suenan en mis oídos como la música de las esferas, . . . y hasta imagino percibir una sutilísima fragancia que su limpio cuerpo despide . . ." (86). After the manhood ritual of riding *Lucero*, the implications resulting from the sense of touch are gradually developed, beginning with the touch of Pepita's hand, which becomes increasingly meaningful: "Cuando Pepita y yo nos damos la mano, no es ya como al principio. Ambos hacemos un esfuerzo de voluntad y nos transmitimos, por nuestras diestras enlazadas, todas las palpitaciones del corazón. Se diría que, por arte diabólico, obramos una transfusión y mezcla de lo más sutil de nuestra sangre. Ella debe de sentir circular mi vida por sus venas, como yo siento en las mías la suya" (89). Next, after their knees have touched "by chance" several times (90), the first embrace is briefly described: "Acerqué mis labios a su cara para enjugar el llanto, y se unieron nuestras bocas en un beso. Inefable embriaguez, *desmayo fecundo en peligros* invadió todo mi ser y el ser de ella. Su cuerpo desfallecía y la sostuve entre mis brazos" (97). Luis is aware of the danger and makes a new effort to overcome his love, saying that it is only a trial: "Lejos de Pepita me voy serenando y creyendo que tal vez ha sido una prueba este comienzo de amores" (98). It is significant that Valera uses the phrase "comienzo de amores." Before the discoveries of modern psychology, he knew intuitively the enormous importance of sex in an awakened sensibility or in any kind of flirtation. Valera is also conscious that Luis is an adolescent, for, in addition to referring to him often as a *colegial* or as a *joven teólogo*, he uses the words "adolescencia" (162, line 23) and "juvenil" (165, line 3).

The typical conflict of masculine and feminine physical characteristics in the adolescent, who is often distinguished by a pale skin, by little hirsute growth on the face, and by a childish voice, the type who is ordinarily the passive agent in his sentimental relations, is observed in Luis too.[8] While in the Casino, he tries to behave with an authority that ". . . ni sus años juveniles, ni su rostro, donde había más bozo que barbas, . . . consentían . . ." (130), and his father jocularly calls him a "teólogo barbilampiño" (199). Luis on several occasions tries to speak in a grave, solemn tone, which may mean that his voice is not fully developed yet. Valera does not tell us precisely what kind of voice Luis has, but certain sound patterns in his letters reveal immaturity of speech, if not of voice, as in: "Todo me parece más chico, mucho más chico, pero también más bonito que el recuerdo que tenía" (5). Yet he does not have the excessively white skin; rather his complexion is dark and Valera states that his bearing is manly (144). Although Montesinos states that Luis is passive, that he is treated like a woman, and that this explains the success of his portrayal since Valera is better at characterizing women than men, it seems more appropriate to relate the feminine elements of his makeup, which are not exaggerated anyway, to his adolescence.[9]

In France, not until after World War I are the visible physical and temperamental effects of the change in the adolescent described, that is, ". . . the ill health, the dark rings under the eyes, the irritability, the depression, the overwhelming disgust with everything."[10] These effects are not so much described in *Pepita Jiménez* as alluded to. Luis writes: "Hace días que no pongo los pies en casa de Pepita, que no la veo. Casi no tengo que pretextar una enfermedad porque

[8] Cf. *ibid.*, pp. 130–131.

[9] Montesinos, *Valera o la ficción libre*, pp. 119, 121.

[10] O'Brien, *The Novel of Adolescence*, pp. 121–122.

realmente estoy enfermo. Estoy pálido y ojeroso . . ." (91). A few days before his projected departure, and after having endured the Count's derision, Luis has become silent and melancholy, has no appetite, spends much time in his room, and gives vent to his irritation upon the entry of Antoñona (133–134). Previous mentions are made of his condition: "No sé cómo el mal que padezco no me sale a la cara. Apenas me alimento; apenas duermo" (88).

According to O'Brien, "When the adolescent finally has had his first sexual experience with a woman, he often looks back and congratulates himself on having left behind the period of indistinct desires and warped instincts."[11] To some extent this happens to Luis; he laughs at his illusions of mysticism and at his former plans. Likewise, what happened to him is no longer referred to as a fall, with the accompanying moral implications, but as a *change*, which has a psychological force. Two elements lacking in Luis are often found in the adolescents of French novels: deviation from the normal sexual instinct and the dissociation of love and sex, although the dissociation does not always occur—this is true, for instance, of Colette's *Le Blé en herbe.*[12]

Some general characteristics of the adolescent are: the fear of the unknown and forbidden, the conflict between new boldness and natural timidity, the invasion of sex into all phases of life, the gradual loss of inhibitions, the exaggeration common to novices, the simultaneous repelling and attracting influence of the loved person, the fleeing from direct temptation, and the seeking for vicarious pleasure.[13] Most of these elements, in varying degrees, are found in Luis. He at once hates and loves Pepita (63, 90), and throughout the novel he attempts to avoid temptation, at least mentally, by justifying his new emotions. He frequently mentions that he does not wish to go to Pepita's house and only goes at his father's insistence; however, such statements can not be taken too seriously, since they may be mere excuses. Undoubtedly he experiences fear and terror. At times the fear is related to his increased sensibility, as when he speaks of the

[11] *Ibid.*, p. 133.
[12] See *ibid.*, pp. 130, 139, and 174, on these three points, respectively.
[13] *Ibid.*, pp. 119–120.

"... *terror* misterioso de las horas nocturnas" (61); at others it is connected with his love, as when he awakes frightened (88). It is also directly related to his initiation into sex, since before and after the crisis it is mentioned: "Conforme se iba acercando, se aumentaba el *terror* que le infundía lo que se determinaba a hacer" (147); and "Al cabo de un largo rato, D. Luis apareció de nuevo, saliendo de la obscuridad. En su rostro se veía pintado el *terror*; algo de la desesperación de Judas" (170). Quite similar to this is the idea of the great mystery of life, which for the adolescent is sex.[14] We may remember that Luis makes frequent remarks about mysteries and that in the first letter he is no doubt alluding to sex when he speaks of "otros misterios" of Pepita's married life (13). Perhaps his concept of Pepita's magic powers, of the way she mesmerizes him, is also involved. Luis begins to overcome his timidity and, to some extent, his inhibitions, by learning to ride horseback, to play cards, and by participating in other diversions. These are the first assertions of his growing manhood, which lead up to the decisive call on Pepita and the subsequent duel. The duel, then, is not purely melodramatic, for it shows the final stage of his development. After experiencing love and renouncing his previous plans, he must defend Pepita against all offenders.

2. THE INTELLECTUAL AND SPIRITUAL AWAKENING. Although the intellectual and spiritual awakening ordinarily follows or occurs at the same time as the physical change, the reverse is true of Luis on account of his training. When the story begins he is already in an arrested precrisis stage of adolescence, since several allusions are made in the novel to his former daydreams and other traits of adolescence. Nevertheless, the characteristics of this stage of development are manifested in Luis too: all the faculties are subordinated to the imagination and even his reasoning is emotional; he has a keen desire for personal glory; he exhibits a marked propensity to imitate and a great tendency toward abstract thought.[15]

It is clear that Luis's overwrought imagination and fantasy are

[14] *Ibid.*, p. 143.
[15] See *ibid.*, pp. 147–154.

constantly at work. When he meets Pepita in the secluded wooded area, he is thinking of the patriarchs, of the pagan heroes and shepherds, and of the apparitions of nymphs, deities, and angels (61–62). Thus he immediately associates Pepita with these daydreams, imagining that she is a sorceress, and later compares her sudden appearance to the famous apparitions or visions of pagan and Christian literature (66–67). The most remarkable work of his imagination, of course, is to have deluded himself into mistaking sensuality and fantasy for mystical experiences. Also, the long speech stating that for years he has lived in his imagination, in the castles of his dreamworld, with the most exquisite and ideal women possible, discloses both his present and past propensity to daydream. We have seen the fantasy of these passages, many of which are used for rationalization and the concealment of guilt. Similarly, Luis's reasoning powers may serve as an excuse to satisfy the demands of his emotions or sensuality, which is simply another form of rationalization. For instance, in order to speak of Pepita, he says of his father: "Apenas si se atreve a decir a Pepita 'buenos ojos tienes'; y en verdad que si lo dijese no mentiría . . ." (38). This is used as a "logical" starting point for a long description of her eyes and a renewed curiosity about why she married Don Gumersindo, thus manifesting Luis's latent and recurring jealousy concerning Don Gumersindo and Pepita's virginity. In another case, the self-deluding description has no logical connection with Pepita's sincerity: "Hay sinceridad y candor en Pepita Jiménez. No hay más que verla para creerlo así. Su andar airoso y reposado, su esbelta estatura . . ." (48). In regard to personal ambition and desire for glory, both elements, as we saw, are contained in Luis's concept of his mission.

Luis has a strong propensity for imitation of others since, in addition to emulating the mystics, he also associates himself with and tries to imitate St. John Chrysostom, St. Vincent Ferrer, St. Edward, and Philemon, to mention but a few. Among the people he actually knows, he has in all probability imitated his uncle in his decision to become a priest and continues to do so for a time after leaving the seminary. Gradually, however, and despite the animosity he bears toward his father, he transfers his ideal from his uncle to his father.

This transference of affection may be seen in the sixth and seventh letters (49–70), since it is here that Luis fully asserts his independence from his uncle, defending himself against the latter's accusations and even blaming him for having made them. The first major step in the imitation of his father is that of learning to ride a horse, and while the lessons take place the natural bond of affection between father and son is strengthened. At the same time, Luis seems to derive a vicarious pleasure from writing of his father's youthful misadventures, his escapades with women, and his present irreverent remarks; but almost immediately he feels guilty about this and adds some afterthought like: "Me pesa en el alma de que mi padre sea así . . ." (70). From this point on, his relations with Pepita are bettered and he imitates his father more and more, learning to play cards, enamoring a woman, and having a duel, all of which activities Don Pedro had performed as a youth.

No doubt Luis, as a seminarian, even more than the typical adolescent, shows a marked tendency toward abstract thought, as is noticed in the various philosophical and spiritual passages and in the dialogue with Pepita. Another characteristic of the adolescent, increased self-knowledge and awareness, directly related to a new love of the world and nature, is also applicable to Luis; in fact, his self-discovery and adjustment to his social and physical environment could be taken as the entire novel's theme.

3. THE SYMPATHETIC IMPULSE. Luis's imitation of others and desire to adapt himself are part of an almost universal sympathy and of a general exteriorization of the ego; thus he feels the urge to get outside his own personality, to identify and to associate himself with others.[16] The adolescent's first step beyond heightened sensibility and vague sympathy is to form friendships, usually with someone like himself of approximately his own age. In *Pepita Jiménez* this process is alluded to in Luis's growing friendship with his cousin Currito, who frequently enters Luis's room to take him somewhere, such as to the Casino. After seeing Luis ride *Lucero*, Currito formed

[16] See *ibid.*, pp. 162–176, for O'Brien's discussion of these and related topics to be dealt with here.

a "superhuman concept" of Luis and now idolizes him: "A D. Luis, que era el ídolo de Currito, le sucedía como a todas las naturalezas superiores con los seres inferiores que se les aficionan. Don Luis se dejaba querer; esto es, era dominado despóticamente por Currito en los negocios de poca importancia. Y como para hombre como D. Luis casi no hay negocios que la tengan en la vida vulgar y diaria, resultaba que Currito llevaba y traía a don Luis como un zarandillo" (126). Since Currito also went along on the excursions and regularly attended Pepita's *tertulias*, we may assume that the relationship between the two was a significant one, although, to be sure, it is not described in detail as, for instance, the relationship between Jacques Thibault and Daniel Fontanin in Roger Martin du Gard's *Les Thibault* is.

Another aspect of the sympathetic impulse is the wish to confide in someone, preferably in the adolescent friend; but in Luis's case, no suggestion is made that Currito filled the role of confidant.[17] Nevertheless, the frequent and intimate conversations between Luis and the Vicar indicate that the latter satisfied that need, along with Luis's curiosity in regard to Pepita. We find out what the Vicar tells Luis about Pepita, though only indirectly do we know what Luis may have told the Vicar.[18] Of course, Luis's greatest confidant is the Dean, in whom he confides almost everything by means of his letters.

The adolescent's attraction to an older woman, through timidity or through identification of her with his mother, is only partially true of Luis. Although Pepita is young, she has the added appeal of being a widow and of occupying the role of an older person in the community because of her wealth and social leadership. The carryover of Luis's childhood oedipal conflict, still manifested by resentment of his father, to the latter's new relations with Pepita seems to be one of the ways in which Luis identifies Pepita with his mother; the other way is the similar idealization of the two, who are directly related to the ideal woman of his daydreams.

[17] Cf. *ibid.*, p. 168.

[18] On these two points, see, for example, *Pepita Jiménez*, pp. 43–49 and p. 109, lines 27–30.

4. THE EGOISTIC IMPULSE. In speaking of the adolescent's "maze of contradictions," of his desire to get outside himself and to assert himself at the same time, O'Brien remarks: "Attractions toward the exterior world and reaction against it—contrasts of this kind are so common in adolescence that they appear as one of the characteristics of that period; the happy realization of new tendencies seems to require the opposition, either successive or simultaneous, of contradictory tendencies. Thus the egoistic and the sympathetic impulses develop side by side. . . . "[19] Luis's chameleonic nature is somewhat difficult to establish since the narration is not continuous, but rather is given from successive points in time in the first half of the novel. However, between one letter and another fluctuations may occur, as when Luis, after earlier remarks that he was bored with his monotonous life in the town, makes such statements as: "En fin, hay aquí una holganza tan encantadora, que más no puede ser. Las diversiones son muchas . . ." (55); and "La vida de aquí tiene cierto encanto" (56). A significant change, a more open admission of how much he was enjoying himself, is also indicated. Luis vacillates within the same letter too. For instance, at the beginning of the seventh letter he claims that in small towns it is difficult to isolate oneself (54), but he modifies this remark: "Hasta la soledad puede lograrse aquí haciendo un esfuerzo" (56). In the same letter he reports other variations: "Me *alegré* de ver a Pepita tan gallarda a caballo; pero desde luego presentí y *empezó a mortificarme* el desairado papel que me tocaba hacer . . ." (59). Then his rage and mortification are forgotten after his conversation with Pepita, and he is serene during the return (66). At one moment Valera represents Luis as being angry after his verbal clash with the Count, but in the midst of his wrath and ill-humor Luis laughs at the memory of comic teaching methods and passes on to happier thoughts (130–131). In a similar way, although it is not always possible to take his statements at face value, Luis's attitudes toward his father, Pepita, and even the Dean vary from direct criticism to open admiration or praise. Of course, the kaleidoscopic nature of his love for Pepita, of his vacillations be-

[19] O'Brien, *The Novel of Adolescence*, p. 177. Also see pp. 177–188 on these matters in general.

tween love and hate, between confidence of victory and abject despair, and between innocence and guilt, is nowhere better observed than in the last seven letters (76–101). Such fluctuations, however, are only part of Luis's overall pattern of self-contradiction, a matter which I shall treat in another context.

Three additional manifestations of the egoistic impulse are also seen in Luis: revolt, escape through imagination, and self-isolation.[20] In a sense, Luis has already rebelled when the novel begins, for, against his father's wishes, he has decided to be a priest. Don Pedro discloses that this is so in a letter to his brother, "Tú fuiste más allá de mis esperanzas y aún de mis deseos, y por poco no sacas de Luisito un Padre de la Iglesia" (199–200), and Luis half admits it in the first letter (18–19). But in the rest of the novel Luis's rebelliousness is indicated by criticism and an underlying note of animosity, as in the following passage: ". . . me dijo que era muy rico y que me dejaría mejorado, aunque tuviese varios hijos más. Yo le respondí que para los planes y fines de mi vida necesitaba harto poco dinero, y que mi mayor contento sería verle dichoso con mujer e hijos, olvidado de sus antiguos devaneos" (24). It is not hard to imagine that this answer was given in a tone of stiff-lipped resentment. Luis's escape through imagination, already mentioned, is bound up with his self-isolation, which is revealed in the fact that he often takes walks alone or shuts himself up in his room. Several references are made to persons entering his room (54, 95, 100, 125, and 134) and to his withdrawal to his room: "—¡Esta flor le faltaba al ramo!—murmuró . . . D. Luis cuando llegó a su casa, y volvió a meterse en su cuarto . . ." (130); and "Solo ya D. Luis, dejó el comedor para no ver a nadie, y volvió al retiro de su estancia para abismarse más profundamente en sus ideas" (134). Such passages also indicate another characteristic of the adolescent, that of spending much time in idleness, satisfied to be engaged in daydreams.

5. OTHER ADOLESCENT CHARACTERISTICS. Unrest and disillusion are common traits in the adolescent. Luis's constant vacillations and interior contradictions amply illustrate his restlessness. The loss

[20] *Ibid.*, p. 178.

of illusions is evidenced by the impossibility of his becoming a priest and a missionary and, successively, of imitating St. Edward, St. Vincent Ferrer, and Philemon. Don Pedro also refers to his son's disillusion (209–212). The resulting desire of suicide, supposedly characteristic of the adolescent after his loss of illusion, does not occur in Luis's case, not only because of his firm Catholic faith but also because he felt a sense of liberation more than total disillusionment.

Perhaps nothing betrays Luis's immaturity so much as his conscious effort to convince himself and others that he is quite mature and that he knows the ways of the world and of women. We may recall that when he says to Pepita, "Desde que vivo, desde que soy hombre, y ya hace años, pues no es tan grande mi mocedad . . ." (164), his pretended maturity is belied by the naive things he tells Pepita about his adolescent daydreams. Several times he pretends to be more experienced than he is: ". . . no soy tímido y conozco las miserias y locuras de esta vida . . ." (7); "Aquí, como en todas partes, la gente es muy aficionada al dinero" (13); and "Me alegro de no ser cándido . . ." (17). He thinks that he knows feminine psychology too, as when he remarks that his father is especially attractive to women because of his past conquests (7–8) or speaks of the *instinto adivinatorio* of women, particularly of young girls, no matter how candid they are (11). He believes that Pepita is perfectly natural and that only a great actress could feign such simplicity of action and dress (38); yet the reader finds out later what he already expected—that her naturalness is a studied one, the result of much preparation (152–153). In contradistinction to these pretenses, Luis states his true ignorance by saying that in the seminary he had only dealt with his companions and teachers and that he knew nothing of the world except by speculation and theory (48–49). More significantly, his inexperience is revealed by his gullible belief in the time-worn threat that the woman will kill herself or die of lovesickness if rejected (137, 170).

The primary problem in the presentation of adolescent psychology is that the emphasis must be on the beginning of the new emotions and relationships. This Valera does, generally speaking, with considerable detail. Even for those actions or attitudes which are only alluded to, the implications are that they were both recurrent and progressive. Therefore we may conclude from the parallels between Luis's behavior and that of the typical adolescent, as outlined by O'Brien, that Valera skillfully depicted the psychology of adolescence in his portrayal of Luis.

B. *Complicating Factors*

The characterization of Luis as an adolescent remains incomplete if one does not consider three important complicating factors: his religious training and commitment to the priesthood, his illegitimacy, and his oedipal conflict. In conjunction with the ordinary adolescent vacillations and self-contradicting behavior, these three elements create great inner tensions in Luis, which are concealed, as we have seen, by exterior mitigating devices and stiltedness. The voice of his conscience, highly developed by his training and avowed purpose in life, constantly reminds him that his sensuality and new activities and thoughts are wrong; hence he tries to evade his feelings of guilt by self-delusion and by all sorts of excuses and rationalizations. The complications derived from this struggle and from Luis's relations with his father and mother are so great that the possibility of pathological behavior presented itself; yet to consider this possibility would surely be a mistake because Luis's disorder is neither sufficiently serious nor persistent to justify such an assumption.[21] Furthermore, ". . . it is nowhere more difficult than in adolescence to distinguish between the normal and the abnormal."[22]

1. RELIGIOUS TRAINING AND ILLEGITIMACY. The struggle within Luis is intensified by his previous training at the seminary, for he knows how wrong his new feelings are according to his purpose in life. Although he relates things to his knowledge of spiritual matters, instead of correcting his attitudes and behavior, this knowledge and

[21] Cf. Norman Cameron and Ann Margaret, *Behavior Pathology* (New York: Houghton Mifflin, 1951), p. 7: "Behavior pathology . . . involves reactions which render the individual persistently tense, dissatisfied, incompetent or ineffectual."

[22] O'Brien, *The Novel of Adolescence*, p. 192.

his conscience increase his guilt to such a point that he must excuse his behavior or drive his emotions underground. Thus almost any reference in the novel to his mission or to a saint or some other spiritual leader is fraught with ambiguity, since it may constitute an effort to resume his former way of life or to combat his new tendencies and simultaneously reveal an awareness of guilt and an attempted rationalization or self-delusion. Moreover, such statements may be related to the situation between Luis and his father, as in the following passage: "Cuando volvemos a casa de cualquiera de estas expediciones, *vuelvo a insistir con mi padre en mi ida con V.*, a fin de que llegue el suspirado momento de que yo me vea elevado al sacerdocio; *pero mi padre está tan contento* de tenerme a su lado . . . que halla siempre . . . fundado pretexto para retenerme aquí. . . . Me retiene contra mi gusto; *aunque* no debiera decir 'contra mi gusto,' porque le tengo muy grande en vivir con un padre que es para mí tan bueno" (41). In his wavering style, Luis begins by mentioning his mission in order to conceal how much he had enjoyed the outing to Pepita's *huerta.* Then he half blames his father for retaining him in the village against his will, but remembering his filial duty he negates this statement. Similar complications and vacillations are frequently prevalent in these remarks, as has been pointed out in relation to Luis's mission, his stiltedness, and the pseudo-spiritual passages.[23]

Luis's decision to become a priest is in part an escape mechanism, an effort to establish his independence from his father; more significantly, however, it is an atonement for the stain of illegitimate birth which normally even excludes one from the priesthood, according to canon law.[24] It is impossible to discuss this problem without mentioning the alluding nature of Valera's style. From the very first, we learn that Luis had been away from home for a long time, that he had been at the seminary with his father's brother, the Dean; but the question immediately raised—about why neither Luis nor his uncle had been to the town in all those years—is never answered.

[23] See *Pepita Jiménez,* pp. 131–133, 142, and 183–184 for longer examples of self-deluding rationalizations.

[24] Cf. Montesinos, *Valera o la ficción libre,* p. 117.

We may only conjecture that there is a certain feeling of animosity between Don Pedro and the Dean and that it may in some way be related to Luis's mother. On the other hand, since Don Pedro is the brother who seems to have inherited the landed property of the family, the Dean was perhaps a second son, as Valera was. Whatever the reasons for the rivalry between the two, it is certain that many of Luis's concepts of his father came to him via the Dean. This we know because of Luis's allusions to what the Dean had told him; for instance: "Aunque V. me tenía prevenido acerca de estas genialidades de mi padre, y de que por ellas había estado yo con V. doce años, desde los diez a los veintidós, todavía me aturden y desazonan los dichos de mi padre, sobrado libres a veces" (73). From this and similar remarks we may infer that the Dean had often spoken to Luis of his illegitimacy, about how his father was to blame, about his mother's being innocent, a martyr, and now an angel, and, in general, about the irreverence and scandalous behavior of his father, his reputation of being a Don Juan, etc. In all fairness to the Dean, it is not possible to separate the transforming effect of Luis's imagination from these concepts. Yet the fact remains that there is a feeling of rivalry between the two and that Luis's character has been partially molded by the rivalry.[25] The indirect way in which these relations are presented is equally true of most other interrelations among the characters.

Careful attention is required to grasp these relationships at first reading. Luis does not speak directly of his illegitimacy because his uncle already knows this and because of his own inhibitions. Yet he hints at the situation several times in the first letter. He speaks of his father's remaining a *soltero* (15, lines 4 and 13); he says that his father has recognized him (18, line 5); and he speaks of the "vínculo de la naturaleza" between them (18, line 27), which implies that there is no legal bond. As if to be absolutely sure that the readers comprehend this relationship, Valera remarks later: "Esta última injuria, que recordaba a D. Luis *la falta de su nacimiento*, y caía

[25] We may recall that Don Pedro wrote to the Dean that he would keep Luis with him this time, even by force, and that he was conspiring against his son's vocation (201). Also, the Dean refused to attend the wedding (203).

sobre el honor de la persona cuya memoria le era más querida y respetada . . ." (191). Also, he has Don Pedro write: "Cuando estaba yo en todo mi vigor no pensaba en las delicias domésticas . . ." (202). But if the reader becomes cognizant of Luis's illegitimacy only at this late stage, it is almost necessary for him to reread the entire novel for a full understanding. The same is true of the exchange of letters between the Dean and Don Pedro (198–202), which occurs chronologically perhaps after Luis's first three or four letters and which provides new insight into Don Pedro's insistence that Luis attend Pepita's *tertulia* and his happiness to learn that Luis, at Pepita's instigation, wished to learn to ride a horse (67), as well as into the reasons for similar passages. Of course, for the reader accustomed to puzzling out the meaning of twentieth-century novels, there is no great difficulty in grasping these relationships in *Pepita Jiménez*, although the ambiguity is nonetheless there.[26]

Luis twice asks himself if his desire to be a priest is not connected to his relations with his father and to his father's mistreatment of his suffering, angelic mother, whom he has undoubtedly romanticized. We are never told why there was no marriage, nor the details of the situation. We are not even certain that Luis even knew her; that is, whether she died sometime in his childhood or soon after his birth. The latter possibility is implied by the fact that as a child Luis had lived in his father's house (5) and by the visit of some five women, all of whom had been his nurses (6). With this stain of illegitimacy lurking in his unconscious, all references to his childhood or to his father become more meaningful. The strange fear, scruple, and remorse he now feels are related to his childhood and probably to fantasies about his mother (31). The awareness of his illegitimacy seems more important than any Platonic ideal (and even as important as his religious commitment) in determining his desire to have chaste relations with Pepita. If Don Pedro does not really love Pepita, he says, ". . . me alegraría de que Pepita permaneciese firme

[26] An indication of the ambiguity is M. Romera-Navarro's remark about Don Pedro: ". . . está para contraer segundas nupcias con cierta bella viudita." *Historia de la literatura española* (New York: D. C. Heath, 1928), p. 560. This error was corrected in subsequent editions.

en su *casta viudez*, y cuando yo estuviese muy lejos de aquí, allá en la India o en el Japón, o en algunas misiones más peligrosas, tendría un consuelo en escribirle algo sobre mis peregrinaciones y trabajos. Cuando, ya viejo, volviese yo por este lugar, también *gozaría mucho* en intimar con ella, que estaría ya vieja, y *en tener con ella coloquios espirituales y pláticas por el estilo de las que tiene ahora el padre Vicario*" (52–53). Luis wishes to emulate St. Edward, whose marriage was unconsummated: ". . . se figuraba que él iba a ser como San Eduardo, y que Pepita era como la reina Edita, su mujer; y bajo la forma y condición de la tal reina, *virgen a par de esposa*, si cabe, mucho más gentil, elegante y poética" (142). Luis expresses this ideal to Pepita also: "¿Por qué, . . . no se eleva V. hasta mí por virtud de ese mismo amor que me tiene, limpiándole de toda escoria? ¿Por qué no nos amamos entonces *sin vergüenza y sin pecado y sin mancha*?" (167). It seems that the awakened sensibility motivated by Luis's return home, by the memories of the circumstances of his birth, and by his adolescence culminates in a transference of the unresolved oedipal conflict of his childhood to the new object of both his and his father's affections, Pepita, thus reproducing in reality what had existed only in his mind or imagination before.[27]

2. OEDIPAL CONFLICT. Since there is no fixation or carry-over into maturity of Luis's infantile relationship, it is perhaps more appropriate to speak of his oedipus or oedipal conflict (relationship, etc.) than of a complex.[28] Whatever the terminology, it is certain that Luis was preoccupied not only with his illegitimacy but also with a potential father-son rivalry for the new object of their attention, Pepita. Luis's switch from third person narrative to the first person, *yo*, in his reporting of his father's statements about winning Pepita's love (25, line 32) already reveals his unconscious rivalry with his father. Then, in the following passage, the latent rivalry is manifested symbolically:

27 Having very few facts, we can merely conjecture about Luis's childhood. Cf. Mario Maurín, "Valera y la ficción encadenada," *Mundo Nuevo*, no. 14 (Aug., 1967), 35–44; no. 15 (Sept., 1967), 37–44.

28 Cf. Karl A. Menninger, *The Human Mind*, 3rd ed. (New York: Alfred A. Knopf, 1948), pp. 310–311.

El otro día cogieron los hijos del aperador de mi padre un nido de gorriones, y al ver yo *los pajarillos sin plumas aún y violentamente separados de la madre cariñosa*, sentí suma angustia, y, lo confieso, se me saltaron las lágrimas. Pocos días antes trajo del campo un rústico *una ternerita que se había perniquebrado*; iba a llevarla al matadero y venía a decir a mi padre qué quería de ella para su mesa: mi padre pidió unas cuantas libras de carne, la cabeza y las patas; *yo me conmoví al ver la ternerita, y estuve a punto, aunque la vergüenza lo impidió, de comprársela al hombre, a ver si la curaba y conservaba viva.* (42)

In the first case, Luis as a child was like a small bird violently separated from his mother, a separation for which his father was to blame, and in the second, the "ternerita que se había perniquebrado" symbolizes his mother. By buying the calf and keeping it alive, he could save it (and redeem his mother), while keeping his father from having it. If Luis is reliving his childhood experience, brought on by the disturbing fact that his father is planning to marry the attractive widow in whom he is already interested and who is largely responsible for his new emotional state, the analogy may be taken one degree farther, and the relationship becomes: *ternerita* = mother = Pepita. But his impulse to preserve the calf's life and ultimately to prevent his father from marrying Pepita is checked by his shame.

His substitution of his father in the relations with Pepita is expressed in other ways too. About Pepita's *tertulia*, he comments, with an underlying note of complaint: "Pepita juega al tresillo con mi padre, con el señor Vicario y con algún otro. Yo no sé de qué lado ponerme" (72). He also tells us that his father is teaching him to play cards (73), and by the next letter he has begun to replace his father in the card game: ". . . yo le sustituyo en la mesa al lado de Pepita" (79). The irony of the whole situation is, of course, that Don Pedro is doing everything possible to bring them together. Luis interprets this effort as his father's carelessness and belief that he (Luis) is not capable of enamoring Pepita, "sin querer" (82), and angrily compares his father's attitude to the cuckoldry of Marcus Aurelius (82).

Luis becomes aware of his conflict with Don Pedro for Pepita's love: ". . . si la mujer a quien mi padre pretende se prendase de mí, ¿no sería espantosa mi situación? Desechemos estos temores, fraguados, sin duda, por la vanidad. No hagamos de Pepita una Fedra y de mí un Hipólito" (82). The fact that this statement is negative does not gainsay the obvious parallel between Luis's situation and that of Hippolytus, although Luis is a more willing participant in love. Don Pedro in this connection, then, is Theseus, being superseded by his son. If we remember that Phaedra claimed to love in Hippolytus the replica of what Theseus was in his youth, a subsequent reference to this story assumes added significance, when it is said of Pepita: "Hubiera recordado a un poeta o a un artista la figura de Ariadna, . . . cuando Teseo la abandonó en la isla de Naxos" (117). The situation has now changed its perspective, however, for Pepita would have reminded a poet of Ariadne because she had been abandoned, or was to be abandoned, by Luis. Thus the sequence from the first allusion to the second is: Theseus = Don Pedro to Theseus = Luis, with Luis replacing his father in the affections of the loved woman. The classical alluding device is ironically climaxed by the most apt description possible of Antoñona's role: "Don Luis se paró a considerar la condición de Antoñona, y le pareció más aviesa que la de Enone y la de Celestina" (141). Valera's aesthetically pleasing way of presenting intricate relationships through cultural-literary references and allusions is also discernible in Luis's desire to emulate St. John Chrysostom: "Y recordaba, sobre todo, aquella entereza de San Juan Crisóstomo, que supo desestimar los halagos de una madre amorosa y buena, y su llanto y sus quejas dulcísimas y todas las elocuentes y sentidas palabras que le dijo para que no la abandonase y se hiciese sacerdote, llevándole para ello a su propia alcoba, haciéndole sentar junto a la cama en que le había parido" (124). Since he imagines himself in the position of St. John Chrysostom, the identification of the latter's mother and Pepita automatically suggests itself. Though his conscious reason for thinking of this example is to fortify his attempt to reject Pepita's love, his unconscious wish is to play the game out, to carry the temptation further, and only at the last moment to demonstrate his great self-control and virtue. In this respect, the mentions of Pepita as Phaedra and of himself as the chaste Hippolytus who rejects love fall into the same pattern, as does the reference to Joseph's rejection of Potiphar's wife. Luis's belief that Joseph's act of "casto desdén" (57) was not so difficult is a hint that he has been deluding himself all along by belittling the danger of his flirtation with Pepita. But it must be remembered that Valera made the second allusion to Luis as Theseus, a fact which indicates that the author is determined for Luis to become a Theseus or Don Juan Tenorio (8) like his father and not to "sin against nature" by renouncing human love for divine love. Thus by the time Pepita has wept and made her "quejas dulcísimas" as St. John Chrysostom's mother had done, Valera has seen to it that nature and natural instincts will assure Luis's inability to resist.[29]

C. *Particular Means of Characterization*

1. INTERIOR CONTRADICTIONS. Despite the light, ironical treatment of the conflicting elements that constitute Luis's characterization, the result of his contradictory feelings and motives is a great interior struggle. It is a struggle between his conscience and his sensuality, his aspiration to be a priest and his vainglory, his resentment and his admiration of both Pepita and Don Pedro, his acceptance of reality and his self-delusion. Luis is conscious of the struggle only as it is motivated by his love for Pepita: "Con todas estas consideraciones procuro hacer aborrecible el amor de esta mujer; pongo en este amor mucho de infernal y de horriblemente ominoso; pero *como si tuviese yo dos almas*, dos entendimientos, dos voluntades y dos imaginaciones, *pronto surge* dentro de mí *la idea contraria; pronto me niego lo que acabo de afirmar*, y procuro conciliar locamente los dos amores" (93). Other comments about the struggle are: "Mi vida, . . . es una lucha constante" (88); "Una tempestad de encontradas afecciones combate ahora en mi corazón" (99); and "Estaba asimismo tan alborotado y fuera de sí por culpa de las encontradas pasiones que se disputaban el dominio de su alma, que no cabía en el cuarto . . ." (143). We have seen that in the first letter Luis's vacillating style is directly connected to his sense of guilt and

29 Another important element of Luis's nature, mentioned earlier, is his stubborn pride, from which is derived his concern about the opinions of others and his dread of appearing ridiculous or adolescent. (See, for instance, *Pepita Jiménez*, pp. 122–123.) Cf. Montesinos, *Valera o la ficción libre*, pp. 115 and 120–122.

to the circumstances of his birth. There and in other places the stilted passages, classical nature descriptions, pseudo-philosophical digressions, and expressions of religious zeal alternate with a more open representation of emotions and reality. The outward manifestation of the interior contradictions, then, is a wavering style, a wave movement of opposing forces which characterizes practically all the letters.

An additional example of the wavering style in the letters is Luis's indecision about whether there is something strange in Pepita's look which betrays her love for him and whether he has become his father's rival (80–83). After stating that Pepita has shown no interest in him, Luis begins to reveal his indecision and self-delusion by a series of contradictory remarks, of which the main ones are: "Quiero y debo, *no obstante*, decir a V., . . . una rápida impresión que he sentido . . ."; "Nada de pasión ardiente, nada de fuego hay en los ojos de Pepita"; "Pues bien, *a pesar de* esto, yo he creído notar . . . un resplandor instantáneo, . . . en aquellos ojos . . ."; "La calma del cielo, . . . es lo que descubro siempre en los ojos de Pepita. Me atormenta, *no obstante*, este ensueño, esta alucinación de la mirada extraña y ardiente"; "Según mi padre, la mujer es quien se declara por medio de miradas fugaces . . ."; "*¿Quién sabe si* estas teorías de mi padre, oídas por mí, porque no puedo menos de oírlas, son las que me han calentado la cabeza y me han hecho imaginar lo que no hay? *De todos modos*, me digo a veces, ¿sería tan absurdo, . . . que lo hubiera? Y *si* lo hubiera . . ." (80–81).

Like the litotes described earlier, self-contradictions or excessive qualifications tend to negate the remark, as in the following shorter examples: "Repito, pues, que *estoy lleno de gratitud hacia mi padre*; él me ha reconocido, y *además*, a la edad de diez años *me envió con usted, a quien debo cuanto soy*. Si hay en mi corazón algún germen de virtud; si hay en mi mente algún principio de ciencia; si hay en mi voluntad algún honrado y buen propósito, a usted lo debo" (18). The implications are clear: Luis is grateful to his father for having sent him away, since every good quality in him was derived from his uncle, not from his father. In another case, his qualifying remarks invalidate a statement: "Yo creo buena a Pepita, y a mí, lo digo sin mentida modestia, me creo insignificante. Ya se entiende que me creo insignificante para enamorarla, no para ser su amigo; no para que ella me estime y llegue a tener un día cierta predilección por mí, cuando yo acierte a hacerme digno de esta predilección con una santa y laboriosa vida" (53–54). Sometimes the contradiction is one of terms: ". . . el anhelo, que cada día siento más vivo, de tomar el estado a que *resueltamente me inclino* . . ." (29); and "Es un *amor de odio* . . ." (93). A conventional way of speaking becomes ambiguous in the following sentence, since "de seguro" applied to the verb is more apt than "Tal vez": "*Tal vez, de seguro*, he pecado de arrogante y de confiado . . ." (164).

Similar contradictory passages are also found in the second half of the novel: "Cuando D. Luis reflexionaba sobre todo esto, . . . la pobre Pepita Jiménez quedaba allá muy lejos. . . . Pero pronto se abatía el vuelo de su imaginación, y el alma de D. Luis tocaba a la tierra . . . y Pepita combatía dentro de su corazón contra sus más fuertes y arraigados propósitos, y D. Luis temía que diese al traste con ellos" (125). After promising Antoñona to visit Pepita, he debates with himself about going and tries to write her a letter excusing himself; but his exaggerated pride and fear of appearing ridiculous prevent him from doing so (141–142). Then he finds momentary relief in the thought that he can imitate St. Edward, although his duty toward his father still bothers him: "Hallaba aún cierto no sé qué de criminal en aquella visita que iba a hacer sin que su padre lo supiese, y *estaba por* ir a despertarle de su siesta y descubrírselo todo. *Dos o tres veces se levantó* de su silla y empezó a andar en busca de su padre; *pero luego se detenía* y creía aquella revelación indigna, la creía una vergonzosa chiquillada. . . . La fealdad y lo cómico y miserable de la acción se aumentaban, *notando* que *el temor* de no ser bastante fuerte para resistir *era lo que a hacerla le movía.* Don Luis se calló, pues, y no reveló nada a su padre" (142–143). In addition to Luis's inner conflict, his excessive dread of doing anything childish and his fear of losing the struggle are also disclosed here. The emotion is suggested even in the syntax, since "notando" has no expressed subject and the end-position of the verb "movía" is arranged by the inversion of "a hacerla." It is noteworthy that in the narration of these conflicts the author allows his style to be affected by the character's in a restrained substitutionary reporting. When Valera steps in as the "editor" to determine whether the Dean wrote the narrative part of the novel, he begins with so many contradictions, reversals of opinion, and qualifications that he seems, in part, to be mocking Luis's wavering style: "Dije al comenzar que *me inclinaba a creer* que esta parte . . . era obra del señor Deán, . . . *pero entonces* aun no había yo leído con detención el manuscrito. *Ahora, al notar*, . . . *dudo* de que el señor Deán. . . . *Sin embargo, no hay bastante razón para negar* que sea el señor Deán el autor de los *Paralipómenos. La duda queda en pie. . . . En cuanto a* lo que sostienen dos o tres amigos . . ." (179).

The short concessive clauses or other qualifying remarks employed by Luis are stylistically the most interesting and the most appropriate in the characterization of his vacillating, self-deluding nature. Previous mention was made of phrases which acted as escape valves for his repressed emotions or real motives;[30] similarly, these phrases, which usually result from his overcautious hedging, serve as "loophole clauses" for the truth or for some significant qualification of the original statement. As may be seen in the following list, most of them are concessive clauses with *aun*, *aunque*, or *si*; although *casi* is frequent too:

Por este lado *se me antoja* a veces que soy más censurable que Pepita, *aun suponiéndola merecedora de censura.* (39)

No hay el menor indicio de que Pepita Jiménez me quiera. *Y aunque me quisiese. . . .* (56)

. . . ni yo soy como Josef, . . . ni Pepita es una mujer sin religión y sin decoro. Y *aunque* fuera así, *aun suponiendo todos estos horrores. . . .* (57)

No creo, sin embargo, *que estoy herido de* lo que llaman *amor* en el siglo. *Y aunque lo estuviera*, yo lucharía y vencería. (76)

[30] Cf. Montesinos, *Valera o la ficción libre*, p. 120: "La revelación por el Vicario de las ansias maternales de Pepita 'le infunde cierto temor' por su padre—al que traspone su propio caso—. Tales frases reveladoras son raras." The example cited by Montesinos is found in our edition on p. 47. It seems that there are more than a few such phrases, although they are half-hidden in the maze of Luis's self-contradictions.

Esto no es verdad; y sobre todo, ¿cómo declarar esto a mi padre, *aunque fuera verdad...*? (83)

Esta duda me asalta y me atormenta a veces; pero *casi* siempre la resuelvo en mi favor, y creo que no soy orgulloso con mi padre. . . . (19)

. . . esta admiración y entusiasmo mío, . . . hoy *casi* me parecen pecaminosa distracción. . . . (30)

. . . lloro tan fácilmente de ternura . . . que *casi* tengo miedo. (33)

. . . ha sido la ruda sospecha de V., que *casi* me ha llevado por un instante a que yo mismo sospeche. (51)

. . . ¿soy tan adefesio para que mi padre no tema que, . . . no pueda yo enamorar, *sin querer*, a Pepita?

Hay un curioso raciocinio, que yo me hago, y por donde me explico, *sin lastimar mi amor propio*, el descuido paterno en este asunto importante. Mi padre, *aunque sin fundamento*, se va considerando ya como marido de Pepita. . . . (82)

Mi compromiso moral, mi promesa de consagrarme a los altares, aunque no confirmada, es para mí valedera y perfecta. *Si algo que se oponga al cumplimiento de esa promesa ha penetrado en mi alma*, es necesario combatirlo. (74)

Escriba V. a mi padre que me dé licencia para irme. *Si es menester*, dígaselo todo. (90)

¡Dios mío, haz que Pepita me olvide; haz, *si es menester*, que ame a otro y sea con él dichosa! (101)

Tal vez soy yo mismo quien provoca las miradas. . . . (86)

On one occasion Luis is led by the hypothetical or, rather, potential nature of what he says to use the rare future subjunctive: "Pepita, *sin duda*, amó a su madre primero, *y luego* las circunstancias la llevaron a amar a Don Gumersindo . . .; *y luego, sin duda*, . . . se encontró *quizás* en una situación de espíritu apacible . . . , en la cual, *si tal vez hubiere algo que censurar*, será un egoísmo de que ella misma no se da cuenta" (38–39). Pepita's mind works in somewhat the same way: "–Está bien, padre; yo me alegraré; *casi* me alegro ya de que se vaya" (117); and "No hay lazo alguno que conmigo te ligue; *y si lo hay*, yo le desato o le rompo" (171). In the latter example, the qualification after the negative indicates the general weakness of negatives in this kind of writing; instead of absolute, final statements, there are only semipromises and false decisions. The large number of these "loophole clauses" and the frequent occurrence of contradictory, qualifying remarks, of such adverbs and conjunctions as *si*, *aun*, *aunque*, *casi*, *pero*, *sin embargo*, *no obstante*, *con todo*, *a pesar de*, *acaso*, *quizás*, *tal vez*, and *de todos modos*, and of verbs and nouns like *disimular*, *excusa*, *excusarse*, *justificarse*, *lisonjearse*, *persuadirse*, *pretextar*, and *pretexto*, with subtle distinctions between the indicative and subjunctive moods, reveal Luis's interior contradictions, his vacillating and self-deluding mind.

2. THE EPISTOLARY METHOD. In addition to Luis's letters, there are also the note from the Dean and the significant exchange of letters between the latter and Don Pedro in the second part, as well as the letters written by Don Pedro, which constitute the epilogue. Valera has recourse to the epistolary method, or to some analogous device, in most of his novels. In *Doña Luz*, Padre Enrique writes down his tortured admission of love, which is subsequently read by Doña Luz.[31] Two meaningful letters are written by Clara in *El Comendador Mendoza*;[32] there are revealing letters in *Pasarse de listo*;[33] and there is Rafaela's confessional life story, which she wrote just before committing suicide, in *Genio y figura . . .*[34]

Before Samuel Richardson, the epistolary method had already been used in two psychological novels: the *Lettres portugaises* (1669), allegedly of Sor Mariana de Alcoforado, and Mme Ferrand's *Lettres de Cléante et de Bélise* (1689).[35] These novels, ". . . along with others of their kind, ushered in the psychological-sentimental novel in the epistolary style. The letter form gave the note of truth and intimacy to such accounts. . . . This, in turn, prepared the way

[31] Valera, *Obras*, I, 90–94.

[32] *Ibid.*, I, 392–393 and 421–422.

[33] *Ibid.*, I, 475–479 and 514–518.

[34] *Ibid.*, I, 681–707.

[35] Charles E. Kany, *The Beginnings of the Epistolary Novel in France, Italy, and Spain* (Berkeley: Univ. of California Press, 1937), pp. 111–119.

for the work of such novelists as Mme de Graffigny, Rousseau, and Richardson."[36] A little later (1774), Goethe published a most influential epistolary novel, *Werther*. In fact, in the disposition of the parts and in the alternation between an epistolary method and third-person narrative, *Pepita Jiménez* is more like *Werther* than its most immediate Spanish forerunner, Fernán Caballero's *Un verano en Bornos*, which is a rather inept epistolary novel set in Andalusia. In both the European and the Spanish traditions, then, Valera followed a long line of predecessors in the use of the epistolary style; but even more important for his success with the method are his own copious, stylized letters, written on a wide variety of topics and always with great charm.[37]

The epistolary method, especially as seen in Luis's letters, has several major closely interrelated functions in *Pepita Jiménez*: it allows the letter writer to reveal his own thoughts and attitudes; it provides the author the opportunity to insert himself unobtrusively into his characters' speech; and it serves as an instrument for the author's alluding style, for his deliberately ambiguous irony, and for a general blending, even a pastiche, of different voices and ways of speaking. We have seen how Valera, starting from the subtle parody of mystical and general spiritual language in the speech of the seminarian, expands the imitation of styles to the epoch style of the *Siglo de Oro*, which already makes of Luis's speech a remarkable, elegant pastiche. Valera was able to do this mainly because of the epistolary method; it would have been extremely affected, awkward, and difficult to have worked in the pseudo-mystical passages, as well as the other spiritual, philosophical, and stilted passages, in straight narrative or in either direct or indirect discourse. (A possible alternative would have been the free indirect style, but in a much more drastic form than the way in which Valera was able or willing

36 *Ibid.*, p. 126. Kany also stresses the importance of the first modern epistolary novels in prose, Juan de Segura's *Processo de cartas de amores* (1548) and Quevedo's *Cartas del caballero de la tenaza* (1627), on pp. 69–72 and 107–109, respectively.

37 Valera, "Correspondencia," *Obras*, III, 11–209. Also see *Correspondencia de don Juan Valera (1859–1905)*, ed. Cyrus C. DeCoster (Madrid: Castalia, 1956). It is interesting to compare Valera's early exercises in prose style and his own self-doubts and ambitions (as seen especially in the letters written from Madrid, Naples, Lisbon, and Río de Janeiro between 1847 and 1853) with Luis's letters.

to use it.) In other words, since no one expects a young, romantic person, with his head full of half-assimilated knowledge and delighted at the opportunity to show off this knowledge and to indulge in adolescent melodramatics, to write in a restrained way, Valera, through the stylization of the letters in accord with the nature and background of the letter writer, was free to parody and to make a pastiche of the prose styles he found most pleasing. Thus he was able to imitate in a refined and selective way, much more freely than he ever could before, the prose style of the *Siglo de Oro* and to make of it an integral part of his personal style, while avoiding the exaggerations of romanticism and naturalism, both of which he disliked intensely.

There would be no point in repeating what has been said concerning the self-revelation, the opportunities for Freudian slips, the confusion of spirituality, eroticism, and poetic, adolescent daydreams in Luis's letters. But I would like to point out, in passing, the blending of voices, an elegant (if limited) sort of free indirect style or substitutionary reporting in the letters, for although the speech of each character is indelibly marked by the author's refined culture, it nevertheless reflects very subtly the character's own way of speaking, which is sometimes imitated by Luis in his mimic-reporting style. It is not always easy to determine whose voice is speaking, that is, whether what Luis writes is phrased in the way he ordinarily speaks, or whether it is modeled after the person or source from which the ideas came to him. The source may be a literary one or, from his actual experience, it may be the speech of the Dean and others at the seminary or the speech of his father, the servants, and the townspeople. Thus two new ingredients are blended into Luis's speech: popular language and Don Pedro's speech. The latter's speech, though spiced with popular elements too, has additional notes of irony, irreverence, and worldly wisdom.

The epistolary method greatly facilitates the author's allusive, evocative style. Not being primarily a descriptive writer, Valera prefers to evoke settings and to allude to the basic situations in order to maintain the ambiguity necessary for his irony. Thus one must read between the lines, so to speak, for a total comprehension of the implicit relationships and situations and of Luis's psychological problems and motives. The psychological validity of the characterization is largely a result of the use of the epistolary method, because the reader, following Luis's self-probings, his constant examinations of conscience, becomes aware of the false motives, rationalizations, and self-delusions and begins to piece together the true motives and attitudes. It is through these letters, too, that the other characters are seen through Luis's personality, filtered and colored by his imagination and his attitudes. Consequently much of the second half of the novel is a correction of the partly false interpretations and perspectives derived from the first half.

Another function of the letter device is to provide vantage points of separate moments in time from which Luis can report previous events after having had the opportunity to analyze his reactions and those of others in accordance with later developments and his present state of mind. For example, after touching Pepita's hand and perceiving her ardent glances (78–81), he has time to probe into his and Pepita's behavior, to explain, interpret, justify, and even falsify his reactions or the reality of the event itself before writing the letter. Then with a mixture of naiveté and an inner awareness of guilt he begins to relate the events; but he often sees his erotic or otherwise guilty behavior reflected in his own words and hastily tries to conceal, rationalize, or mitigate his feelings. The reader is thus brought into close contact with the functionings of Luis's mind—the processes and the results of the workings of both intellect and imagination, as well as reflections, afterthoughts, and so on. The time factor is important in the achievement of this psychological artistry, for despite the logical sequence of the letters and the rapid development of the plot, with the apparently logical movement from stimulus to response, from cause to effect, there are surprising shifts in time which generally correspond to Luis's shifts from one aspect of his nature or from one attitude to another. Luis may move with equal facility from dim memories of his childhood to wishful daydreams or he may even anticipate some situation dependent on the fulfillment of his daydreams, as when he speaks of returning to the town as an old man, after spending most of his life in distant lands, in order to enjoy then a platonic relationship with Pepita (52–53) or as when he pretends Pepita is dead only to bring her back to life, like Galatea (93–94).

The emphasis placed on Luis's characterization, as viewed through his letters, does not detract from the inner cohesion of this characterization and the development of the plot. On the contrary, the action and situations are seen causing change in his character, while our knowledge of the events and situations is channeled through the characterization, with a confining intensification of the dramatic action. The fact that Luis's evolution from adolescence to maturity is inextricably interwoven with the progression of the plot gives the novel its dramatic qualities. Everything moves toward the solution of tensions and conflicts, nothing is extraneous, and even what Gerald Brenan objected to as Luis's "lengthy excuses and theological disquisitions" are a result of the happenings and a part of the characterization.[38] The novel is dramatic in structure, though not tragic, of course, since Valera's irony and humor are always present. Space and settings are of secondary importance whereas time is highly significant in the progression of the plot and in the dramatic evolution of Luis's character.[39] In this connection, it is important to remember that the change occurs in only three months and to bear in mind the dates of the letters.[40] For instance, although the interval between the letters varies from four days to a week in all cases but one, two weeks elapse between the sixth and seventh letters. During that time the main step toward the ultimate change was taken: Luis's decision to try to please Pepita by learning to ride *Lucero*. Luis delayed his letter, perhaps because he was busy taking lessons and because of his reluctance to inform his uncle of this; but significantly, within the following eight days he wrote two letters: to report his progress first and then his triumphant success.

The successful and artistic representation of the adolescence, the oedipal conflict, and the interior contradictions of the protagonist

[38] Gerald Brenan, *The Literature of the Spanish People*, 2nd ed. (Cambridge: Cambridge Univ. Press, 1953), p. 382.

[39] Cf. Edwin Muir, *The Structure of the Novel*, 6th impression (London: Hogarth Press, 1954), especially pp. 63–64.

[40] Cf. Montesinos, *Valera o la ficción libre*, p. 119.

were facilitated by the use of the epistolary method, without a loss of unity or of dramatic interest. The psychological depiction of Luis and of his change is identical with the plot in the first half of the novel. There the reader is introduced to the other major characters, none of whom has precisely the role or qualities that one is led to believe at the completion of the letters.

II. OTHER CHARACTERS AND THEIR INTERRELATIONS

A. *Ironical-Critical Treatment of Other Characters*

Although the other characterizations of the novel are psychologically impressive, they are still in keeping with Valera's general critical empathy and his alluding style. No character is completely bad or entirely without fault, without some share in the responsibility for Luis's behavior. Thus the treatment of the characters alternates between ironical criticism and varying degrees of empathy, graded according to Valera's approval or disapproval of the person and of what he represents. The characters with theological training are considered more blameworthy because they appear to go against natural laws and do not want Luis to marry Pepita. Luis is particularly at fault, but the criticism is softened by the author's irony and by the fact that others—Luis's parents, the Dean, even the whole system which produced him—are also to blame.

1. CHARACTERS ON THE SIDE OF NATURE (PEPITA, DON PEDRO, AND ANTOÑONA). The representation of feminine psychology in Pepita is excellent. Her use of all the tricks and ruses, of all the "preparativos, . . . *cosméticos*, indumentarios y religiosos . . ." (153), becomes clear in the second half of the novel, where Luis's romantic conception of her is corrected and enlarged.[41] In the first letters, there exists the implied criticism that Pepita married for money, a fact remembered by everyone. A later example of the attitude of the towns-

[41] Cf. *ibid.*, p. 114.

people and of the author's criticism by ironical allusion occurs at the end of the *Paralipómenos*: "Aunque en el lugar es uso y costumbre, jamás interrumpida, dar una terrible cencerrada a todo viudo o viuda que contrae segundas nupcias, no dejándolos tranquilos con el resonar de los cencerros en la primera noche del consorcio, Pepita era tan simpática y D. Pedro tan venerado y D. Luis tan querido, que no hubo cencerros ni el menor conato de que resonasen aquella noche: caso raro, que se registra como tal en los anales del pueblo" (204–205). The reason for the inhabitants' failure to make the usual charivari—surely not only because of great respect and admiration—may be either that Pepita's first marriage was not a true, consummated marriage or that that night was not "la primera noche del consorcio."

Brief mentions are made of possible mystical qualities in Pepita's makeup;[42] but her religious fervor is mainly pretended, especially in relation to her *Niño Jesús*, which she had neglected since falling in love: ". . . bajó a la sala donde estaba el Niño Jesús. Encendió primero las velas del altarito, que estaban apagadas; vió con cierta pena que las flores yacían marchitas; pidió perdón a la devota imagen por haberla tenido desatendida mucho tiempo . . ." (152). Such neglect had already been presaged in the second letter, where Luis reports his father's statement that no mortal had come along yet capable of making Pepita forget her *Niño Jesús*, and then: ". . . añadía mi padre, *yo* me lisonjeo aún de ser ese mortal dichoso" (25). Our original interpretation, that here, by the unique change to the first person, Luis unconsciously takes his father's place, is confirmed by the later passage; Luis is the one who makes Pepita forget her *Niño Jesús*, not Don Pedro.

Notwithstanding the light criticism of Pepita, there is no doubt that she is the incarnation of the author's ideal woman and appears, with slight variations, in other novels by Valera.[43] She is characterized by studied moderation, by a calm exterior that hides her passionate nature, and by a more refined, erudite manner of speaking than one might expect. We saw that this last characteristic was

[42] Cf. *ibid.*, p. 112.

[43] See *ibid.*, pp. 110–113, where Pepita is compared to Mariquita.

in part derived from her repetition of the phrases and ideas of Luis and the Vicar as well as from her effort to combat her foe with his own weapons and to mitigate her inhibited feelings of love. This type of speech, then, has greater *raison d'être* in Pepita than it seems to have in Valera's other heroines. Even where it is most exaggerated —in her dialogue with Luis—her femininity and passion are not thereby diminished.[44] There is no question about her role in the novel; she is the motivating force behind the change in Luis and all the action. She is the center of attraction, the nucleus around which all the characters revolve; yet she is not the main figure, nor does she necessarily eclipse the characterization of Luis.[45]

Don Pedro is undoubtedly the third most important character of the novel and is Luis's main interest after Pepita. It has been noted that underneath Luis's critical, resentful attitude toward his father lies a secret note of admiration, which gradually changes to true filial love as the novel progresses. In many passages Luis reveals his constant preoccupation with his father by repeating, like a refrain, the phrase *mi padre*, instead of using a pronoun or simply the verb in the third person: "Antes de lo que yo pensaba, querido tío, me decidió *mi padre* a que montase en *Lucero*. Ayer a las seis de la mañana, cabalgué en esta hermosa fiera, como le llama *mi padre*, y me fuí con *mi padre* al campo. *Mi padre* iba caballero en una jaca alazana" (76). Of course, the repetition sometimes indicates resentment rather than affection, though always great interest.[46] One of the most appealing features of the novel is that Luis's resentment of his father changes to admiration and love. The new warmth and understanding of their relationship is briefly depicted after Don Pedro's reading of the two letters: "Así acabó D. Pedro de leer su carta, y al volver a mirar a D. Luis, vió que D. Luis había estado escuchando con los ojos llenos de lágrimas. El padre y el hijo se dieron un abrazo

[44] Cf. *ibid.*, p. 113.

[45] See *ibid.*, p. 116, where Montesinos says of the two: "El protagonista y fictivamente autor de casi una mitad de estas páginas, aunque encarne tantos sentimientos que en Valera mismo alentaron, es de menos relieve y se tiene menos presente, no obstante ocupar siempre la escena."

[46] Other examples: *Pepita Jiménez*, p. 33, lines 24–27; p. 34, lines 10–15; p. 37, lines 22–26; p. 40, lines 20–23; and p. 41, lines 10–12 and 26.

muy apretado y muy prolongado" (202–203). This simple, even clichéd scene nevertheless expresses true feeling. Similar scenes that indicate warm human relationships in *Pepita Jiménez* and other novels by Valera, although they may be surrounded, as this scene is, by more critical, ironical, or humorous passages, belie the often repeated charge that Valera is cold, incapable of feeling and passion.

Another significant thing about Don Pedro is that, in spite of his ironically irreverent remarks (which are never said in a serious vein and which the reader should not take as seriously as Luis does) and his past mistakes, he fits the author's conception of what a hard-working, responsible Spaniard should be. He, like most of the characters, receives a blow to his pride, but quickly recovers and sensibly yields to his son: "Aunque me precio de listo, confieso mi torpeza en esta ocasión: La vanidad me cegaba . . . me mortificó y afligió un poco este desengaño en el primer momento; pero después lo reflexioné todo con la madurez debida, y mi mortificación y mi aflicción se convirtieron en gozo" (199). Henceforth he does everything to further his son's cause, thus correcting Luis's suspicious remarks about his father. Valera is least critical of Don Pedro because of the resemblance between the two.

Antoñona is the most successfully delineated of the secondary characters. The first mention of her, in which she is compared to Doña Casilda, hints at her role as an intermediary, with the ironical reversal of the usual situation, since here the male is the recalcitrant party. Luis says that Antoñona is clever, more discreet than Doña Casilda, and that she often visits his house. We know from Don Pedro's letter that her part in the conspiracy began early, that she is the "soplete utilísimo" who has already told Don Pedro that Pepita loves Luis (202) and who helps him bring the two together. Though a comic character, her genuine affection for her mistress is shown by the tender care with which she picks her up: "Aunque Pepita no fuese una paja, Antoñona la alzó del suelo en sus brazos, como si lo fuera, y la puso con mucho tiento sobre el sofá, como quien coloca la alhaja más frágil y primorosa para que no se quiebre" (118). Antoñona betrays her emotion in the passage following Pepita's statement that she must renounce her plan to marry Luis even if it kills her: "Antoñona, aunque era recia de veras y nada sentimental, sintió, al oír esto, que se le saltaban las lágrimas. –Caramba, niña–dijo Antoñona–, vas a conseguir que suelte yo el trapo a llorar y que berree como una vaca" (121). Valera never reproduces popular speech exactly or phonetically, since he prefers to refine it, while adhering to its inner form, as he does in the representation of Antoñona's speech.[47] Her relative eloquence in the dialogue with Luis (134–138) is a result not of Valera's forgetfulness, however, but of a deliberate effort on her part to speak in such a way that Luis will be persuaded to visit Pepita; it is her variety of the dialectical skill possessed by most of Valera's characters. Her role, of course, is that of a modern-day Celestina, as is evident from her visits to Luis and her elaborate preparations to assure that Luis and Pepita will be alone at their decisive meeting. Furthermore, Valera was able to characterize her and to suggest the nature of the love tryst with one accurate detail: "Bastante más tarde, *con previas toses y resonar de pies*, entró Antoñona en el despacho . . ." (174).

2. THE VICAR AND THE DEAN. It is typical of Valera's irony that the unwitting intermediary, the Vicar, had interrupted the lovers' first kiss in the same fashion that Antoñona interrupted their tryst: "Quiso el cielo que oyésemos *los pasos y la tos* del padre Vicario, que llegaba, y nos separamos al punto" (97). This is another case of the subtle cross-reference or recurrence of themes which one should notice to get the full effect of the author's ironical criticism. Don Pedro states ironically that the Vicar is more help than Antoñona and that he has become an unwitting go-between (202). Luis, in his attempt to evade his responsibility for what is happening, frequently blames the Vicar (76), as does Pepita (109), although she immediately withdraws her charge. Even if the Vicar is outwardly praised for his goodness and for his holiness, the treatment of him is no doubt ironical-critical in the entire novel and Valera implies that he is ignorant (even of theology), sometimes through Luis's voice, but in other passages too, as in the Vicar's dialogue with Pepita. Here it is suggested that the mistakes in theology (the promise of union

[47] Cf. Montesinos, *Valera o la ficción libre*, pp. 115–116.

or betrothal in Heaven) are caused by the Vicar's ignorance or by his attempt to console Pepita and to persuade her to renounce her designs on Luis. The Vicar is also criticized for being too fond of Pepita (112) and for his vanity (117). Indeed, practically all references to him are ironical, even in Luis's letters, where the irony is implied.[48] Obvious examples of the ironical portrayal of the Vicar are the adjectives "cándido" (47 and 108) and "virtuoso" (112) applied to him and passages like the following one: "Casi siempre se me adelanta el excelente padre Vicario, que atribuye nuestra amistad a la semejanza de gustos piadosos, y la funda en la devoción, como la amistad inocentísima que él le profesa" (89). Even the circumstances of his death and his "eulogy" are ironized in the epilogue, where he is called "un varón excelente," "un intercesor," and "un hombre, . . . simple y de cortas luces, pero de una voluntad sana, de una fe profunda y de una caridad fervorosa" (209). We may recall that Pepita's mother was also "de cortas luces" (10); and yet the last remarks indicate the Vicar's essential piety. Valera softens his criticism with his irony; by implication he is criticizing the educational system more than the man.

The Dean, who also undergoes a certain *desengaño* (198), is largely responsible for Luis's decision to become a priest and perhaps for his resentment of his father. His probable humoring of Luis as a child is alluded to by such statements as: "Confieso que algún sentimiento profano se ha mezclado con esta pureza de afecto. Usted lo sabe, se lo he dicho mil veces; y *usted, mirándome con su acostumbrada indulgencia*, me ha contestado que el hombre no es un ángel, y que sólo pretender tanta perfección es orgullo; que debo moderar esos sentimientos y no empeñarme en ahogarlos del todo" (32). The advice, while not unsound, reveals overindulgence, as does a previous remark: ". . . la excesiva indulgencia de usted para conmigo . . ." (26). The occasional references to Luis's early formation under the Dean's tutelage also show a certain indulgence in the kind of ideas Luis was allowed to entertain, ideas for which, in the final analysis,

48 The most outstanding example of the ironical-critical treatment of the Vicar occurs on pages 43–45. The delightful irony of this passage was superbly analyzed by R. Romeu, "Les divers aspects de l'humour dans le roman espagnol moderne," *Bulletin Hispanique*, XLVIII (1946), 97–100.

the Dean was primarily responsible: "El señor Vicario me va reconciliando mucho con el clero español, a quien algunas veces he tildado yo, hablando con V., de poco ilustrado" (43). In fact, Luis had been spoiled all his life: "Don Luis, que desde niño había estado acostumbrado a que nadie se descompusiese en su presencia ni le dijese cosa que pudiera enojarle, porque durante su niñez le rodeaban criados, familiares y gente de la clientela de su padre, que atendían sólo a su gusto, y después en el Seminario, así por sobrino del Deán, como por lo mucho que él merecía, jamás había sido contrariado, sino considerado y adulado . . ." (129). Valera subtly criticizes the fact that Luis had been granted a dispensation to be ordained before the age of twenty-five (131 and 141). Also, at some point Luis must have received, probably through the Dean, a dispensation of his illegitimacy. We see that in general, then, Valera is critical of the Dean and of the others who were responsible for Luis's poor theological training.

B. *Intricate Relations*

1. ALLUDING STYLE. Valera's style is made intricate and ambiguous by its alluding nature, which is primarily a consequence of the epistolary method, with its preclusion of well-defined relationships and situations. These are shrouded in mystery and must be gradually unraveled by the reader, with constant corrections and enlargements of the original interpretations. The most important interrelations, those of Luis's family, are implicit. Such ambiguity was not always Valera's goal or achievement; for instance, Doña Luz's origin, unlike Luis's, is treated quite directly (although not altogether factually): "Huérfana de madre desde que tenía dos años, había quedado sola en el mundo al morir el marqués. Este, que jamás había sido casado, había tenido aquella hija en una mujer oscura; pero le había dado su nombre y la había legitimado."[49] The true relations among Pepita, her mother, and Don Gumersindo are alluded to by irony and litotes, as are the true interpretations of the characters. We never know whether Tía Casilda and Currito are related to Luis on his

[49] Valera, *Obras*, I, 36.

mother's or father's side, although we assume the latter possibility, since no mention is made of her family.

The references and allusions to saints and to other historical or literary personages are integral parts of the characterizations and the plot; references to St. John Chrysostom, St. Edward, Theseus, Phaedra, and others indirectly indicate Luis's own situation and psychological problems. The allusive style occurs on a lower level of importance too, as in the representation of Antoñona: "La nodriza de Pepita, hoy su ama de llaves, es, como dice mi padre, una buena pieza de arrugadillo; picotera, alegre y hábil como pocas. Se casó con el hijo del maestro Cencias, y ha heredado del padre lo que el hijo no heredó: una portentosa facilidad para las artes y los oficios. La diferencia está en que el maestro Cencias componía un husillo de lagar, arreglaba las ruedas de una carreta o hacía un arado, y esta nuera suya hace dulces, arropes y otras golosinas. El suegro ejercía deleite inocente, o lícito al menos" (95). In the first place, an allusion is made to Maestro Cencias of Valera's earlier work, *Mariquita y Antonio*;[50] then there is the comparison of one character to another, with implied criticism of Maestro Cencias's son, who is an idler.

We have seen that the criticism of the clergy and of the characters is ordinarily rendered by implication or through some character's voice. Similarly, Valera shows his awareness of social problems and presents minor criticism by allusion. Thus Don Pedro, in the epilogue, refers to the problem of alcoholism and idleness in the comment about Antoñona's husband (207). Businessmen and social climbers are censured in the remark that Pepita's brother, after going bankrupt, ". . . que viene a ser para ciertos hombres de negocios como una buena poda para los árboles, la cual hace que retoñen con más brío . . ." (210), has earned a fortune and is seeking a title. Valera is critical of absentee ownership and management of estates (211), although less so than in *Doña Luz*. The men's idleness is indicated by the fact that they spend all day in the Casino (54–55) and by Currito's lack of an occupation except that of a "paseante" (77). A brief allusion is made to the poor: "Las luces de las tiendas

[50] Cf. Montesinos, *Valera o la ficción libre*, pp. 109–110.

y puestos de la feria se habían apagado y la gente se retiraba a dormir, salvo los amos de las tiendas y otros pobres buhoneros, que dormían al sereno al lado de sus mercancías" (177). In the same way, local color and customs are not so much described, in the manner of the *costumbristas*, as alluded to or evoked, and then only as part of the general atmosphere or tone (for example, the festival of St. John's Day).

Another feature is that important events mentioned only a few times are alluded to as being frequent. Such is the case with the following activities: Luis's walks alone and with the Vicar, his talks with the Vicar and the early ones with Pepita (none of which is directly represented), the excursions, the work in the vineyard or on the farm, the visits to the *tertulia*, Antoñona's calls on Luis, the lessons in horseback riding, the physical contact and exchange of glances between Luis and Pepita, the relations between Luis and Currito, and the visits to the Casino. Naturally, the avoidance of needless repetition is to be expected; but even so, condensation is part of Valera's "classical" economy of means. Important relationships, situations, and events are given by the briefest of allusions and in the fewest possible words.[51]

2. CROSS-REFERENCE. By cross-reference I mean the thematic repetition of images, ideas, allusions, phrases, and even of single words which often establishes new associations or modifies some previous concept.[52] It is the author's subtle way of adding depth and of indirectly suggesting the intricate plot and interrelationships. Hence it is closely connected, on the one hand, to the alluding qualities of the style, while on the other hand it is one of the dialectical devices employed. When Antoñona coughs before interrupting Luis

[51] In this respect, as well as in others, such as ambiguity, characterization, and critical empathy, Valera is not altogether unlike his French predecessor, Flaubert. See R. A. Sayce, *Style in French Prose* (Oxford: Oxford Univ. Press, 1953), p. 123, concerning Flaubert's condensation, and, on indirect characterization, which supposedly originated with Flaubert, see Anna G. Hatcher, "Voir as a Modern Novelistic Device," *Philological Quarterly*, XXIII (1944), 354–374.

[52] Since many cases of ordinary repetition and of more subtle cross-references have already been pointed out, only a brief recapitulation of salient examples and typical features need be given here.

and Pepita, the reader's recollection of the time the Vicar had done the same thing induces him to associate the two situations and to admire the author's subtle irony. If, when the Dean employs the unusual phrase, *candor selvático,* we recall that Luis had used it earlier, we briefly stop to ponder the significance of the linguistic relationships. The same is true of Pepita's repetition of previous phrases and ideas; we wonder to what extent her somewhat artificial speech is determined by her imitation of Luis and the Vicar.

The cross-references which suggest new relationships are the most significant ones; but, as has been pointed out, they may also have the useful function of characterizing speech and attitudes. For instance, the argument that the love between Pepita and Luis should be renounced because it would be shocking for the son to become his father's rival is used by both the Vicar (114) and the Dean (199). A minor indication of the author's free indirect style is his use of phrases or ideas that were previously used by Luis; for example, Luis compares himself and is compared by the author to Judas (97, 170); and both use the phrases, "pecar de prolijo" (19, 122) and "ejemplar escarmiento" (56, 179). At times repetition simply reinforces the idea, as in the following three sentences: "Era un mar de flores el que *engalanaba* la cruz" (70); "Pepita . . . , está ahora más *galana* y vistosa con trajes ligeros . . ." (71); and "La novia, muy bien *engalanada,* pareció hermosísima a todos . . ." (203). The ironical trick of comparing one character to another or to a previous evaluation, with the result of a new, more complete evaluation, has been noted. We also saw that Don Pedro, by an ironical reversal of roles, reports Luis's speech in the epilogue. The cross-references, then, may be said to call forth new interpretations or corrections of the truth and to further the author's ironical criticism and characterizations in a clever, indirect way.

The consummate portrayal of Luis is chiefly a result of the following factors: traditional Spanish introspection heightened by Valera's knowledge of the mystics and ascetics, which is presented as Luis's misuse of the learning that he acquired at the seminary; the use of casuistic vocabulary to describe Luis's self-probings; thinking in terms of images and symbols; the use of the epistolary method; and the author's critical empathy. Yet the psychological validity of Luis's characterization as such would be of little interest if it could not be related to other features and elements in the novel's aesthetic structure, for ". . . psychological truth is an artistic value only if it enhances coherence and complexity. . . ."[53] In this respect, a minute analysis of Luis's characterization is clearly indispensable for a full understanding of the plot and other characters; thus the novel loses neither in unity nor in dramatic intensity because of the stress on Luis's portrayal.

[53] René Wellek and Austin Warren, *Theory of Literature* (New York: Harcourt, Brace, 1949), p. 88.

CHAPTER IV: *Critical Empathy*

Just as Don Pedro is the author's spokesman in *Pepita Jiménez*, so does Luis have many of the same qualities—pride, ambition, illusion, idealism—that Valera had had as a youth. In fact, the penetrating characterization of Luis is largely attributable to Valera's introspective probings into his own youthful behavior and attitudes and to the resultant ironical self-correction, which also helps explain his critical empathy for his protagonist. Montesinos clearly saw the relationship between Valera the youth and the mature novelist: ". . . mientras que toda su obra de juventud está basada en un misticismo y un afán de absoluto . . . , en un momento de plenitud se revolverá contra esa antigua exigencia suya de orden ideal y tratará de poner en armonía la carne y el espíritu. La ironía . . . indica que las ilusiones de antaño no han sido abandonadas como abominables errores; una experiencia más madura las ha superado, pero siguen alentando en el recuerdo con un prestigio de poesía."[1] Valera's novels, says Montesinos, are the exposition and ironical corrective of that youthful idealism, the longing for the absolute, which Valera shared with those of his contemporaries who, like himself, could no longer find complete satisfaction in Catholicism.[2] This self-corrective pro-

[1] José F. Montesinos, *Valera o la ficción libre: Ensayo de interpretación de una anomalía literaria* (Madrid: Gredos, 1957), p. 94.
[2] *Ibid.*, p. 98.

cess is one of the main elements in Valera that makes him representative of his age in some respects, although it is partly responsible for those features of his style that distinguish him from his contemporaries too. Valera was drawn by his liberal, humanitarian feelings of empathy and concern, not only toward his fictional characters, but also toward nineteenth-century Spain in general, while he simultaneously withdrew to ironical-critical aloofness. Hence his total position in *Pepita Jiménez* was one of a special kind of pseudo-objectivity, a semidetached vantage point from which he could criticize the Spanish society of his day, while unobtrusively expounding his views on it and on the solutions to its problems.[3] Valera was not merely an aesthete; he had underlying didactic purposes and his ideas and dialectics became integral parts of his novels. The polemical and dialectical qualities of his work and style, though mitigated by refined irony and verbal evasion, manifest his critical empathy toward contemporary Spain. A study of these problems will serve as an aid in the fixing of Valera and the novel, both in regard to artistic value and to historical localization.

I. PSEUDO-OBJECTIVITY

A. *Juan Valera's Relations to His Age and the Problem of 'Art for Art's Sake'*

"Yo soy más que nadie partidario *del arte por el arte.*" So said Valera near the end of his essay, "De la naturaleza y carácter de la

[3] The term "pseudo-objectivity" was applied, in a somewhat different sense, to Charles-Louis Philippe's work by Leo Spitzer, *Linguistics and Literary History* (Princeton: Princeton Univ. Press, 1948), p. 13. See also Erich Auerbach, *Mimesis: The Representation of Reality in Western Literature,* trans. Willard Trask (Garden City, N.Y.: Doubleday, 1957), pp. 432–433, concerning Flaubert's implied criticism and "objective seriousness," which is in reality only "pseudo-objective," as other critics have shown. Cf., for instance, B. F. Bart, "Aesthetic Distance in Madame Bovary," *PMLA,* LXIX (1954), 1112–1126. Also of interest, because of the importance of "art for art's sake" and Platonism in Flaubert's theory of the novel, which may be contrasted with Valera's, is Bart's article, "Flaubert's Concept of the Novel," *PMLA,* LXXX (1965), 84–89.

novela" (1860).[4] He added: "no condeno, sin embargo, que las doctrinas se divulguen por medio de las novelas." But the doctrines would have to be of high quality. Valera's frequent statements that his only purpose was to please, that he was trying to prove nothing, have been accepted at face value by many critics who believed that he was an exponent of art for art's sake and that in some or most respects he was not a man of his age. Jean Krynen concluded that Valera was "romantic" rather than "classical" and derived Valera's originality from his *idée maîtresse*, aestheticism, about which he said: "L'esthétisme, . . . n'est pas chez J. Valera une doctrine, mais un style de vie."[5] Although placing Valera in the Generation of 1868, Alberto Jiménez was still able to say: "Lejos de la intención de Valera, la pintura exacta de las costumbres: tan lejos como ninguna preocupación moralizadora o docente. *En sus escritos sólo persigue la belleza.*"[6] Revuelta y Revuelta insisted that Valera's only object was to please.[7] Montesinos treated Valera as a literary anomaly and placed his roots in the eighteenth century.[8] Finally, Gerald Brenan said: "Valera was a man who by temperament belonged more to the late Italian Renaissance than to his own age."[9]

These commentators, among others, share the somewhat antihistorical belief that Valera was not primarily a product of his age and that he had little or no didactic purpose. One of the reasons which in some measure justifies this point of view is Valera's eighteenth-century philosophy, modeled primarily after that of Kant, with some influences from the German romantic school of philosophy.[10]

[4] Valera, *Obras*, II, 200. See Manuel Olguín, "Juan Valera's Theory of Art for Art's Sake," *Modern Language Forum*, XXXV (1950), 24–34, on these matters.

[5] Jean Krynen, *L'Esthétisme de Juan Valera, Acta Salmanticensia*, "Filosofía y Letras," vol. II, no. 2 (Salamanca: Universidad de Salamanca, 1946), p. 87.

[6] Alberto Jiménez, *Juan Valera y la generación de 1868* (Oxford: Dolphin, 1956), p. 173 (italics mine).

[7] Luisa Revuelta y Revuelta, "Valera, estilista," *Boletín de la Real Academia de Ciencias, Bellas Letras y Nobles Artes de Córdoba*, XVII (1946), 42.

[8] Montesinos, *Valera o la ficción libre*, pp. 8 and 13; see also pp. 77–79.

[9] Gerald Brenan, *The Literature of the Spanish People*, 2nd ed. (Cambridge: Cambridge Univ. Press, 1953), p. 381. Brenan also said that Valera was a believer in art for art's sake.

[10] Cf. Jiménez, *Juan Valera y la generación de 1868*, p. 177. Sherman H. Eoff, *The Novels of Pérez Galdós* (St. Louis: Washington Univ. Studies, 1954), p. 137, summarizes the philosophical background as follows: "Along with the nineteenth-

Yet it is certain that Valera avoided any binding limitations to his freedom, as was shown by Alberto Jiménez when he said that what really dominates in Valera's philosophy is: ". . . el desdén a los arrogantes sistemas doctrinales que encadenan la razón robándole el valor de la incertidumbre y privándola de responsabilidad personal y del sentido de sus limitaciones."[11] Most critics have pointed out the strong element of freedom in Valera's philosophy, which only amounts to a lack of strict adherence to any organized system of thought.[12]

There are inconsistencies between Valera's professions of faith in religion or of belief in philosophical systems and his ironical-critical statements about them. For instance, his professions of faith in Catholicism were said to have been for political expediency,[13] although passages could be adduced to assert his sincerity. Similarly, he alternately defended and criticized the Krausists. In his essay, "Sobre las enseñanzas de la filosofía en las universidades," he defended the Krausists against the attack from *El pensamiento español* and clearly stated his belief that tolerance and liberalism were essential if Spain was to produce great thinkers and to overcome her backwardness.[14] In a review of Gumersindo Laverde's *Ensayos críticos*, Valera proclaimed the need for a reform in Spanish education and for the establishment of a *Seminario Central* to provide a much more thorough education of the priests.[15] Such educational reformatory zeal, which was an essential part of Krausism, is a direct expression of what is only implied in *Pepita Jiménez*. On the other

century discussion of the natural and social sciences, a top layer of metaphysical thought is present in the belief that the individual, while being a social organism that develops in a natural, maturational process through community of experience, is bound to that self-hood which includes all individuality. This thinking is pervaded with a good portion of post-kantian idealism, manifest in the "self and others" concept . . . with emphasis resting on conciliation of the two components, and with a tendency to see in organisms a purposeful activity of reciprocal influence."

[11] Jiménez, *Juan Valera y la generación de 1868*, p. 177.

[12] Manuel Azaña, in his prologue to the "Clásicos Castellanos" edition of *Pepita Jiménez* (Madrid: Espasa-Calpe, 1953), p. xxxiii, immediately relates this "freedom" to art for art's sake, although the relationship is not necessarily a causal one.

[13] Cf. *ibid.*, p. xxxviii.

[14] Valera, *Obras*, II, 1461–1474.

[15] *Ibid.*, II, 364–371.

hand, Valera sometimes ridiculed the Krausists and their predecessors, as in his dialogue, "El racionalismo armónico," in which he particularly makes fun of such German terminology as *el yo, el no-yo, el otro que yo*, etc.[16] This dialogue, which was written in 1873, just before the publication of *Pepita Jiménez*, actually gives Valera's overall, mixed position in regard to Kant, Hegel, and Krause, for while Filateles and Filodoxo express some of the author's views, including the erroneous belief that sixteenth-century Spanish mystics were close to pantheism, Gláfira expresses his ironical criticism, the other half of his nature which always remained aloof. In "Notas a *La metafísica y la poesía*," written in 1890, Valera expounded his disapproval of the followers of the top Krausist educator, Sanz del Río, and his ultimate inability to embrace unreservedly any philosophy: "La filosofía de Krause, por tanto, y cuantas se le semejan, deben de ser también vano ensueño."[17] He added that he could not be a Kantian and that man knows so little, even with his experimental sciences, that ". . . tan absurdas son las afirmaciones como las negaciones." It seems that beyond his faith in natural reason, progress, and art, Valera's philosophical beliefs, even his post-Kantian idealism, were always subject to doubt and fluctuations. Valera shared with the men of his generation a belief in the efficacy of reason and intuition and in progress, as well as the restlessness which led them to seek new explanations of the supernatural and new solutions for contemporary social problems.[18]

Beyond doubt Valera's main purpose was to please and he had no overt thesis to prove as the naturalists had;[19] yet he also had didactic purposes. Both Montesinos and Jiménez[20] stress the general lesson against pride and illusion and point out other works in which Valera treated the same problem, namely, *Mariquita y Antonio*, *Asclepigenia*, and *Las ilusiones del doctor Faustino*; but more specific intentions in *Pepita Jiménez* were to expose false mysticism and to criticize the selection and education of candidates for the priesthood.

16 *Ibid.*, II, 1520–1553.
17 *Ibid.*, II, 1679–1693; the quote is from 1691.
18 See Jiménez, *Juan Valera y la generación de 1868*, p. 176.
19 See Montesinos, *Valera o la ficción libre*, p. 24.
20 *Ibid.*, pp. 103–104; Jiménez, *Juan Valera y la generación de 1868*, pp. 139–140.

With some of his contemporaries, Valera exhibits anticlericalism, although never in the more severe manner of the early Galdós.[21] Valera, according to Montesinos, had little liking for the novels of his contemporaries, especially Pereda's, and supposedly shared with Alarcón only an aversion to realism.[22] However, notwithstanding his refinement, idealism, and verbal evasion toward the *Siglo de Oro*, it seems that in several respects Valera was essentially realistic. He participated in the general reaction against romanticism and in the search for the more restrained language that the realistic novelists had to find for adequate description, psychological analysis, and representation of everyday speech, for which purposes neither the oratorical nor the journalistic styles then prevalent were suitable.[23] Valera was typical of his age in regard to the relations between idealism and reality, as well as in the expression of concern about the general problems of his time. Perhaps his ironical-critical approach and pseudo-objectivity explain those aspects of his work which have led to an overemphasis of his position as a follower of art for art's sake.[24]

The problems involved in the classification of nineteenth-century novelists are in part derived from a faulty understanding of the terms. As Eoff has shown in his study of Pereda's concept of realism, the terms "idealism" and "realism" are not incompatible, although Pereda "might well have made a comparison between classicism, romanticism, and realism, since certain essential differences in these literary traditions are clear both in technique and attitude."[25] Eoff adds that revealing differences would be: ". . . the emotionalism and extremism of romanticism as opposed to the moderation and the insistence upon logical development of action in classicism; the selec-

[21] Cf. Eoff, *The Novels of Pérez Galdós*, p. 161: ". . . his [Galdós's] youthful belligerence and his novels of thesis are in keeping with the controversial atmosphere of the 1870's and the emphasis on 'ideas' in literature." See also Montesinos, *Valera o la ficción libre*, p. 124.

[22] Montesinos, *Valera o la ficción libre*, pp. 212–215.

[23] Rafael Lapesa, *Historia de la lengua española*, 3rd ed. (Madrid: Escelicer, 1955), pp. 272–273.

[24] The emphasis placed by Jiménez and Montesinos on these characteristics in Valera's work is, as the passages cited indicate, offset by their many remarks which reveal truer understanding.

[25] Sherman H. Eoff, "Pereda's Conception of Realism as Related to His Epoch," *Hispanic Review*, XIV (1946), 283.

tiveness, directness, and concentration of the latter as opposed to the multiplicity and diversity of realism; and the realistic emphasis upon the usual as contrasted to the romantic tendency to magnify the unusual." It is in accordance with these beliefs that Eoff calls Valera a "classical idealist," and it is no doubt true that Valera should be placed somewhere along the trajectory—a trajectory complicated in Spain by time lags and eclecticism—of classicism-romanticism-realism. The exact position would vary somewhat according to the novel by Valera under discussion; *Las ilusiones del doctor Faustino* and *Pasarse de listo*, for instance, are probably more realistic than Valera's other novels of the 1870's, both in themes and technique.

The precise and manifold relationships between Valera and realism would require a separate study of some length. Suffice it to say that unlike Flaubert, a typical realist, Valera followed Aristotle in separating the novel, as part of poetry, from history, since the true (things as they are) and the beautiful (things as they should be) are separated and since the ugliness of reality should be excluded from poetry, except for the purpose of catharsis.[26] Again unlike Flaubert, Valera relegates verisimilitude to secondary importance, since for him it can include both the probable and the possible. Also, like the classicists, Valera uses types and general qualities to represent the true, but without documentation and without direct and detailed treatment of social problems.

Although in his criticism Valera opposed didacticism in literature and the thesis novel, it can be shown that in practice his novels of the 1870's share certain characteristics, not to mention thematic resemblances, with the "novel of ideas" which came into favor during that decade.[27] More precise parallels could be established between other novels of the 1870's and *Pepita Jiménez*, which, as Montesinos remarks, is something of an exception in Valera's total work.[28] Two significant features which further characterize the novels of the

[26] See Valera, "De la naturaleza y carácter de la novela," *Obras*, II, 190 *et passim*.

[27] See Sherman H. Eoff, "The Spanish Novel of 'Ideas': Critical Opinion (1836–1880)," *PMLA*, LV (1940), 531–558, especially 541, for a detailed treatment of the critical reaction to transcendentalism and didacticism in the novel, and Valera's role as a critic.

[28] Montesinos, *Valera o la ficción libre*, p. 108.

1870's are their important ideological content and their polemical nature, as has been noted by Juan López Morillas:

> El despotismo de las ideas es, pues, lo que da carácter polémico a la novela española del período 1870–1880, como da también carácter polémico a la filosofía, a la religión, a la política, en suma, a todas las actividades españolas de ese decenio. Por eso no parece muy adecuado el calificativo de "realista" que de ordinario se aplica a esa manera de entender la ficción novelesca. Si bien se mira, es todo lo contrario, por su intención al menos: es una novela "idealista", alimentada por ese deseo de que las cosas sean distintas de lo que son. . . .[29]

The "novela 'idealista' " is but one manifestation of the ideological polemics of the time, which were broadly reflected in the great, insatiable taste for oratory and rhetoric.[30] López Morillas was no doubt correct in stressing the importance of ideas and polemics in his description of the 1870's. In this connection, it is of interest to show Valera's similarity to the spirit of the times by illustrating his polemical characteristics.

B. *Polemical Elements in* Pepita Jiménez

Valera's argumentative nature—one must remember that he was trained in law and in dialectics—is manifested by several polemics such as the ones with Donoso, Castelar, and Campoamor.[31] His mental reservations and the periphrastic mitigation of his criticism are often disconcerting to the modern reader.[32] As Azaña has seen:

> Poseía Valera inclinación natural a contradecir. . . . Emparedado entre la duda y la mesura, apestándole cualquier dogmatismo, propenso a la sátira, su opinión se precipitaba al oponerse a otras, más por argumento que por razón, más para decir: *no es eso*, que para probar: *esto es*. Tan fuerte contradictor, a veces se cargaba si alguien venía a demostrarle lo que él mismo, por moción espontánea y sin hostigo, solía profesar.

[29] Juan López Morillas, *El krausismo español* (México: Fondo de Cultura Económica, 1956), pp. 137–138.

[30] A popular book was F. Cañamaque's *Los oradores de 1869* (Madrid, 1879).

[31] See Valera, *Obras*, II, 1383–1399, 1399–1434, and 1630–1693, respectively.

[32] See Azaña, *Pepita Jiménez*, "Prólogo," pp. xxxvi–xxxvii.

Preso en este espíritu, dejábase arrastrar por la fuerza de sus argumentos al paso que los tejía. Valera lo confiesa. . . . La oposición a lo contiguo, a lo presente, se halla en su carácter y en su intelecto.[33]

Azaña suggests Valera's critical empathy when he adds that Valera was prevented from being more of a polemicist by: "Muchas causas . . . , ya provengan de su natural benigno, con más 'ternura que odio', ya de cuanto había de diletante en su espíritu, gustador de lo bello en la vida . . . Le detuvo también el respeto mundano. . . ."[34]

Other critics have suggested these qualities in Valera too. Jiménez has pointed out the mixed attitude of criticism and respect in the relations between the Generation of 1868 (including Valera) and the Church, while stating that many of the Krausists were trained in law and forensics.[35] Such training lent a strong note of formality to the polemics in which they became involved. Montesinos frequently mentions the dialectical and polemical aspects of Valera's work and recalls that *Pepita Jiménez* was first conceived as a polemical intervention, as Valera himself claimed.[36] We have seen several of the apparent dialectical traits of the novel: the author's utilization of his opponents' weapons—mystical and ascetical language—the corrections of original interpretations of reality, along with Luis's refutations of the Dean's charges, his weighing of pros and cons, his half-promises, and his rationalizations.

Another, most important dialectical feature is the use of formal, polemical dialogues. Critics of Valera's time censured the implausibility in the speech of his characters, especially the female ones, who were said to speak with all the elegant erudition of the author.[37] To some extent this charge is true, although the inner truth of particular modes of speech is usually adhered to. The lack of verisimilitude is a result of the deliberate stylization of speech in accordance with the author's cultural background and ideals of expression. A further explanation of the formal characteristics of such speech

[33] *Ibid.*, p. xxxiv.
[34] *Ibid.*, p. xxxv.
[35] Jiménez, *Juan Valera y la generación de 1868*, pp. 22–23.
[36] Montesinos, *Valera o la ficción libre*, p. 123.
[37] See *ibid.*, pp. 74–78, 151–152, and 218–220.

is that each character, when engaged in a serious conversation, is represented as making a conscious attempt to speak with formality and eloquence, almost as if participating in a public debate. We have seen that the formalized, dialectical qualities of speech in the long conversation between Luis and Pepita serve to mitigate the real emotions and constitute a stylized debate in which each character expresses himself at length in a highly formal way, while the other waits patiently, taking mental notes of the opponent's arguments and of his own plan of attack and rebuttal. Thompson, who likewise noted these characteristics, says of formalized speech in Valera's novels: "The reason for such monologues is perhaps to be found in the fact that in most cases the author is indulging in a further spiritual auto-analysis, completing Valera's preceding expository remarks. The situation in itself is completely artificial; consequently the dialogue appears correspondingly strained. In the cases where no mental problems are concerned and the conversation is the natural result of the circumstances, Valera handles the speeches with appropriate spontaneity and lightness."[38]

Although less formal, with shorter, more naturally expressed remarks, the dialogue between Pepita and the Vicar is likewise a stylized debate. The situation is carefully set up, with a note of suspense, and the dialogue is initiated rather formally: "Después de los saludos de costumbre, y arrellanado el padre Vicario en una butaca al lado de Pepita, se entabló la conversación" (106). Pepita begins with an indirect statement of the problem by admitting her error and claiming to be a victim of Leviathan, Mammon, and Asmodeus (107). She finally tells the Vicar that her impure love is not for Don Pedro, as the Vicar expected, but for Luis, thus provoking the Vicar's disapproval (108–109). Pepita then says that the Vicar is partly to blame, a fact which he professes to admit, though it is really a trick to make Pepita avow her guilt (109–110). After she does so and relates the beginnings of her love for Luis, the Vicar tries to persuade her that this love should be renounced, in return for which she and Luis would be rewarded in Heaven (112). Pepita protests vehemently

[38] Frank R. Thompson, "The Classicism of Don Juan Valera," Ph.D. Diss., Univ. of Wisconsin, 1941, p. 140.

and switches her attack to Luis: "¡Se acordará de mí! ¡Me la pagará! Si es tan santo, si es tan virtuoso, ¿por qué me miró prometiéndomelo todo con su mirada? Si ama tanto a Dios, ¿por qué hace mal a una pobre criatura de Dios? ¿Es esto caridad? ¿Es religión esto? No; es egoísmo sin entrañas" (113). Upon seeing Pepita weep, "El Vicario sintió la más tierna compasión; pero recobró su brío al ver que el enemigo se rendía" (114). Beginning with the aphorism that this life is short, the Vicar again promises a future reward, praises Pepita's discretion, and lists several reasons why she should give up her love for Luis, including the possible rivalry of father and son and the townspeople's disapproval (114). He tells her what the results would be if she were to accept his advice: Luis would become a priest and she would recover, retaining only a lingering, poetic memory of the incident (115). After the Vicar repeats the promise of a reward, Pepita seemingly yields and the Vicar encourages her (115–116). Then, in a last effort to win his sympathy, Pepita belittles herself. But the Vicar skillfully corrects her and has her repeat her acceptance of his advice. The Vicar leaves, pleased with ". . . la influencia que ejercía sobre el noble espíritu de aquella preciosa muchacha" (117). The agreement, however, is not kept, for Pepita tells Antoñona that she cannot give up her love for Luis and that (in what must be the author's opinion too) the Vicar's reasonings now seem ". . . vano juego de palabras; mentiras, enredos y argucias" (119). The outcome of the debate is revealed in her remark: "Yo amo a D. Luis, y esta razón es más poderosa que todas las razones" (120).

Even Antoñona's colloquial speech is stylized in her dialogue with Luis, which is a debate on a farcical level (134–138). She is determined to have a serious talk with Luis and has asked ". . . no se sabe si al cielo o al infierno le diese habla, y habla no chabacana y grotesca, como la que usaba por lo común, sino culta, elegante e idónea para las nobles reflexiones y bellas cosas que ella imaginaba que le convenía expresar" (134). Here the author is being ironical, of course, since her speech, though somewhat more refined than usual, is not "culta, elegante e idónea," nor does she say beautiful, noble things. In other words, the author's refined irony moves her speech one step closer to his ideal of elegant speech, allowing her to win her debate with Luis through her native cunning and argumentative skill. Alternately blaming and praising Luis, appealing to his vanity, and even using a sort of theological cant to convince him, she has him completely at her mercy: "Don Luis, aturdido, no sabía qué objetar a estos raciocinios. . . . Además, le repugnaba entrar en metafísicas de amor con aquella sirvienta" (136). Then Antoñona demonstrates her shrewdness and knowledge of psychology by telling Luis that Pepita might kill herself, thus attaining his promise to visit Pepita.

Many passages in Luis's letters are polemical, and occasionally an entire letter, like the sixth one, is a secondary stylized debate (49–54). It is one-sided, since the Dean's charges are only revealed through the allusions and recapitulations made by Luis. Luis initiates the debate with a *captatio benevolentiae* by praising his uncle's discreet advice; then he depreciates himself while stating the charges and confessing his impatience and pride, before beginning his defense with an appeal for God's help and with a remark that the advice is good but pointless, since he is not yet guilty of the offense (i.e., of evincing too much interest in Pepita) (49–50). Citing precedents and illustrative cases, he recognizes his vulnerability, professes humility, promises to remember the advice and to pray, but finds nothing to fear in his behavior (50–51). Luis then blames his father and the Vicar for the favorable statements about Pepita in his letters, charges that the Dean's accusations have almost led him to suspect himself, claims to feel for Pepita only the innocent admiration inspired by a work of art made by God, and states that since he must live in the world and lead an active life, as the Dean wants him to, he cannot help noticing Pepita (51). After employing this sanctimonious self-deception as a pretext to describe Pepita's beauty, which comes from God, he adds that one with evil thoughts would be in danger but not he, because he only loves her like a sister (52). Again blaming others, professing altruistic motives, he indulges in daydreams about returning to the town as an old man and having pure relations with Pepita, although now, being young, he avoids her (52–53). Next he defends the charge that Pepita is interested in him by maintaining, with meaningful reservations, that she would not care for a person so lacking in social graces and manly pursuits as himself; he feels too insignificant to gain Pepita's love, but not her friendship and esteem (53–54). He concludes by asking pardon for his heated self-defense and states that if the Dean was wrong in accusing him, it was only because he had his (Luis's) interests at heart (54). Luis loses even this one-sided debate because his rationalizations are so flimsy that he reveals the truth of the charges in his attempted refuting of them.[39]

Stylized debates also occur in Valera's other novels, for instance, the dialogues in *El Comendador Mendoza* between Doña Blanca and Padre Jacinto and between Doña Blanca and Don Fadrique.[40] Eloquence and dialectical skill are indispensable elements in the author's concept of ideal self-expression; thus it is not surprising that his characters aspire to greater eloquence and powers of persuasion than usual when they become engaged in some vital, decisive conversation.[41] These are necessary attributes in the characters' concept of the ideal woman. Pepita speaks of great ladies who ". . . disertan de política, de filosofía, de religión y de literatura . . ." (158); and Luis heard his ideal women ". . . discurrir como Aspasia o Hipatia, maestras de elocuencia . . ." (162). Antoñona flatters Luis by praising his eloquence and polemical skill: "Tú irás allí, y con esa cháchara que gastas y esa labia que Dios te ha dado, le infundirás en los cascos la resignación y la dejarás consolada . . ." (317). In general, the characters wish to speak with ceremony and gravity in order to persuade others; therefore, in the representation of these serious dialogues, the verbs *discurrir* and *disertar*, with their formal implications, are often used.[42] Contrariwise, the greatest insult is to accuse one's opponent of sophistry[43] or, as Don Fadrique does, to apply such verbs as *discretear* and *filosofar* to the opponent's speech.[44] That Don Pedro is also clever in argumentation is shown by his ironical rep-

[39] For a similar passage, see *Pepita Jiménez*, pp. 56–58.
[40] Valera, *Obras*, I, 407–416 and 432–436, respectively.
[41] See *Pepita Jiménez*, p. 134, concerning Antoñona's aspirations to eloquence, and p. 142: "Don Luis confortó su espíritu con la esperanza de que iba a tener mucha serenidad y de que *Dios iba a poner en sus labios un raudal de elocuencia*, por donde persuadiría a Pepita. . . ."
[42] See *ibid.*, p. 157, line 11, and p. 159, lines 25–31.
[43] See *ibid.*, p. 159, line 29, and p. 161, line 1.
[44] Valera, *Obras*, I, *El Comendador Mendoza*, 433.

artees to the Dean's statements in his letter (200–202). We may conclude, then, that Valera, by deliberately endowing his characters with eloquence and dialectical skill, particularly in formal, decisive dialogues, reflected the polemical characteristics of his epoch, despite his seemingly detached position.[45]

In addition to the polemical influence of his time, there are contradictions and vacillations in the author which suggest a deeper reason for his argumentative nature. That reason is his critical empathy. First of all, he is strongly attracted to Luis, who embodies the idealism of his youth, although he nevertheless criticizes him for this very idealism, for his illusions, ambition, pride, and so forth. Yet he is aware that Luis is a product of his poor theological education and is an adolescent with psychological problems not entirely of his own making; thus the criticism is tempered with empathic understanding. It would not be amiss, perhaps, to term Luis's interior contradictions, his wavering between the sympathetic impulse and the egoistic impulse of adolescence, his fluctuations between love and hatred, submission and rebellion, in his relations with his father, Pepita, and the Dean, as his own highly personalized form of critical empathy. Through him, in the first half of the novel, the author expresses his own critical empathy toward the same characters. Valera's treatment is thus made more impartial and ironical, although his approach is still not entirely objective. Then in the second half of the novel, Valera demonstrates his empathy toward Luis by a moderate form of free indirect style ("moderate" because the speech of each character is originally placed one or more degrees above everyday speech, thus making the borrowings much more subtle than they would be, for example, in a writer who uses the slang and technical language of a homogeneous group, as Zola does with the language of miners in *Germinal*). Valera's epilogue, which relates the satisfactory solution of all problems, compensates with empathy the criticism voiced throughout the novel.

45 We may compare, for example, the formal and often polemical, even heated conversations in Galdos's *Doña Perfecta, Gloria,* and *La familia de León Roch,* which also treat religious questions.

Valera was undoubtedly a man given to criticism, even in regard to himself and his work; for instance, his mature evaluations of some of his youthful poems include such frank remarks as "Versos tontos y embusteros; nunca conocí ni sé que haya existido en el mundo la Laureta de que se trata en ellos"; and "Todo esto es mentira y necedad."[46] His evaluation of his early poem, "La divinidad de Cristo," discloses his true attitude toward Catholicism:

> Cualquiera diría al leer estos versos en su principio, que, aunque pobres de gracias poéticas y de ciencia teológica, están escritos *corde puro, conscientia bona el* [*sic, et*] *fide non ficta*, como dice el apóstol. Por desgracia mía, sin embargo, en esto de catolicismo yo soy como los gitanos, que si no la pegan a la entrada, la pegan a la salida; y así es que, con decir a lo último que la Humanidad se llenó de entusiasmo y llamó a Cristo hijo de sus entrañas, vengo a dar a conocer lo falso de mi fe y que, a pesar de que entonces no había yo aún leído nada de lo que hoy se llama humanismo y egoteísmo, era ya un tanto cuanto egoísta, sin saberlo ni sospecharlo siquiera.[47]

In his essay, "El concepto sobre España," however, Valera shows his great admiration for the Catholic writers of the *Siglo de Oro* when he says that Spaniards should be grateful to Rousselot, notwithstanding his criticism of Spain, because he praised the two Luises, Santa Teresa, and other mystics, who were then undeservedly neglected by the Spanish. Then he quotes Rousselot: " 'Guardada la debida proporción—dice—, fray Luis de León y fray Luis de Granada son para España lo que Bossuet y Bourdaloue son para Francia'; pero en la frase *guardada la debida proporción* afirma nuestra inferioridad grandísima, aun en esto del misticismo, única cosa que nos concede. Y, sin embargo, cualquiera de los dos Luises vale tanto en absoluto como su Bossuet, o su Fenelón, o sus otros autores devotos. Fray Luis de León, sólo considerado como poeta lírico, no tiene igual en Francia."[48] While criticizing what he considered the fanaticism and

46 Valera, *Obras*, I, 1511 and 1512, respectively.

47 *Ibid.*, I, 1513.

48 *Ibid.*, III, 748. This essay, written in 1868, is one of the many indications of Valera's consistent interest in the mystical and ascetical writers of the sixteenth century.

ignorance of the Catholics of his day, as well as the watering down of a great Spanish tradition in the seminarians' textbooks, Valera always exhibited great curiosity in religious matters and genuine admiration for the Catholic literary tradition in Spain—an overall attitude of critical empathy, for he was attracted by what he criticized.[49]

The same attitude is seen in Valera's view of contemporary Spanish society, because he always had in mind the past glory of Spain and was truly interested in improvement. In the essay just cited, he tells his compatriots:

> . . . yo entiendo que todos los españoles, hasta los que hallan peor y más perdida a España, tienen conciencia del gran ser de esta nación y de sus altos destinos, y que la contraposición entre esta conciencia y la realidad presente es quien tanto los lleva a maldecir de la patria. Mas no por eso debe desesperarse ni prever la muerte. Antes el exceso mismo de nuestro mal, y todo cuanto lo lamentamos, y lo mal sufridos que somos, y el prurito con que los extranjeros nos censuran, son indicios de que no hemos caído para siempre, son casi un buen agüero.
>
> Lo que importa ahora es no adularnos en público, ni jactarnos de lo que fuimos, sino señalar nosotros mismos todas nuestras faltas, procurando el remedio. . . . Lo que nos importa es abrir puerta franca a los frutos de esa inteligencia, vengan de donde vinieren; no fingirnos un ideal de Batuecas; no creernos una Arcadia tonta a lo místico, y esperar confiados en que nuestro porvenir ha de ser venturoso.[50]

It is difficult to believe that Valera, a man with such strong convictions, who by the exemplary criticism in the person of Luis and by the alluded criticism of other ills showed his concern about contemporary problems, and whose style reflects the current interest in polemics, was a completely aloof believer in art for art's sake. As a youth he had political and social ambitions; he became a politician,

[49] Cf. Brenan, *The Literature of the Spanish People*, p. 382: ". . . we feel . . . a certain *malaise* at the ambiguous tone in which these subjects are treated, which comes from Valera's being one of those sceptics who reject with their intellect the dogmas of the church, but are drawn back to religious matters by a sort of prurient curiosity."

[50] Valera, *Obras*, III, 751.

a diplomat, an intellectual leader, and a member of the Spanish Academy.[51] Having attained this responsible position of leadership, Valera no doubt felt a certain moral obligation to his fellow man, and through his letters, his critical writings, and even his fiction, to a large extent, he showed himself to be vitally concerned about the problems, polemics, aspirations, and ideals of his time. Hence his true position, we may repeat, was one of partial involvement and not a complete withdrawal into a world of art and form.

c. *Free Indirect Style*

One indication of Valera's critical empathy is his restrained free indirect style. Stephen Ullmann, writing of Flaubert, for whom this device was more important than for Valera, has given a valuable summary of its main uses:

> 1. The very existence of the construction makes for variety in style. The author can now choose between three different forms of reported speech and can alternate them in a number of ways.
> 2. Free indirect style combines the advantages of the two orthodox methods. The author is not committed to an exact reproduction of words or thoughts; yet he is able to dispense with explicit subordination and to retain the emotive and expressive features and the very inflexions of the spoken language.
> 3. Free indirect style is reported speech masquerading as narrative. It means a break in continuity and a certain shock to the reader. It is essentially an oblique construction and provides a discreet but effective vehicle for irony and ambiguity, and for the description of reveries, dreams and hallucinatory states.[52]

[51] Valera was much more active in contemporary affairs than Flaubert, who really withdrew to an ivory tower but whose position was also one of critical empathy.

[52] Stephen Ullmann, "Reported Speech and Internal Monologue in Flaubert," in *Style in the French Novel* (Cambridge: Cambridge Univ. Press, 1957), pp. 94–120. The quotation is from p. 117. Concerning these matters, also see Marguerite Lips, *Le style indirect libre* (Paris: Payot, 1926), Sister Anne Gertrude Landry, *Represented Discourse in the Novels of François Mauriac* (Washington: Catholic Univ. of America Press, 1953), and, for additional bibliography, Ullmann's footnotes.

Ullmann further states that Flaubert's main reason for preferring the free indirect style lay in both his objective, impassive attitude and his "capacity for sympathetic self-identification with the protagonists of the story."[53] These seemingly contradictory attitudes are actually complementary and constitute, in Flaubert as in Valera, an overall position of critical empathy. Free indirect style, which creates a blurring of contours, is particularly useful to Valera for parody, irony, and characterizations.

In the first half of *Pepita Jiménez*, a moderate free indirect style, in the form of substitutionary reporting, results in a general blending of voices. In his mimic-reporting style, Luis repeats colloquialisms of the townspeople and the ironical, irreverent remarks of Don Pedro, incorporating these new elements into his stilted, rationalizing speech. Apart from easily recognized colloquialisms, we see that Luis indirectly reports popular language. When it is introduced by verbs like *decir*, the discursive element is still evident: "Apenas hay aquí quien acierte a comprender lo que llaman mi *manía de hacerme clérigo*, y esta buena gente me *dice*, *con un candor selvático*, que *debo ahorcar los hábitos*, que *el ser clérigo está bien para los pobretones*; pero que yo, que soy un rico heredero, debo casarme y consolar la vejez de mi padre, *dándole media docena de hermosos y robustos nietos*. Para adularme y adular a mi padre, *dicen* hombres y mujeres *que soy un real mozo, muy salado, que tengo mucho ángel, que mis ojos son muy pícaros* . . ." (6–7). The italicized phrases are statements of the townspeople that Luis would not ordinarily make, with the notable exception of " con un candor selvático." Although the only direct representations of the Dean's speech are the note and the letter to Don Pedro, it is probable that Luis learned this rather unusual phrase from him, for the Dean wrote that Pepita fell in love with Luis ". . . con un *candor* y un ímpetu *selváticos*" (183). (In this connection, we may add that the Dean's speech, like Luis's, is briefly characterized by a mixing of popular and spiritual language and by a similar use of analogy and illustrations [181–183 and 198–199].) Shortly after the passage cited above, Luis uses a

[53] Ullmann, *Style in the French Novel*, p. 119.

popular phrase without an introductory verb: "Está visto: *quieren cebarme*" (7).

Similar elements occur in the reporting of Pepita's background and of her marriage to Don Gumersindo, after which there occurs another mixing of learned and popular language: "Mi padre no está más adelantado ni ha salido mejor librado, según dicen, que los demás pretendientes; pero Pepita, para cumplir el refrán de que *lo cortés no quita a lo valiente, se esmera* en mostrarle la amistad más franca, afectuosa y desinteresada. *Se deshace con él en obsequios y atenciones;* y siempre que mi padre trata de hablarle de amor, *le pone a raya echándole un sermón dulcísimo,* trayéndole a la memoria sus pasadas culpas, y tratando de desengañarle del mundo y de sus *pompas vanas*" (14). Of the italicized phrases, all are of popular language except "se esmera," "Se deshace con él" etc., "dulcísimo," and "pompas vanas." After the first letter, such combinations also occur (though less frequently), especially in short phrases like the mentioned uses of *llevar calabazas.*

Don Pedro's humorous, ironical-critical speech, which is seen in his letter, in the epilogue, and in a few cases of direct discourse, is often reported indirectly by Luis, not without occasional insertions of his own.[54] A good example of this is Luis's narration of what his father told him about his relations with Pepita (24–25), of which a few phrases are:

> *Para ponderarme el mérito* de la novia y la dificultad del triunfo, me refirió las condiciones . . . de los . . . novios . . . , y que todos habían llevado calabazas. . . . Además, la causa del desvío de Pepita tenía para mi padre *un no sé qué de fantástico y de sofístico* que al cabo debía desvanecerse. Pepita no quería retirarse a un convento ni se inclinaba a la vida penitente: a pesar de su recogimiento y de su devoción religiosa, harto se dejaba ver que se complacía en agradar. El aseo y el esmero de su persona poco tenían de cenobíticos. . . . [Ella] *es un ser superior por la voluntad y por la inteligencia,* por más que con modestia lo disimule: ¿cómo, pues, ha de entregar su corazón a los palurdos que la han pretendido hasta ahora? (25)

[54] See Friedrich Todemann, "Die erlebte Rede im Spanischen," *Romanische Forschungen,* XLIV (1930), 103–184, especially 165, on this point.

In this case, I have italicized the words Don Pedro, according to his usual speech habits, would not be likely to say and which are characteristic of Luis's speech.[55] The device of having Luis report Don Pedro's comments allows the author to present his own views, as was seen by Montesinos: "Cuando D. Luis, inexperimentado como quien no ha visto el mundo sino por un agujero, debe callarse, es por boca de su padre por la que habla la experiencia mundana; con mayor habilidad y circunspección que otras veces puede así el autor introducirse en la novela y apuntar una idea útil para la interpretación de sus personajes."[56] With such a blending of voices it is less awkward for the author to insert his own ironical criticism even more directly, as when Luis says of the Spanish clergy: "¿Hay verdadera vocación en los que se consagran a la vida religiosa y a la cura de almas, o es sólo un modo de vivir como otro cualquiera, con la diferencia de que hoy no se dedican a él sino los más menesterosos, los más sin esperanzas y sin medios, por lo mismo que esta *carrera* ofrece menos porvenir que cualquier otra?" (20–21). Such passages as these and Luis's two semi-identifications with his father (25) and with Pepita (26–28) (used to replace his father and to reveal his own nature while censuring others), in addition to the general pastiche of styles, lend a surprising complexity of form and ambiguity to almost everything said in the stylized letters.

Friedrich Todemann has shown that Valera was one of the first of his generation to use free indirect style to depict thought processes (more than speech, which was successfully represented along with thought from 1880 on), although *Pepita Jiménez*, because of its epistolary method and first person narrative, shows less advance in this technique than *Doña Luz*.[57] Valera's use of the device is restrained and there is usually, but not always, a verb of mental activity close to the passage in free indirect style. One of the first examples in the narrative part of the novel, already cited by Todemann, is the following passage, in which the free indirect style is indicated by Valera's ironical borrowing from Luis's exaggerated speech, "con

[55] For similar passages of blended voices and the reported speech of Don Pedro, too long to quote, see *Pepita Jiménez*, pp. 67–69 and 73–74.

[56] Montesinos, *Valera o la ficción libre*, pp. 111–112.

[57] Todemann, "Die erlebte Rede im Spanischen," pp. 162–167.

titánica pujanza," and by the lack of an introductory verb before the question, which is Luis's: "Contra esto se rebelaba el orgullo de D. Luis *con titánica pujanza.* ¿Qué se diría de él, y sobre todo, qué pensaría él de sí mismo, si el ideal de su vida, el hombre nuevo que había creado en su alma, si todos sus planes de virtud, de honra y hasta de santa ambición se desvaneciesen en un instante, se derritiesen al calor de una mirada, por la llama fugitiva de unos lindos ojos, como la escarcha se derrite con el rayo débil aún del sol matutino?" (123). The rest of this passage (123–125), with some introductory verbs, is also in free indirect style.

Valera skillfully represents Antoñona's plans for Luis's visit (138–139) as well as the following passage, in which the *pero* clause is Luis's thought, in free indirect style, with a characteristic use of the conditional tense: "Impulsado por tales razones, lo primero que *pensó* D. Luis fué faltar a la cita sin dar excusa ni aviso, y que Antoñona le aguardase en balde en el zaguán; *pero* Antoñona anunciaría a su señora la visita, y él faltaría, no sólo a Antoñona, sino a Pepita, *dejando de ir*, con una grosería incalificable" (141). An interesting feature of many of the passages in free indirect style is the use of present participles, as in this case, to represent hypothetical actions. The next two pages, in which Luis considers various aspects of and possible courses of action concerning his promise to visit Pepita, are in the same vein, especially the following: "Dos o tres veces se levantó de su silla y empezó a andar en busca de su padre; pero luego se detenía y creía aquella revelación indigna, la creía una vergonzosa chiquillada. *El podía revelar sus secretos; pero revelar los de Pepita para ponerse bien con su padre, era bastante feo.* La fealdad y lo cómico y miserable de la acción se aumentaban, *notando* que el temor de no ser bastante fuerte para resistir era lo que a hacerla le movía. Don Luis se calló, pues, y no reveló nada a su padre" (142–143).

In the narration of Luis's approach to Pepita's house, Valera again represents Luis's thoughts without any subordination to introductory verbs, and, at the beginning, even uses a schematic verbless sentence: "Nada de aviso, nada de signo, nada de pompa fúnebre: todo vida, paz y deleite. *¿Dónde estaba el Angel de la Guarda? ¿Había* *dejado a D. Luis como cosa perdida, o, calculando que no corría peligro alguno, no se cuidaba de apartarle de su propósito? ¿Quién sabe? Tal vez de aquel peligro resultaría un triunfo.* San Eduardo y la reina Edita se ofrecían de nuevo a la imaginación de D. Luis y corroboraban su voluntad" (147). Other significant examples of free indirect style are:

> Con cierta mortificación de la vanidad *reflexionaba*, no obstante, D. Luis en el cambio que en él se había obrado. *¿Qué pensaría el Deán? ¿Qué espanto no sería el del Obispo? Y sobre todo, ¿qué motivo tan grave de queja no había dado D. Luis a su padre?* Su disgusto, su cólera cuando supiese el compromiso que ligaba a Luis con Pepita, se ofrecían al ánimo de D. Luis y le inquietaban sobremanera. (177)

> . . . D. Luis se sonreía y *sospechaba* que no había estado por completo en su juicio. Todo había sido presunción suya. *Ni él había hecho penitencia, ni él había vivido largos años en contemplación, ni él tenía ni había tenido merecimientos bastantes para que Dios le favoreciese con distinciones tan altas.* (178)

> En cuanto al mal éxito que tuvo la proyectada imitación de San Eduardo, también trataba de cohonestarle y disculparle. *San Eduardo se casó por razón de estado, porque los grandes del reino lo exigían, y sin inclinación hacia la reina Edita; pero en él y en Pepita Jiménez no había razón de Estado, ni grandes ni pequeños, sino amor finísimo de ambas partes.* (184)

The passages of free indirect style in *Pepita Jiménez* indicate the author's critical empathy. Empathy is denoted by Valera's use of expressions ordinarily employed by Luis in the ironical-critical representation of Luis's thoughts (see also page 194, lines 7–23), which are smoothly presented, usually without any subordination, although it is evident that they are thoughts because of the context.

II. REFINED IRONY AS THE INFORMING STYLISTIC PRINCIPLE

Despite Valera's reflection of the fundamental problems and aspirations—primarily centered around the Krausist and anticlerical movements—which were part of the spirit of the 1870's, his ideological commitment is offset by a partial escape from the prosaic, backward Spain of his day into a more refined, beautiful, and idealistic world—the world of art and form. In most of his novels the escape is not complete, as it is in several of his short stories with their fairy-tale atmosphere, but is always checked by his strong interest in his time and by his critical attitude; or, to put it conversely, his critical approach is concealed behind the veneer of a cosmopolitan, humanistic, liberal irony and sense of humor, on the psychological plane, and behind a restrained, well-proportioned surface elegance, on the linguistic plane. Again the criticism is softened by irony and by elegance. In an all-inclusive sense, then, Valera's critical empathy can be formulated as ideological commitment and verbal evasion (toward the *Siglo de Oro*), which, unified by refined irony, inform all aspects of *Pepita Jiménez* and its style.

Without actually stating it thus, the critics have suggested Valera's critical empathy and the importance of irony in his literary production. Alberto Jiménez mentions Valera's "natural burlonamente benigno,"[58] and says, after pointing out the speculative nature of Valera's essays: "Bajo *su elegante decir* y amables temas, a no menos altas especulaciones se entregan las novelas de Valera. . . . En sus novelas *expresó* Valera, *en forma* tan *elevada* que bien merece el título de 'segundo modo de poesía,' *los pensares y sentires de su edad*, llevando a sus lectores a vislumbrar la *beldad* y la *armonía* que lo más profundo y brioso de su generación perseguía."[59] Revuelta y Revuelta speaks of Valera's "*sentido crítico* y a la vez *benévolo* y complaciente, equilibrado . . . ," of his "serenidad optimista," with a "*matiz burlón o irónico*, siempre *lleno de bondad*."[60] Concerning Valera's attitude toward his characters, Brenan remarks: "We feel a mind at work that likes to survey the field of human action from a certain distance and not to be emotionally mixed up in it. But if he is Olympian like Goethe, he can also be sentimental and unctuous. *He flatters his characters* in the soft Andalusian way, though often

[58] Jiménez, *Juan Valera y la generación de 1868*, p. 95.
[59] *Ibid.*, p. 176 (italics mine).
[60] Revuelta y Revuelta, "Valera, estilista," pp. 41–42 (italics mine).

under his flattery there *lies* a good deal of *malice*."[61] Montesinos likewise intimates Valera's critical-empathic treatment of his characters: "En la actitud de Valera al contemplar cómo caen estos personajes *se mezclan la admiración, la socarronería, un desengaño a un tiempo melancólico e irónico*."[62] Valera often evinced at least a partial awareness of his critical empathy in his nonfictional writings; for instance, he said of himself and Pedro A. de Alarcón: ". . . usted y yo . . . estamos dotados, . . . de singular *doblez de carácter*. Ambos somos espiritualistas, idealistas hasta rayar en misticismo, y a la vez muy aficionados a lo real y sólido. . . ."[63]

We have seen that Valera's criticism of the contemporary world and of his characters is tempered by empathy and refined irony. The element of refinement in the irony is extremely important; through it we become aware of the author's sophistication and gain insight into his subtlety, which must be understood for a complete appreciation. Valera's irony is refined, first of all, because with his classical restraint he carefully avoids vulgarity, obviousness, exaggeration, and affectation in general. For instance, in resuming the traditional ironical use of the absolute superlative, he never goes to Cervantes's farcical, linguistically innovative extreme; rather, in Luis's statement that his father was *finísimo*, or in the *toque delicadísimo* of Pepita's hand (with the accompanying insinuations and mystical reminiscence), the irony is not immediately discernible. In the treatment of Luis and his speech, Valera establishes and maintains a line of demarcation between sincerity and irony which is so fine that even competent critics have failed to detect the irony. This subtlety is particularly existent in the pseudo-spiritual passages, because without a close examination of them in relation to Luis's emotional, psychological state, one may be misled into believing that he is sincere. In the same way, one must recognize the attenuating digressions for what they are in order to comprehend Luis's self-delusions, rationalizations, and interior stiltedness. The subtlety should cause the reader to pause and reflect on the mental processes of the pro-

[61] Brenan, *The Literature of the Spanish People*, p. 384 (italics mine).
[62] Montesinos, *Valera o la ficción libre*, p. 122 (italics mine).
[63] In Valera's letter to Pedro A. de Alarcón (1887), *Obras*, II, 617.

tagonist; when this occurs, the psychological portrayal of Luis becomes more impressive.

The twofold parody, which is directed toward false mysticism and poor theological training and which points to the sixteenth century on the linguistic level, with indirect criticism of all mysticism, of German idealistic philosophy and Krausism, is of such subtle refinement that it has usually been ignored or, at best, only summarily treated. When Luis, the Vicar, the Dean, and Pepita use spiritual language, the underlying irony is only discernible from the viewpoint of the ironical structure of the novel. Indeed, Luis is allowed to attain such a high degree of seriousness in the last few letters that the irony becomes almost imperceptible. However, in the second half of the novel, Luis's speech is more obviously ironical, as in his wrath-motivated paraphrase of the Sermon on the Mount or in his stilted dialogue with Pepita. Spiritual language is consciously ironized, with an added note of irreverence, in the speech of Don Pedro and Antoñona, and, since their speech is represented mainly in the second half, there is a resulting progressive intensification in the irony, which is climaxed by the sly mixture of Christianity and paganism at the conclusion of the epilogue. The irony, then, is graded from the barely perceptible to the farcical, depending on the speaker, the context, and the reader's recognition of phrases from mystical-ascetical literature. The evident cases of irony, such as "el misticismo de Luisito había salido huero" (203) or "cantarle el gorigori y rociarla con el hisopo" (118), and the key words of the parody—*místico*, etc.—point to the author's ironical-critical purposes and hint at the less obvious irony of other passages. Once it is realized, for example, that Luis's pseudo-mystical experiences are directly motivated by physical contact with Pepita, the overall ironical mixture of spirituality and eroticism becomes apparent.

The ironical use of *Siglo de Oro* stylistic expressions often creates refined irony in the different degrees of stiltedness of the lovers, occasioned by their inhibitions and attempted concealment of sensuality. The scale of stiltedness is also a widely diversified one, ranging from tightly organized, oratorical periods that skillfully blend doublets and triads with more extensive *pluralidades*, thus masking true feelings behind a symmetrical facade, to minor devices like the use of stock phrases and stereotyped comparisons. Highly significant are the euphemistic devices, which objectify the relationships by removing them to the relative anonymity of the third person, and the extended litotes, mainly used for characterization, which stress certain aspects while actually disclosing opposite ones, as in the masterful portrayal of Don Gumersindo or the representation of the local attitude toward Pepita. Then there is the frequent use of the enhancing adverb *tan*, which likewise stresses the opposite of the stated qualities. Within the symphonic structure, the thematic recurrence of phrases and allusions subtly points to new ironical relationships among the characters.

The irony is culturally refined by the author's unobtrusive use of his vast erudition. This feature of the novel is manifested, first, by literary-cultural allusions, the comprehension of which is indispensable for an understanding of Luis's portrayal. We may recall the very important references to Theseus, Phaedra, and Hippolytus in connection with Luis's gradual replacement of his father as Pepita's suitor. There are new, ironical juxtapositions of Christianity and paganism too, as in the mentions of St. Edward and St. John Chrysostom, models of chastity, and Philemon and Baucis, or to Ruth and Booz and Daphnis and Chloe. One often encounters literary reminiscences in characters and situations, such as the fact that Antoñona, like Aldonza Lorenzo, possessed great physical strength; or, when the reminiscences are linguistic ones, the result may be humor or ironical incongruity. On a strictly linguistic level, irony is caused by the use of archaic or semi-archaic words, the mixture of erudition and colloquialisms, erudite periphrases used jocularly, and the relatively frequent occurrence of the *cursus tardus*, composed of learned spiritual proparoxytones and absolute superlatives.

Refined irony permeates the entire novel and informs all phases of it and its style, thus providing unity and delightful ambiguity. The parodistic and ironical features and the *Siglo de Oro* expressions are not always readily discernible as such, a fact which reveals a significant avoidance of extremes, true classical restraint, in this subtle and elegant style. There is a wholesale mitigation on a higher level because Valera softens his ironical-critical approach to the problems of his age and to his characters by means of his sophisticated irony and empathy. Thus, while Valera attenuates his criticism with refinement and verbal evasion, he shares significant attributes and attitudes of his contemporaries concerning the polemics revolving around Krausism and religion. He also joined his fellow novelists in the reaction against prevailing styles and in the search for a more moderate, verisimilar prose style. In this quest, they ordinarily had to be content with the utilization of existent, conventional modes of expression. It is, therefore, inappropriate to blame them for a lack of originality, or of linguistic innovation, or of sustained attempts at writing poetic prose. Valera was one of the few among them to mold a personal style that was at once distinctive and artistic and yet highly effective for analysis, description, evocation, and representation of speech and thought.

SUMMARY

Valera's underlying purposes in writing *Pepita Jiménez*, partly to give a moral lesson against pride, but mainly to ridicule the subordination of human love to divine love, led him to utilize the Spanish ascetical-mystical literature of the sixteenth century in his subtle parody of the seminarian and false mystic. He was particularly attracted to the works of Santa Teresa and San Juan de la Cruz, from which unobtrusive borrowings may be seen in several aspects: the depiction of Luis's three pseudo-mystical experiences, imagery like Santa Teresa's *alegorías marciales* or San Juan de la Cruz's net-images, and on a secondary level of parody, the parallels between Luis's progression toward the consummation of his human love and the ascent of the *preprincipiante* to mystical union. Paradoxical statements similar to Santa Teresa's serve to depict the seminarian's inhibited love, and the frequently occurring verbs, *acertar*, *atinar*, and *procurar*, which were an outgrowth of Santa Teresa's true humility, are used to indicate false humility and psychological probing in *Pepita Jiménez*. Valera's firm knowledge of mystical language is attested by the appearance of such terms as *conversación interior*, *la vía unitiva*, and *la oración de quietud*, as well as by the important term, *el centro* (*abismo*, etc.) *del alma*, which, for Valera, acquires a new meaning, quite close to the modern concept of the unconscious mind.

From casuistic terminology Valera felicitously drew his introspective and psychological vocabulary, including such probing verbs as *abismarse*, *analizar*, *confesar*, *desnudar*, *escudriñar*, *penetrar*, *profundizar*, and *registrar*. A great deal of ascetical language appears in Luis's sham examinations of conscience and in his romantic, self-deluding references to his calling. The characters' use of spiritual language, of illustrations for mock-purposes, and of specious reasoning constitutes theological cant. Direct paraphrases from the Bible are made in new combinations that are always ironical and sometimes poetic, as in the borrowings from the Psalms and the Canticle. Mystical-spiritual imagery and allusions are given a pleasing ambiguity because of their surface beauty, underlying irony, and psychological significance. In short, all that Valera took from mystical-spiritual language for his purposes of parody, characterization, and ironical criticism acquires a new, subtle, and ambiguous aesthetic value and makes the style of *Pepita Jiménez* essentially mock-spiritual.

By employing the epistolary method, Valera unobtrusively expanded the parody of spiritual language, primarily of mystical-ascetical writings of the sixteenth century, to a general pastiche of the *Siglo de Oro* epoch style, especially that of Cervantes in *Don Quijote*. Always avoiding affectation, Valera made a linguistically sure choice among *Siglo de Oro* forms of expression, including: borderline archaisms like *cuán* with a verb and *sobrado* as an adverb; words and constructions, relatively rare in modern usage, which are *castizos* and immediately evocative of the *Siglo de Oro*, such as *cuitas* and *Mediando*, *como media* . . . ; literary and elegant words and phrases like *de cortas luces*, *en punto a*, and the frequent use of *cuanto* to avoid relative clauses introduced by *que;* and stock phrases and comparisons, often ironized, like *la dama de sus pensamientos* and *ojos verdes como los de Circe*.

Above all, one finds in *Pepita Jiménez* the devices which, in the *Siglo de Oro*, served the basic though not unique purpose of mitigation. The most obvious feature of Valera's prose style is the almost constant appearance of *pluralidades*, particularly manifested by: binary combinations, especially verb doublets which often have assonance or rhyme, as in *le cuidaba y regalaba, le atendió y veló*, or which recall Cervantine ones like *no he tenido ni tengo* and *quiero y debo*; a general pattern of binary combinations mixed with ternary constructions; amplification and gradation in the more extensive occurrences of *pluralidades*; and didactic-planned enumerations which rarely exceed five members and of which the logical disposition is frequently reinforced by a summation phrase. Luis employs *pluralidades* in tightly organized periods which mask his sensual emotions and guilt behind a well-balanced, formalized exterior; but concessive clauses and qualifying remarks often serve as escape valves for his repressed feelings, thus ironically revealing his interior stiltedness, as do the occasional cases in which there is unexpected complexity in the apparently intellectual organization. *Pluralidades* in the pseudo-philosophical and seemingly altruistic digressions, such as Luis's remarks about his mission, and in the mock-spiritual and classical-descriptive passages are used by Luis for rationalization and mitigation. Since these passages are interspersed with self-revealing phrases and franker expressions of his true nature, there is a resultant wave-movement between the two extremes which again reflects his general stiltedness.

Other important attenuating devices are: summation phrases like *en resolución*, *en suma*, *todo esto*, and *por último*; smooth linking phrases, especially at the beginning of paragraphs, such as *En esto*, *Dicho esto*, and *Oído el señor Vicario*; a traditional quality and evocativeness in the descriptions attained by the pre-position of adjectives in literary epithet-substantive combinations like *verdes sembrados* and *tímida gacela*; *no parecer sino* and a graded use of the indicative and subjunctive after *tal vez*; litotes; and euphemisms. The euphemisms are used on a grand scale by Luis because he is afraid to tell the truth; thus he describes Pepita's servants in detail only to be able to describe Pepita by comparison. Luis and Pepita, as a result of their inhibitions, try to impersonalize their relationship by referring to themselves in the third person with words like *el prójimo*, *alguien*, *esta mujer*, and *zafia aldeana*. This procedure sometimes becomes a veiled means of flirtation.

Siglo de Oro style elements other than mitigating devices are also found in Valera. The main ones are perceptible *clausulae*, especially the *cursus tardus*; rhyme, assonance, and alliteration; repetition; and the latinizing end-position of the finite verb. Their importance is heightened by the fact that they appear in clusters and in meaningful contexts. It seems that Valera's prose is thus distinguished from that of his nineteenth-century contemporaries, who make no significant use of these elements. The same is true of the *Siglo de Oro* expressions in general because, although they are found in Spanish prose of most epochs, in none of Valera's contemporaries do they appear in such meaningful constellations or with functions so similar to those of the *Siglo de Oro*. Yet a sure sense of style enabled Valera to give these traditional forms original values and functions.

Notwithstanding the great differences in subject matter and scope, *Pepita Jiménez* bears rather striking structural and thematic resemblances to *Don Quijote*. In each work the protagonist exemplifies a common folly of his time, confuses reality and illusion, reflects his reading in ironized stilted speech, and is revealed as a psychologically complex person; but while Cervantes's ironical treatment of these matters is hyperbolic and is generally within the Catholic tradition, Valera's is marked by refinement and, underneath the genial humor, subtle anticlericalism. The essential difference in the treatment of the reality problem is that Luis, instead of grossly misinterpreting external events, twists and colors his true inner feelings and attitudes to fit his guilt-ridden rationalizations. In each novel there appear the leitmotifs of the protagonist's alleged mission, the return-motif (in which Luis, like Sancho, expresses the desire to return to his former way of life, although in a different relationship), and the motifs of magic and the supernatural. Then, too, there are similarities in devices and techniques, such as Valera's use of ironical concessive clauses, litotes, and stilted circumlocutions for characterization; the brief, evocative descriptions of characters, especially their gestures and poses; and the occasional closed phrases, *frases espectativas*, and contrary-to-fact conditional sentences—all in the Cervantine tradition.

Valera deviated from the "renunciative" Contreras-Cervantes tradition, however, in his treatment of youth and love, to which he imparted modern implications of eroticism and inhibitions. By means of his critical empathy, his ironical insistence on what he considered excusable, his allusions and symbols, like the central *Lucero* manhood-symbol, his utilizations of probing vocabulary in the analyses of motives and attitudes, and his felicitous use of the epistolary method, which brings the reader close to the character's mental processes, Valera wrote the first modern psychological novel in Spanish literature. The psychology, which is primarily that of the adolescent, though greatly complicated by Luis's religious training, commitment to the priesthood, illegitimacy, and unresolved oedipal conflict, is presented with such artistry and truth that Valera's work must be placed well in the forefront of European efforts along these lines. Luis's rapid progression toward maturity is skillfully depicted from his early heightened sense of awareness and awakened sensuality to the climactic love tryst and his reactions to it. Typical conflicting traits of adolescence are even more serious in Luis and result in great interior contradictions that are revealed by concessive clauses and other hedging statements, or "loophole clauses." The frequent appearance of clauses with *aun*, *aunque*, *si*, *casi*, and *tal vez*, and of such words as *pero*, *sin embargo*, *a pesar de*, *disimular*, *excusarse*, and *pretextar* is indicative of Luis's interior contradictions and his self-deluding, wavering style.

The implicit relations among the characters and the subtle cross-reference of phrases impart nuances of irony and call forth revisions of previous concepts. Such complexity, directly implemented by the epistolary method, indicates the important quality of allusiveness in Valera's style. The circumstances of Luis's birth and childhood, his early relations with his father, and the animosity between the latter and the Dean are only hinted at. The late exchange of letters between Don Pedro and the Dean provides additional irony and ambiguity to Luis's blaming of his father for remaining in the town and for attending Pepita's *tertulia*, and, in fact, points out the irony of what Luis supposes is his rivalry with his father, who actually does everything possible to have Luis fall in love with Pepita. Valera's criticism of the other characters is graded according to the degree of his empathy; thus he is least critical of those on the side of nature and most critical of those with theological training. Then, through his critical empathy and Luis's mimic-reporting style in the letters, there occurs a restrained, elegant blending of voices, a substitutionary reporting in which each character's voice, however refined, still has its distinguishing characteristics.

Valera's critical empathy toward his characters and contemporary Spain shows that he was not a completely detached follower of art for art's sake, but rather a product of his age, a man who demonstrated vital interest in the problems centering around Krausism, idealism, and anticlericalism and was actively engaged in the polemics of his time. The polemical nature of the 1870's is reflected in dialectical aspects of *Pepita Jiménez*, particularly the formalized, suasive speech of the characters and the stylized debates. Though Valera's style in *Pepita Jiménez* is essentially derived from *Siglo de Oro* traditions, it has the refinements of the nineteenth century. Quasi-parody in the language eliminates sarcasm, cynicism, and criticism by elegant and refined empathy, which provides understanding of the sadder implications of spurious mysticism and a misguided or ill-trained clergy.

The prominent features of Valera's artistic achievement in *Pepita Jiménez* are psychological complexity in his depiction of adolescent love; the "classical restraint" with which he adapts borrowed elements to his purposes; expressiveness and condensation, as in indirect characterizations and telescoping of means;[1] and ambiguity and "multivalence"[2]—surface beauty and elegance with underlying stiltedness, refined irony with psychological significance.[3] Valera's style in *Pepita Jiménez* may best be characterized as evocative, allusive,

[1] See R. A. Sayce, *Style in French Prose* (Oxford: Oxford Univ. Press, 1953), pp. 123 and 133–134, in particular, and pp. 126–136, concerning related matters of value judgments.

[2] See René Wellek and Austin Warren, *Theory of Literature* (New York: Harcourt, Brace, 1949), pp. 253–259, and in general, pp. 248–262.

[3] José F. Montesinos aptly calls *Pepita Jiménez* an "esperpento," in this general sense: ". . . lo característico del esperpento es que nos ofrezca la personalidad de los personajes que acoge en reflejos múltiples que juntos componen un complejo haz de realidad" (*Valera o la ficción libre* [Madrid: Gredos, 1957], p. 120).

ironical, and refined. Above all, that which causes intellectual pleasure and ambiguity on the psychological level causes, on the stylistic level, verbal pleasure and ambiguity: namely, an overall irony which informs the novel's structure and becomes the unifying principle of its psychology and style.

APPENDIX: *Considerations on the Problem of Supposed Gallicisms and Barbarisms in* Pepita Jiménez

I

The relationships between traditional modes of expression and new ones among Spanish novelists of the second half of the nineteenth century are clouded by an overzealous purist reaction. It has become such a commonplace in the twentieth century to criticize nineteenth-century prose writers for carelessness, lack of elegance and variety, overwrought, elaborately rhetorical phraseology, and even faulty constructions and poor diction, that it is surprising to see the vitriolic manner in which the purists rejected a great number of words and locutions because they were supposedly pernicious Gallicisms or barbarisms.

An early leader of the purist reaction was Rafael María Baralt. His *Diccionario de galicismos* (1st ed., 1855; 2nd ed., 1874) was widely influential. His chief followers were José María Sbarbi and, more importantly, Padre Juan Mir y Noguera. The latter's mammoth two-volume lexical study, *Prontuario de Hispanismo y Barbarismo* (Madrid, 1908), contains thousands of examples of so-called Gallicisms and barbarisms from writers of the eighteenth and nineteenth centuries. Supposedly superior words or phrases for each expression are quoted from "classical" or Golden Age Spanish writers. Although Mir possessed great knowledge of the Spanish lexicon and corrected many of Baralt's mistakes, he was an antiquated lexicographer and transmitted to noted lexicographers and academicians of the twentieth century his excessively purist and stylistically blind criteria. Like Baralt's, however, Mir's work is none the less useful as a guide to many of the important lexical questions of the day.

The Spanish Academy Dictionaries of the time, although far too conservative, are of interest because they enable us to trace the development of the language in the acceptance of certain expressions and meanings. The eleventh edition of the Academy Dictionary (1869) is particularly useful for the study of the major nineteenth-century novelists' vocabulary because of its date (prior to the publication of the important novels) and because of the inclusion of many new words. The label of archaicness (*anticuado*) is removed from many words and Latin equivalents are suppressed for the first time. Gradual acceptance of some supposed Gallicisms and barbarisms is noted in the next few editions.

The information found in the very complete dictionaries published during the early years of the twentieth century by Aniceto Pagés de Puig and by Elías Zerolo *et al.* may today be supplemented by Corominas and by Martín Alonso's three-volume *Enciclopedia del idioma* (Madrid, 1958). The latter work lays claim to being the most complete historical dictionary yet written for the Spanish language. But its dates are at times erroneous or too vague (for example, items are attested to be from the seventeenth to the twentieth centuries), or important meanings are omitted.

In view of these limitations and the lack of a complete up-to-date historical dictionary of the Spanish language, it will be useful, though difficult, to study the meanings of selected words and phrases used by Valera in *Pepita Jiménez*. More importantly, however, such considerations will facilitate comprehension of certain stylistic and psychological nuances in *Pepita Jiménez*'s vocabulary. But there will be no pretension here of anything like the vastly detailed and precise study that such a problem merits.

The Andalusian priest, José María Sbarbi, in an essay published shortly after the appearance of *Pepita Jiménez*, ironically criticized its language, claiming that he did not know until finishing the essay that the novel was by the distinguished academician, Juan Valera. This little study, called "Un plato de garrafales," was written in 1874, although it was not published in a book until much later.[1] Sbarbi attacked the language of *Pepita Jiménez* to show the bad effect being produced on Spanish literary style by carelessness and by thoughtless imitation of French. For whatever it is worth, Valera recognized partial justification for Sbarbi's criticism but said that he was glad because it proved his style was spontaneous and not affected.[2]

That Juan Valera was not unaware of the problem of Gallicisms is evidenced by comments scattered throughout his works. In one of the *Nuevas cartas americanas* (Dec. 20, 1896), he is concerned lest Spanish-American writers, like Rubén Darío and Carlos Reyles, imitate French models too closely. He finds what he calls "el galicismo de pensamiento," as seen in Reyles's *Academias*, much more harmful than the use of Gallicisms. He enters a firm plea for tolerance and common sense in the whole matter of additions to Spanish vocabulary:

No sería justo que me atribuyesen por lo expuesto una afición intolerante a lo castizo. No ya sólo para los pensamientos, hasta para las palabras, frases y giros, repugno yo las aduanas y las fronteras y pido libertad de comercio. Todo pensamiento, si es bueno, tomémoslo, aunque no sea español. Y aceptemos también vocablos y modos de expresarse de otros países, con tal de que falten en nuestro idioma y con tal de que sepamos acomodarlos a él con arte y con gracia. Tan firme estoy yo en esta opinión, que la mitad de las expresiones que don Rafael María Baralt pone como galicismos en su *Diccionario de galicismos*, o me parece que no lo son, o bien que, aun siéndolos, no son vitandos. Así, por ejemplo, cuando Baralt condena el término de *elegante négligé* o *deshabillé*,

[1] José María Sbarbi, "Un plato de garrafales," in *Ambigú literario* (Madrid: Fuentenebro, 1897), pp. 1–14.

[2] In a letter written by Valera, May 15, 1897, *Correspondencia de don Juan Valera (1859–1905)*, ed. Cyrus C. DeCoster (Madrid: Castalia, 1956), p. 245. Valera mentioned Sbarbi's work earlier, Oct. 24, 1891 (*Obras*, III, 435).

y sostiene que debemos decir *elegante trapillo*, yo no puedo menos de reírme. La palabra *trapillo* implica pobreza, suciedad u ordinariez, y brama de verse junta con el epíteto elegante. . . .

De notar es, además, que muchas frases y palabras que se suponen galicismos no son sino neologismos, malos o buenos; y si son buenos, no sé por qué han de desecharse. A menudo ocurre también que en España, y acaso por ahí, se considere galicismo tal o cual frase castellana semejante a otra francesa, pero que tiene en francés un valer muy diferente. *Hacer el amor*, verbigracia, vale hoy en España, sobre poco más o menos, tanto como requebrar, enamorar, obsequiar, servir y pretender a una dama para conseguir lo que en francés se llama hacer el amor, *faire l'amour* con ella. Es, pues, evidente que ni la frase está tomada del francés ni significa lo mismo en francés que en castellano.[3]

Manuel Azaña showed that the proper balancing of old and new words and constructions had been a primary concern of Valera's much earlier, ever since his "apprenticeship" under Estébanez Calderón.[4] Estébanez made Valera study areas of Spanish literature that he did not know, aroused some interest in him regarding folklore and colloquial language, and criticized his use of so-called impure vocabulary. But, as Azaña said, "Valera no secundó ni en la doctrina ni con el ejemplo el riguroso purismo de su maestro."[5] Azaña then cites the following comment from Valera's "Discurso de . . . recepción en la Real Academia Española" (1862): "Tampoco soy yo de los que por amor al lenguaje y a su pureza se desvelan y afanan en imitar a un clásico de los siglos XVI y XVII. Prefiero una dicción menos pura, prefiero incurrir en los galicismos que censuro a hacerme premioso en el estilo o duro y afectado."[6] In short, Valera sought an amenable, unmannered style. But, with his vast erudition and excellent memory, many details, phrases, and constructions remained in his mind. To appreciate fully his style, it would be necessary to study his vocabulary as a happy blending of the traditional and literary with the modern.

[3] Valera, *Obras*, III, 482–483.
[4] Manuel Azaña, "Estébanez Calderón y Valera," *Contemporáneos* (México), no. 18 (Nov., 1929), 296–317, and no. 9 (Dec., 1929), 339–353.
[5] *Ibid.*, p. 317.
[6] Valera, *Obras*, III, 1056.

The most vitriolic and detailed criticism of Valera's vocabulary in *Pepita Jiménez* is a curious, little-known work by Luis de Ocharan Mazas called *Incorrecciones deslizadas en las páginas de "Pepita Jiménez."*[7] Ocharan Mazas, who used, and practically reproduced, everything found in Sbarbi's " Un plato de garrafales," did not have a modern, well-formed judgment of lexical matters. He criticized sarcastically or ironically what he should have tried to explain. Perhaps he was right in a few cases, but in general it appears that twentieth-century usage has corroborated Valera's choice of what Ocharan Mazas called Gallicisms, many of which could have come from other languages, since Valera knew, in addition to French, Latin, Greek, English, German, Portuguese, and Italian.

Ocharan Mazas also adapted material from other purists, especially Baralt and Mir, but not always correctly. Only rarely did he go against the purists and approve Valera's choice of words.

Despite the lack of a modern perspective in Ocharan Mazas (and his predecessors), what he (and they) wrote may serve us today as a stimulus for the investigation of: (1) the vocabulary of *Pepita Jiménez* (and, eventually, of other works by Valera), especially in regard to Gallicisms, neologisms, foreign words, as well as pure and elegant locutions; (2) the stylistic and, at times, psychological values reflected in the choice of words; (3) the relationships between Valera's usage and the spirit of his times (and, ideally, the period style).

It is, of course, impossible for me to undertake at this point such a task in the desirable dimensions. It will be necessary, therefore, to limit myself to key words and phrases.

II

References to *Pepita Jiménez* (*PJ*) will be to the "Clásicos Castellanos" edition. Ocharan Mazas will be referred to as OM. When known, his most likely sources are indicated within parentheses. The dictionaries and vocabulary studies mentioned above will be cited

[7] Luis de Ocharan Mazas, *Incorrecciones deslizadas en las páginas de "Pepita Jiménez"* (Madrid: Tipografía de la "Revista de arch., bibl. y museos," 1924).

by the authors' names. When the Academy Dictionaries are mentioned, only the 11th (1869), 12th (1884), and the 13th (1899) editions are meant. Individually they will be cited as *DRAE* (*Diccionario de la Real Academia Española*) with the year.

I have not as a rule tried to reproduce the typography of the various sources. In regard to equivalents proposed by OM, I have quoted them in succession whenever it was feasible to do so without including unnecessarily repeated phrases or irrelevant remarks. Otherwise, his equivalents are quoted individually. A statement to the effect that a given word or phrase is (or is not) in a particular dictionary means that it appears (or does not appear) there in the meaning or usage under discussion. Comments or definitions are quoted only when necessary. In the case of M. Alonso, I have quoted, whenever possible and useful, from the number of the definition on, and have changed the centuries from Roman to Arabic numerals. Supporting examples and my comments are given only when directly appropriate. There is, inevitably, some overlapping in the topical groupings, which are intended merely as guides to understanding. Although it was usually considered unnecessary to explain the relationships between an item and its heading, in a few cases explanations or comments are included.

The abbreviations used or quoted are the standard ones in English and Spanish lexical studies. A list follows:

adj.	adjective	*ms. advs.*	*modos adverbiales*
ex.	example	*met.*	*metafórico*
exs.	examples	*n.*	noun; *neutro*
F.	*francés*	*Patol.*	*Patología*
fig.	*figurado*	*pl.*	plural
Filos.	*Filosofía*	*port.*	*portugués*
fr. fig. y fam.	*frase figurada y familiar*	*Psicol.*	*Psicología*

inf.	infinitive	*r.*	*reflexivo*
m.	*substantivo masculino*	*s.*	*siglo, siglos*
m. adv.	*modo adverbial*	*Teol.*	*Teología*
		tr.	*verbo transitivo*

Vestiges of Older Usage and Possible Regionalisms

ABANDONO. "Siento una dejadez, un quebranto, un *abandono* de la voluntad" (*PJ*, p. 33, line 13). OM (following Baralt and Mir): "descaecimiento, dejamiento, dejación, desmayo, flaqueza, desfallecimiento, abatimiento . . ." (pp. 46–47). ". . . con la humildad y el *abandono* completo con que se ofreció a Booz la nuera de Noemi" (*PJ*, p. 157, line 3). *DRAE*: *abandonar*. "Entregarse a la ociosidad, a los vicios; descuidar uno sus intereses u obligaciones . . ."; *abandono*. "Acción y efecto de abandonar o abandonarse." M. Alonso lists, among others, the following meaning, which could have influenced Valera: "3. Teol. Entre los místicos, entrega total del alma a Dios, para que la trate o pruebe como quiera."

Supporting examples indicate a much wider spread, and perhaps a regional, though still psychologically interesting usage. Exs.: "¡Con qué expresión y juego/ de talle y brazos Silvia/ En amable *abandono*/ Su Palemón esquiva!" (Juan Meléndez Valdés, *Poesías*, "Clásicos Castellanos," no. 64, pp. 13–14. ". . . recogíme en el cuadro de flores que yo mismo cultivo a gozar del triste y dulce *abandono* que inspira una tarde serena . . ." (S. Estébanez Calderón, *Obras*, *BAE*, II, 355); "Amémonos con *abandono*" (Valera, in a letter to his future wife, 1867: C. C. DeCoster, *Correspondencia de don Juan Valera*, p. 38); two examples from Valera in the new, still incomplete *Diccionario histórico de la lengua española*. Cf. "La noche de la Nava se presentaba viva en su imaginación, con su *abandono*, con su deleite, con todos sus hermosos delirios . . ." (Valera, *Las ilusiones del doctor Faustino*, *Obras*, I, 315).

ALTA NOCHE. "Si me despierto en el silencio de la *alta noche* y oigo que algún campesino enamorado canta, . . . suelo enternecerme . . ." (*PJ*,

p. 42, line 8). OM (following Sbarbi): "muy noche," "media noche" (p. 53). Not in the Academy Dictionaries or Zerolo. M. Alonso gives only "alta hora" and "alto día." Corominas, I, under *alto*, says that Baralt was wrong to call "altas horas de la noche" a neologism and adds: "se ha dicho también *alta noche* [Zorrilla, 1852], port. *alta noite*. . . ."

Also: Valera, *Obras*, I, 255; Bécquer, *Rimas*, xvi and xxviii; Juan Ramón Jiménez, *Libros de poesía* (Madrid: Aguilar, 1959), pp. 332, 354, 364–365, and *Platero y yo*, ch. lxvi. Since, besides these examples among Andalusians, the expression is also found in Azorín, R. Gómez de la Serna, C. J. Cela, and Juan Rulfo, it must be more common than generally recognized.

DE DIARIO (ADV.). "Todo esto, . . . ocupa aquí *de diario* a los hidalgos . . ." (*PJ*, p. 55, line 20). OM (following Mir): "cada día, diariamente, todos los días" (p. 68). The Academy Dictionaries and Zerolo give neither *de diario* or *a diario*. Mir, I, under *a*, calls Valera's usage erroneous, but lists *a diario*, as does M. Alonso. Cf. Valera, *Obras*, I, 1107; and Echegaray: ". . . al ocupar en su mesa/ *de diario* el mismo sitial" (*El gran Galeoto*, I, ii).

EN EL DÍA. ". . . y como *en el día* se publica todo . . ." (*PJ*, p. 4, line 11). OM (following Mir): "hoy, hoy en día, hoy día, el día de hoy" (p. 13). "Pepita, . . . se ve *en el día* considerada y respetada extraordinariamente" (*PJ*, p. 14, line 7). OM: "hoy en día" (p. 26). The Academy Dictionaries, Zerolo, and M. Alonso do not give this expression; but the usage is close to that given in *DRAE* (1869): "*El día de hoy* mod. adv. El *día* presente, en esta época." *En el día*, very frequent in Valera, is also more common than the dictionaries indicate. Examples were seen in Larra (*Artículos escogidos*; Buenos Aires: Estrada, 1957, p. 98); F. Martínez de la Rosa (*Obras dramáticas;* Madrid: Espasa-Calpe, 1933, p. 410); E. Pardo Bazán (*Los Pazos de Ulloa*, ch. xxv); José Yxart (*El arte escénico en España;* Madrid, 1896, II, 115). The meaning also occurs in *del día* and *hasta el día.*

GENTES. "A veces se interrogaban en balde las *gentes* unas a otras a ver si alguien le había visto estrenar una prenda" (*PJ*, p. 9, line 26). ". . . tal vez sería más difícil empresa el moralizar y evangelizar un poco a estas *gentes*" (*PJ*, p. 20, line 14). OM (following Baralt): "gente," "puesto que en buen romance *gentes* representa multitud de personas que habitan diversas regiones, hablan distintas lenguas y tienen diferentes costumbres" (p. 32). Also *PJ*, p. 111, line 22; p. 197, line 16; cf. OM, pp. 116–117 and 148. *DRAE* (1869): "pl. Los gentiles. Hoy sólo tiene uso en la expresión: el Apóstol de las *gentes*." Mir (I, 903–905), in addition to giving the Academy Dictionary definition a somewhat more ample interpretation, says that *gentes* is also used for "hombres," "personas," etc., and even for "criados" and "miembros de la familia." Zerolo gives examples of the plural use of *gente* and tries to make distinctions between *gentes* and *personas*, and *gentes* and *gente*. Thus it is odd to find M. Alonso and Corominas mistaken in their treatments of *gentes*. M. Alonso: "12. pl. *Gentiles*. Hoy sólo tiene uso en la expresión" [*sic*]. Corominas: "En el período arcaico predomina el uso plural (*las yentes*), al fin de la Edad Media el singular gana terreno y el plural va quedando relegado después al estilo eclesiástico (*el apóstol de las gentes*), hasta el punto de que en el S. XIX y hoy en día sólo lo emplean los escritores afrancesados, como observa Baralt." Nevertheless, the use of the plural must be more widespread, since it is found in American Spanish, in phrases like "todas las gentes." Also, two usages were observed in Pereda's *El sabor de la tierruca* ("Biblioteca Contemporánea," Losada, no. 47, pp. 127, 140). Cf. C. Laforet: "Aquellas *gentes* [relatives and a servant], . . . parecían haberme cargado con todo el calor y el hollín del viaje . . ." (*Nada*, ch. i).

PÁSEME USTED LA PALABRA. ". . . quién sabe si . . . se propone, *páseme V. la palabra*, molerle antes con sus desdenes . . ." (*PJ*, p. 40, line 25). OM (following Sbarbi): "con perdón sea dicho, disimule usted la frase, dicho sea sin ofender a usted . . ." (p. 52). The Academy Dictionaries do not list the expression with this meaning, but the verb *pasar* has appropriate meanings. *DRAE* (1869): *pasar*. "No poner reparo, censura o tacha en alguna cosa. Callar u omitir algo. . . . Disimular o no darse por entendido. . . ." Cf. M. Alonso: *pasar*. "10. s. 16 al 20. Sufrir, tolerar." Other exs. by Valera: " 'En el conjunto *sinfónico* (*páseme usted la palabrilla*) de la música alemana se cree oír la voz misma del espíritu del mundo' " (1855; *PJ*, Intro., pp. xxviii-xxix); ". . . *páseme* usted la metáfora" (1862; *Obras*, II, 326); ". . . *pásame* lo grosero de la palabra" (*Pasarse de listo*; *Obras*, I, 524).

New or Modern Meanings and Usages

CARÁCTER. "¿Tendrá por fundamento, en parte al menos, el *carácter* de mis relaciones con mi padre?" (*PJ*, p. 17, line 25). "Mi triunfo fué grande y solemne, aunque impropio de mi *carácter*" (*PJ*, p. 78, line 6). OM (following Mir): "temperamento, índole, natural, condición, inclinación, genio, etc." (p. 28). Also *PJ*, p. 44, line 10; p. 58, line 17; p. 123, line 29; p. 156, line 11; p. 185, line 26; cf. OM, pp. 56, 72, 119, 136, 147. *DRAE* (1869): "La índole, genio y condición de cada uno." M. Alonso: "9. s. 19 y 20. Indole, condición: conjunto de rasgos o circunstancias con que se da a conocer una cosa distinguiéndose de las demás. 10. s. 19 y 20. Natural o modo de ser peculiar . . . de cada persona por sus cualidades morales."

DARSE CUENTA. ". . . Pepita apenas *se* había *dado cuenta* de que amaba a D. Luis . . ." (*PJ*, p. 104, lines 5-6). OM (following Mir): "dar en la cuenta, caer en la cuenta"; "echar de ver, advertir . . ." (pp. 104–105). Not in the Academy Dictionaries. Zerolo: "*Darse cuenta de* una cosa. fr. fig. y fam. Echarla de ver, notarla" (ex. from *PJ*).

DESTACARSE. "El sol acababa de ocultarse . . . , haciendo que las pirámides, agujas y rotos obeliscos de la cumbre *se destacasen* sobre un fondo de púrpura y topacio . . ." (*PJ*, p. 145, line 9). OM (following Baralt and Mir): "sobresaliesen, resaltasen" (p. 129). The Academy Dictionaries and Zerolo give only the military and pictorial meanings, which are explained by Corominas. M. Alonso gives the modern meaning: "4. r. fig. s. 19 y 20. Sobresalir, descollar . . ." (with examples from Azorín and G. Miró).

FORMULAR. ". . . las ideas que expresaba y *formulaba*" (*PJ*, p. 103, line 25). OM (following Mir): "declaraba" (p. 104). Not in the Academy Dictionaries or Zerolo. M. Alonso: "3. Expresar, manifestar."

INVEROSÍMIL; INVEROSIMILITUD. *PJ*: p. 11, line 5; p. 105, line 1; p. 129, line 4. OM (following Academy Dictionaries and Mir) prefers the spelling of these words with *i*, not *o*. M. Alonso lists both spellings, the one with *o* since the 18th C.

LEJOS DE + INF. ". . . *lejos de* ser favorable a esta mujer, estaba yo prevenido contra ella con prevención injusta" (*PJ*, p. 51, line 8). "*Lejos de* dejar de ir a casa de Pepita, voy más temprano todas las noches" (*PJ*, p. 89, line 9). "*Lejos de* llevarte al chico otra vez, le retendré aquí, hasta por fuerza, si es necesario" (*PJ*, p. 201, line 14). OM: "en vez de," "en lugar de" (pp. 61–62). This construction is not given in the Academy Dictionaries or in Zerolo. In Mir: II, 153–158. M. Alonso: "Al contrario, de un modo opuesto."

MISIÓN. "¿Está en España [el clero] a la altura de su *misión*?" (*PJ*, p. 20, line 30). OM (following Baralt and Mir): "cargo, obligación, ministerio . . ." (pp. 34–35). In *DRAE* (1869): "2. Encargo, comisión."

MODO DE SER. "En fin, vivo como fuera de mi centro y de mi *modo de ser*" (*PJ*, p. 29, line 8). OM (following Mir): "genio, natural, costumbre, condición, hábito, índole" (p. 41). *DRAE* (1869) gives "modo de existir" as a meaning of *ser*.

NADA DE. "*Nada de* pasión ardiente, *nada de* fuego hay en los ojos de Pepita" (*PJ*, p. 80, line 29). "*Nada de* aviso, *nada de* signo, *nada de* pompa fúnebre: todo vida, paz y deleite" (*PJ*, p. 147, lines 14–15). OM (following Mir): "Ni . . . , ni . . ."; "No . . . , no . . ." (p. 93). This meaning is not given in the Academy Dictionaries or Zerolo. M. Alonso: "2. s. 14 al 20. Carencia de todo ser. . . ." *Nada de* is not given, but it is understood from the meanings of *nada* and *de* and is more emphatic than *ni . . . ni*, or *no . . . no*.

PERFUME. "Las hierbas y flores vertían más generoso *perfume*" (*PJ*, p. 146, line 15; also p. 161, line 24; p. 170, line 17). OM: "olor, aroma y fragancia" (p. 130; also pp. 138–139, 144). In *DRAE* (1869). M. Alonso: "4. fig. s. 18 al 20. Cualquier olor bueno o muy agradable."

DE PIE. "Pepita, . . . quedó sola, *de pie* . . ." (*PJ*, p. 117, line 21). OM: "*en pie* o *de pies*" (pp. 118–119). Not in Academy Dictionaries. Zerolo: "*De pie.* m. adv. *En pie.* 'Pertenecía el discurso que se pronunciaba *de pie*.' " M. Alonso: "*De pie. De pies.* ms. advs. En pie."

PORVENIR. ". . . esa *carrera* ofrece menos *porvenir* que cualquiera otra" (*PJ*, p. 21, line 5). OM (following Baralt): "buena suerte, bienandanza, provecho . . ." (p. 35). ". . . todo el *porvenir* que se había creado se deshacía al punto . . ." (*PJ*, p. 130, line 30). OM: "lo por venir" (p. 121). The Academy Dictionaries and subsequent ones give only "suceso o tiempo futuro."

PREOCUPACIÓN; PREOCUPARSE. "Tales son, querido tío, las *preocupaciones* y ocupaciones de mi padre en este pueblo (*PJ*, p. 26, line 1). OM (following Mir): "cuidados," "aflicción," "zozobra" (pp. 38–40). "Sobre este caso de conciencia harto alambicado y sutil para que así *preocupe* a una lugareña" (*PJ*, p. 27, line 19). OM: "para que ande *confusa y turbada* una lugareña" (p. 40). In the Academy Dictionaries. M. Alonso: *preocupación.* "4. s. 17 al 20. Cuidado, desvelo, previsión de alguna contingencia azarosa o adversa." *preocupar.* "3. Poner el ánimo en cuidado, embargarle. . . ."

REPUGNAR. "Además, le *repugnaba* entrar en metafísicas de amor con aquella sirvienta" (*PJ*, p. 136, line 19). OM (following Mir): "disgustar, fastidiar, desazonar, aburrir . . ." (p. 124). In the Academy Dictionaries. M. Alonso: "3. s. 18 al 20. *Rehusar,* hacer de mala gana una cosa o admitirla con dificultad."

SENO. "Pero hoy, que la moral evangélica ha penetrado más profundamente en el *seno* de la sociedad cristiana . . ." (*PJ*, p. 57, line 27). OM: "gremio" (pp. 69–70). Baralt finds the figurative usage of *seno* acceptable, but prefers "entrañas," "corazón," "pecho," "centro," etc. *DRAE* (1869): "La cavidad del pecho. Regazo"; also "Se dice de las cosas espirituales." M. Alonso: "7. fig. s. 16 al 20. Parte interna de alguna cosa."

That the usage was common is attested by these earlier examples: L. F. de Moratín: "Esta es la felicidad más alta;/ . . . Vive contenta en el *seno*/ de tu familia, estimada, querida y en dulce paz" (*El barón*, II, xviii); Espronceda: ". . . Levantóse en su cóncavo hueco/ semejante a un aullido una voz/pavorosa, monótona, informe,/ que pronuncia sin lengua su boca,/ cual la voz que del áspera roca/ en los *senos* del viento formó" (*El estudiante de Salamanca*, "Clásicos Castellanos," no. 47, p. 252); Valera: "El natural discurrir de una mujer, que ha corrido siempre en el *seno* de la verdad, . . . no es empeño fácil" (1861; C. C. DeCoster, ed., *Artículos de "El Contemporáneo"*; Madrid: Castalia, 1966, p. 44); Valera: ". . . El mal . . . no tardó en penetrar en el *seno* del ministerio . . ." (1871; C. C. DeCoster, ed., *Obras desconocidas de Juan Valera*; Madrid: Castalia, 1965, p. 404, also used again pp. 404 and 406).

DE SIEMPRE. "Sigo haciendo la misma vida *de siempre*, y detenido aquí a ruegos de mi padre" (*PJ*, p. 43, line 2). OM (following Sbarbi): "de costumbre," "acostumbrada," "habitual" (p. 55). Not in Academy Dictionaries and subsequent ones, perhaps because the meaning seemed obvious.

TERNURA. ". . . lloro tan fácilmente de *ternura* al ver una florecilla bonita o al contemplar el rayo . . . de una remota estrella, que casi tengo miedo" (*PJ*, p. 33, line 15). "Me quejo . . . de disipar mi *ternura* en objetos pueriles" (*PJ*, p. 49, line 17). "Don Luis sintió una invencible *ternura*, una piedad funesta" (*PJ*, p. 170, line 4). OM: "amor, cariño, afecto" (p. 60). Baralt, as in OM, but clearer: "Es en castellano *la calidad de tierno*; y también *terneza*, esto es, afecto, cariño y sentimiento *explicado* con palabras y acciones atractivas y suaves. Pero es galicismo cuando se usa por *la pasión misma del amor*."

TODO. "*Toda otra* consideración, *toda otra* forma, no destruye la imagen de esta mujer" (*PJ*, p. 75, line 33). "*Todo otro* amor era imposible para ella" (*PJ*, p. 156, line 10). OM (following Baralt and Sbarbi): "cualquier(-a) otro (otra)" (pp. 88, 136). Academy Dictionaries say only that the construction may have a plural meaning; later dictionaries do not explain it.

DE VEZ EN CUANDO. ". . . *de vez en cuando* me pica y enoja la tal seguridad" (*PJ*, p. 82, line 9; also p. 180, line 4). OM (following Mir): "de cuando en cuando," "de tiempo en tiempo," etc. (pp. 44, 146). In *DRAE* (1869) and subsequent dictionaries.

Misinterpretations or Evident Mistakes

JAMÁS. "Yo, como *jamás* he aprendido a montar . . ." (*PJ*, p. 59, line 11). OM (following Mir): "nunca" (pp. 72–74). OM wants *jamás* to be accompanied by a particle or complement. *DRAE* (1869): "Nunca." Baralt (1874; pp. 325–327) and Zerolo, while recognizing the negative value of *jamás* when used alone, distinguish between it and *nunca*.

RECURSO. "No me queda más *recurso* que huir" (*PJ*, p. 88, line 30). OM (following Baralt and Mir): "no . . . más remedio" (p. 97). Also *PJ*, p. 120, line 33; p. 142, line 8; p. 151, line 6; cf. OM, pp. 119, 126, 134–135.

SER. ". . . pero D. Gumersindo era un *ser* extraordinario" (*PJ*, p. 8, line 23). OM: "hombre, persona, sujeto" (p. 21). Also *PJ*, p. 25, line 23; p. 28, line 3; p. 46, line 22; p. 87, lines 27, 28; p. 97, line 33; cf. OM, pp. 38, 56, 59, 96–97, 101. *DRAE* (1869): "Esencia o naturaleza. Ente." M. Alonso: "3. s. 18 al 20. Ente, lo que es y existe." This usage by Valera is perhaps a result of philosophical usage, as among the Krausists.

SER DE. ". . . mi padre quiere que yo *sea de* la tertulia" (*PJ*, p. 71, line 26). OM: "acudir, asistir o concurrir" (p. 85). *DRAE* (1869): "Pertenecer o tocar, hablando de alguna comunidad o número o persona de calidad; y también se junta con la preposición *de*; como: *Es* del consejo, etc." M. Alonso: *ser*. "2. s. 12. *Asistir*, tomar parte en una acción."

SIMPLICIDAD. ". . . por temor . . . de salir con doscientas mil *simplicidades* . . ." (*PJ*, p. 65, line 20). OM (following Sbarbi): "simplezas" (pp. 81–82). The Academy Dictionaries and Zerolo do not give this meaning. According to M. Alonso's treatment, the distinctions made by OM are not valid.

SOLO. "Me complacía y me afligía al mismo tiempo estar *solo* con aquella mujer" (*PJ*, p. 63, line 19). OM: "a solas" (pp. 78–79). *Solo* in the sense of *a solas*, though found in the Academy Dictionaries, Zerolo, and M. Alonso, is not explained well.

MÁS TARDE. ". . . ella misma niega *más tarde* a su propia conciencia . . ." (*PJ*, p. 81, line 19). OM (following Sbarbi): "después" (pp. 93–94). The dictionaries do not explain this obvious meaning of *más tarde*.

AL TRAVÉS. ". . . toda su forma corporal, en suma, que me enamora y seduce, y *al través de* la cual, y sólo *al través de* la cual se me muestra el espíritu invisible, vago y lleno de misterios" (*PJ*, p. 168, line 31). OM (following Mir): "por entre" (p. 143). "Luisito me escribe hace días extrañas cartas, donde descubro *al través de* su exaltación mística . . ." (*PJ*, p. 198, line 11). OM: "envuelta en" (p. 149). Baralt: Not ". . . *A través* (F. *A travers*) sino *Al través*, esto es *Por entre*." In the Academy Dictionaries. M. Alonso: *Al través*. "m. adv. A través. 2. de través. A través. m. adv. por entre."

VÍCTIMA. "—Pues de los tres soy *víctima* . . ." (*PJ*, p. 107, lines 16 and 19). OM: "esclava, juguete, mártir" (pp. 106–107). ". . . ¿no cree V. que la [la pasión] compartirá y que será *víctima* de ella?" (*PJ*, p. 159, line 5). OM: "esclavo, mártir" (p. 137). In the Academy Dictionaries and Zerolo. M. Alonso: "2. fig. s. 16 al 20. Persona que se expone u ofrece a un grave riesgo en obsequio de otra. . . . 3. fig. s. 18 al 20. Persona que padece daño por culpa ajena o por causa fortuita."

VOLUPTUOSO. "Don Luis se sintió dominado, seducido, vencido por aquella *voluptuosa* naturaleza, y dudó de sí" (*PJ*, p. 146, line 25). OM: "embriagadora, regalada" (p. 132). ". . . en voluptuosos gabinetes" (*PJ*, p. 158, line 9). OM: "cómodos, elegantes, suntuosos" (p. 137). In the Academy Dictionaries and Zerolo. M. Alonso: "s. 17 al 20. Que inclina a la voluptuosidad ['Complacencia en los deleites sensuales.'], la inspira o la hace sentir. . . . 2. s. 18 al 20. Dado a los placeres o deleites sensuales."

Grammatical Usage

USE OF THE PRESENT PARTICIPLE. "Pepita, pues, con dinero y *siendo* además hermosa, y *haciendo*, . . . buen uso de su riqueza . . ." (*PJ*, p. 14, lines 5–6). ". . . pero esta . . . pasión, ya que existe en mí, *importando* desecharla, celebra V. que no se mezcle con la oración . . ." (*PJ*, p. 58, line 3). Other exs., *PJ*: p. 71, line 1; p. 94, line 18; p. 111, lines 7–9; p. 133, line 24; p. 135, line 20; p. 141, lines 9–10. OM (following Mir) opposes these usages of the present participle, either because he considers them too free in the time referred to or ambiguous. See OM, pp. 26, 84, 101, 109–116, 122, 125. Cf. Mir, I, 905–913, and J. P. Wonder, "Some Aspects of Present-Participial Usage in Six Modern Spanish Novelists," *Hispania*, XXXVIII (1955), 193–201.

HACER + INF. "Yo agradezco a usted que me haya *hecho conocer*, ... todo lo malo y todo lo bueno ..." (*PJ*, p. 17, lines 2–3). OM (following Baralt and Mir on all of this): "enseñar" (p. 27). *PJ*: "*hacerle ver*" (p. 42, line 29). OM: "mostrar, enseñar, sacar a luz" (pp. 54–55). *PJ*: "*hacer nacer*" (p. 80, line 25). OM: "causar, engendrar, ocasionar, producir" (p. 93). *PJ*: "¿Por qué la he *hecho creer* que la quería?" (p. 100, line 3). OM: "persuadir, convencer, evidenciar" (p. 102). *DRAE* (1869): *Hacer*. "Junto con algunos verbos, es obligar o precisar; como: *hacer* venir, *hacer* que se vaya." Mir says that *hacer* + infinitive should only be used in cases of strong obligation (II, 14). M. Alonso: "21. s. 16 al 20. Obligar a que se ejecute la acción de un infinitivo."

OMISSION OF THE REFLEXIVE PRONOUN. "... cuando veo a Pepita después, ... *imagino* que todo lo hace candorosamente ..." (*PJ*, p. 34, line 20). OM: "me imagino" (p. 48). Other exs. of *imaginar* in *PJ*: p. 43, line 23; p. 59, line 22; p. 64, line 13; p. 149, line 14. Cf. OM, pp. 55–56, 74, 134. Adequate definitions and usages of *imaginar* in *DRAE* (1899) and Zerolo, but curiously lacking in M. Alonso.

"Cuando, ya viejo, volviese yo ... gozaría mucho en *intimar* con ella ..." (*PJ*, p. 53, lines 2–3). OM: "intimarme" (p. 65). According to OM, "intimar vale declarar, notificar una cosa." The Academy Dictionaries and Zerolo only give the definitions used by OM. M. Alonso does not give *intimar* with the sense of Valera's usage.

PJ: "cuando *sonríe*" (p. 90, line 21). OM: "se sonríe" (p. 100). Nonreflexive use indicated in *DRAE* (1884), not in *DRAE* (1869).

"... mi fervor religioso disminuye ..." (*PJ*, p. 41, line 30). OM: "se disminuye (p. 53).

Reflections of Romanticism

CREACIÓN. "Todo mi valer, si yo le tuviese, mi padre le consideraría como *creación* suya ..." (*PJ*, p. 18, line 18). "La mano es el ... medio por donde la inteligencia reviste de forma sus pensamientos artísticos, y da ser a las *creaciones* de la voluntad ..." (*PJ*, p. 37, line 2). "¿Será quizás la idea que V. tiene de mí, la idea que ama, *creación* de esa fantasía tan eficaz ...?" (*PJ*, p. 161, line 18). "Sobre todos los ensueños de mi juvenil imaginación ha venido a sobreponerse y entronizarse la realidad que en V. he visto; sobre todas mis ninfas, reinas y diosas, V. ha descollado; por cima de mis ideales *creaciones*, . . . se levantó en mi alma la imagen fiel . . . de la viva hermosura que adorna, que es la esencia de ese cuerpo y de esa alma" (*PJ*, p. 165, line 7). Cf. OM (following Mir): pp. 29–30, 51, 165. *DRAE* (1869): *creación*. "Hiperbólicamente se suele dar este nombre a la obra original, artística o literaria, de mérito relevante." Cf. "[Después de] las monstruosas *creaciones* del arte oriental . . . , hemos contemplado, llena el alma de *entusiasmo* y regocijo, esa *creación* admirable que se llama *Consuelo*" (1878; Revilla, *Críticas*, I, 45). Cf. CREAR.

CREAR. "No se podía decir que *crease* riqueza . . ." (*PJ*, p. 8, line 24). "En las grandes ciudades es fácil no recibir, aislarse, *crearse* una soledad, una Tebaida en medio del bullicio . . ." (*PJ*, p. 54, line 20). ". . . hay muchos álamos y otros árboles altos que . . . *crean* un intrincado laberinto y una sombría espesura" (*PJ*, p. 61, line 22). Also *PJ*, p. 123, line 22; p. 130, line 30; p. 160, line 19. OM (following Mir): "hacer," "formar," "componer," "producir," "concebir," "fabricar," etc. (pp. 21–22, 66–67, 77–78, 120–121, and 138). *DRAE* (1869): "Criar, por sacar o producir alguna cosa de la nada." *DRAE* (1899): "fig. Establecer, fundar, introducir por vez primera una cosa; hacerla nacer o darle vida, en sentido figurado." M. Alonso repeats this definition (dating it from the 18th C. to the 20th C.) and adds: "6. Producir, componer obras literarias con originalidad."

The modern meanings would seem to come from the philosophical-religious use of *crear* and *creación* combined with the romantic exaltation of the products of "creative geniuses." Cf. Valera: "Alfieri concibió los caracteres sobrenaturales; pero los ha *creado* como los concibió" (1861; *Obras*, II, 246).

ENTUSIASMO; ENTUSIASMADO (ENTUSIASMARSE). ". . . esta admiración y *entusiasmo* mío . . . hoy casi me parecen pecaminosa distracción . . ." (*PJ*, p. 30, line 2). ". . . cuando tengo . . . algún rapto de *entusiasmo* . . ." (*PJ*, p. 31, line 18). ". . . Pepita me recibió *entusiasmada* . . ." (*PJ*, p. 78, line 23). OM (following Baralt and Mir): *entusiasmo*. "aplauso, festejo, loor, aclamación"; "alborozo," "júbilo," "contento," etc. (pp. 44–45, 92). *DRAE* (1869); *entusiasmo*. "El vigor y vehemencia con que hablan o escriben los que son o parecen inspirados. Dícese comúnmente del furor o arrebatimiento de la fantasía de los poetas." *DRAE* (1889) adds: "Exaltación y fogosidad del ánimo, excitado por cosa que la admire o cautive"; and, under *entusiasmar*, it adds to "infundir entusiasmo": "causar ardiente y desapoderada admiración. Usase también como reflexivo."

Zerolo, M. Alonso, and Corominas give about the same information. The romantic qualities of these words are evident.

IDEAL. "El padre Vicario nota que Pepita sueña con la madre *ideal* y con el hijo *ideal*, inmaculados ambos, al rezar a la Virgen Santísima, y al cuidar a su lindo niño Jesús de talla" (*PJ*, p. 46, lines 29–30). OM (following Mir, and distorting Valera's meaning): "la madre sin mancha, santísima, y el hijo perfecto, divino" (p. 57). ". . . mis *ideales* creaciones" (*PJ*, p. 165, line 7). OM: "primorosas fantasías, sonrientes ilusiones, quiméricos sueños, fantásticos pensamientos, celestiales imaginaciones" (p. 140). In the Academy Dictionaries. Zerolo: "Ideal, en el uso común, significa una cosa que no tiene nada de realidad, y que no existe más que en la imaginación o en la opinión. Pero cuando se trata de bellas artes, esta expresión, lejos de ser tomada en mal sentido, designa muchas veces el más alto punto de perfección. Esta expresión se aplica particularmente a la pintura y a la escultura." M. Alonso: "4. s. 19 y 20. Excelente, perfecto en su línea. 5. m. Prototipo, modelo o ejemplar de perfección. Filos. Modelo o patrón de la actividad práctica."

The growing prominence of *ideal*, adj. and n., in the nineteenth century is probably a result of the convergence of philosophical idealism and romantic longing for the absolute. Cf. Valera, ". . . los *ideales* y metafísicos padecimientos del héroe enamoran y seducen a quien empieza a vivir, cuyos arranques de entusiasmo y de ternura producen . . . reacciones contrarias . . ." (1864; *Obras*, II, 273). See also J. López Morillas, who stresses the importance of the ideal in the 1870's and among the Krausists (*El krausismo español*, pp. 71, 137–138, *et passim*).

INSPIRAR. "Una poesía melancólica *inspiraba* a la naturaleza . . ." (*PJ*, p. 145, line 23). OM (following Baralt and Mir): "La naturaleza inspiraba una poesía melancólica, es como debe decirse; porque inspirar . . . es infundir o engendrar en el ánimo o la mente afectos, ideas, etc." (p. 129). (OM ignores the fact that, immediately afterwards, Valera adds ". . . todo [including *la naturaleza inspirada*] entonaba un himno al Creador.") Similar meanings in the Academy Dictionaries and Zerolo. Cf. M. Alonso: "6. fig. s. 15 al 20. Iluminar Dios al entendimiento de uno o excitar y mover su voluntad. 7. r. fig. s. 18 al 20. Enardecerse y avivarse el genio del orador, del literato o del artista con el recuerdo o la presencia de una persona o cosa, o con el estudio de obras ajenas."

Again, the traditional metaphysical (religious in this case) and the romantico-emotional meanings seem to be joined.

Concern about Public Opinion and Social Position

DARSE LUSTRE. "Cualquiera persona regular hubiera vivido con las rentas de este mayorazgo en continuos apuros, llena tal vez de trampas, y sin acertar a *darse el lustre* y decoro propios de su clase . . ." (*PJ*, p. 8, line 21). OM: "mostrar ufanía" (p. 19). This phrase not in Academy Dictionaries or Zerolo, but cf. *DRAE* (1869), *lustre*: "met. Esplendor, gloria." Corominas: " 'brillo, esplendor'. . . . Hoy es sólo popular hablando de los zapatos y de alguna superficie bruñida, pero en sus sentidos figurados sigue siendo palabra de tono noble." But cf. A. Alcalá Venceslada: "*Lustre.* m. En la frase 'Darse lustre', darse tono, darse charol" (*Vocabulario andaluz*; Madrid, 1951). Cf. Valera, "En medio de sus apuros sostenía esta dama respetable el *lustre* señorial de la casa" (*Las ilusiones del doctor Faustino*, 1875, *Obras*, I, 211).

DARSE TONO. "–No seas tonto . . . . Lo digo para *darme tono* de perspicaz" (*PJ*, p. 197, line 28). OM (following Baralt and Mir): "ufanarme," "jactarme," "bravear," "preciarme," "blasonar" (p. 148). *DRAE* (1884): "Darse importancia." In Zerolo and M. Alonso. Cf. Mir, I, 498–499; II, 928–931.

DISTINCIÓN. ". . . en las ciudades . . . , hay otras *distinciones* que se ambicionan . . . ; pero en los pueblos pequeños, donde ni la gloria . . . , ni tal vez la *distinción* en los modales, ni la elegancia, . . . suelen estimarse . . ." (*PJ*, p. 13, lines 29, 33). OM (following Mir): "cortesanía, cortesía, urbanidad, gracia, hidalguía, comedimiento, finura" (p. 25). "Había . . . en el porte y continente de D. Luis aquel indescriptible sello de *distinción* y de hidalguía que parece, aunque no lo sea siempre, privativa calidad y exclusivo privilegio de las familias aristocráticas" (p. 144, line 14; not cited by OM). Cf. *PJ*, p. 22, line 5; p. 110, line 21; OM, pp. 37–38, 109. This meaning not in Academy Dictionaries. Zerolo: "Elegancia, cortesía, buen tono" (*Suplemento*, p. 430). M. Alonso: "5. s. 18 al 20. Elevación sobre lo vulgar, especialmente en elegancia y buenas maneras" (examples from L. F. de Moratín).

DISTINGUIDO. ". . . ella es naturalmente elegante, *distinguida*; es un ser superior . . ." (*PJ*, p. 25, line 23). OM (following Mir): "eximia," "afamada," "principal," "aristócrata," "egregia," etc. (pp. 37–38). "¡Es tan *distinguido*, tan aristocrático, tener una linda mano!" (*PJ*, p. 36, line 28). Also *PJ*, p. 166, line 8; OM, pp. 49–50, 142. In *DRAE* (1884): "Illustre, noble, esclarecido." M. Alonso dates it "s. 16 al 20."

HACER UN PAPEL. "Usted está lastimado de las bromas de Currito y de *hacer* (hablando profanamente) *un papel* poco airoso, montado en una mula mansa . . ." (*PJ*, p. 64, lines 24–25). OM: "representar un papel." Similar usages are found in the Academy Dictionaries and subsequent ones.

Valera's characters, often victims of pride and vanity, are very concerned about the impression they make. This is especially true of Doctor Faustino: "Don Faustino empezaba a *hacer un papel* bastante desairado" (*Obras*, I, 257; other examples: 260, 277, 288).

PONERSE EN RIDÍCULO. "A no *ponerme en ridículo*, cerrando en su presencia los ojos, fuerza es que yo vea y note la hermosura de los suyos . . ." (*PJ*, p. 51, line 33, to p. 52, line 1). OM (following Mir): "tenerme por burlado y escarnecido" (p. 63). "Con no ir, . . . *me pondría en ridículo*" (*PJ*, p. 72, line 27). OM: "mofarían de mí, haría platillo de mentecato, sería objeto de risa" (p. 86). Cf. *PJ*, p. 64, line 18, and OM, pp. 79–80. Baralt (1874): "*Poner* y *ponerse en ridículo* son expresiones consagradas ya por el uso moderno." In *DRAE* (1884), Zerolo, M. Alonso, etc.

This expression reflects the natural concern of a proud young man in others' reactions to him.

Of Special Psychological and Stylistic Interest

ABANDONO. (See under "Vestiges of Older Usage and Possible Regionalisms" for examples.) The use of this word and of the verb *abandonar* often reveals Valera's modern interest in depicting the psychological state of those on the verge of yielding completely to feelings of sensuality and eroticism.

APARECER(SE). "Pepita . . . hace olvidar todo esto, y *aparece* como un ser peregrino, venido de alguna tierra lejana, de alguna esfera superior . . ." (*PJ*, p. 48, line 7). OM (following Baralt): "se presenta" (p. 59). "En cuanto a Pepita, . . . me sorprendió, *apareciendo* en un caballo tordo muy vivo . . ." (*PJ*, p. 59, line 24). OM: "pareciendo, presentándose, dejándose ver, mostrándose" (p. 75). "En aquellos sitios agrestes *se* me *apareció* más hermosa" (*PJ*, p. 62, line 21). "No hay duquesa . . . , ni emperatriz . . . , ni reina . . . , que valgan lo que valen las ideales . . . criaturas con quienes yo he vivido, porque *se aparecían* en los alcázares . . . , que yo edificaba . . ." (*PJ*, p. 162, line 19). In all of these examples there is a strong note of surprise or of a quasi-supernatural appearance. Cf. *PJ*, p. 170, lines 19, 29; p. 206, line 19; OM, pp. 144, 150.

DRAE (1869): "Manifestarse, presentarse a la vista inopinadamente algún objeto. Parecer, encontrarse, hallarse." Also in subsequent dictionaries. Cf. Mir: "Pero el *aparecer* castizo es un mostrarse repentinamente, con sorpresa, sin expectación" (I, 150).

APLOMO. ". . . se sentó [Antoñona] enfrente de D. Luis con *aplomo* y descaro" (*PJ*, p. 135, line 5). OM (following Baralt and Mir): "serenidad, desparpajo, cordura, confianza, gravedad" (p. 123). In *DRAE* (1899), M. Alonso. This neologism, applied to Antoñona, has an ironic, incongruous effect. But cf. Bécquer: "con qué admirable *aplomo*, / me dijo al presentarnos / un amigo oficioso / . . ." (*Rima* xl).

COQUETEAR. "No, no tengo la menor prueba de que Pepita desee siquiera coquetear conmigo" (*PJ*, p. 83, line 15). OM, using awkward periphrases with verbs like "procurar atraer," "gitanear," "halagar," "embelesar," shows how completely inappreciative he is of the stylistic nuances of *coquetear*, *coqueta*, etc., words which are fully attested from the Academy Dictionary of 1843 on. Cf. examples not cited by OM, *PJ*, p. 157, line 15; p. 163, line 5; p. 200, line 16. Cf. Mir, I, 428–429.

ENCANTAR (ENCANTADO, ENCANTO). "Yo estoy *encantado* con las huertas . . ." (*PJ*, p. 6, line 11). OM (following Mir): "embelesado," "hechizado," "maravillado," "fascinado," etc. (pp. 19–20). Cf. *PJ*, p. 56, line

3; p. 110, line 26; OM, pp. 69, 109. Cf. Baralt: "Sin embargo, usado [*encantar*] con discreción da a las veces gracia y energía al discurso." Not in the Academy Dictionaries. Zerolo makes interesting distinctions between *hechizar* and *encantar*, with the latter applying more to imaginative than sensory effects. M. Alonso: "3. s. 16 al 20. Suspender, embelesar."

There can be little doubt that nature and Pepita combine to "cast a spell" over Luis.

EXISTIR. ". . . *existiendo* una notable desproporción de edad . . ." (*PJ*, p. 50, line 8). OM (following Mir): "habiendo" (pp. 60–61). This matter-of-course usage implies an equivalence between *existir* and *haber* not found in nineteenth-century dictionaries, though fully attested in the twentieth century. Some of the examples from *PJ* suggest the strong reality, the "ser real y verdadero" (*DRAE*, 1869), of psychological values. ". . . esta afeminada pasión de ánimo, ya que *existe* en mí . . ." (*PJ*, p. 58, line 3; cf. OM, pp. 70–71). "De aquí provino, . . . que *existiera* un secreto entre ambos . . ." (*PJ*, p. 66, line 6).

FIJARSE. "Si Pepita ha desairado todo esto, ¿cómo ha de *fijarse* en mí . . . ?" (*PJ*, p. 53, line 28). OM (following Mir): "reparar, considerar, atender" (p. 66). "*Me he fijado* además en la gallardía de su persona . . ." (*PJ*, p. 110, line 20). OM, pp. 107–109. Cf. *PJ*, p. 124, lines 12–13; p. 144, line 21; OM, pp. 120, 126–127. Not in Academy Dictionaries, 1869 and 1884. *DRAE* (1899): "Dirigir o aplicar intensamente." Cf. M. Alonso: "13. s. 17 al 20. Atender, reparar, notar."

The two quoted usages in *PJ* could reflect how intensely the loved person was noticed.

OBSESIÓN, OBSESO. "Imaginé mil extravagancias, me creí presa de una *obsesión*" (*PJ*, p. 64, line 14). OM (following Baralt and Mir): "pesadilla," "asedio inoportuno," "persecución," etc. (p. 79). "Encuentro tan natural como el de Pepita se trastrocaba en mi mente en algo de prodigio . . . al notar la consistencia de esta imaginación, me creí *obseso* . . ." (*PJ*, p. 67, line 6). Not in Academy Dictionaries. Zerolo: *obsesión*. "Por extensión, estado del que se halla dominado por una idea fija." M. Alonso: "2. *Patol. y Psicol.* Persistencia irresistible de una idea o de una emoción" (under *obseso* he cites the above example from *PJ*).

PENETRANTE. "Poco tuvo . . . que confiar a una criada tan *penetrante* y tan zahorí de cuanto pasaba en lo más escondido de su pecho" (*PJ*, p. 104, line 15). OM: "sagaz" (p. 105). This meaning not in the Academy Dictionaries. Zerolo lists *penetrante* as a synonym of *sutil*, but with a greater degree of perspicacity. M. Alonso: "2. s. 16 al 20. *Profundo*, que entra mucho en alguna cosa."

PENETRAR EN. "Por otra parte, ¿cómo *penetrar en* lo íntimo del corazón, en el secreto escondido de la mente juvenil de una doncella . . . ?" (*PJ*, p. 12, lines 20–21). "Si algo de esto . . . pensó la muchacha, y en su inocencia no *penetró en* otros misterios . . ." (*PJ*, p. 12, line 33, to p. 13, line 1). OM objects to the use of *en* with *penetrar* in the sense of *descubrir* (pp. 24–25). Appropriate meanings of *penetrar* are given from *DRAE* (1869) on. Only Zerolo treats the added nuance of difficulty when *en* is used: "*Penetrar en*, se dice de los lugares en los que se entra con alguna dificultad." This nuance is, of course, very appropriate to describe Luis's attempts to understand Pepita.

RELEVADO. " . . . los labios finos, aunque *relevados*, lo cual le daba un aspecto desdeñoso . . ." (*PJ*, p. 144, line 9). OM (following Sbarbi): "abultados, llenos, carnosos" (p. 127). Not in the Academy Dictionaries or in Zerolo, although a similar meaning could be derived from the definitions of *relevar*, especially as a pictorial term. Cf. M. Alonso. Clearly, OM's equivalents do not give the note of disdain which Valera intended.

RETENER. ". . . en suma, me *retiene* aquí contra mi gusto . . ." (*PJ*, p. 41, line 23). ". . . mi padre me *retiene* a pesar mío . . ." (*PJ*, p. 56, line 23). ". . . mi padre me *retendrá* . . ." (*PJ*, p. 71, line 31). "Lejos de llevarte al chico otra vez, le *retendré* aquí, hasta por fuerza, si es necesario" (*PJ*, p. 201, line 15). OM (following Sbarbi): "detener," "guardar a su lado" (pp. 52, 69, 86, 149). In Academy Dictionaries and Zerolo. M. Alonso: "tr. s. 12 al 20. *Detener*, conservar, guardar en sí o para sí." There is perhaps a stylistic value in all of these examples that *detener* would not have, the idea being that Luis's father "holds him back," against his wishes. Cf. *PJ*, p. 43, line 2: "Sigo . . . *detenido* aquí a ruegos de mi padre."

SIN EMBARGO. This expression, fully attested and so very frequent, along with the related expressions, *no obstante* and *de todos modos*, etc., that it constitutes a real stylistic leitmotif in *PJ*, where it reinforces Luis's interior contradictions, is objected to by OM because it lacks complements, as in "sin embargo de lo dicho (esto, eso, etc.)." Cf. *DRAE* (1869): " No obstante. Sin que sirva de impedimiento."

DE TODOS MODOS. "*De todos modos*, me digo a veces, ¿sería tan absurdo, tan imposible que lo hubiera?" (*PJ*, p. 81, line 32). "De todos modos, no se negaba D. Luis . . ." (*PJ*, p. 184, line 21). OM (following Baralt and Mir): "como quiera que sea" (pp. 94, 147). Not in *DRAE* (1869, 1884). *DRAE* (1899) mentions related expressions. In Zerolo, but missing in M. Alonso.

TENER LA HONRA. ". . . en un lugar de Andalucía, y sobre todo *teniendo la honra* de ser hijo del cacique, es menester vivir en público" (*PJ*, p. 54, line 22). OM: "teniendo a gran suerte (felicidad, suerte, etc.)" (pp. 67–68). Similar usage in *DRAE* (1884) and Zerolo. Not in M. Alonso.

Selected Bibliography

Valera y Alcalá-Galiano, Juan. *Obras completas*. ed. Luis Araujo Costa. 3 vols. I, 3rd ed. II, III, 2nd ed. Madrid: Aguilar, 1947–1949.

———. *Pepita Jiménez*. ed. Manuel Azaña. "Clásicos Castellanos." Madrid: Espasa-Calpe, 1953.

WORKS ON VALERA

BOOKS

Azaña, Manuel. *Valera en Italia: amores, política y literatura*. Madrid: Paez, 1929.

DeCoster, Cyrus C. "The Theory and Practice of the Novels of Valera: A Study in Techniques." Ph.D. Diss., Univ. of Chicago, 1951.

Fishtine, Edith. *Don Juan Valera, the Critic*. Bryn Mawr, 1933.

González López, Luis. *Las mujeres de don Juan Valera*. Madrid: Espasa-Calpe, 1934.

Jiménez, Alberto. *Juan Valera y la generación de 1868*. Oxford: Dolphin, 1956.

Krynen, Jean. *L'Esthétisme de Juan Valera*. *Acta Salmanticensia*, "Filosofía y Letras," vol. II, no. 2. Salamanca: Universidad de Salamanca, 1946.

Montesinos, José F. *Valera o la ficción libre: Ensayo de interpretación de una anomalía literaria*. Madrid: Gredos, 1957.

Ocharan Mazas, Luis de. *Incorrecciones deslizadas en las páginas de "Pepita Jiménez."* Madrid: Tipografía de la "Revista de arch. bibl. y museos," 1924.

Romero Mendoza, Pedro. *Don Juan Valera*. Madrid: Ediciones Españolas, 1940.

Thompson, Frank R. "The Classicism of Don Juan Valera." Ph.D. Diss., Univ. of Wisconsin, 1941.

WORKS ON VALERA

ARTICLES, ESSAYS, ETC.

Alas, Leopoldo ["Clarín"]. "Don Juan Valera en Francia." *La literatura en 1881.* Written in part by Armando Palacio Valdés. Madrid: Alfredo de Carlos Hierro, Editor, 1882, pp. 175–180.

———. "El libre examen de nuestra literatura presente." *Solos de Clarín.* 2nd ed. Madrid: Alfredo de Carlos Hierro, Editor, 1881, pp. 51–62.

———. "Valera," *Obras selectas.* Madrid: Biblioteca Nueva, 1947, pp. 1191–1195.

Azaña, Manuel. "La novela de Pepita Jiménez." *Obras completas.* ed. Juan Marichal. 4 vols. México: Oasis, 1966, I, 1035–1058.

———. "Prólogo" to the "Clásicos Castellanos" ed. of *Pepita Jiménez.* Madrid: Espasa-Calpe, 1953, pp. ix–lxviii.

Clavería, Carlos. "En torno a una frase en *caló* de don Juan Valera." *Estudios sobre los gitanismos del español.* Madrid: CSIC, 1951, pp. 97–128.

DeCoster, Cyrus C. "Valera and Andalusia." *Hispanic Review,* XXIX (1961), 200–216.

Ellis, Havelock. "Juan Valera." *The Soul of Spain.* 2nd impression. London: A. Constable, 1908, pp. 244–272.

Krynen, Jean. "Juan Valera et la mystique espagnole." *Bulletin Hispanique,* XLVI (1944), 35–72.

Martínez Ruiz, José [Azorín]. "Valera." *De Valera a Miró.* Madrid: A. Aguado, 1959.

Maurín, Mario. "Valera y la ficción encadenada." *Mundo Nuevo,* no. 14 (Aug., 1967), 35–44; no. 15 (Sept., 1967), 37–44.

Olguín, Manuel. "Juan Valera's Theory of Art for Art's Sake." *Modern Language Forum,* XXXV (1950), 24–34.

Pageard, Robert. "*Pepita Jiménez en France.*" *Bulletin Hispanique,* LXIII (1961), 28–37.

Palacio Valdés, Armando. "Don Juan Valera." *Obras completas.* Madrid: Aguilar, 1945, II, 1179–1182.

Pérez de Ayala, Ramón. "Don Juan Valera o el arte de la distracción." *Divagaciones literarias.* Madrid: Biblioteca Nueva, 1958, pp. 67–85.

Revilla, Manuel de la. "Don Juan Valera." *Obras.* Madrid: Víctor Saiz, 1883, pp. 47–55.

Revuelta y Revuelta, Luisa. "Valera, estilista." *Boletín de la Real Academia de Ciencias, Bellas Letras y Nobles Artes de Córdoba,* XVII (1946), 25–71.

Ríos de Lampérez, Blanca de los. "De la mística y de la novela de D. Juan

Valera." *Raza Española* (Madrid), año VII, nos. 75–76 (March–April, 1925), 4–18.

Romeu, R. "Les divers aspects de l'humour dans le roman espagnol moderne." *Bulletin Hispanique*, XLVIII (1946), 97–146, 340–364; XLIX (1947), 48–83. On Valera: XLVIII, 97–126.

Sbarbi, José María. "Un plato de garrafales." *Ambigú literario.* Madrid: Fuentenebro, 1897, pp. 1–14.

Urmeneta, Fermín de. "Sobre la estética valeriana." *Revista de Ideas Estéticas*, XIV, no. 54 (1956), 161–164.

Vidart, Luis. "Recuerdos de una polémica acerca de la novela de don Juan Valera–'Pepita Jiménez.'" *Revista de España*, LIII (Nov.–Dec., 1876), 269–284.

GENERAL WORKS

BOOKS AND ARTICLES

Alonso, Amado. *Ensayo sobre la novela histórica: El modernismo en "La gloria de don Ramiro."* "Estudios Estilísticos," III. Buenos Aires: Instituto de Filología, 1942.

———. *Materia y forma en poesía.* Madrid: Gredos, 1955.

Alonso, Dámaso. *La poesía de San Juan de la Cruz.* Madrid: Aguilar, 1946.

———. *Poesía española.* 3rd ed. Madrid: Gredos, 1957.

———. *Seis calas en la expresión literaria española.* 2nd ed. Madrid: Gredos, 1956.

Arbiol, Padre Fr. Antonio. *Desengaños mysticos.* Barcelona: Thomas Piferrer, 1772.

Auerbach, Erich. *Mimesis: The Representation of Reality in Western Literature*, trans. Willard Trask. Garden City, N.Y.: Doubleday, 1957.

Bécquer, Gustavo A. *Obras completas.* 2nd ed. Buenos Aires: Joaquín Gil, Editor, 1944.

Bello, Andrés and Cuervo, Rufino J. *Gramática de la lengua castellana*, ed. Niceto Alcalá-Zamora y Torres. 4th ed. Buenos Aires: Sopena Argentina, 1954.

Biblia Sacra iuxta Vulgatam Clementinam. Madrid: Biblioteca de Autores Cristianos, 1946.

Blanco García, Padre Francisco. *La literatura española en el siglo XIX.* 3 vols. 2nd ed. Madrid: Sáenz de Jubera, Hermanos, Editores, 1899–1903.

Brenan, Gerald. *The Literature of the Spanish People.* 2nd ed. Cambridge: Cambridge Univ. Press, 1953.

Brunetière, Ferdinand. "La casuistique dans le roman." *Revue des Deux Mondes*, 3rd period, XLVIII (Nov. 15, 1881), 453–464.

Cameron, Norman and Margaret, Ann. *Behavior Pathology*. New York: Houghton Mifflin, 1951.

Casalduero, Joaquín. *Sentido y forma del "Quijote."* Madrid: Insula, 1949.

Castro, Américo. "La estructura del *Quijote*." *Semblanzas y estudios españoles*. Princeton: Princeton Univ. Press, 1956.

Cejador y Frauca, Julio. *Fraseología o estilística castellana*. 4 vols. Madrid: Tipografía de la "Revista de arch. bibl. y museos," 1921–1923.

———. *La lengua de Cervantes*. 2 vols. Madrid: J. Rates, 1905–1906.

Cervantes Saavedra, Miguel de. *Don Quijote de la Mancha*, ed. Francisco Rodríguez Marín. 8 vols. 6th ed. "Clásicos Castellanos." Madrid: Espasa-Calpe, 1952–1957.

Contreras, Jerónimo de. *Selva de aventuras*, in *Novelistas anteriores a Cervantes*. 2nd ed. "Biblioteca de Autores Españoles," III. Madrid: Imprenta de la Publicidad, 1849, pp. 471–505.

Díaz-Plaja, Guillermo. *Modernismo frente a Noventa y ocho*. Madrid: Espasa-Calpe, 1951.

Edel, Leon J. *The Psychological Novel: 1900–1950*. New York: J. B. Lippincott, 1955.

Eoff, Sherman H. *The Novels of Pérez Galdós*. St. Louis: Washington Univ. Studies, 1954.

———. "Pereda's Conception of Realism as Related to His Epoch." *Hispanic Review*, XIV (1946), 281–303.

———. "The Spanish Novel of 'Ideas': Critical Opinion (1836–1880)." *PMLA*, LV (1940), 531–558.

Fernández Luján, Juan. *Pardo Bazán, Valera y Pereda (Estudios críticos)*. Barcelona: Luis Tasso, 1889.

Giancarlo, Guido Mancini. *Espressioni letterarie dell'insegnamento di Santa Teresa de Avila*. Modena: Società Tipografica Modence, 1955.

Gómez de Baquero, Eduardo. *El renacimiento de la novela española en el siglo XIX*. Madrid: Mundo Latino, 1924, pp. 68–74.

González-Blanco, Andrés. *Historia de la novela en España*. Madrid: Sáenz de Jubera, Hermanos, Editores, 1909, pp. 323–345.

Goode, Helen Dill. *La prosa retórica de Fray Luis de León en "Los nombres de Cristo."* Madrid: Gredos, 1969.

Hatzfeld, Helmut. "Artistic Parallels in Cervantes and Velázquez." *Estudios dedicados a Menéndez Pidal*, III (1952), 265–297.

———. "A Clarification of the Baroque Problem in the Romance Literatures." *Comparative Literature*, I (1949), 113–139.

———. *Estudios literarios sobre mística española*. Madrid: Gredos, 1955.

———. *El "Quijote" como obra de arte del lenguaje*. Madrid: Patronato del IV Centenario del Nacimiento de Cervantes, 1949.

Herman, J. Chalmers. "Quotations and Locutions from *Don Quijote* in Galdós's Novels." *Hispania*, XXXVI (1953), 177–181.

Highet, Gilbert. *The Anatomy of Satire*. Princeton: Princeton Univ. Press, 1962.

Howells, William Dean. *Criticism and Fiction and Other Essays*, ed. C. M. Kirk and R. Kirk. New York: New York Univ. Press, 1959.

Icaza, Sister Rosa María. *The Stylistic Relationship between Poetry and Prose in the "Cántico espiritual" of San Juan de la Cruz*. Washington: Catholic Univ. of America Press, 1957.

Juan de la Cruz, San. *Vida y obras de San Juan de la Cruz*, ed. Crisógono de Jesús, O.C.D. Madrid: Biblioteca de Autores Cristianos, 1950.

Kany, Charles E. *The Beginnings of the Epistolary Novel in France, Italy, and Spain*. Berkeley: Univ. of California Press, 1937.

Lapesa, Rafael. *Historia de la lengua española*. 3rd ed. Madrid: Escelicer, 1955.

La Vida de Lazarillo de Tormes, ed. Julio Cejador y Frauca. "Clásicos Castellanos." Madrid: Espasa-Calpe, 1952.

León, Luis Ponce de. *De los nombres de Cristo*. 3 vols. "Clásicos Castellanos." Madrid: Espasa-Calpe, I, 1938.

Levin, Harry. "The Example of Cervantes," "Society and Self in the Novel." *English Institute Essays, 1955*. New York: Columbia Univ. Press, 1956. pp. 3–25.

———. *The Gates of Horn*. New York: Oxford Univ. Press, 1966.

López Morillas, Juan. *El krausismo español*. México: Fondo de Cultura Económica, 1956.

Luis de Granada. *Guía de pecadores*, ed. Matías Martínez Burgos. "Clásicos Castellanos." Madrid: Ediciones de "La Lectura," 1929.

Luis de San José. *Concordancias de las obras y escritos de Santa Teresa de Jesús*. Burgos: Tipografía de "El Monte Carmelo," 1945.

———. *Concordancias de las obras y escritos del Doctor de la Iglesia San Juan de la Cruz*. Burgos: Tipografía de "El Monte Carmelo," 1948.

Menéndez [y] Pelayo, Marcelino. *Historia de los heterodoxos españoles*, ed. Enrique Sánchez Reyes. 8 vols. Santander: Aldus, 1946–1948.

Menéndez Pidal, Ramón. *La lengua de Cristóbal Colon: El estilo de Santa Teresa y otros estudios sobre el siglo XVI*. "Colección Austral." Buenos Aires: Espasa-Calpe Argentina, 1942.

Menninger, Karl A. *The Human Mind*. 3rd ed. New York: Alfred A. Knopf, 1948.

Mercier, Vivian H. S. "James Joyce and an Irish Tradition," "Society and Self in the Novel." *English Institute Essays, 1955*. New York: Columbia Univ. Press, 1956, pp. 78–116.

Morreale, Margherita. "El superlativo en *issimo* y la versión castellana del *Cortesano*." *Revista de Filología Española*, XXXIX (1955), 46–60.

O'Brien, Justin. *The Novel of Adolescence in France*. New York: Columbia Univ. Press, 1937.

Ortega y Gasset, José. "Una polémica." *Obras completas*. 2nd ed. Madrid: Revista de Occidente, 1950, I, 156–163.

Pardo Bazán, Emilia. *La cuestión palpitante. Obras completas*. Madrid: 1891, I, 262–265.

Parente, Pascal P. *The Mystical Life*. St. Louis: B. Herder, 1946.

Peers, E. Allison. *Studies of the Spanish Mystics*. 2 vols. London: Sheldon Press, 1927.

Pfandl, Ludwig. *Historia de la literatura nacional española en la Edad de Oro*, trans. Jorge Rubió Balaguer. 2nd ed. Barcelona: Gustavo Gili, 1952.

Predmore, Richard L. *El mundo del Quijote*. Madrid: Insula, 1958.

Quevedo Villegas, Francisco de. *Los sueños*, ed. Julio Cejador y Frauca. 2 vols. "Clásicos Castellanos." Madrid: Espasa-Calpe, I (1954).

Sayce, R. A. *Style in French Prose: A Method of Analysis*. Oxford: Oxford Univ. Press, 1953.

Siebenmann, Gustav. *Über Sprache und Stil im Lazarillo de Tormes*. Bern: A. Francke, 1953.

Sobejano, Gonzalo. *El epíteto en la lírica española*. Madrid: Gredos, 1956.

Spitzer, Leo. *La enumeración caótica en la poesía moderna*. Buenos Aires: Instituto de Filología, 1945.

———. *Linguistics and Literary History*. Princeton: Princeton Univ. Press, 1948.

Switzer, Rebecca. *The Ciceronian Style in Fr. Luis de Granada*. New York: Instituto de las Españas, 1927.

Teresa de Jesús, Santa. *Las moradas*, ed. Tomás Navarro Tomás. 6th ed. "Clásicos Castellanos." Madrid: Espasa-Calpe, 1951.

———. *Obras de Santa Teresa de Jesús*, ed. P. Silverio de Sta. Teresa. 2 vols. 2nd ed. Buenos Aires: Poblet, 1943.

Todemann, Friedrich. "Die erlebte Rede im Spanischen." *Romanische Forschungen*, XLIV (1930), 103–184.

Ullmann, Stephen. *Style in the French Novel*. Cambridge: Cambridge Univ. Press, 1957.

Urbano, Luis de. "Las alegorías predilectas de Santa Teresa de Jesús." *Ciencia Tomista*, XXVII (1923), 52–71; XXVIII (1923), 364–383; XXIX (1924), 350–370.

Wellek, René and Warren, Austin. *Theory of Literature*. New York: Harcourt, Brace, 1949.

Zorrilla, José. *Don Juan Tenorio*. "Colección Austral." Mexico: Espasa-Calpe Mexicana, 1956.

Index of Subjects and Terms

Index of Names

A Note on the Author

Robert E. Lott, a native of Miami, Florida, received his B.A. from Athens College in 1951, his M.A. from the University of Alabama in 1952, and his Ph.D. from the Catholic University of America in 1958. After eight years of teaching at the University of Georgia, in 1966 he joined the faculty of the Department of Spanish, Italian, and Portuguese of the University of Illinois, where he is professor of Spanish. His fields of research and his special teaching interests have been in the modern literature of Spain, particularly the novel and stylistics. Among his publications are articles on Valera and Azorín and a book, *The Structure and Style of Azorín's "El caballero inactual"* (1963). Professor Lott's current project, a general study on Valera, his fiction, and his style, has been supported by the University Research Board and by a grant from the American Philosophical Society which enabled him to use the archives of the Valera family in Madrid during the summer of 1970.

UNIVERSITY OF ILLINOIS PRESS